Term	Meaning
SCOPE(S)	Scope of definition S (p.178)
STAT	Statement set of the program (p.56)
STAT(L)	Statement set of loop L (p.135)
S_DEFS	Set of definitions (p.71)
S_USES	Set of uses (p.71)
t_j	Lower bound of I_j in loop L_j (p.118)
u_j	Upper bound of I_j in loop L_j (p.118)
UD(n,v)	Use-definition chain for n and v (p.74)
USE(n)	Outward exposed variables used in n (p.72)
USE(S(i))	Input execution set of $S(\mathbf{i})$ (p.128)
VAR	Set of (declared) variables of the program (p.54)
var(p)	Set of declared variables in p (p.54)
VARX	$\cup\{varx(p):p \in \mathrm{P}\}$ (p.54)
varx(p)	Set of declared variables and subscripted variables occurring in p (p.54)
visible(p)	$local(p) \cup formal(p) \cup global(p)$ (p.53)
z^+	Positive part of z (p.145)
z^-	Negative part of z (p.146)
δ	Data dependence (pp.129, 134)
δ^a	Anti dependence (p.130)
δ^o	Output dependence (p.130)
δ^t	True dependence (p.130)
$\delta\mu$	Dependence with distance specification (p.134)
$\delta\theta$	Dependence with direction specification (p.134)
δ_c	Loop carried dependence (p.134)
δ_∞	Loop-independent dependence (p.134)
θ	Direction vector (p.125)
Ω	Monotone dataflow system (MDS) (p.84)
$<$	Lexicographical order (p.116)
$<_c$	$\mathbf{x} <_c \mathbf{y}: \iff (\forall j \in [1:c-1]: x_j = y_j) \wedge x_c < y_c$ for $\mathbf{x},\mathbf{y} \in \mathbb{Z}^n$ (p.116)
$\leqslant$	Dominance relation (p.59)
$\ll$	Standard execution order (p.121)

Supercompilers for Parallel and Vector Computers

Supercompilers for Parallel and Vector Computers

Hans Zima

University of Vienna

with

Barbara Chapman

University of Bonn

ACM Press
New York, New York

Addison-Wesley Publishing Company
Wokingham, England • Reading, Massachusetts • Menlo Park, California
New York • Don Mills, Ontario • Amsterdam • Bonn
Sydney • Singapore • Tokyo • Madrid • San Juan

ACM Press Frontier Series

Copyright © 1991 by the ACM Press. A Division of the Association for
Computing Machinery, Inc. (ACM).

The programs in this book have been included for their instructional value. They
have been tested with care, but are not guaranteed for any particular purpose.
The publisher does not offer any warranties or representations, nor does it accept
any liabilities with respect to the programs.

Many of the designations used by manufacturers and sellers to distinguish their
products are claimed as trademarks. The publisher has made every attempt to
supply trademark information about manufacturers and their products mentioned
in this book. A list of the trademark designations and their owners appears on
p. xvi.

Cover designed by Marshall Henrichs
and printed by The Riverside Printing Co (Reading) Ltd.
Typeset by CRB Typesetting Services, Ely, Cambs.
Printed and bound in Great Britain by TJ Press (Padstow) Ltd, Cornwall.

First printed 1990. Reprinted 1992.

British Library Cataloguing in Publication Data

Zima, Hans
  Supercompilers for Vector and Parallel Computers
  ACM Press
  1. Supercomputers – Programming   2. Compilers
3. Parallel processing   4. Vector processing (Computer
Science)
I. Barbara Chapman   II. Title
006.3'3

ISBN 0–201–17560–6

Library of Congress Cataloging in Publication Data

Zima, Hans.
  Supercompilers for parallel and vector computers/Hans Zima, Barbara
  Chapman.
     p.   cm. – (ACM Press frontier series)
  Includes bibliographical references (p.).
  ISBN 0–201–17560–6
  1. Supercomputers–Programming.   2. Compilers (Computer programs)
3. Parallel processing (Electronic computers)   4. Vector processing
(Computer science)   I. Chapman, Barbara. date.   II. Title.
III. Series.
QA76.6.Z56   1990
004'.35–dc20   90–317
                                                                  CIP

Foreword

The practice of compiler optimization has, over the past decade and a half, been deeply influenced by the development of the theory of dependence, originated by Professor David J. Kuck at the University of Illinois. Originally developed as a tool to aid in automatic vectorization and parallelization, Kuck's theory has been applied to a number of other compiler optimizations, including register allocation and memory hierarchy management. Because of the successes of this technology, I predict that every optimizing compiler that does not use dependence analysis in some form will be considered obsolete and that the quality of a compiler will be measured, in large part, by the quality of its dependence analysis.

In spite of these advances, no satisfactory textbook on dependence analysis and its applications to vectorization and parallelization has yet emerged. Given the importance of the subject, this is quite surprising. *Supercompilers for Parallel and Vector Computers*, by Professor Hans Zima and Barbara Chapman, promises to fill this gap.

Professor Zima is highly qualified to produce this book. During his tenure at Bonn University, he supervised the implementation of SUPERB, a parallelization and vectorization tool designed to support parallel programming for the SUPRENUM, a distributed memory machine with a vector unit on each processor. SUPERB includes rigorous dependence analysis and uses the results to guide the application of program transformations. In addition, Professor Zima spent a year at Rice University while he was writing this book. During that year, he learned everything there is to know about PFC, our own vectorization and parallelization system, which has influenced his thinking substantially. Thus, he has intimate knowledge of the implementation details of two of the best-known research prototypes.

Through his background as a mathematician, Professor Zima has brought rigor to the presentation of the material, which heretofore has been described primarily in an informal way. The result is a book that cleanly presents a broad range of the techniques used in practical programming support systems.

It is my hope that this text will make the techniques of program analysis and transformation in parallel programming systems accessible to a significant fraction of the compiler-writing community, so that the exciting advances of the last decade will find their way into every compiler.

Ken Kennedy
Rice University
Texas
May 1990

Preface

The aims of this book

One of the most fundamental challenges facing computer science today is the need to develop the algorithms and programming tools required to harness the vast computing power of modern supercomputers. The term **supercomputer** was coined to describe the most powerful machines that exist at any given point in time; the commercially available machines that fall into this (roughly defined) class today include vector and array computers, and massively parallel architectures containing a large number of autonomous communicating processors. These machines provide their users with a peak performance of up to 10 billion floating point operations per second, thus opening the way for the solution of problems which seemed computationally quite out of reach until recently, and spawning interest in a whole range of new problems.

The full potential of supercomputers as instruments for conducting scientific and industrial research can only be reached when they are programmed effectively, which has proved to be a difficult task. The efficiency of concurrent programs depends critically on the proper utilization of specific architectural features of the underlying hardware, which makes automatic support of the program development process highly desirable. Work in the field of programming environments for supercomputers spans several broad areas, including the design of very high-level specification tools, the development of new programming languages, and **super-compilers** that transform code written in a sequential programming language into equivalent concurrent code that can be efficiently executed on a target machine. The focus of this book is in the latter area, which is also known as **automatic restructuring**; it concentrates on the transformation of numerical programs for large-scale scientific and engineering applications.

Automatic restructuring relieves users of a supercomputer from the burden of manually transforming old, 'dusty deck' programs; thus many applications can be up and running on a new machine with a minimum of programmer effort. Moreover, many users in science and engineering have been encouraged to continue programming in conventional languages (Fortran in particular), which they know well and use efficiently. Although new languages and algorithms will play an increasingly important role in the future, automatic restructuring will be of use for a long time to come as a method by which programs within a large class of important scientific problems may be suitably adapted to perform well on supercomputers. Moreover, a welcome side-effect of the activity in this area is the development of new compiling techniques which will have a profound influence on the design and implementation of future languages with explicit concurrency.

This book is a systematic presentation of automatic restructuring techniques for numerical programs, reflecting the significant progress that has been made in this field over the past 15 years. It covers **vectorization** – automatic restructuring for vector or array computers – as well as **parallelization**, with a particular emphasis on massively parallel target architectures. Not only is vectorization a theoretically well-established discipline today, it has also resulted in the development of many commercially successful systems. In contrast, parallelization is still largely the domain of universities and research institutions, and is only slowly reaching the maturity necessary for broader application. Nevertheless, even in parallelization the principal problems have been recognized and many of them have been tackled successfully, although some open questions still remain.

The book is an outgrowth of a four-year period of research and development at the University of Bonn, which led to SUPERB, the first interactive restructuring system for a massively parallel distributed-memory machine (SUPRENUM), in late 1989. A research stay at Rice University during that period proved to be exceptionally stimulating. The material has been covered in courses at the Universities of Bonn and Vienna. It is intended for use in graduate courses in computer science and engineering, and addresses researchers and system developers working in the field of programming environments for concurrent computer systems.

The material in this volume offers a comprehensive treatment of the subject area, illustrating the theoretical development with a large number of examples, and providing an extensive bibliography. It is reasonably self-contained; the mathematics required is either to be found in the appendix or developed directly in the text. We emphasize the basic principles and methods used, and their application to the solution of problems for typical architectures, rather than dealing with the idiosyncrasies of any particular concurrent machine in detail. A working knowledge of Fortran or a similar procedural high-level programming language is assumed. Readers with a basic knowledge of machine architectures and compilers for sequential machines will be able to attain a deeper understanding of the material.

Since Fortran plays a dominating role in the world of scientific programming, it has been chosen as the basis for the presentation of the material in the text. A supercompiler will be taken to be a programming system that performs a source-to-source transformation, translating Fortran 77 into an extended version of Fortran with explicit concurrency. Machine-dependent code generation, which, for concurrent computers, is a far more important issue than for sequential machines, will be treated within this framework as well.

How the contents are organized

Each chapter begins with a section which gives an overview of the material covered and introduces its main topics, with the aim of providing an intuitive understanding of the subject matter; a concluding section puts the preceding discussion into perspective, points out problems and alternative approaches, and gives references.

Chapter 1 shows the need for restructuring systems, traces the history of their development and outlines the manner in which they perform.

In Chapter 2, we describe basic features of computer architectures, classify modern supercomputer systems, and discuss register-to-register vector supercomputers as well as various multiprocessing systems in some detail. Performance issues are considered, and several example systems are presented.

Chapter 2 was included to keep the book as self-contained as possible. It is hoped that the reader will gain an understanding of basic facts in the field; however, it was not our intention to cover architectures in depth. The knowledgeable reader may prefer to proceed directly to Chapter 3.

The core of the book consists of Chapters 3–7. While the first two of these deal with the analysis of programs, the subsequent chapters show how the results of analysis can be used to actually transform programs into concurrent form.

Chapter 3 describes the principal tasks of program flow analysis and gives methods for their solution. This is a condensed reproduction of many important concepts and results in the field, and includes control flow analysis, data flow analysis, monotone data flow systems, call graph construction in the presence of formal procedure parameters, and a collection of interprocedural data flow analysis algorithms.

Program flow analysis is a prerequisite for dependence analysis, which is at the heart of any restructuring system. Dependence analysis is treated in depth in Chapter 4. It computes a relation between statements of a loop that essentially determines whether or not they can be executed concurrently. After introducing the concepts of loop iteration space, execution orders, distance and direction vectors, the problem of dependence testing is precisely formulated as the problem of determining solutions for a diophantine equation in a certain region. A range of algorithms is then presented, describing both exact and approximate methods.

Chapter 5 describes a set of standard transformations for normalization and simplification which convert the program into a form that is a more convenient basis for analysis, vectorization and parallelization.

Chapter 6 (vectorization) discusses criteria and methods for rewriting statements in a loop as vector statements. The basic transformations, such as statement reordering, loop distribution, and vector statement generation are individually introduced and characterized with respect to semantic validity. After establishing the main result of the chapter, which essentially states that a statement can be vectorized if it is not contained in a dependence cycle, a general algorithm for the vectorization of straight-line code in nested loops is presented. The remainder of the chapter deals with auxiliary transformations and machine-dependent aspects.

Chapter 7 (parallelization) treats the problem of transforming sequential programs into programs for a parallel computer. The methods adopted differ significantly, depending on whether code for a shared-memory or a distributed-memory architecture has to be generated.

For shared-memory systems we can use similar techniques and transformations as for vectorization. The objective is to rewrite loops in such a way that their iterations are distributed across the existing processors. However, parallelization induces an overhead for scheduling and synchronization; so in contrast to vectorization, we do not attempt to parallelize single statements, but regions of maximum size.

Parallelization for distributed-memory systems requires a fundamentally different approach, because communication between different processors may be very costly. We introduce a method that is based on a user-specified partition of the sequential program's data domain, which maps the portions of the data domain to the local memories of processors. The specification of the partition must be guided by the local behavior of the program, in an effort to minimize communication. The restructuring system must guarantee that each process will access only its local data, and that synchronization and communication between processes are automatically inserted as required.

Finally, Chapter 8 (conclusion) discusses a few existing restructuring systems and addresses some general issues concerning programming environments for supercomputers. The basic scheme for an interactive restructuring system is developed and directions for future research are indicated.

Acknowledgements

The idea to write a book on supercompilers originated in 1985, when one of the authors became involved in the German supercomputer project SUPRENUM, taking on the responsibility for developing an automatic parallelization system for the distributed-memory SUPRENUM multi-processor. It soon became clear that the relevant research work was scattered among hundreds of papers, technical reports and theses, and that neither a comprehensive book nor a generally acknowledged common terminology existed for the field. Thus a significant portion of the work consisted of reviewing, concentrating and unifying the large body of literature on automatic vectorization and parallelization. Much of the material is based on the pioneering contributions of David Kuck, Ken Kennedy and their associates.

The SUPRENUM project, in particular the cooperation with Ulrich Trottenberg and his group, provided an excellent environment for the exchange of ideas. A large debt of gratitude goes to the members of the SUPRENUM research group at the University of Bonn, especially Heinz Bast, Hans Michael Gerndt and Michael Grindel, who not only developed and implemented some of the new concepts presented in the chapter on parallelization, but also reviewed the book and contributed many useful ideas and improvements. The collaboration with Ken Kennedy is deeply appreciated, as is his generous support in providing a stimulating and exceptionally productive and enjoyable research environment at Rice University, where much of this book was written.

Numerous other people have directly or indirectly contributed to the book; it was a special pleasure to work with the students at Bonn and Rice Universities, who showed so much enthusiasm and competence in dealing with difficult research problems. We are grateful to Markus Theissinger, who helped in the production of the book, and to Marek Karpinski for his encouragement. Finally, it is a pleasure to acknowledge the support and advice of Simon Plumtree and the editorial staff of Addison-Wesley, UK.

Hans Zima
Barbara Chapman
May 1990

To our parents

Contents

Trademark Notice

Butterfly Parallel Processor^{TM} is a trademark of BBN Incorporated

Cray X-MP^{TM}, Cray X-MP/48^{TM}, Cray Y-MP^{TM}, Cray-1^{TM} and Cray-2^{TM} are trademarks of Cray

Cyber-205^{TM} is a trademark of Control Data Corporation

Facom VP-200^{TM} is a trademark of Fujitsu Limited

IBM GF-11^{TM}, IBM RP3^{TM}, IBM System/360 Model 91^{TM}, IBM System/370^{TM}, IBM 3090^{TM} and IBM 3838^{TM} are trademarks of International Business Machines

iPSC and iPSC-VX^{TM} are trademarks of Intel Corporation

occam^{TM} is a trademark of INMOS

SX2^{TM} is a trademark of NEC

S-810^{TM} and S820^{TM} are trademarks of Hitachi

T1-ASC^{TM} is a trademark of Texas Instruments

Chapter 1

Supercomputers and Supercompilers

1.1   Supercomputer applications

Supercomputers have become a fundamental tool of science. While computers have long been used to organize and control scientific experiments and to analyze their results, supercomputers can do much more than that: they play an important role in theoretical science too, enabling scientists to construct and test models in their search for theories to describe natural phenomena. These highly complex mathematical models are typically governed by partial differential equations, whose solution in a discretized version may require a supercomputer to perform trillions of operations. It is not going too far to say that supercomputers are beginning to play a role in modern-day science similar to that of the telescope in seventeenth-century astronomy: the unprecedented increase in computing power at reasonable cost has opened up an exciting new avenue for the exploration of the universe, from dissecting the behavior of subatomic particles to simulating the collision of galaxies.

Supercomputers allow the implementation of more realistic models that improve the quality of existing applications: the transition from a two-dimensional to a three-dimensional numerical simulation model, for example, may require a 100-fold increase in computing power; a mesh size of 150 km in a weather prediction system based on Navier–Stokes equations will lead to about 10^{13} floating point operations for a one-day forecast. A supercomputer with a peak rate of 10 billion floating point operations per second can produce the result within half an hour.

1

Among the manifold application areas for the power of modern high performance computing systems are to be found biology, energy research, high energy physics, astrophysics, aerospace science and engineering, seismology, petroleum exploration, image processing, pattern matching, VLSI design, tomography, industrial automation and genetic engineering.

Supercomputers are used in many areas of energy research to investigate processes that involve physical and chemical interactions. This includes fusion research, simulating the behavior of nuclear reactors, studying combustion processes, improving our ability to harness solar energy, studying the effects of pollution, and modeling climatic changes.

In quantum chromodynamics – a theory of the forces governing atomic and subatomic particles – supercomputers are employed to investigate the properties and the behavior of elementary particles. The computation of the mass of the proton, for example, requires 10^{17} operations, which corresponds to a computation time of 3000 years on an IBM 3081, 18 years on a Cray-1 supercomputer, and four months on the GF-11, a research supercomputer developed at IBM with a processing power of 11 billion operations per second.

Important examples of supercomputer application are to be found in structural biology. The ability to calculate the structure of proteins synthesized from a gene with a known DNA sequence will help to detect the results of genetic defects. It has become feasible to determine the atomic structure of simple viruses consisting of about 1 million atoms: the common cold virus has been analyzed using a three-dimensional fast Fourier transform model with 108 million grid points in 60 cycles, each 200 minutes long, on a Cyber-205 supercomputer.

Supercomputers produce results at such a speed that it far exceeds the ability of human beings to deal with them, if they are represented in a conventional form. A graphical display of the information is indispensable, and new tools and techniques are being devised for visualizing data intelligibly. The flow of air through a jet engine, for example, may be illustrated by a film, using a pattern of colors to represent such parameters as temperature, pressure, and velocity.

1.2   Supercomputer architecture and software

Although many supercomputers provide operating system support for multi-user operation, their typical application is the solution of single, large-scale scientific programs. In this book, we focus our attention exclusively on the latter type of application.

The two major sources contributing to the power of supercomputers are hardware technology and multilevel architectural concurrency. Their architectures vary widely: they span the range from vector and array computers which can handle entire arrays with a single instruction to parallel systems with hundreds or even thousands of processors, each of which is capable of executing an independent instruction stream. Any given class of supercomputers is specialized in the sense that it may perform extremely well on one set of applications and very poorly on another. It is not unusual that an application which is well tuned to the architecture of a specific machine runs with almost 100 per cent efficiency, while another application for the same machine may reach only a small fraction of that rate. For example, a vector computer may operate at near peak performance when applied in a regular fashion to uniformly structured data, whereas it may deal rather inefficiently with list-processing problems or database management.

The programming paradigm for vector computers is closest to the familiar sequential programming model and therefore fairly well understood. In contrast, the management of parallelism in a multiprocessing system adds a new dimension to the complexity of programming. Parallel programming has to deal with systems of processes – individual (sequential) threads of execution – which may, in principle, run independently of each other at unspecified speeds. Such systems can only work in a predictable way when processes are synchronized appropriately, thereby avoiding conditions such as deadlock and preventing race conditions or unintentional data sharing. Moreover, programs for a supercomputer cannot only be judged by the absence of logical errors; they must also be rated according to their efficiency. The diversity of architectures makes this a highly machine-dependent problem.

Current software technology is not yet able to handle the complete range of problems indicated above. For this reason, many of the clerical tasks of programming still have to be performed by the users. Although the pace of change in this area is rapid, only partial solutions can be expected within the next few years. The main directions of current research include the design of concurrent algorithms and languages, and the construction of increasingly powerful tools to support software development and analysis; knowledge-based systems will play a growing part in all of these fields.

Certain aspects of concurrent architectures can be modeled by appropriately extending a standard procedural programming language, such as Fortran, Pascal, or C. Fortran 90, for example, provides vector extensions to allow the declaration, allocation, and manipulation of arrays. Languages with features for the explicit control of parallelism include, among many others, PL/I, ALGOL 68, Ada and occam.

Such languages permit the programmer to formulate concurrent algorithms explicitly. Extensions may be classified according to their degree of machine-dependence: while they are sometimes designed for a specific machine only, others provide a more abstract model that can be efficiently implemented on a large class of suitable architectures. Vector language features are more or less standardized today, while no widely accepted language standard has been developed for parallel languages as yet.

In recent years, several new languages have been designed that promise to raise concurrent programming to a more abstract level by shielding the user from the details of concurrency management. In the long run, high-level programming environments incorporating domain knowledge may well supersede current low level programming tools.

An important problem faced by supercomputer installations is the conversion of the large body of existing code – millions of lines of Fortran programs which have been developed over the past 35 years – into a form suitable for concurrent processing. The exclusive use of language extensions or new languages would force the user to transform each program manually, an extremely time-consuming and error-prone process.

Supercompilers, which perform automatic restructuring, have been developed to deal with precisely this task. They analyze sequential programs, in particular their loops, to detect hidden concurrency, and use this information for the creation of concurrent programs. We speak of **vectorization** if vector code is generated, and of **parallelization** if code for a parallel machine is produced. The transformation strategy can be influenced by user-specified assertions and commands, which are either attached to program statements or entered within a dialog in an interactive system.

The merits of automatic restructuring go beyond the transformation of 'dusty deck' programs: despite the existence of concurrent languages, there are some definite advantages to be had in writing programs in such a well-understood sequential language as Fortran, and then having them automatically transformed into concurrent form. Few computer scientists will readily recognize this – for understandable reasons, as Fortran does not fit into the modern understanding of programming languages – but it is a widespread conviction among practising scientists and engineers. Fortran has been successfully used in countless applications; the design, development, verification and debugging of sequential programs is well understood, and several software environments provide efficient support for programming. Furthermore, retaining programs in Fortran may well be a good way to achieve portability between different supercomputer architectures.

Supercompilers cannot transform every program efficiently; the quality of the results will depend on the structure of the algorithm and the architecture of the target machine. More specifically, supercompilers can detect hidden concurrency in sequential algorithms but, at the current state of the art, they are not able to construct a new algorithm that is better suited to a concurrent architecture. Many algorithms exist which display inherently sequential behavior; for example, it would be extremely difficult to convert a highly specialized sequential sorting algorithm into an efficient concurrent algorithm automatically. Moreover, while vectorization has evolved into a well-understood technique and many of the principal problems of parallelization have been successfully attacked, the variety and structural complexity of parallel systems has so far prevented a general solution of the parallelization problem. Finally, supercompilers rely on the adherence of programs to the language standard: whenever features of a particular machine or system are exploited in a program (a common practice among some Fortran programmers), the technique fails and the program has to be manually rewritten.

In general, the complexity of the relationships between algorithm structure, computer architecture and transformation strategies prevents optimal global solutions – because of their undecidability or intractability – and forces us to use heuristics. Many factors imply that restructuring is best tackled in an interactive system, where the user can make strategic decisions and supply the system with information that cannot be obtained automatically.

Our interest will focus on compiling techniques for restructuring the code of Fortran 77 programs at the statement and procedure level. Whenever we refer to Fortran in the text, Fortran 77 (ANSI, 1978) is meant. Examples will be written in a modified syntax, the meaning of which should be obvious. Although we base our discussion on Fortran, the techniques developed remain fairly general and are thus applicable to a wide range of languages and problems.

1.3   Early work in automatic restructuring

The semantics of procedural languages such as Fortran or Pascal imposes a total order on the execution of statements in a program. However, it is often possible to relax this order without changing the effect of the program, as these two statements demonstrate:

$$S_1: A = B + C$$
$$S_2: D = E * F$$

If there are no equivalences between any two different variables here, then the statements S_1 and S_2 can be executed in reverse order or concurrently without changing the program's semantics. Under such circumstances we speak of a **hidden** or an **implicit concurrency** in the program.

As early as 1966, Bernstein (1966) investigated the semantic validity of executing two segments of a sequential program concurrently. He showed the general problem to be undecidable, but formulated a sufficient condition, which can be written as follows for two statements S_1, S_2:

$$(DEF_1 \cap USE_2) \cup (USE_1 \cap DEF_2) \cup (DEF_1 \cap DEF_2) = \varnothing$$

DEF_i and USE_i are the sets of variables written and read respectively in statement S_i ($i = 1,2$). (The notation is motivated by a terminology in which 'defining' and 'using' a variable are used synonymously with respectively writing and reading the variable (see Chapter 3).) This condition essentially expresses the absence of data dependence between the statements involved, a concept which will play a dominating role in this book: assume that S_1 is executed in the sequential program before S_2, and that there exists a variable $v \in DEF_1 \cap USE_2$, such that S_2 reads the value of v which was written in S_1. Then we say that there is a **true dependence** from S_1 to S_2. Similarly, let v denote a variable such that there is no assignment to v between S_1 and S_2: if S_1 reads v and S_2 writes v, then we speak of an **anti dependence**, and, if S_1 and S_2 both write v, of an **output dependence**. In all of these three cases, any transformation of the program that does not maintain the original execution order of S_1 and S_2 may modify the output of the program and therefore be semantically invalid.

Data dependence is one factor that can prevent concurrent execution; another one is **control dependence**. For example, in the conditional statement IF A < 0 THEN A = -A ELSE A = A + 1 FI, both statements A = -A and A = A + 1 are control dependent on the condition A < 0: the condition must be evaluated before either of these statements can be executed.

If we ignore special cases such as input/output statements, then it turns out that any rearrangement of statements that respects the dependence relation suffices to maintain the semantics of the program.[†] In other words, program transformations are free to reorder statements or to execute them concurrently whenever these statements are not involved in the dependence relation. As an immediate consequence, restructuring must be guided and controlled by dependence. The role to be played by the dependence relation was already apparent in the earliest approaches to parallelization (Ramamoorthy and Gonzalez, 1969; Russell, 1969; Roucairol, 1977), which detect parallelism by analyzing and transforming a graphical representation of the program. They do not modify the original program except to insert code for controlling parallel execution. Kotov (Kotov and Narinyani, 1969; Kotov, 1984) uses program transformations to delete anti and output dependences in a semantically valid way by renaming variables.

The methods we have so far discussed either do not deal at all with loops, or do not provide any means by which different loop iterations can be executed as independent processes. Urschler (1973) proposes a strategy for the transformation of flowchart programs which can also handle loop iterations. The drawback of his method is that it does not analyze subscripted variables and thus is not able to handle most of the cases that are interesting from a practical point of view.

In this respect, the work of D. Kuck, L. Lamport and others in the early 1970s (Kuck *et al.*, 1972; Kuck, 1973a, 1973b; Lamport, 1974; Towle,

---

[†] There are, however, transformations that eliminate dependences without changing the semantics of the program. An example is the renaming of a scalar variable in a region of the program (this is discussed in Section 5.4). Therefore, maintaining the dependence relation is not necessary for the semantic validity of a transformation.

1976) was a major breakthrough, since they were the first to include subscripted variables with symbolic subscript expressions in the analysis. The basic ideas which were developed at that time still dominate the reasoning about automatic vectorization and parallelization.

The object of the transformation strategy developed by Kuck is a sequential Fortran program, which is analyzed at the statement level. All data dependences are eliminated in the program's basic blocks (which are sequences of assignment statements that are always executed in textual order) by renaming variables and substituting expressions for their uses; the statements can then be executed concurrently. The computation of the expressions generated can be optimized by applying standard algebraic laws (Stone, 1967; Ramamoorthy and Gonzalez, 1971; Beatty, 1972; Baer, 1973).

For a do-loop, the dependences are computed using tests that also analyze subscripted variables. The dependence relation is represented by a directed graph. The strongly connected components of the dependence graph ('PI-blocks') are determined, and code is generated for the loop by processing the PI-blocks in topological order according to the following criterion: if a statement is involved in a cyclic PI-block (that is, in a cyclic dependence relationship), then sequential code must be generated; other-wise the instances of the statement in different loop iterations are indepen-dent, and vectorization or parallelization is semantically valid.

1.4   Components of a supercompiler

We describe the principal components of a supercompiler which performs a source-to-source transformation (Figure 1.1). The input language is Fortran 77, the output language a Fortran superset which we call VP-Fortran (for **vector parallel** Fortran). It contains language features for the specification and control of vector and parallel operations. Elements of the language will be defined in subsequent chapters as required.[†]

The system consists of two main modules: the **front end** and the **back end**. When presented with a Fortran 77 program P as input, the super-compiler produces a semantically equivalent VP-Fortran program P_{VP} by first applying the front end, which analyzes the program and transforms it into an internal representation, and then synthesizing P_{VP} according to the architecture of the target machine.

The first phases of the front end perform the analysis tasks of a conventional compiler, that is scanning, parsing and static semantic

---

[†] Actually, VP-Fortran is not a well-defined language but rather a loosely defined set of – sometimes unrelated – features which will be used as needed in specific contexts.

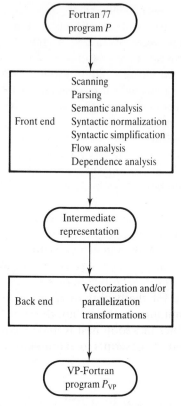

Figure 1.1   Structure of a supercompiler.

analysis, and create an internal representation of the program; this is typically an attributed abstract tree with associated symbol table. We refer the reader to the standard compiler literature, for example Aho *et al.* (1986) and Zima (1989), for further details. Note that the use of an internal representation is not a matter of principle, but a means of improving the efficiency of the translation process. There is at least one system (Parafrase) that transforms programs at the source level. In the rest of the book we shall ignore the internal representation and discuss programs and their transformations at the source level only.

   Among the other tasks performed by the front end are program analysis (including flow analysis and dependence analysis) and syntactic normalization and simplification.

   In the past, program analysis was mainly used in optimizing compilers to reduce execution time and program memory requirements (Hecht, 1977; Muchnick and Jones, 1981), or in software development tools to reveal programming errors caused by certain data flow anomalies

(Fosdick and Osterweil, 1976). With the advent of concurrent computers, analysis proved to be successful in supporting the automatic mapping of sequential programs to these new architectures.

The methods of analysis can be classified into two basic groups, flow analysis and dependence analysis, where flow analysis is a prerequisite of dependence analysis. **Flow analysis** derives information about the flow of scalar data during program execution, such as cross-reference listings associating definitions with uses of variables. **Data flow analysis** – which is the means of obtaining such information – must be preceded by a **control flow analysis** that determines the control structure of the program. Flow analysis is treated in Chapter 3.

The task of **dependence analysis** is to determine the dependence relation and represent it in the **dependence graph**. This relation controls the restructuring process. The crucial difference between data flow analysis and dependence analysis lies in the treatment of subscripted variables: while data flow analysis can handle a subscripted variable only as a representative for the whole array, dependence analysis examines subscripted variables individually. The resulting gain in the precision of the analysis information is decisive for the quality of restructuring. Whereas the general problem of determining whether or not there is a dependence between two subscripted variables in a loop nest is undecidable, effective tests can be developed if we restrict subscripts to expressions which are linear in the loop variables. These techniques were first used in two automatic vectorizers, Parafrase and PFC, which were respectively developed by D. Kuck at the University of Illinois, Urbana–Champaign, and K. Kennedy at Rice University, Houston (Wolfe, 1982; Allen, 1983; Kuck *et al.*, 1984a; Padua and Wolfe, 1986; Allen and Kennedy, 1987). We shall discuss dependence analysis in Chapter 4.

During program analysis, we convert the program into a standardized form, via a number of normalization and simplification procedures, to make our subsequent application of the transformations simpler and more efficient. We may, for example, normalize do-loops so that the increment is equal to 1, simplify subscript expression according to the laws of algebra and eliminate useless code. These transformations are the subject of Chapter 5.

The task of the back end is to construct P_{VP} from its internal representation, using the analysis information gathered in the front end. The back end can be viewed as a collection of transformations, the (**transformation) catalog**, whose application to the program is governed by certain strategies that depend on the program characteristics, the quality of the analysis information, and the target machine. It is often convenient to classify the transformations of the catalog into three categories, general, architecture specific, and machine specific, which may serve as a guide to a structured translation process.

The principal uses of analysis information in the control of the transformation process can be summarized as follows:

(1)   verify the existence of preconditions necessary for the application of transformations, and help to establish criteria for making a selection from a number of valid transformations;

(2)   determine the effect of a transformation on the program;

(3)   provide the information to clean up after a transformation sequence has been applied.

The two main methods of restructuring treated in this book will be vectorization and parallelization. The related properties of the catalog and associated transformation strategies will be discussed in Chapter 6 (vectorization) and Chapter 7 (parallelization).

1.5   Examples of restructuring

In the first example, we illustrate the main steps in the vectorization of a sequential Fortran program. We do not use the internal representation, but specify the effect of each step at the source program level.

Example 1.1

```
DO I = 100, 1, -1
  A(I - 2) = B(I + 1) + C(I)
  E(I)     = F(I - 3) / A(I - 2)
END DO I
```

do-loop normalization
$\Longrightarrow$

```
DO %I = 1, 100
  A(100 + (%I - 1) * (-1) - 2) = B(100 + (%I - 1) * (-1) + 1)
                                 + C(100 + (%I - 1) * (-1))
  E(100 + (%I - 1) * (-1))     = F(100 + (%I - 1) * (-1) - 3)
                                 / A(100 + (%I - 1) * (-1) - 2)
END DO %I
I = 0
```

Dead-code elimination
$\Longrightarrow$

```
DO %I = 1, 100
  A(100 + (%I - 1) * (-1) - 2)= B(100 + (%I - 1) * (-1) + 1)
                               + C(100 + (%I - 1) * (-1))
  E(100 + (%I - 1) * (-1))    = F(100 + (%I - 1) * (-1) - 3)
                               / A(100 + (%I - 1) * (-1) - 2)
END DO %I
```

Simplification and subscript standardization
$$\Longrightarrow$$

```
DO %I = 1, 100
  A(99 - %I)  = B(102 - %I) + C(101 - %I)
  E(101 - %I) = F(98 - %I) / A(99 - %I)
END DO %I
```

Loop distribution
$$\Longrightarrow$$

```
DO %I = 1, 100
  A(99 - %I)  = B(102 - %I) + C(101 - %I)
END DO %I

DO %I = 1, 100
  E(101 - %I) = F(98 - %I) / A(99 - %I)
END DO %I
```

Vector code generation
$$\Longrightarrow$$

```
A(-1:98) = B(2:101) + C(1:100)
E(1:100) = F(-2:97) / A(-1:98)
```

The first step shown is **do-loop normalization**. This transformation converts the original loop into one with a new compiler-generated do-variable %I whose initial value is 1 and which is incremented in steps of 1. The value of I in iteration i is $100 + (i - 1) * (-1)$; therefore each occurrence of I in the loop body can be replaced by $100 + (\%I - 1) * (-1)$. Finally, the assignment $I = 0$ immediately following the loop must be generated so that I has the same value as in the original program when execution of the loop terminates.

The second step, **dead-code elimination**, removes statements whose effect is empty. Such statements are called **useless** or **dead code**. We assume that in our program I is not used before it is assigned a new value: so the assignment $I = 0$ is dead code and can be eliminated.

The third step simplifies and standardizes all subscript expressions which are integer linear functions in the loop variable by writing them in the form $a_0 + a_1 * \%I$, where a_0 and a_1 are integer constants. After this step we have already constructed the dependence graph, which here indicates a dependence from the first to the second statement: this dependence is caused by the fact that, in each iteration of the loop, the second statement uses the value assigned to the variable A(99 - %I) in the first statement.

The steps described so far, and the representation of the program in an internal form to which analysis information is attached, are all performed in the front end. The remaining steps, which are associated with transformations of the catalog, belong to the back end and synthesize a vectorized version of the program.

First, **loop distribution** produces a program with loops whose body consists of a single statement. **Vector code generation** can be applied to such loops. If the statement in the body is not cyclically dependent on itself – which is guaranteed in our example – then the generation of vector code is semantically valid. Now consider the first vector statement. The notation A(-1:98) refers to the vector with components (A(-1), A(0), ... A(98)); similarly, B(2:101) and C(1:100) represent vectors with 100 components. The operator + is applied to all pairs of corresponding components, that is it produces the sum vector (B(2) + C(1), B(3) +C (2), ..., B(101) + C(100)), whose components are finally assigned to the corresponding components of A(-1:98). All component operations are executed concurrently; thus we cannot assume any specific order of processing. This is the reason why we stipulate that the statement within the distributed loop may not be dependent on itself.

Example 1.2

Here, we illustrate the transformation of a sequential program for matrix multiplication into a parallel program for a shared-memory machine. We use the doall-loop to express parallelism: in the loop

```
DOALL I = 1, N
  SEQ
ENDALL
```

where SEQ is a statement sequence, all iterations can be executed in parallel without synchronization. If a sufficient number of processes is available, every process can execute exactly one iteration; if there are fewer than *N* processes, two or more iterations must be mapped to one process.

We begin with the sequential program:

```
DIMENSION A(N, N), B(N, N), C(N, N)

DO J = 1, N
  DO I = 1, N
    C(I, J) = 0.0
```

```
    DO K = 1, N
     S: C(I, J) = C(I, J) + A(I, K) * B(K, J)
    END DO K
  END DO I
END DO J
```

Assume that the values of I and J are fixed, and consider the execution of statement S for the iterations K = 1, 2, ... of the innermost loop:

```
C(I, J) = C(I, J) + A(I, 1) * B(1, J)
C(I, J) = C(I, J) + A(I, 2) * B(2, J)
...
```

The value assigned to C(I, J) in the first iteration is used in the second one; thus there exists a true dependence from S to S. This cyclic dependence suffices to prevent concurrent execution of the K loop. In contrast, the J loop and the I loop can be executed in parallel. Since we want to keep the cost of scheduling as low as possible, we select the outermost loop and transform the program accordingly. This yields:

```
DOALL J = 1, N
  DO I = 1, N
    C(I, J) = 0.0
    DO K = 1, N
      C(I, J) = C(I, J) + A(I, K) * B(K, J)
    END DO K
  END DO I
ENDALL J
```

Now assume that N processes p_j $(1 \leqslant j \leqslant N)$ are available for the execution of the doall-loop. Then we can assign the work in such a way that for each j, process p_j executes the code:

```
DO I = 1, N
  C(I, j) = 0.0
  DO K = 1, N
    C(I, j) = C(I, j) + A(I, K) * B(K, j)
  END DO K
END DO I
```

Thus, process p_j computes the jth column of the result matrix C: for I = 1, 2, ... the scalar product of the Ith row of A and of the jth column of B is calculated. Whereas the elements within each column are computed sequentially (in one process), different columns are processed in parallel.

For each I, p_j references the variable C(I, j) $2N + 1$ times. It is realistic to assume that p_j has a local memory which can be accessed much faster than the shared memory in which C(I, j) is located. So we can improve the efficiency of the code by introducing a local variable of p_j, %T; then the code for p_j is as follows:

```
DO I = 1, N
  %T = 0.0
  DO K = 1, N
    %T = %T + A(I, K) * B(K, j)
  END DO K
  C(I, j) = %T
END DO I
```

Now, only one memory access is required for each C(I, j) in p_j.

The final version of the program can then be given as follows (LOCAL x introduces a separate local variable in each process):

```
DIMENSION A(N, N), B(N, N), C(N, N)
DOALL J = 1, N
  LOCAL %T
  DO I = 1, N
    %T = 0.0
    DO K = 1, N
      %T = %T + A(I, K) * B(K, j)
    END DO K
    C(I, j) = %T
  END DO I
ENDALL J
```

If the processors have a vector facility, then the program can be further transformed by vectorizing the I loop (after an interchange with the K loop). We do not discuss details.

BIBLIOGRAPHICAL NOTES

There is a large body of literature on supercomputer applications and parallel algorithms. We mention just a few of them (Quinn, 1987; Fox *et al.*, 1988; Bertsekas and Tsitsiklis, 1989).

Vectran (Paul and Wilson, 1978), Fortran 8x (ANSI, 1989) and Actus (Perrot, 1979; Perrot *et al.*, 1983) are among the languages which provide vector extensions. Vectran and Fortran 8x are based upon Fortran, while Actus is a superset of Pascal.

Languages which allow explicit control of parallelism include PL/I (ANSI, 1976), ALGOL 68 (van Wijngaarden *et al.*, 1975), Concurrent Pascal (Brinch Hansen, 1975), CSP (Hoare, 1978), Ada (Department of Defense, 1981), Concurrent C (Gehani and Roome, 1986), occam (INMOS, 1988), IBM Parallel Fortran (IBM, 1988), and PCF (Leasure *et al.*, 1988). Karp and Babb (Karp and Babb, 1988; Babb, 1988) compare several parallel Fortran dialects. SUPRENUM Fortran (Ehses and Mevenkamp, 1986) provides vector as well as parallel extensions. Fortran extensions for the Cray and Sequent multiprocessing architectures are described in Booth and Misegades (1986) and Osterhaug (1989) respectively.

Recently developed languages at a higher level of abstraction include SISAL (McGraw *et al.*, 1985), BLAZE (Mehrotra and Rosendale, 1985), and SUSPENSE (Ruppelt and Wirtz, 1988, 1989; Wirtz, 1989).

Chapter 2

Supercomputer Architectures

2.1 Introduction

Any restructuring system has to take into account the specific features of the target architecture. It is the intention of this chapter to provide the reader with an understanding of typical supercomputer architectures and their components, together with the specific advantages and disadvantages of particular design decisions. However, this is by no means a comprehensive treatment of the area and the interested reader is referred to the literature (Hockney and Jesshope, 1981; Hwang and Briggs, 1984; Hwang, 1984a, 1984b; Stone, 1987; Dongarra, 1987; Quinn, 1987; Babb, 1988; Bertsekas and Tsitsiklis, 1989).

The history of computing has been characterized by a continual growth in the computing power of available systems, coupled with a continued demand for even better performance. Part of this increase in power is due to a series of technological advances, and part of it is the accumulated result of a number of improvements in system design. One of the major features of the design decisions taken over the past decades was that they introduced more and more concurrency into computer architectures. Thus memory was organized into banks to enable concurrent access to different locations, I/O devices were duplicated within a system where they operated independently, and pipelining meant that several instructions could be undergoing execution simultaneously. Today, a modern supercomputer may well have a large number of processors, each of which is able to execute its own instruction stream independently of the others. The provision of multiple units in the processing component and the memory, the basic idea behind both vector and parallel supercomputers, was the single most important design innovation to date, providing a new dimension of computing performance.

We begin this chapter by introducing the important components of modern high performance computing systems and then discuss a method for their classification which is based on the way in which these components are put together. We look at the problem of measuring a supercomputer's performance and see what factors can be expected to put an upper limit on the computing power they provide. This is followed by an analysis of vector supercomputers, with several example systems, in Section 2.2, and a discussion of parallel computing systems (Section 2.3).

2.1.1 Components of a computer system

We can think of a modern computer system as being a structured collection of independent modules. These modules, which include processors, memories, input/output channels, and peripheral devices are functionally independent units that can operate concurrently. The way in which they are selected and organized determines the **architecture** of a system.

The processing component may execute one or more independent instruction streams. It is made up of one or more control units (CUs) and arithmetic–logical units (ALUs). A CU preprocesses the instructions in a stream: it fetches and decodes the instructions, executes certain control instructions, such as branches, and sends all others on to an appropriate unit (such as an ALU, or an input/output subsystem) for further processing. We call the combination of one CU and one ALU a **processor** or **processing unit** (PU); a PU with attached memory will be referred to as a (processing) **node**. Nodes are self-contained units that can execute one instruction stream.

A supercomputer needs access to vast amounts of data that have to be processed effectively. However, since processing units operate much faster than memories, a serious organizational problem arises here: any system designer must find some way of ensuring that the memory does not reduce the performance of the entire system significantly. This inherent imbalance is known as the **von Neumann bottleneck** and many different methods have been developed to eliminate it. In today's supercomputers, memory is organized as a hierarchy which may consist of five or more levels, ranging from a small, high speed cache to main memory – which may be divided into fast local process memories and a slower global memory – to mass storage, and, finally, to the virtually unlimited capacity of long-term archival memory. In order to keep the processing units busy, programs must manage the hierarchy in such a way that a constant flow of data to and from the units is maintained. Main memory can be divided into interleaved banks such that consecutive locations are allocated to banks in a round-robin manner. The different banks operate independently, enabling memory accesses to be overlapped when linear instruction or data streams are being processed.

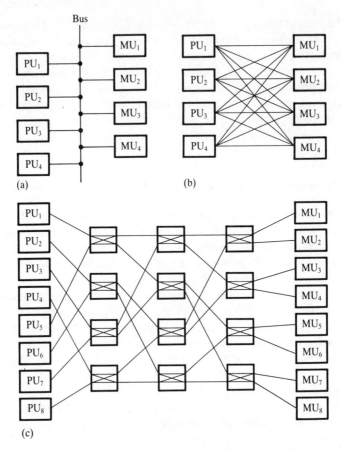

Figure 2.1   Interconnection networks (PU, processing unit;
MU, memory module). (a) Common bus; (b) crossbar switch;
(c) multilevel switch network.

The **bandwidth** of a memory system is the maximum number of bytes
that can be transferred in one second between the processing component
and the memory. This concept can be extended to describe the rate at which
other system components involved in the transport of data can operate.

Any system with a number of independent functional modules has to
provide some sort of interconnection network for the transfer of data and/or
control signals. Processors must be connected to memory modules, to other
processors and to the input/output subsystem; I/O channels must be linked
to the memory. A variety of networks have been hitherto realized in the
hardware: they vary both in their efficiency and their cost, and some can
only be implemented for small systems. We briefly characterize three
important methods of implementing a network connecting processors to
memory modules: buses, crossbar switches and multilevel switching networks (Figure 2.1).

A (**common**) **bus** is a communication path shared by the processors, connecting them to the memory units. The bus must have an arbitration mechanism with which it can resolve conflicting access requests. Buses are inexpensive to build and easy to reconfigure, but their performance is in general too poor to support a large number of modules. If we want to avoid a critical bottleneck, we will have to use more than one bus and/or the processors must be supplemented by local memories and local I/O subsystems.

A **crossbar switch** will connect each processor directly with every memory module, so network contention is entirely eliminated. This is the most efficient interconnection mechanism; however, the cost of connecting n processors with n memory modules – which can be expressed as a function of the number of crosspoints required in the system – is $O(n^2)$, compared with $O(n)$ for the bus. For large n, a crossbar switch cannot be constructed.

Multilevel switching networks establish a connection between two points via a number of intermediate switching stages. They exist in a variety of designs, some of which are similar to the familiar telephone networks: each time a processor accesses a memory module, it uses a path through the network; a delay occurs if two simultaneous requests for memory access use the same switch. A typical example is the Ω-network (Lawrie, 1975), which is characterized by a path length of $O(\log_2 n)$ and a cost of $O(n \log_2 n)$.

2.1.2 Flynn's classification of computer architectures

There are several different ways in which modern supercomputers can be classified. One of these is to assign them to classes based on the type and number of their processors; another is to take the nature of the interconnections between individual processors as the major criterion. Here, we group architectures into three categories according to a classification scheme developed by Flynn (1966); this scheme, which could be said to characterize the global control in a system, assigns a particular computer to a category on the basis of the structure of its processing components and the ability of the system to execute one or more instruction and/or data streams simultaneously. We call these classes SISD, SIMD, and MIMD; they are defined below. (In Flynn's classification there is a fourth class, MISD (multiple instruction stream–single data stream), which does not seem to be of any practical relevance.)

SISD (**single instruction stream–single data stream**) architectures consist of a single processing node. This class comprises all conventional uniprocessor systems (although, as implied above, these too generally exhibit a high degree of internal concurrency, it cannot be exploited by the programmer). **Vector computers**, which have instructions that operate on entire arrays rather than on scalar entities, are included here. We illustrate the basic structure of an SISD machine in Figure 2.2.

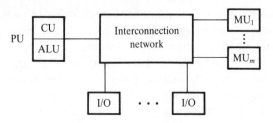

Figure 2.2   An SISD machine with m memory units (MU_j, memory unit j ($1 \leqslant j \leqslant m$); I/O, input/output subsystem).

SIMD (single instruction stream–multiple data stream) architectures are synchronous parallel machines.[†] The processing component of an SIMD computer consists of one CU and a number of processing elements (PEs), each of which is made up of one ALU and one local memory (LM). The PEs operate in parallel in a lock-step fashion: an instruction is broadcast by the CU to all PEs and is then executed synchronously by the PEs on data in their local memory. Note that the PEs cannot decode instructions. The basic structure of an SIMD machine is shown in Figure 2.3. SIMD machines are also referred to as **array computers** or **processor arrays**.

The first SIMD machine built was the ILLIAC IV; it was designed at the University of Illinois in the 1960s and went into operation in 1972. The ILLIAC IV has 64 PEs, each of which is connected via a 64-bit data path with four neighbors; the system is managed by a Burroughs B6500 host computer and can perform up to 200 million floating point operations per second. Other computers of this type are the ICL DAP (Flanders *et al.*, 1977), Burroughs BSP (Kuck and Stokes, 1982), and Goodyear MPP (Batcher, 1980; Gilmore, 1986). The largest SIMD machine currently in existence is the Connection Machine CM-2 from Thinking Machines Corporation (Hillis, 1985), which consists of 65536 1-bit PEs. SIMD machines can be used successfully in applications dominated by repetitive operations on regularly structured data, as for example in image analysis and pattern matching. The programmer is responsible for partitioning the data domain in such a way that all data required in an operation executed by a PE are allocated in its local memory. This makes SIMD machines much harder to program than vector computers.

[†] Some authors (for example Stone (1987)) define SIMD as an architecture in which a single instruction can manipulate an entire data structure. This allows the inclusion of vector computers in the SIMD class. We do not follow this practice.

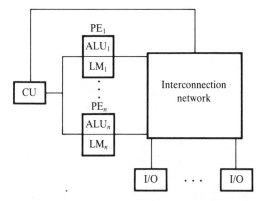

Figure 2.3 An SIMD machine with n processing elements ($PE_i = (ALU_i, LM_i)$, processing element i; ALU_i, arithmetic–logical unit of PE_i; LM_i, local memory of PE_i; $1 \leq i \leq n$).

Example 2.1

Assume we have an SIMD machine with 64 processing elements $PE_i = (ALU_i, LM_i)$ ($1 \leq i \leq 64$), where each ALU_i contains a floating point register R_i. Suppose that a vector addition $C = A + B$ is to be performed, where $A(1:64)$, $B(1:64)$, and $C(1:64)$ are one-dimensional real arrays distributed over the PEs such that $A(i)$, $B(i)$ and $C(i)$ are allocated in LM_i.

This vector addition can be implemented by a sequence of three instructions, which are decoded by the CU and then sent to all ALUs for synchronous execution:

For every ALU_i: LOAD $A(i)$ into R_i
For every ALU_i: Execute $R_i \leftarrow R_i + B(i)$
For every ALU_i: STORE R_i in $C(i)$

MIMD (multiple instruction stream–multiple data stream) architectures are asynchronous parallel machines, which will be referred to in the following as **parallel** or **multiprocessing systems**. (Synchronous parallel systems (SIMD systems) will no longer be considered, so this terminology is unambiguous.) An MIMD system contains two or more processors, each of which can execute an instruction stream independently of the other processors. Depending on the method of communication between processors, we further distinguish between two classes, namely **shared-memory** or **tightly coupled** MIMD systems (**SMS**), and **distributed-memory** or **loosely coupled** MIMD systems (**DMS**).

Figure 2.4 illustrates an SMS with n processors sharing the input/output subsystems and the global memory. The processors communicate via

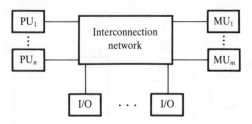

Figure 2.4   A shared-memory system with n processors and m memory units (PU$_i$, processing unit i $(1 \leq i \leq n)$; MU$_j$, memory unit j $(1 \leq j \leq m)$; I/O, input/output subsystem).

the memory, which allows them to share code and data. This organization makes an SMS highly versatile and relatively easy to program. The drawback is that the system design is highly complex, primarily because it is necessary to reduce the effect of the von Neumann bottleneck. The limit on the number of processors in such systems implemented using a bus or crossbar network is currently on the order of 64. Larger systems may be constructed with a multilevel switching network.

In Figure 2.5 we have a DMS with n processors. Each of these processors has its own local memory and an I/O subsystem; there is no global memory at all. Processors communicate by exchanging messages via an interconnection network. While the distance between processors and the global memory is the same for each processor of an SMS, a processor in a DMS may be able to access its local memory several orders of magnitude faster than it can access non-local memory via the network. Furthermore, the communication paths between two processors may have different lengths, depending on the topology of the network (see Section 2.3.5). Thus

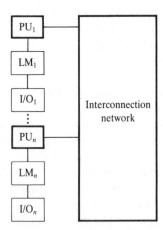

Figure 2.5   A distributed-memory system with n processors (PU$_i$, processing unit i; LM$_i$, local memory of PU$_i$; I/O$_i$, input/output subsystem of PU$_i$; $(1 \leq i \leq n)$).

one of the main concerns in a DMS is to keep the communication:comput-ation ratio low: algorithms must display a predominantly local behavior to be efficiently run on such a system. DMSs are relatively easy to build; their most significant advantage is the scalability to a large number of nodes.

There are a wealth of different MIMD systems in existence today; many of them are hybrid systems which may, for example, exhibit a mixture of local and shared memory, or have shared memory distributed among clusters of processors.

A number of issues will concern us in connection with MIMD systems that have no counterpart in sequential computers: among other things, the workload of a system must be suitably divided up into tasks, communication must be provided for, and synchronization must be arranged where required.

2.1.3 Performance

The single most important criterion for a supercomputer is its perfor-mance. However, there exists no commonly accepted metric for perfor-mance measurement, and performance data actually observed when running an application on a supercomputer may be one or two orders of magnitude lower than the specifications supplied by the manufacturer. One reason for this is that the computational efficiency of a problem solution depends to a great extent on the characteristics of the problem, such as uniformity of operations, locality of references and communication and synchronization requirements, and how well a particular machine is suited to handle precisely these characteristics. As a consequence, we restrict ourselves to stating a few basic facts and relationships informally, and return to the topic in Sections 2.2.5 and 2.3.3.

The **peak rate** of a computer system is the maximum computational rate that can be theoretically achieved when all modules are fully utilized. The **sustained rate** for a given computational task is the rate that can actually be achieved for the solution of this task. We usually specify the computational rate by the number of floating point operations (FLOPS) that can be executed in one second (see Appendix C, Section C.9).

Let A be a given computational task, M_1 and M_2 two machines, and T_1 and T_2 the times required to execute task A on machines M_1 and M_2 respectively. Assume that M_2 is more powerful than M_1 with respect to the given problem, that is $T_2 < T_1$. The ratio T_1/T_2 is called the **speed-up** of task A on machine M_2 with respect to machine M_1.

2.2 Vector supercomputers

Current vector processors belong to two classes: attached processors and vector supercomputers. **Attached processors** are pipelined arithmetic

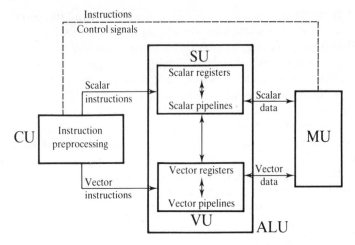

Figure 2.6 The structure of a vector supercomputer.

processors that are connected to a host – a minicomputer or a standard mainframe – as a peripheral device. They include Texas Instruments' Advanced Scientific Computer (TI-ASC) and Control Data Corporation's STAR-100 (which were installed in 1972 and 1973), the IBM 3838 (Hwang and Briggs, 1984) and the FPS-164 systems (Charlesworth, 1981).

We restrict our attention to **vector supercomputers**, a class of SISD computers operated in conjunction with a host. The first of these were the Cray-1 and the Cyber-205; there are a number of others closely related to the Cray-1. The installation of Cray Research's first Cray-1 at Los Alamos National Laboratory in 1976 marked the beginning of commercially successful vector computers.

Vector supercomputers are classified as either **memory-to-memory** or **register-to-register** architectures, depending on whether the operands and results of vector instructions are in main memory or in vector registers within the processor. The only systems of note with the former type of architecture are the Cyber-205 and the processors of the ETA[10]. The majority of vector supercomputers, including the Cray-1 and its successors, are register to register, and it is this class which we discuss in the following.

2.2.1 Register-to-register vector architectures

We base our discussion on a register-to-register vector supercomputer, VSC, (Figure 2.6) which satisfies the following:

1. VSC = (CU, ALU, MU), where CU is the control unit, ALU the arithmetic–logical unit, and MU the main memory. The distinctive feature of VSC is the structure of its arithmetic–logical unit, which is

composed of a scalar unit, SU, and a vector unit, VU. The control unit executes an instruction stream which may contain scalar as well as vector instructions, and passes individual instructions for processing to SU or VU, depending on their type. SU and VU may work concurrently.

2. The instruction set of SU corresponds to that of a standard mainframe, such as the IBM System/370.[†]

3. The vector unit executes vector instructions. It is organized as a register-to-register architecture, whose main components are (functional) pipelines and vector registers. Each functional pipeline implements one specific operation such as floating point addition, multiplication, or logical and. The registers provide a high speed buffer storage between main memory and the pipelines. Different pipelines can work concurrently. The vector unit is discussed in Section 2.2.3.

4. Vector supercomputers are built upon the principle of pipelining. Pipelines are not only used in the vector unit but are to be found throughout the entire system: in the control unit, in the mechanisms for transferring data between registers and memory, and in the scalar unit. Pipelining is discussed in Section 2.2.2, and we see how pipelines can be 'chained' to improve performance in Section 2.2.4.

2.2.2 Pipelining

Pipelining is a method of processing objects that has been used for a long time in industrial mass production. To understand how it works, consider for a moment the way an automobile is put together on the assembly line: the task of assembling a car is divided into many small subtasks, each of which is performed at a particular assembly station (stage). While each particular car is built sequentially, many cars – at different stages – are assembled concurrently. Suppose that the assembly line consists of k stages $F_1, \ldots, F_k$, each of which does its job in the same fixed amount of time (say 10 minutes). The assembly of each individual car thus takes $10k$ minutes, but the assembly line outputs one car every 10 minutes. So after the first $10(k - 1)$ minutes of operation, production is increased by a factor of k compared with purely sequential operation. Computers can be organized to process instructions in a similar way.

Pipelining as a form of internal concurrency is not new; a prominent early example is the IBM System/360 Model 91 which was built in the 1960s (Andersen et al., 1967). Example 2.2 illustrates a hypothetical single-processor machine with a pipelined instruction cycle.

[†] Some vector supercomputers (such as the Amdahl Vector Processor (Amdahl, 1984) or the IBM 3090 (Buchholz, 1986)) are direct extensions of the IBM System/370.

Example 2.2: Pipelining in a single-processor machine

Assume that we have an SISD machine M = (CU, ALU, MU) and want to execute a program containing only instructions of the form (op, R, x), where op specifies a binary arithmetic or logical operation, R is a register and x a memory location. An instruction applies op to the contents of R and x, and returns the result value to R.

The control of sequential program execution can be described by the following loop, which processes one instruction per iteration. At the right-hand side we indicate the unit responsible for the execution of each step:

> **repeat**
>   Step 1: fetch instruction;   [MU]
>   Step 2: decode instruction;   [CU]
>   Step 3: fetch operand;   [MU]
>   Step 4: execute operation   [ALU]
>
> **until** last instruction

Supposing that each step takes one unit of time, the processing of n instructions requires $4n$ time units.

Now assume we have two independent memory units MU_1 and MU_2 in our system, and that all four units can work concurrently. We are thus able to organize our machine as a four-stage pipeline $PL = (MU_1, CU, MU_2, ALU)$. As before, the execution of each particular instruction takes 4 units; but subsequent instruction executions are overlapped, and after initialization the pipeline completes the processing of one instruction in every time unit. This is illustrated in Figure 2.7, where instruction I1 is completed at time 4, instruction I2 at time 5, and so on.

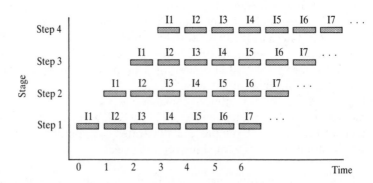

Figure 2.7   Operation of an instruction pipeline (I1, I2, ... denote the instructions of a program).

We assume a simplified functional pipeline F, such that:

1.   F is divided into $k \geqslant 2$ stages F_i $(1 \leqslant i \leqslant k)$. The different stages are independent functional units.

2.   Each single task to be performed by F is processed sequentially in the stages F_1, F_2, ... F_k: when a stage has completed its share of processing a task, it hands the job over to the next one by transferring its output to the successor's input.

3.   Different tasks may be processed in different stages of F concurrently.

4.   Every stage needs one time unit to process one task. The operation of the pipeline is synchronized by a common clock.

In the first $k - 1$ time units, pipeline F will produce no result. This is called the **start-up phase**. Beginning at time unit k, one result is produced in every unit. Thus the time required by F to process m tasks is $T_{PL} = k - 1 + m$. It takes time $T_1 = mk$ to process m tasks serially, so F's speed-up over serial operation is:

$$\sigma = \frac{T_1}{T_{PL}} = \frac{mk}{k - 1 + m}$$

From this we can conclude that the speed-up of a k-stage pipeline may asymptotically approach k.

In practice, we cannot assume that a pipeline is able to work without interruption. This is prevented, for example, by the occurrence of a branch in the instruction stream, which enforces a clean-up and a start-up phase before work continues at the instruction's target, or as the result of a conditional operation or an interrupt. There will be delays due to the necessity of satisfying a data dependence or as a result of memory contention. Also, in contrast to property (4) above, different stages of a pipeline may take different amounts of time to complete their tasks. Moreover, not all pipelines are linear, that is, characterized by a sequential flow of data as in property (2). A non-linear organization is required to implement an operation involving recurrence, such as a dot product: feedforward and feedback connections cause data to flow from some stage F_i to another one, F_j, where $j > i + 1$ or $j \leqslant i$.

Pipelines are most effective when a large number of similar tasks are executed. An obvious paradigm is the execution of single operations on a large data stream, the ideal situation for vector computers, which are primarily designed to process long vectors efficiently in a uniform way.

Many functions can be realized well by a pipeline. This includes instruction preprocessing, arithmetic and logical operations, and the transfer of vectors between memory and registers (load/store pipelines). The pipelining concept may be also used in a more general context, involving whole processing elements or processors as stages.

2.2.3 The vector unit

The vector unit consists of the following components:

(1)   a vector instruction processor,
(2)   a collection $\mathbf{R}$ of r (vector) registers: $\mathbf{R} = \{R_j : 0 \leqslant j \leqslant r - 1\}$,
(3)   a vector length register VL,
(4)   a mask register MASK, and
(5)   a set of functional pipelines.

Vector registers provide a fast buffer storage between the functional pipelines and main memory. Each register $R \in \mathbf{R}$ has a constant **length** s, the number of words that can be stored in it. R is to be interpreted as an array of scalar component registers $R(i)$ $0 \leqslant i \leqslant s - 1$. All arithmetic and logical vector operations are register-to-register operations, that is their operands and results are in registers. A number of vector instructions are introduced on the following pages.

A **vector operand** D of length h $(1 \leqslant h \leqslant s)$ is a list $(D(0), \ldots, D(h - 1))$ of h words, called the **components** of D. A vector operand may reside in memory or in a register. If an instruction sequence manipulates vector operands of length h, then h must be loaded into the vector length register VL.

The mask register MASK may hold a boolean array of length s to restrict the execution of vector instructions to those components of registers for which the associated element of the mask is **true**.

It is instructive to see how a simple Fortran program might be run on the Cray-1, for which $r = 8$ and $s = 64$.

Example 2.3

Suppose that A, B, and C are declared as one-dimensional arrays: DIMENSION A(N), B(N), C(N), where $N \leqslant 64$. The following Fortran statements

```
DO I = 1, N
  A(I) = B(I) + C(I)
END DO
```

can be translated into the vector instruction sequence shown below. Here, A represents the vector operand (A(1), A(2), ..., A(N)), and similar conventions hold for B and C.

```
VL ← N          /* load vector length register */
R₀ ← B          /* load vector operand B into R₀ */
R₁ ← C          /* load vector operand C into R₁ */
R₂ ← R₀ + R₁    /* add contents of R₀ and R₁ and store the result
                   in R₂ */
A  ← R₂         /* store contents of R₂ in A */
```

The maximum length of a vector operand for the Cray-1 is 64. So for the general case, suppose that $N = q * 64 + rem$, where q, rem are positive integers, $q \geq 0$, and $0 \leq rem < 64$. Then the loop must be partitioned into $q + 1$ sections to process the subscript ranges $1{:}64$, $65{:}128$, $\ldots$, $(q - 1) * 64 + 1{:}q * 64$, $q * 64 + 1{:}N$. Each individual section can be executed by a sequence of vector operations as shown above, but consecutive sections must be processed sequentially. Thus, the Fortran loop must be split into an outer loop L_1 and an inner loop L_2. L_1 is executed $q + 1$ times and remains sequential; L_2 is translated into vector code, with the vector length 64 for the first q iterations of L_1, and rem for the last iteration. This process is called **loop sectioning** or **strip mining** and is further examined in Chapter 6.

All vector instructions have a fetch before store semantics (FS-semantics). Example 2.4 shows what this term means.

Example 2.4

Suppose that A and B are declared as in the previous example, and that the initial value of A(1) is a_{old}. The execution of the vector instruction $A = B * A(1)$ is equivalent to the N scalar assignments $A(i) = B(i) * a_{old}$ ($1 \leq i \leq N$). The assignment of a new value, $a_{old} * B(1)$, to A(1), does not affect the outcome of the operation.

Thus the input is completely independent from the output, in the sense that no component of the result produced may affect any of the input values. Further, we do not make any assumptions about the order in which the component operations are executed.

We now discuss two important classes of vector instructions: the LOAD and STORE instructions and the arithmetic–logical operations.

LOAD and STORE instructions

LOAD and STORE instructions are used to transfer vector operands between memory and a register. Whereas the components of vector operands are densely packed when they reside in a register, they may be stored in various ways in memory. Consider for example a two-dimensional array $C(1:m, 1:n)$ stored in column-major order in a contiguous block of main memory locations: $C(1, 1)$, $C(2, 1)$, ..., $C(m, 1)$, $C(1, 2)$, ... Then the elements of the columns of C are in adjacent locations (in this discussion, locations are always associated with words), while the elements of rows are m words apart. If a row is to be used in a vector operation, it becomes a vector operand of **stride** m. Similarly, if $m = n$, then the main diagonal of C is a vector operand of stride $m + 1$.

Basic LOAD and STORE

The basic version of LOAD provides for the different ways in which we may want to access the elements of an array by allowing us to specify an increment. It has the form:

$$R \leftarrow A(x_1{:}x_2 \, [{:}incr])$$

where $R \in \mathbf{R}$, A is a one-dimensional array[†], x_1, x_2 are integer subscripts which specify the first and last element of A to be loaded, and $incr$ is a constant integer increment which may be of either sign (we assume here for simplicity that $x_2 = x_1 + q * incr$, where q is a non-negative integer). If $incr$ is not explicitly specified, it is assumed to be 1. The execution of this instruction creates a vector operand of length $h = (x_2 - x_1) / incr + 1$, with the components $A(x_1)$, $A(x_1 + incr)$, ..., $A(x_2)$, and transmits it to R by the set of assignments $\{R(i) := A(x_1 + i * incr): 0 \leqslant i < h\}$. The instruction is well defined only if $h \leqslant s$. We assume throughout that this condition is satisfied unless it is explicitly stated otherwise.

Similar instructions are provided to STORE a vector operand in memory.

Extended LOAD and STORE

The basic LOAD/STORE instructions can be extended by masked and indirect LOAD/STORE, often referred to as COMPRESS/EXPAND or GATHER/SCATTER.

Let $A(0:N - 1)$ be an array and assume we want to form a vector operand by selecting those elements of A which satisfy a certain predicate p (for example, $A(i) < 0$). Let $i_1, i_2, \ldots, i_k$ be the indices of all elements of A for which p yields **true**. If $N \leqslant s$, we can form the vector operand $D = (A(i_1), A(i_2), \ldots, A(i_k))$, and load it into a register R as follows:

$$\{MASK(i) := p(A(i)): 0 \leqslant i < N\}$$
$$R \leftarrow MASKED\_LOAD(A)$$

MASKED_STORE can be similarly defined.

[†] Note that any declared Fortran array, and, in fact, the memory itself, can be interpreted as a one-dimensional array.

A more general alternative to this method is **indirect loading**. Let $X(0:h - 1)$ be an index vector of length h, whose elements are integer numbers in the range $[0:N - 1]$ which specify subscripts for the array A. A specific subscript of A can occur zero or more times in X. Then we define $D := A(X)$ as the vector operand $D := (A(X(0)), A(X(1)), \ldots, A(X(h - 1)))$. The vector code to load this operand is:

$$R \leftarrow \text{INDIRECT\_LOAD}(A(X))$$

INDIRECT_STORE can be similarly defined. One use of the indirect LOAD/STORE is to perform operations upon the nonzero elements of a sparse matrix.

Arithmetic–logical operations

- **Binary vector operations** take the form $R \leftarrow R' \mu R''$, where μ might be '+', '−', '*', '/', 'MAX' or another arithmetic or logical operator. $R \leftarrow R' \mu R''$ is equivalent to the set of h component operations $R(i) \leftarrow R'(i) \mu R''(i)$, $0 \leqslant i < h$. Remember that we make no assumptions about the order in which the component operations are executed. If one of the operands is a scalar, SC, it is interpreted as being an abbreviation for SC^h. Unary vector operations $R \leftarrow \sigma R'$ are similarly defined.

  The **mask register** can be defined by instructions of the form:

  $$\text{MASK} \leftarrow R \text{ rel } R'$$

  where $R, R' \in \mathbf{R}$ and $\text{rel} \in \{\leqslant, <, =, \neq, >, \geqslant\}$. Their effect is described by:

  $$\{\text{MASK}(i) := R(i) \text{ rel } R'(i): 0 \leqslant i < h\}$$

- **Linked triads** are operation patterns with three operands (and two operators) that frequently occur in application programs. A typical case is a combination of multiply and add or subtract ($A * B + C$ and $A * B - C$). The efficiency of such operations is enhanced when they can be expressed as single vector instructions.

- **Reduction operations** reduce a vector or a pair of vectors to a scalar value. Such operations may for example yield the sum of the elements of a vector, its maximum element, or the scalar product of two vectors (see Table 6.1).

Conditional vector processing

Unary and binary vector operations may be controlled by a mask; they are then called **masked operations** and are represented in the form

$$\text{WHERE (MASK) } R \leftarrow R' \mu R''$$

The effect of this is that $R \leftarrow R' \mu R''$ is performed for precisely those vector components for which the corresponding mask element is **true**. The WHERE statement also permits negation of the mask.

Example 2.5: Masked vector operation

Consider the following Fortran loop:

```
DO I = 1, s
  IF B(I) ≠ 0
    THEN C(I) = A(I) / B(I)
    ELSE C(I) = MAXNUMBER
  FI
END DO
```

It can be translated into vector code as shown below:

$$
\begin{aligned}
\text{VL} &\leftarrow s \\
R_0 &\leftarrow A \\
R_1 &\leftarrow B \\
R_2 &\leftarrow \text{MAXNUMBER} \\
\text{MASK} &\leftarrow R_1 \neq 0 \\
\text{WHERE (MASK) } R_2 &\leftarrow R_0/R_1 \\
C &\leftarrow R_2
\end{aligned}
$$

The time required for the execution of a masked vector instruction depends on the length of the vector operands involved, not on the number of mask components which are **true**. If that number is small compared with the vector length, it may well be more efficient to use masked loading or indirect addressing, together with unmasked vector operations.

2.2.4 Chaining

Each functional pipeline is dedicated to the execution of one specific operation. For frequently used operations such as floating point add or multiply, there may be more than one pipeline in the vector unit.

In this section we discuss **chaining**, where the output stream of one pipeline is linked to the input stream of another one. Each component result produced in the first of these is then immediately fed into the second pipeline. We illustrate this by an example which is based on the design of the Cray-1.

Example 2.6: Chaining (Cray-1)

The vector instruction sequence

$$I_1: R_2 \leftarrow R_0 + R_1$$
$$I_2: R_4 \leftarrow R_2 * R_3$$

is to be executed; registers R_0, R_1 and R_3 are preloaded. Without chaining, execution of I_2 would not begin before the execution of I_1 has been completed. However, with chaining, the output of the add pipeline is connected via R_2 with the input of the multiply pipeline. Thus, the two form a single virtual add–multiply pipeline and the execution of I_2 is begun as soon as output starts to come from R_2. We assume that the component operations are executed sequentially, in the order $0, 1, \ldots, h - 1$.

The add and multiply pipelines require 6 and 7 cycles respectively. It takes one cycle to transfer two operand components from their registers to the pipeline input, or a result component to a register. The time required to execute the instruction sequence is thus calculated by summing the times taken to perform the following elementary steps:

t1: transfer of operands from R_0 and R_1 to the add pipeline   (1)
add: computation of sum in the add pipeline   (6)
t2: transfer of result to R_2 (1)
t3: transfer of operands from R_2 and R_3 to the multiply pipeline   (1)
mul: computation of product in the multiply pipeline   (7)
t4: transfer of result to R_4 (1)

Without chaining, the total time required to execute the instruction sequence amounts to the sum of the execution times for I_1 and I_2, that is $(7 + h) + (8 + h) = 15 + 2h$ cycles (Figure 2.8).

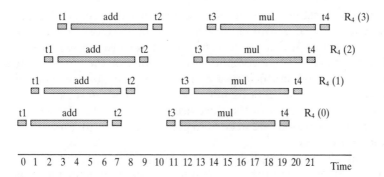

0 1 2 3 4 5 6 7 8 9 10 11 12 13 14 15 16 17 18 19 20 21   Time

Figure 2.8   Instruction execution without chaining ($h = 4$).

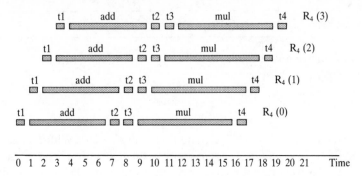

Figure 2.9   Instruction execution with chaining.

With chaining, the multiply pipeline can start operating as soon as it receives the first component result from the add pipeline via R_2, that is after the ninth cycle. From then on, the add and multiply pipelines work concurrently until the first pipeline has processed all components. The total time required is $16 + h$ cycles (Figure 2.9). Thus, execution with chaining is up to twice as fast as execution without chaining.

This method can be more generally applied: three or more pipelines may be chained in this way. Both the availability of chaining capabilities and the fact that different pipelines may operate concurrently mean that the compiler (or the user) must attempt to schedule vector instructions in a way that exploits these features efficiently. We return to this problem in Chapter 6.

2.2.5 Performance issues

There are several factors that may prevent an actual application program from reaching peak performance when run on a vector computer. It may deal with vectors which are too short to utilize the full length of vector registers, or may involve conditional processing; or the effective memory bandwidth may be insufficient. An important source of performance degradation is that some code is inherently serial and must be executed in scalar mode, as a result of the existence of certain dependences. In addition, scalar instructions are needed to prepare and control the execution of vector instructions.

Amdahl's law (Amdahl, 1967) expresses the fact that the inherent sequentiality of an algorithm is the ultimate limiting factor for its performance on any machine. We shall discuss this in more detail.

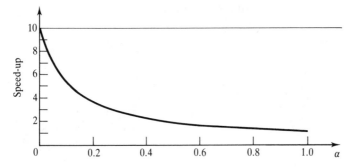

Figure 2.10   Speed-up $\sigma(\alpha, \tau)$ as a function of α for $\tau = 10$.

Let α denote the fraction of code that must be executed in scalar mode and assume that in any time unit one operation may be performed in the scalar unit, and τ component operations may be carried out in the vector unit.

We can then execute a sequence of m operations in time m in scalar mode, and in time $m[\alpha + (1 - \alpha)/\tau]$ using vector operations. Thus our speed-up is

$$\sigma(\alpha, \tau) = \frac{1}{\alpha + (1 - \alpha)/\tau}$$

For all α and τ $(0 \leqslant \alpha \leqslant 1, \tau \geqslant 1)$ we have $1 \leqslant \sigma(\alpha, \tau) \leqslant \tau$; and for every τ, $\sigma(0, \tau) = \tau$ and $\sigma(1, \tau) = 1$. In any given system, τ is constant and typically on the order of 10. Under this assumption, σ becomes a function of α (Figure 2.10). A slight increase in α may lead to a significant drop in the speed-up. Table 2.1, which lists the speed-up values for $\tau = 10$ and $\tau = 20$ and selected values of α, makes this even more explicit. Note in particular that where 90% of the code can be run in vector mode, only about one-half $(\tau = 10)$ or one-third $(\tau = 20)$ of the peak performance can be reached.

Keep in mind, however, that α is a dynamic measure, and that it does not count the fraction of scalar statements contained in the program text. Most of the execution time of a program (80–90%) is spent in rather small sections (10–20%) of the code, primarily in loops. This reinforces an observation stated earlier, that we must concentrate our optimization efforts on these critical portions of the code.

We conclude by informally characterizing two performance measures (Hockney and Jesshope, 1981) for pipeline vector processing, both of which are related to the fact that the start-up time degrades the throughput of a pipeline. This effect is inversely proportional to vector length; for very short vectors processing in scalar mode will be more effective than in vector mode.

Table 2.1   Selected values for
$\sigma(\alpha, 10)$ and $\sigma(\alpha, 20)$.

α	$\tau = 10$	$\tau = 20$
0	10	20
0.1	5.26	6.90
0.25	3.08	3.48
0.5	1.82	1.90
1	1	1

Half-performance length is the vector length that produces half the maximum throughput; **vector breakeven length** is the minimum vector length that makes operating in vector mode more efficient than in scalar mode. This is approximately the ratio between the start-up time and the time to execute one scalar operation. For more details see Hockney and Jesshope (1981) and Ercegovac and Lang (1986).

2.2.6   Case studies

We briefly review three commercial vector supercomputers, the Cray-1 (Russell, 1978), the Fujitsu Facom VP-200 (Miura and Uchida, 1984; Amdahl, 1984), and the IBM 3090 (Buchholz 1986), all of which are register-to-register architectures conforming closely to our model. Both the Cray-1 and Fujitsu VP systems operate in conjunction with a host computer (for example, an IBM System/370), which performs global system management such as the control of batch job entries, input/output, and file management. The host connection is established via I/O channels. In contrast, the IBM 3090 is a direct extension of the scalar IBM System/370 architecture.

The Cray-1 has a main memory that consists of up to 1 MW in 16 interleaved banks. Only the basic forms of LOAD and STORE are supported. The memory cycle time is 50 ns; the memory bandwidth reaches $320 \times 10^6 \, \text{W s}^{-1}$. The vector unit contains 8 vector registers of length 64; the total number of registers in the vector processor amounts to more than 800. It has 12 functional pipelines for address, scalar, and vector computations, and supports add, multiply, reciprocal approximation, shift, and logical vector operations. The processor cycle time is 12.5 ns, yielding a theoretical peak rate of 160 MFLOPS. The start-up time is very low, resulting in a breakeven vector length of about 2–4.

The Fujitsu Facom VP-200 processor was introduced in 1982; its architecture is similar to that of the Cray-1. Main memory can contain up to 32 MW; in contrast to the Cray-1, which contains only one path between memory and the vector unit, the Fujitsu has two separate paths, both of which can be used for loading and storing operands.

The scalar unit of the machine is compatible with the IBM System/370. The cycle time of the vector unit is 7.5 ns, leading to a peak rate of about 500 MFLOPS. The Fujitsu differs from the Cray-1 with respect to its register organization and the support it provides for conditional operations. All the features for conditional vector processing discussed in our model (including masked and indirect LOAD/STORE) are supported in the Fujitsu's hardware.

The register organization in the Fujitsu is unique: the machine has a 64 KB register cache which can be dynamically reconfigured. The user may select any of the following configurations, whereby the number of registers and their length must be a power of 2:

   256 registers of length 32
   128 registers of length 64
      . . .
       8 registers of length 1024

What is best depends on the processing characteristics of the program; the tradeoff is between register space (which may be wasted if registers are too long) and transfer time between main memory and registers (which may be high if registers are too short).

The vector processing facility of the IBM 3090 vector processor is integrated into the IBM System/370 design in such a way that it may be viewed as an addition to the basic scalar System/370 machine. It has 8 vector registers of length 128. (The register set actually contains 16 registers of length 128, based on 32-bit words. Adjacent 32-bit components can be combined to form a 64-bit register.) In addition to the instructions in our model, IBM 3090 vector instructions can directly specify an operand in main memory. The result of a vector operation is always placed into a vector register. Masked and indirect LOAD/STORE instructions are supported in the hardware; the processor cycle time is 18.5 ns.

Other register-to-register architectures are the Hitachi S-810 (Odaka *et al.*, 1986) and the NEC SX2 (Watanabe *et al.*, 1986).

As mentioned in the introduction to this section, the Cyber-205 (Lincoln, 1986) differs from the machines primarily discussed here in that it is a memory-to-memory architecture: vector instructions fetch their operands directly from main memory, and store their results there. It differs significantly from the Cray-1 type machines in two respects: first, the length of vector operands can be very large (up to 65 535 W), which renders the loop sectioning procedure discussed in Section 2.2.3 superfluous in almost all cases. Further, the breakeven vector length is very long, lying somewhere near 50. This means that a significant fraction of potential vector code is more efficiently executed in scalar mode, with the obvious consequences for performance (Section 2.2.5).

The performance of current SISD vector supercomputers ranges from 160 MFLOPS to 2 GFLOPS. There are organizational and technological limits to this type of architecture: an increase in the number of functional pipelines does not necessarily lead to a linear increase in processing power (there may be a speed-up limit of about 8 that can be gained in this way), and many of the machines are already at the technological edge, which means that the cost of building and maintaining them is very high.

2.3   Parallel computing systems

Parallel computing systems contain a number of processors which cooperate to solve a common task. An application program is run as a system of **parallel processes**, where each process is the execution of one sequential instruction stream. Processes are dynamic entities; they must be created to come into existence, they can communicate with other processes, and may terminate. No specific assumptions regarding the relative speeds of parallel processes can be made, unless explicit synchronization takes place.

The non-determinism in a process system makes parallel programming an extremely difficult task if it is not tightly controlled by an appropriate set of language constructs and programming rules. For example, the fact that one execution of a parallel program has yielded correct results for a given set of input values is no guarantee that this behavior can be repeated: even with the same set of input values, another execution of the program may fail if the processes are not correctly synchronized. Similarly, errors observed in one execution of a parallel program may not be reproducible in a debugging run, where tracing and/or monitoring facilities are attached to the program and thereby modify its dynamic behavior.

In this section, we provide an overview of some basic concepts of parallel programming: after discussing processes in Section 2.3.1, we treat synchronization and communication (Section 2.3.2), and deal with performance issues (Section 2.3.3). We conclude by discussing several existing parallel architectures.

2.3.1   Processes and their creation

Numerous proposals have been made for language primitives that permit the creation of processes. One of the first mechanisms proposed (Conway, 1963) was FORK/JOIN, where the FORK statement spawns a new process and JOIN is used to synchronize the termination of processes. In procedural programming languages, procedures are most often the objects of parallel execution: for example, the execution of

CREATE(SUB, PID, PROC)

in a process p_1 may create a new process, p_2, by initiating the execution of subroutine SUB on processor PROC, and assigning an identification for p_2 to the variable PID. p_1 and p_2 may proceed in parallel. A more structured, but less flexible, technique defines a cobegin statement in the form:

$$\text{COBEGIN } S_1, S_2, \ldots, S_n \text{ COEND}$$

The execution of this statement creates n parallel processes p_i, where p_i is an execution of statement S_i, and terminates when all p_i $(1 \leq i \leq n)$ have terminated. This construct was proposed by Dijkstra, and is included in Algol 68 (van Wijngaarden et al., 1975).

2.3.2 Synchronization and communication

Cooperating processes must be able to communicate and to synchronize their actions. There are two types of synchronization, namely mutual exclusion and condition synchronization.

Mutual exclusion is required if two or more processes exclusively access a common resource in a critical region, and the relative order of accesses is irrelevant. As an example, consider two processes p_1 and p_2 which both update a shared variable SUM by 1. If each process simply executes the statement S: SUM = SUM + 1, then one of the updates may be lost. Let

$$
\begin{aligned}
R_i &\leftarrow \text{SUM} \\
R_i &\leftarrow R_i + 1 \\
\text{SUM} &\leftarrow R_i
\end{aligned}
$$

be the instruction sequence which realizes S in p_i, where R_i is a local register of the processor on which p_i is executed $(i = 1, 2)$. While each single memory access is an atomic operation, memory references in one process may be interleaved with memory references in other processes. Specifically, the actions of p_1 and p_2 could be executed in the following order:

$$
\begin{aligned}
R_1 &\leftarrow \text{SUM} \\
R_1 &\leftarrow R_1 + 1 \\
R_2 &\leftarrow \text{SUM} \\
R_2 &\leftarrow R_2 + 1 \\
\text{SUM} &\leftarrow R_2 \\
\text{SUM} &\leftarrow R_1
\end{aligned}
$$

However, now the total effect is to increment SUM by 1, rather than 2 as desired.

We speak of **condition synchronization** if a process can proceed only when a certain condition in its environment is fulfilled. Examples for such a condition are the termination of another process, the completion of an I/O transfer, or the accessibility of a data item which the process needs for its further work.

In shared memory systems (SMSs), mutual exclusion and condition synchronization can be solved by tools such as semaphores, event variables, conditional critical regions, or monitors (Andrews and Schneider, 1983; Zima, 1986; Perrot, 1987). The details of these mechanisms fall outside the scope of this text; however, we do see how they are implemented. Dijkstra and Knuth have both shown that the indivisibility of loads and stores with respect to a single memory cell suffice, but their results are of academic interest only. The key to a practical solution is to provide an instruction that combines a load and a store into one atomic operation. Such an instruction is TEST_AND_SET, which can be defined as follows:

```
TEST_AND_SET(x, R): begin
                    {R := x;
                      if R = 0 then x := 1 fi}
                    end
```

x is a shared memory location, R a local register of the process executing TEST_AND_SET, and the brackets '{' and '}' indicate indivisibility of the enclosed action sequence: the test of x and the conditional setting take place in one memory cycle, making the intervention of another process impossible. x takes only two values, that is 0 and 1, which respectively express the accessibility or non-accessibility of a resource associated with x. The assignment $x := 1$ can be thought of as reserving exclusive access to the resource in question, while $x := 0$ releases it.

We return to the above example and show how mutual exclusion can be realized using TEST_AND_SET. Suppose that a shared variable *SUM_LOCK* has been associated with *SUM* and initialized to 0. Then the sequence:

```
repeat TEST_AND_SET(SUM_LOCK, R) until R = 0
SUM = SUM + 1
SUM_LOCK = 0
```

is a correct solution of the problem. On some systems, the repeat-loop is realized in hardware; such an instruction is called a **spin-lock**. Note that the repeated execution of TEST_AND_SET results in a form of busy waiting which is tolerable only at a low level, for example in the context of a semaphore implementation.

The execution of the repeat-loop may create a 'hot spot' in memory which can seriously degrade system performance if the number of processors is large, as TEST_AND_SET instructions that are issued simultaneously by different processors must be serialized. A method invented by the designers of the NYU Ultracomputer can significantly reduce hot spot contention (Gottlieb *et al.*, 1983): a FETCH_AND_ADD instruction essentially performs the task of the TEST_AND_SET, but combines simultaneous requests by a number of processors in such a way that only one memory access is required.

Let us now turn to distributed memory systems (DMSs). In a DMS, synchronization and communication must be realized by **message passing** primitives SEND and RECEIVE, which combine the transmission of data with process synchronization:

(1)   SEND $exp_1, \ldots, exp_m$ TO p_2

(2)   SEND $exp_1, \ldots, exp_m$ TO ALL

(3)   RECEIVE $v_1, \ldots, v_m$ FROM p_1

Here, the exp_i are expressions with respective values a_i, the v_i variables, and p_1, p_2 are processes ($1 \leqslant i \leqslant m$). The list $\mathbf{a} = (a_1, \ldots, a_m)$ is called a **message**. If SEND $exp_1, \ldots, exp_m$ TO p_2 is executed in process p_1, and RECEIVE $v_1, \ldots, v_m$ FROM p_1 is executed in process p_2, then the two statements are said to **match**, and the message $\mathbf{a}$ can be transmitted from p_1 to p_2 by performing the assignments $v_1 := a_1, \ldots, v_m := a_m$.

SEND $exp_1, \ldots, exp_m$ TO ALL transmits the message $\mathbf{a}$ to all processes in the system with a matching RECEIVE; this is called a **broadcast**.

Message passing accomplishes synchronization, since a message can be received only after it has been sent. If a SEND or RECEIVE statement is delayed until a matching RECEIVE or SEND is executed, we speak of **blocking** or **synchronous**, otherwise of **non-blocking** or **asynchronous**, statements. Three variants have been implemented in current systems: both SEND and RECEIVE as non-blocking operations (Seitz, 1985), non-blocking SEND and blocking RECEIVE (Ehses and Mevenkamp, 1986) – the most frequent version – and blocking SEND and RECEIVE (CSP (Hoare, 1978), Ada (Department of Defense, 1981)). The implementation of non-blocking primitives requires the buffering of messages, for example in private mailboxes of processes. For a detailed discussion see Andrews and Schneider (1983).

In real systems, the primitives must allow additional flexibility, permitting for example a process to inspect the contents of the message buffer, tag messages, and so on. We do not go into details.

2.3.3 Performance issues

Suppose that M_1 is an SISD machine, and M_2 is an MIMD system with n processors, each of which is identical to the processor of M_1. Furthermore, suppose that an application program is given, which requires T_i time units to execute on machine M_i $(i = 1, 2)$. Then we assume that the speed-up, $\sigma(n) = T_1/T_2$, satisfies $1 \leq \sigma(n) \leq n$.[†] The **efficiency**, $\tau(n) := \sigma(n)/n$, measures the speed-up per processor. It is normally not possible to achieve **linear speed-up**, n, since multiprocessing also involves overheads and inefficiencies, when compared with a single processor's operation:

(1)   When multiple processors cooperate in the solution of a task, communication and synchronization are necessary.

(2)   It may not always be possible to balance the total system load evenly. Some processors may be idle in certain time intervals.

(3)   There is an operating system overhead associated with the scheduling and management of processes.

(4)   Some parts of an algorithm may be inherently serial.

Observation (4) leads to Amdahl's law (see Section 2.2.5), which can be roughly formulated as follows: if α $(0 < \alpha \leq 1)$ is the fraction of a task which is inherently sequential, the speed-up of the task for any number of processors has an upper bound of $1/\alpha$. While there are certain problems that only allow very limited parallelization (for example, following a chain of pointers in a complicated data structure), there are other tasks for which α is very close to zero, so that an almost linear speed-up is feasible (for example, Fox and Otto (1984) report an efficiency of 97 per cent for a Monte Carlo lattice gauge theory computation on a Caltech Cosmic Cube (Seitz, 1985) with 64 nodes).

An important factor in assessing the efficiency of DMSs is the **communication overhead**, which measures the ratio between the time spent for communication and that for computation in a given interval. The communication overhead in a system may increase if new processors are added to it.

2.3.4   Case studies

Current parallel systems that either exist as working prototypes or are already available on the market consist of between two and 8192 processors, and yield a peak performance of up to 10 GFLOPS. In this subsection, we discuss four such architectures, namely the Cray X-MP, the IBM RP3 research processor, the Cosmic Cube, and the SUPRENUM machine.

[†] This may seem trivial, but it is not. (1) There are some cases where superlinear speed-up is possible. We do not discuss this aspect further (see Faber *et al.* (1986), Parkinson (1986), Helmbold and McDowell (1989)). (2) If the overhead associated with parallel operation is higher than the gain of parallelism, $\sigma(n) < 1$.

The Cray X-MP

The Cray X-MP (Chen, 1984) is a family of computer systems which was first installed in 1983 and includes a one-processor system and parallel configurations with two and four processors. We discuss only the largest configuration, the Cray X-MP/48. This is a pure SMS, with four processors and a total shared memory of 8 MW. Each processor is an advanced version of the Cray-1; it has an instruction set including extended versions of LOAD/STORE, and four parallel memory ports, two of which are dedicated to vector LOAD, one to vector STORE, and one to the input/output system. This means that in every clock cycle and every processor the following actions can occur simultaneously: two words can be loaded, one word stored, one word sent to the I/O, and an arithmetic/logical operation performed in each functional pipeline. The processor cycle time is 9.5 ns. The main memory is organized into 64 interleaved banks with a cycle time of 38 ns; the total memory bandwidth of the system is 1.6 GW s^{-1}. The input/output subsystem is accessible to all processors and the host, and provides up to four I/O processors with local memories, a global buffer memory and maximum disk storage space of 38 GB, consisting of 32 1.2 GB disks with an average access time of 20 ms and a 10 MB s^{-1} data transfer rate. This may be additionally supplemented by a solid-state random-access storage device which provides storage space of up to 1 GB and a transfer rate of 1 GB s^{-1}. The I/O subsystem is supported by three types of channel with transfer rates of 6, 100, and 1000 MB s^{-1}. The peak rate of the system is around 1 GFLOPS.

The Cray-2 (with four processors and a processor cycle time of 4.1 ns) and the Cray Y-MP (with eight processors) are more recent MIMD extensions of the Cray-1.

The IBM RP3 research processor

The RP3 computer (Pfister *et al.*, 1987) is being developed in an IBM research project conducted in cooperation with the Ultracomputer Project of New York University (Gottlieb *et al.*, 1983). Although both the RP3 and the Cray X-MP/48 are MIMD systems, there are significant structural differences between them: the RP3 processing node is based on a microprocessor, a maximum system configuration consists of 512 nodes, and the system may contain a variable combination of local and shared memory. A system with 64 nodes is already operational.

We shall discuss the properties of a maximum configuration. The processing node consists of the following components (see Figure 2.11):

(1)   a 32-bit microprocessor (the processor of the IBM RT PC);
(2)   a floating-point unit;
(3)   a memory map unit;

(4)   8 MB of main memory;

(5)   a 32 KB cache;

(6)   an interface to an I/O and support processor.

A unique feature of the RP3 is the way it manages storage: the memory associated with each node can be dynamically (that is, by software) partitioned into a local and a global memory area. The local memory may be directly accessed only by the node with which it is associated, while the global memory is shared among all nodes: the system's global shared memory is the union of the global memories of the processing nodes; every node can access this memory by traversing a switching network. Each memory reference issued in a node is automatically interpreted and translated by the memory map unit, which also supports segmentation, paging and cache maintenance. The access time ratio between cache, local, and global memory is 1:10:16.

One of the major goals of the RP3 project is to examine the relationships between the shared-memory and distributed-memory paradigms. The hardware provides optimal support for this objective, as it enables the modeling of not only a pure SMS (all node memories are wholly global), and a pure DMS (all node memories are purely local), but also any intermediate combination.

The RP3 provides a combining multilevel switching network, which can execute multiple synchronization statements (FETCH_AND_ADD) directed to the same memory location in parallel. This task is partially performed in the network switches, and partially in the memory. In other networks, synchronization statements of this kind (for example, TEST_AND_SET) must be serialized and thus contribute to memory contention.

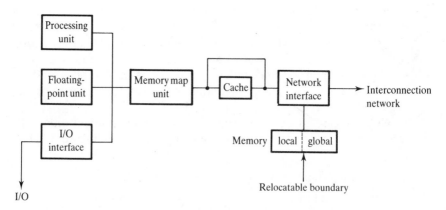

Figure 2.11 Structure of an RP3 processing node.

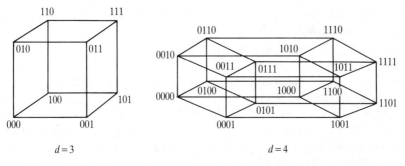

Figure 2.12   Hypercube network for $d = 3$ and $d = 4$ (the nodes are represented by their numbers).

These figures illustrate the overall power of the machine: the maximum configuration is expected to reach 1.3 GIPS and 800 MFLOPS, the total memory amounts to 4 GB, the interprocessor communication rate will be 13 GB s^{-1}, and the I/O bandwidth 192 MB s^{-1}.

The Cosmic Cube

The Cosmic Cube (Seitz, 1985) is a pure DMS that has been developed at the California Institute of Technology. The nodes of the Cosmic Cube are based on a microprocessor, with an interconnection network structured as a hypercube.

Let $d \geqslant 1$. A Cosmic Cube of dimension d is a computer system consisting of $n = 2^d$ nodes. We can think of the nodes as being positioned at the corners of a d-dimensional unit cube, that is identified by the set of all d-tuples whose elements are either 0 or 1. Each node contains a microprocessor, local memory and support for communication. There is a bidirectional asynchronous point-to-point communication channel connecting each node to its d neighbors. Any two nodes can be reached from one another in at most d steps. Figure 2.12 illustrates the hypercube network for $d = 3$ and 4. For example, in the three-dimensional hypercube, node $(1, 0, 1)$ has the neighbors $(1, 0, 0)$, $(0, 0, 1)$ and $(1, 1, 1)$. A message from node $(1, 0, 1)$ to one of its neighbors can be transferred in one step; a message to node $(0, 0, 0)$, $(1, 1, 0)$, or $(0, 1, 1)$ takes two steps, and a message to node $(0, 1, 0)$ takes three steps, the maximum number required.

Communication is established between two nodes of a Cosmic Cube via non-blocking message-passing primitives. Each node contains an operating system that supports the following functions:

(1)   scheduling of processes in the node;
(2)   memory management for the node;

(3)   message-passing primitives SEND and RECEIVE for the communication between nodes;

(4)   routing of messages through nodes.

The Cosmic Cube has been extensively studied in the C³P project at the California Institute of Technology (Fox *et al.*, 1988). The largest hypercube machine currently in existence is the 8192-node NCUBE (see Benner *et al.*, 1988). Other commercially available hypercube systems include the FPS T Series Parallel Processor (Miller *et al.*, 1988), and the Intel iPSC Concurrent Computer (Pase and Larrabee, 1988).

The SUPRENUM machine

The SUPRENUM machine (Giloi, 1988; Zima, 1988) is a DMS architecture that offers MIMD parallelism as well as vector features. The interconnection network is implemented as a two-level bus system.

The basic processing node is a 32-bit microprocessor from Motorola, connected to an 8 MB local memory, a vector unit, and a dedicated communication processor (Figure 2.13). The pipelines of the vector unit can be fed from local memory or a vector cache.

A **cluster** contains up to 16 nodes which communicate via a parallel bus (the **cluster bus**) with a bandwidth of 256 MB s⁻¹. In addition, there are dedicated nodes supporting access to a cluster disk, system monitoring and communication with the global network (Figure 2.14).

The **kernel system** consists of a 4 × 4 mesh of clusters. A separate host machine manages the global resources, input/output, the distribution of the workload, and system recovery. Program execution in the kernel system is handled by local node operating systems. The global system structure is shown in Figure 2.15.

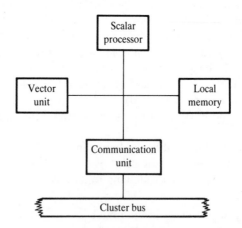

Figure 2.13   Structure of a SUPRENUM processing node.

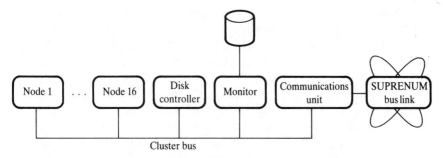

Figure 2.14   A SUPRENUM cluster.

2.3.5 Concluding remarks

Two different networks were featured in the last two examples of the previous section. However, individual processors of a DMS may be connected in a large number of ways. The design of a **network topology** is one of the major architectural decisions: sometimes a particular topology is selected to enable the system to deal particularly well with a certain kind of problem. For example, a mesh system, which connects adjoining nodes ('nearest neighbors') in a d-dimensional grid ($d = 2$ or 3), seems a natural pattern for a large variety of problems, including image processing and numerical algorithms operating on grids. Other topologies include the linear array, ring, tree, and perfect shuffle (Hwang and Briggs, 1984). All of these can be mapped to a hypercube.

Our treatment of parallel architectures here is, of necessity, far from complete. Many other interesting systems have been built. They include

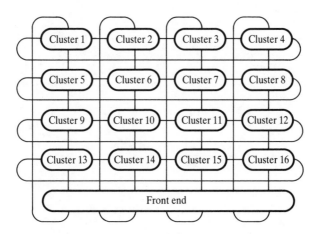

Figure 2.15   A global view of the SUPRENUM system.

the Denelcor Heterogeneous Element Processor HEP (Denelcor, 1981; Smith, 1981), the IBM 3090 multiprocessing system (Tucker, 1986), the Alliant FX/8 (DiNucci, 1988), the CEDAR machine (Kuck *et al.*, 1986), the transputer, the BBN Butterfly (BBN Laboratories, 1986), the Sequent Balance (Osterhaug, 1989) and the Japanese Super-Speed Computer Project (Kashiwagi, 1984). Overviews of some of these and other systems can be found in Dongarra *et al.* (1987) and Babb (1988).

At universities and in research laboratories the next generation of machines is already being designed; these machines will have tens of thousands and, in the long term, possibly millions of processors, reaching peak performances in the TFLOPS range.

Chapter 3

Scalar Analysis

3.1 Introduction

This chapter discusses the basic problems, concepts and techniques of scalar analysis. **Scalar analysis** refers to a set of methods which use static program analysis (that is, analysis performed in the compiler) to derive assertions about the usage of scalar program variables at run time. The variables analyzed may include arrays, but only in the sense that every subscripted variable with a non-constant subscript expression is considered to represent the whole array. Scalar analysis is a prerequisite for data dependence analysis and is needed to determine the applicability and effect of many restructuring transformations which are discussed in later parts of the book.

The following example shows us what kind of information we can expect to obtain from scalar analysis. Consider the statement sequence:

$$S_1: A = \ldots$$
$$S_2: B = \ldots$$
$$\ldots$$
$$S_3: C = A + B$$
$$S_4: DO \ I=1, \ C$$
$$\ldots$$

We refer to the assignments S_1, S_2, and S_3 as **definitions** of the variables A, B, and C respectively, which are assumed to be allocated at disjoint locations. We may, for instance, want to know whether the value of C is a known constant when it is used in the do-loop: if so, we could significantly improve dependence analysis inside the loop. This problem – determining the value of a variable at a given point of the program whenever this value is constant – is called the **constant propagation** problem. It is, in general, undecidable, but methods exist which are sufficiently powerful to handle many interesting cases successfully. One such method looks at the uses of variables A and B in S_3 and attempts to find all definitions which 'reach' these uses. These information sets are called **use–definition chains** (UD chains). If we can prove that S_1 and S_2 are the only definitions of A and B reaching S_3, and we know the values assigned to A and B in S_1 and S_2 – let us assume S_1: A = 100 and S_2: B = 900 – then we can conclude that the right-hand side of S_3 evaluates to 1000, which is the value assigned to C. We then know the upper bound of the loop variable.

It turns out that UD chains (and their inverse, DU chains) are at the heart of many analysis problems of interest, and that they can be applied to a variety of optimization problems. One such problem is dead-code elimination (the elimination of statements that do not contribute to the effect of a program).

A further example for a scalar analysis problem is the following. Assume that an expression, say U * SIN(W), occurs at the right-hand side of an assignment statement S. If we can prove that this expression has already been computed whenever S is reached, and U and W have not been defined again in the meantime, then the expression is **available** in S, and the computation of U * SIN(W) in S is redundant and can be replaced by a reference to the value yielded by the previous computation(s).

We perform scalar analysis as a **flow analysis**, in the sense that information is obtained by examining the flow of control and data through the program. We distinguish between three levels of flow analysis. These are, in order of increasing complexity, local, intraprocedural and interprocedural analysis. **Local analysis** is concerned with basic blocks, which are sections of straight-line code that can only be entered via the first, and only be exited via the last, statement. Local analysis will not be considered further (for a detailed discussion of related problems see, for example, Aho *et al.* (1986)). **Intraprocedural analysis** is performed at the level of a single procedure, while **interprocedural analysis** takes the whole program into account. An orthogonal classification of flow analysis distinguishes between control flow analysis and data flow analysis (see Figure 3.1).

Control flow analysis (CFA) determines the **control structure** of a procedure or a program, that is the set of all possible execution paths. Intraprocedural CFA constructs a **program graph**: this is a **flowgraph** – a directed graph with an initial node from which all other nodes can be reached – whose nodes correspond to basic blocks, and whose edges represent transfers of control between basic blocks. Interprocedural CFA constructs a **call graph**, based on procedures and their calling relationships.

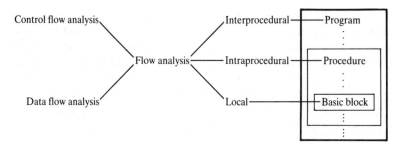

Figure 3.1   Two orthogonal classifications of flow analysis.

Data flow analysis (DFA) examines the flow of scalar values through a program. It solves data flow problems by propagating data flow information along the paths of a flowgraph.

In order to discuss intraprocedural DFA, we introduce the concept of a **monotone data flow system** (MDS). An MDS consists of a semilattice, an associated monotonic function space, and a program graph. The semi-lattice represents the data flow information, and the functions serve to model the way data flow information is modified when control passes through a basic block. Virtually all data flow problems may be elegantly formulated in terms of MDSs; the associated solution mechanism is a very simple iterative fixpoint algorithm.

When DFA is restricted to local and intraprocedural analysis, then worst-case assumptions must be made for each procedure call to ensure the correctness of program transformations based on data flow information. For example, if we are analyzing a procedure in whose body a CALL $q(...)$ occurs and we know nothing about the effect of the call, then we must assume that every variable argument and every global variable accessible to q is changed by the execution of the call.

The growing importance of structured programming techniques even in the Fortran world has led to the increasing modularization of programs, which nowadays often consist of a large number of relatively small procedures. As a consequence, interprocedural DFA has become very important. We shall discuss methods for the construction of the call graph in the presence of formal procedure parameters, and solve a number of standard problems, including the detection of side effects and aliases caused by reference parameters.

Chapter 3 consists of eight sections. In Section 3.2 we introduce a program model. Then intraprocedural analysis is treated (Sections 3.3–3.6): a discussion of CFA is followed by a number of data flow problems and related optimizations, the theory of MDSs, and the application of this theory to a set of selected data flow problems. Interprocedural analysis is discussed in Section 3.7 and we then round off the chapter with an assort-ment of concluding remarks and bibliographic notes.

A final remark is in order here: this chapter concentrates on a small number of important concepts from scalar analysis which will be required later on, and on a limited number of methods which demonstrate possible solution approaches for the problems posed. Thus the discussion is sometimes brief, and there are relatively few examples illustrating the theory. Some of the methods developed in this chapter can be immediately carried over to the analysis and optimization of statements that manipulate entire arrays (and thus of the code generated by vectorization).

3.2 The program model

In this section we introduce an intermediate language model, which is related to Fortran 77 (ANSI, 1978). We extend our model later as required.

A **program** P is a set of $n \geq 1$ declared procedures. **Procedures** correspond to Fortran program units (except for BLOCK DATA subprograms); they are non-recursive and their declarations cannot be nested. Procedures are called **functions** (FUNCTION subprograms) or **proper procedures** (SUBROUTINE subprograms), depending on whether or not their execution yields a result. Formally:

> **Definition 3.1**   A **program** P is a set $P = \{P_i\colon P_i$ is the identifier of procedure i, $1 \leq i \leq n\}$, where $P_1 = $ MAIN represents the main program. ∎

Associated with a program is a two-level **name space**: one global space for the whole program, and a local space for each procedure.

The **global** space includes a set of objects that are in principle accessible in any procedure of the program. Each procedure declares which objects of the global space will be accessed in its body (COMMON). The **local** space of a procedure contains all objects which are known only inside that procedure.

We assume that every object in the program has a unique name, and that there are no naming conflicts, that is, different objects have distinct names. Any global object is denoted by the same identifier wherever it is accessible. Furthermore, different identifiers (excluding formal parameters) are associated with non-overlapping storage sections. Thus, EQUIVALENCE, COMMON and all related conflicts with respect to naming and storage allocation are assumed to have been resolved. (This restricts the model in so far as it does not cover equivalencing of variables and arrays, and of objects with different data types. Aho *et al.* (1986) gives an algorithm for storage allocation in Fortran that takes EQUIVALENCE and COMMON into account.) The following definitions specify the structure of a program's name space. For each procedure p there is a set of identifiers that are visible in p.

It can be partitioned into three disjoint subsets as shown below (note that the elements of P – which are accessible in every procedure – have not been included here for pragmatic reasons).

Definition 3.2 Let $p \in P$ be arbitrarily selected.

(1) $local(p)$ is the set of locally declared variables and arrays.
(2) $formal(p)$ is the set of formal parameters of p. The **parameter vector** of p, that is the list of formal parameters in the order of their occurrence in the procedure's declaration, is denoted by pv_p.
(3) $global(p)$ is the set of global variables and arrays accessible in p.
(4) $visible(p) := local(p) \cup formal(p) \cup global(p)$ ■

For each $p \in P$, the local name space of procedure p is given by the union $local(p) \cup formal(p)$. The sets $local(p)$, $formal(p)$ and $global(p)$ are mutually disjoint. For any $p, p' \in P$ with $p \neq p'$, the local name spaces are disjoint, whereas $global(p) \cap global(p')$, the set of global variables available in both p and p', may be non-empty.

Definition 3.3 We associate the following sets with a program P:

(1) $LOCAL := \cup \{local(p): p \in P\}$
(2) $FORMAL := \cup \{formal(p): p \in P\}$
(3) $GLOBAL := \cup \{global(p): p \in P\}$ ■

$GLOBAL$ constitutes the global name space of the program.

Every identifier that is associated with a declared or formal procedure is called a **procedure identifier**.

Example 3.1

```
PROGRAM MAIN
DIMENSION A(5)
INTEGER I1, I2
REAL B, C
COMMON I1, I2

...
S1: A(I1) = 1
S2: CALL SUB(B)
S3: I1 = A(I2 + 1) - 1
S4: CALL SUB(C)
...
END
```

```
SUBROUTINE SUB(F1)
REAL F1
INTEGER I1, I2, I3, I4
COMMON I1, I2
...
S5: I3 = ...
S6: I2 = I3 * 2
...
END
```

For this program, some of the sets defined above have the following contents:

$P = \{\text{MAIN}, \text{SUB}\}$

$local \ (\text{MAIN}) = \{A, B, C\}$
$formal(\text{MAIN}) = \varnothing$
$global \ (\text{MAIN}) = \{I1, I2\}$
$visible \ (\text{MAIN}) = \{A, B, C, I1, I2\}$

$local \ (\text{SUB}) = \{I3, I4\}$
$formal(\text{SUB}) = \{F1\}$
$global \ (\text{SUB}) = \{I1, I2\}$
$visible \ (\text{SUB}) = \{I3, I4, F1, I1, I2\}$

$GLOBAL = \{I1, I2\}$

We must now be more precise about what we mean by a variable. Let $p \in P$ be arbitrarily chosen. A **variable** of p is either simple or subscripted. A **simple** (or **scalar**) **variable** is any object in $visible(p)$ which is not an array. A **subscripted variable** consists of an array identifier in $visible(p)$, followed by a list of subscript expressions.

Definition 3.4   Let P be a program, and $p \in P$.

(1) $var(p) := \{v: v \in visible(p) \wedge v$ is not an array$\} \cup \{ae: ae$ is an array element name for an array in $visible(p)\}$

   $var(p)$ is called the set of (**declared**) **variables** of p.

(2) $varx(p) := var(p) \cup \{sv: sv$ is a subscripted variable occurring in $p\}$

(3) $VAR := \cup \{var(p): p \in P\}$

   VAR is the set of (**declared**) **variables of the program**.

(4) $VARX := \cup \{varx(p): p \in P\}$.   ∎

For every $p \in P$, $var(p)$ contains the simple variables and all array elements associated with declared arrays, but not the arrays themselves. $varx(p)$ is

Table 3.1   Program syntax.

program	→	*procedure*[+]
procedure	→	*entry-statement declaration* statement* exit-statement*
statement	→	*assignment* | *goto* | *conditional* | *read* | *write* | *call*
assignment	→	*variable* "=" *expression*
goto	→	"GOTO" *label*
conditional	→	"IF" *variable* "THEN" "GOTO" *label* "FI"
read	→	"READ" "(" *variable* ")"
write	→	"WRITE" "(" *expression* ")"
call	→	*procedure-identifier* "(" *argument** ")"
argument	→	*expression*

the set of variables in $var(p)$, augmented by the set of all subscripted variables occurring in the program text with at least one non-constant expression in a subscript position. In Example 3.1, $var(\text{MAIN}) = \{A(1), A(2), A(3), A(4), A(5), B, C, I1, I2\}$, and $varx(\text{MAIN}) = \{A(1), A(2), A(3), A(4), A(5), B, C, I1, I2, A(I1), A(I2+1)\}$.

We now introduce the concept of a state. The **universal domain** Γ contains all values a variable may assume, and in addition the artificial value *undef*, representing undefined. The set $\Gamma_r := \Gamma - \{undef\}$ is called the set of **proper** values.

Definition 3.5   Let P be a program, VAR its variable set, and $V \subseteq VAR$. A **state** of V is a total function $\beta: V \to \Gamma$, which associates each variable in V with a value (possibly *undef*).   ∎

The notion of a state can immediately be extended to cover expressions: if *exp* is an expression, and V the set of variables on which *exp* depends, then the state of *exp*, denoted by $\beta(exp)$, is the value yielded by an evaluation of *exp* after all variables $v \in V$ occurring in *exp* have been replaced by $\beta(v)$.

An abstract syntax for programs is given in Table 3.1 (the notation used is defined in Appendix C, Section C.7). Note that programs are modeled at an intermediate language level. In examples we shall often use source-level statements such as general conditional statements and do-loops: such statements – which do not occur in the model – are interpreted as abbreviations of constructs that conform to the model (see Example 3.4).

The syntax given in Table 3.1 is, of course, incomplete and abstracts from such details as statement labels and separators in statement and argument lists. Non-terminals that are not specified (for example, *declaration* and *expression*) are assumed to be defined as in Fortran. The concrete Fortran syntax will be changed in a number of points (for example, adjacent

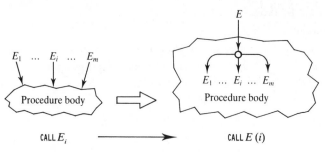

Figure 3.2   Enforcing the single-entry condition.

statements of a statement sequence are separated by '; ', if written on one line); the meaning will be obvious when these changes are used in examples.

The set of all statements in a program, augmented by the entry and exit statements of procedures, is denoted by *STAT*.

In the following, we add a few more remarks concerning the model.

(1)   *Each procedure has exactly one entry point*
This rules out the use of Fortran ENTRY statements. However, if we have a procedure p with $m \geqslant 2$ entry points E_i $(1 \leqslant i \leqslant m)$, we can create a new unique entry point for p, and link it, for example via a computed GOTO (which can be further transformed into a conditional simple GOTO), to the original entry points. Each call must then be modified to identify the entry with which it is associated, and some additional syntactic transformations, such as renaming of parameters, may be necessary (see Figure 3.2).

Alternative approaches to deal with multiple entry points are, first, in-line expansion of the procedure and, secondly, the creation of m separate copies of the procedure, one for each entry point. In practice, these two solutions are applicable only under certain conditions (see Section 3.7.3).

(2)   *Each procedure has exactly one exit point*
This condition rules out alternative returns; it can be enforced by a transformation which is in a sense inverse to that used above. It transforms a procedure which contains multiple exits so that it is always terminated at the same point, whereby the number of the original exit point is communicated (via a new formal parameter) to the calling procedure. After each call, a statement has to be inserted that redirects control to the correct statement (see Program 3.1).

(3)   *Procedure exits*
Upon exit from a procedure, all variables in its local name space become undefined. The values of global variables are not changed (this means that SAVE and certain aspects of named common blocks will not be considered).

Program 3.1   Enforcing the single-exit condition.

`SUBROUTINE P(*,...,*)`	`SUBROUTINE P(F)`
`...`	`...`
`RETURN i`	`F = i; RETURN`
`...`	`...`
`RETURN`	`F = 0; RETURN`
`...`	`...`
`RETURN j` $\Longrightarrow$	`F = j; RETURN`
`...`	`...`
`END`	`F = 0`
	`END`
`CALL P(*L`$_1$`,...,*L`$_n$`)` $\Longrightarrow$	`CALL P(I)`
	`GOTO (L`$_1$`,...,L`$_n$`) I`

(4)   *Statement functions are not considered*
A simple syntactic transformation will always be able to perform in-line expansion of statement functions.

3.3   Control flow analysis

This section is devoted to intraprocedural control flow analysis. We assume that a program P, consisting of a single procedure, is given and discuss various properties of the flowgraph representing the control structure of P. This includes the dominance relation (Section 3.3.1), loops (Section 3.3.2), reducibility (Section 3.3.3), and depth-first search (Section 3.3.4). Finally, Section 3.3.5 uses the concept of dominance to introduce control dependence.

3.3.1   Flowgraphs and the dominance relation

Definition 3.6   A **flowgraph** G is a triple $G = (N,E,s)$, where (N,E) is a directed graph, $s \in N$ is the **initial node**, and there is a path from s to every node of G.   ■

Flowgraphs can be used to model the control structure of programs at the desired level of abstraction. Their nodes may correspond to single Fortran statements, statements in an intermediate language (such as triple or quadruple notation), or sequences of statements. The edges of flowgraphs represent control transfers between nodes.
     If not explicitly stated otherwise, we shall assume henceforth that each node represents a **basic block**: this is a maximum length sequence of

statements $S_1, \ldots, S_r$ ($r \geq 1$) with exactly one entry point (S_1) and exactly one exit point (S_r). The initial node corresponds to the basic block containing the program entry point (PROGRAM). Such a flowgraph is called a **program (flow) graph**. During the construction of this graph, nodes that cannot be reached from the initial node must be eliminated. In our model, every node of a program graph may have at most two immediate successors.

Whenever necessary, we shall assume that every occurrence of a statement in the program, including entry and exit, is uniquely identified by a label. This will allow us to use statement labels and statement occurrences synonymously and to interpret programs as (linearly ordered) sets of labels. Declarations will often be omitted. The basic block structure implies a partition of the statement set $STAT$ into sets $STAT(n)$ for all nodes n of the flowgraph. A call will always be enclosed in a basic block of its own.

We illustrate these concepts below in a program which computes SQRT(L) if the input value L is a non-negative integer.

Example 3.2

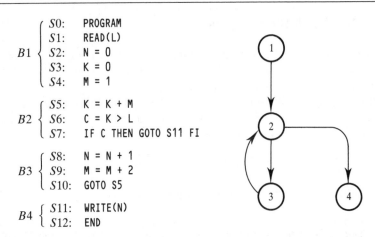

```
        S0:   PROGRAM
        S1:   READ(L)
   B1   S2:   N = 0
        S3:   K = 0
        S4:   M = 1

        S5:   K = K + M
   B2   S6:   C = K > L
        S7:   IF C THEN GOTO S11 FI

        S8:   N = N + 1
   B3   S9:   M = M + 2
        S10:  GOTO S5

   B4   S11:  WRITE(N)
        S12:  END
```

For this program, $STAT = \{Si: 0 \leq i \leq 12\}$.

We construct the first basic block, $B1$, beginning with PROGRAM. Statements can be successively entered into $B1$ until we encounter $S5$: $S5$ is the target of a GOTO (statement $S10$) and therefore does not belong to this block. So $STAT(B1) = \{S0,S1,S2,S3,S4\}$. The next basic block, $B2$, ends with the conditional statement: $STAT(B2) = \{S5,S6,S7\}$. Similarly, we obtain $STAT(B3) = \{S8,S9,S10\}$ and $STAT(B4) = \{S11,S12\}$. The program flowgraph is then given by $G = (\{B1,B2,B3,B4\}, \{(B1,B2), (B2,B3), (B2,B4), (B3,B2)\})$, and is shown above, with the nodes labeled by the indices of the basic blocks.

In the next step we introduce the concept of dominance as a relation in the node set of a flowgraph. This will be used to identify loops in flowgraphs, control iterative algorithms and define control dependence.

Definition 3.7   Let $G = (N,E,s)$ denote a flowgraph, and $n,n' \in N$.

(1) n **dominates** n', written $n \leqslant n'$:$\Longleftrightarrow$ each path from s to n' contains n.

(2) n **properly dominates** n', written $n < n'$:$\Longleftrightarrow$ $n \leqslant n'$ and $n \neq n'$.

(3) n **directly dominates** n', written $n <_d n'$:$\Longleftrightarrow$ $n < n'$ and there is no $n'' \in N$ such that $n < n'' < n'$.

(4) $DOM(n) := \{n'' : n'' \leqslant n\}$ is the **set of dominators** of n.   ■

Example 3.3

The dominance relation for the flowgraph of Example 3.2 can be determined as follows: $\leqslant = \{(1,1), (1,2), (1,3), (1,4), (2,2), (2,3), (2,4), (3,3), (4,4)\}$. The direct dominance relationships are $1 <_d 2$, $2 <_d 3$, and $2 <_d 4$. Finally, $DOM(1) = \{1\}$, $DOM(2) = \{1,2\}$, $DOM(3) = \{1,2,3\}$, and $DOM(4) = \{1,2,4\}$

Lemma 3.1, which is given without proof, summarizes some important properties of dominance.

Lemma 3.1   Let $G = (N,E,s)$ denote a flowgraph with dominance relation $\leqslant$.

(1) $DOM(s) = \{s\}$.

(2)   For every $n \in N$: $s \in DOM(n)$.

(3) $\leqslant$ is a reflexive partial order on N.

(4)   For every $n \in N$, $DOM(n)$ is linearly ordered by $\leqslant$.

(5)   The direct dominator of every node $n' \in N - \{s\}$ is unique.

(6)   Let $n' \in N - \{s\}$, and $n <_d n'$. Then n is the last dominator of n' on any path from s to n'. Furthermore, for any node n'': if $n'' < n'$ and $n'' \neq n$, then $n'' < n$.   ■

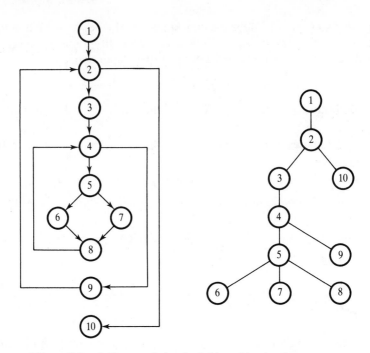

Figure 3.3   A flowgraph (at the left) and its dominator tree.

Note that a direct dominator of a node need not be an immediate predecessor in the flowgraph. This is illustrated in Figure 3.3, where $5 <_d 8$, but $pred(8) = \{6,7\}$. The properties (5) and (6) imply that $<_d$ can be represented by a tree, whose root is the initial node of the flowgraph. This is called the **dominator tree**. Figure 3.4 shows the dominator tree for the flowgraph of Example 3.2. We give a simple method for computing the dominance relation in Section 3.6.3. (Efficient algorithms for the construction of the dominator tree have been provided by Lengauer and Tarjan (1979) and Harel (1985), with respective complexities of $O(e\alpha(e))$ and $O(e)$, where $e = |E|$ and $\alpha(e) \geq 1$ is a very slowly growing function.)

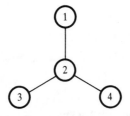

Figure 3.4   Dominator tree for the flowgraph of Example 3.2.

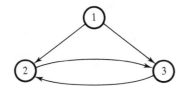

Figure 3.5   An irreducible graph.

3.3.2 Loops

In this section we define **loops** as single-entry strongly connected subgraphs of a flowgraph. Loops represent program regions that may be executed many times; thus their optimization is crucial for the overall run-time efficiency of programs.

> **Definition 3.8**   Let $G = (N,E,s)$ denote a flowgraph.

(1)   A flowgraph $G' = (N',E',s')$ is a **subflowgraph** of G :$\Longleftrightarrow$ (N',E') is a subgraph of (N,E).

(2)   A flowgraph $G'' = (N',E'',s')$ is a **partial flowgraph** of G :$\Longleftrightarrow$ (N',E'') is a partial graph of G.   ∎

If $G' = (N',E',s')$ is a subflowgraph of $G = (N,E,s)$, then G' is said to be **generated** by N'. Note that $E' = E \cap N' \times N'$.

> **Definition 3.9**   Let $G = (N,E,s)$ be a flowgraph. A subflowgraph $G' = (N',E',s')$ of G is a **loop with entry point** s' :$\Longleftrightarrow$

(1)   for every $(n,n') \in E: n' \in N' \Longrightarrow n' = s'$ or $n \in N'$, and

(2)   for every pair of nodes $n,n' \in N'$ there are non-trivial paths from n to n' and vice versa.   ∎

The first condition requires that each path reaching a loop from outside must pass through the entry point. Thus the entry point dominates all nodes of the loop, and is unique. Note that not every strongly connected subflowgraph need be a loop: a counterexample is given in Figure 3.5, where the subflowgraph generated by $\{2,3\}$ with initial node 2 satisfies condition (2) but not condition (1) of the loop definition. The same is true if node 3 is chosen as the initial node. The graph in Figure 3.5 displays a structure that is characteristic of **irreducible graphs** (see Definition 3.10). Note that neither $2 \leqslant 3$ nor $3 \leqslant 2$ holds here.

Example 3.4

Consider the flowgraph G of Figure 3.3. G can be interpreted as a program graph for a program containing a doubly nested do-loop, with a conditional statement contained in the inner loop:

```
PROGRAM
S1
DO I = 1, N
  S2
  DO J = 1, M
    IF C THEN S3 ELSE S4 FI
  END DO J
END DO I
S5
END
```

A mapping between the nodes of G and the statements of this program can be established as follows:

- 1   MAIN, $S1$, initialization of I
- 2   loop control for the I loop
- 3 $S2$, initialization of J
- 4   loop control for the J loop
- 5   computation of C
- 6 $S3$
- 7 $S4$
- 8   incrementation of J
- 9   incrementation of I
- 10 $S5$, END

Here it is assumed that none of the statements Si $(1 \leqslant i \leqslant 5)$ results in a transfer of control.

We can identify two loops in G:

(1)   The subflowgraph G_1' generated by $N_1' = \{2,3,4,5,6,7,8,9\}$ with initial node 2 is a loop with entry point 2. This corresponds to the I loop.

(2)   The subflowgraph G_2' generated by $N_2' = \{4,5,6,7,8\}$ with initial node 4 is a loop with entry point 4. This corresponds to the J loop.

There are no other loops in this flowgraph. Note that G contains exactly two edges (n,n') such that $n' \leqslant n$, namely $(9,2)$ and $(8,4)$.

We have seen that the formal concept of a loop captures do-loops; it can be easily verified that the for, while and repeat loops of Pascal and other 'structured' looping constructs are also included. Furthermore, our definition also covers loops which are programmed 'explicitly', using GOTO and conditional statements. We want to recognize such loops as well and subject them to the same treatment as do-loops, if they meet the additional constraints required.

The dominance relation immediately gives us a method for determining all loops in a flowgraph. We already noted in Example 3.4 that the entry points of the two loops are the only nodes in the flowgraph that are the endpoints of edges whose direction is inverse to the direction of dominance. It turns out that this property actually characterizes the entry points of loops in an arbitrary flowgraph. We formalize this observation in the following theorem, which also leads to a method for the construction of the maximum loop associated with an entry point.

Theorem 3.1 Let $G = (N,E,s)$ denote a flowgraph.

(1) A node $s' \in N$ is the entry point of a loop in G iff there exists a node $n' \in N$ such that $(n',s') \in E$ and $s' \leqslant n'$.

(2) Let s' be an entry point of a loop in G. Then the maximum loop with entry point s' is the subflowgraph G' with initial node s' that is generated by the set N':

$$N' = \{n'' \in N: \quad \text{there exists a path from } n'' \text{ to } s' \text{ which only contains nodes that are dominated by } s'\} \quad \blacksquare$$

The maximum loop associated with an entry point s' can be found by determining the 'natural loop' associated with s' and an appropriate edge (n',s'), as specified by Algorithm 3.1 (Aho *et al.* (1986), Algorithm 10.1). The algorithm begins by entering s' into the loop and then, starting with $n'' = n'$, inserts n'' into the loop; it proceeds recursively by successively identifying n'' with the predecessors of the previously selected node. The process terminates when it cannot find a predecessor that is not already in the loop. If a loop is elementary, $G' = (\{s'\}, \{(s',s')\}, s')$, then the insertion process sketched above is empty.

The notation for the specification of algorithms is described in Appendix C, Section C.8.

ALGORITHM 3.1: Construction of the natural loop

> ***Input***   (1)   A flowgraph $G = (N,E,s)$.
>
> (2)   A loop entry point $s' \in N$, and an edge (n',s') with $s' \leqslant n'$.
>
> ***Output***   The set N' which generates the natural loop associated with s' and (n',s').
>
> ***Method***

```
procedure insert(x);
  begin
    if x ∉ N'
      then N' plus {x}; push(x)
    fi
  end insert;
begin
init_stack;
N' := {s'};
insert(n');
while ¬ empty_stack do
  n := top_of_stack;
  pop;
  for every n'' ∈ pred(n) do insert(n'') end for
end while
end                                               ■
```

Example 3.5

Let us apply Algorithm 3.1 to the flowgraph of Figure 3.3, loop entry point 2, and the edge (9,2). We begin by setting $N' := \{2\}$, then add 9 to N' and push 9 onto the stack. Now 4, 3, 8, 6, 5, and 7 are successively included in N' (assuming that the set of predecessors is visited in the order of increasing node labels). Note that the outcome of the algorithm does not depend on the order in which the predecessors are visited.

3.3.3   Reducibility

An important subclass of the class of all flowgraphs is the one characterized by a property called **reducibility**. Flowgraphs for programs that are written using only structured control such as do, while, and repeat loops, conditional statements and loop exit branches, are reducible. A number of important data flow analysis methods can only be applied to reducible graphs; furthermore, reducible flowgraphs can often be processed more efficiently than irreducible ones.

There are many equivalent definitions of reducibility: we have selected the following one.

Definition 3.10   Let $G = (N,E,s)$ be a flowgraph.

G is **reducible** $:\Longleftrightarrow E$ can be partitioned into sets E_1 and E_2 such that:

(1) $D = (N,E_1,s)$ is a maximal acyclic partial flowgraph (**DAG**) of G, and

(2)   for every edge $(n,n') \in E_2$: $n' \leq n$.   ∎

A corollary of Definition 3.10 is that a flowgraph is reducible iff it has a unique DAG.

Example 3.6

We examine the flowgraphs of Example 3.2 and Figures 3.3 and 3.5.

The flowgraph of Example 3.2 is reducible, with $E_1 = \{(1,2), (2,3), (2,4)\}$ and $E_2 = \{(3,2)\}$ defining the partition of the edges.

The flowgraph of Figure 3.3 is likewise reducible; there, $E_2 = \{(9,2), (8,4)\}$ and $E_1 = E - E_2$.

In contrast, the flowgraph of Figure 3.5 is irreducible. There are two DAGs: those obtained by removing either the edge $(2,3)$ or the edge $(3,2)$. However, neither $2 < 3$ nor $3 < 2$, and therefore condition (2) of Definition 3.10 cannot be satisfied.

3.3.4   Depth-first spanning trees

In many algorithms, all nodes of a flowgraph must be traversed in a systematic manner. An example is the iterative algorithm (see Algorithms 3.4 and 3.6), which propagates data flow information across a flowgraph by processing all nodes iteratively in a round-robin fashion. The specific order in which the nodes are visited may be strongly correlated to the number of iterations required by the algorithm.

In this subsection, we introduce the concept of a depth-first spanning tree, show how such a tree can be constructed by depth-first search, and use the construction process to find a linear order for the nodes of a flowgraph. This order will be called rPostorder (for reverse postorder) and topologically sorts the dominance relation (Kam and Ullman, 1976).

ALGORITHM 3.2: Depth-first spanning tree

Input   Flowgraph $G = (N,E,s)$

Output (1)   An ordered tree $T = (N,E')$ with root s and $E' \subseteq E$. T is called a **depth-first spanning tree** (DFST) of G.

(2)   A linear order rPostorder on N.

Method

```
/* Each node n has associated with it a boolean value mark(n), which is
   initially false, and is set to true when the node is first visited via a call to
   search(n). The algorithm performs a depth-first search by applying the
   search procedure first to the initial node and then recursively to all
   successors which have not yet been visited. The order in the sets succ(n) of
   the tree is established by the order in which edges are added to E' */
function unmarked_successors(n: node): set;
   begin unmarked_successors: = {n' ∈ succ(n): ¬ mark(n')} end;
procedure search(n: node);
   begin
      mark(n) := true;
      while unmarked_successors(n) ≠ ∅ do
         n' := select(unmarked_successors(n));
         E' plus {(n,n')};
         search(n')
      end while;
      rPostorder(n) := i;
      i minus 1
   end search;
/* MAIN PROGRAM: */
begin
E' := ∅;
i := |N|;
for every n ∈ N do mark(n) := false   end for;
search(s)
end
```

■

Note that the DFST constructed in the algorithm may depend on the order in which the successors of a node are selected. As a consequence,

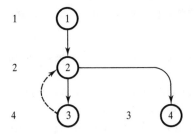

Figure 3.6   A DFST and rPostorder for the flowgraph of Example 3.2.

rPostorder is in general not uniquely determined by the flowgraph. It can, however, be shown that each such order topologically sorts the dominance relation (Hecht, 1977).

In Figures 3.6 and 3.7 we illustrate DFSTs that may be obtained by an application of Algorithm 3.2 to the flowgraphs of Example 3.2 and Figure 3.3. The numbers outside the circles are the rPostorder numbers of the nodes. The solid lines represent the edges of the DFSTs, while the dotted lines are those edges of the original graph which were eliminated

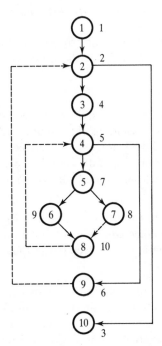

Figure 3.7   A DFST and rPostorder for the flowgraph of Figure 3.3.

during the construction process. These edges are grouped into three categories:

(1)   edges that connect a node with a descendant are called **forward edges**,

(2)   edges that connect a node with an ancestor, and edges of the form (n,n), are called **back edges**, and

(3)   all other edges in $E - E'$ are called **cross edges**.

In Figure 3.6, (3,2) is a back edge. In Figure 3.7, (8,4) and (9,2) are back edges, whereas (7,8) is a cross edge.

We make the following observation (for a proof see Hecht (1977)):

Lemma 3.2   Let $G = (N,E,s)$ be a flowgraph, and $T = (N,E')$ a DFST of G.

(1)   Every edge in $E - E'$ can be uniquely characterized as a forward, back, or cross edge.

(2)   An edge (n,n') is a back edge iff rPostorder$(n') \leqslant$ rPostorder(n).

(3)   Every cycle in G contains at least one back edge.

(4)   rPostorder sorts the dominance relation, that is, for any nodes n,n':

$$n \leqslant n' \implies \text{rPostorder}(n) \leqslant \text{rPostorder}(n')$$

(5)   If G is a reducible flowgraph, then its DAG $D = (N,E_1,s)$ can be constructed by defining E_1 as the union of E' and all forward and cross edges.   ∎

Note that the construction of D described in property (5) is independent of the choice of the DFST, yielding the unique DAG of G. In contrast, different choices of a DFST for an irreducible flowgraph may lead to different DAGs (see Figure 3.5 and Example 3.6).

Finally, we define loop-connectedness (Kam and Ullman, 1976).

Definition 3.11   Let $G = (N,E,s)$ be a flowgraph, and $T = (N,E')$ a DFST of G. The **loop-connectedness**, d, of G with respect to T is the largest number of back edges in any cycle-free path of G.   ∎

It can be shown that for reducible flowgraphs d is independent of T, and that the number of iterations required in the iterative algorithm depends on d (see Section 3.5.5). Knuth (1971) examined a large sample of programs to compute an average value for d; it turned out to be 2.75, and indeed it seems improbable that real programs exist where $d > 5$.

3.3.5   Control dependence

If the execution of a statement S_1 determines whether or not a statement S_2 is to be executed, then we say that S_2 is **control dependent** upon S_1. A typical case for such a situation is the conditional statement, where the value of the condition decides whether or not the statements in a branch are to be performed. Control dependence imposes an order on the execution of statements and thus is an important factor in restructuring.

We formally define the concept of control dependence in Definition 3.15 (Ferrante *et al.*, 1987).

Definition 3.12   A **single-exit flowgraph** is a quadruple $G = (N,E,s,t)$, where (N,E,s) is a flowgraph, $t \in N$ is the **exit node** of G, and there is a path from every node of G to t.   ∎

Note that all the flowgraphs that have been discussed so far in examples are single-exit graphs.

Definition 3.13   Let $G = (N,E,s,t)$ be a single-exit flowgraph. Then G^{-1}, the **reverse** of G, is given as $G^{-1} := (N,E^{-1},t,s)$.   ∎

If G is a single-exit flowgraph, then obviously the same is true for its reverse.

Definition 3.14   Let $G = (N,E,s,t)$ be a single-exit flowgraph, and $n,n' \in N$.

n is **post-dominated** by n' $:\Longleftrightarrow$

(1) $n \neq n'$, and
(2)   every path from n to t contains n'.   ∎

Note that post-dominance in G is the reflexive reduction of the dominance relation in G^{-1}.

Definition 3.15   Let $G = (N,E,s,t)$ be a single-exit flowgraph, and $n,n' \in N$.

n' is **control dependent** on n $:\Longleftrightarrow$

(1)   there exists a non-trivial path from n to n' such that every node n'' in the path $(n'' \neq n,n')$ is post-dominated by n', and
(2) n is not post-dominated by n'.   ∎

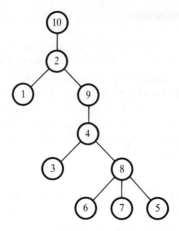

Figure 3.8   Post-dominator tree for the flowgraph of Figure 3.3.

Example 3.7

If we look at the the flowgraph G of Figure 3.3 we will see that Definition 3.15 captures the intuitive meaning usually associated with control dependence: by examining Figure 3.8, which shows the post-dominator tree for G, we can determine all control dependences for G as follows:

(1)   each of the nodes 2,3,4,9 is control dependent on 2,

(2)   each of the nodes 4,5,8 is control dependent on 4,

(3)   6 and 7 are control dependent on 5.

If n' is control dependent on n, then n must have at least two successor nodes. So there must be two distinct paths π_1 and π_2 that both connect n with the exit node, such that π_1 contains n', and π_2 does not contain n'.

If $n = n'$ and condition (1) of Definition 3.15 is satisfied, then condition (2) is satisfied trivially (so the loop entries 2 and 4 in the example above are control dependent on themselves).

It is a simple matter to compute the set of control dependences if the post-dominator tree has been constructed. We do not discuss details here (see Ferrante *et al.* (1987)).

3.4   Data flow problems and optimization

In this section we define a number of data flow problems and show how their solution can be applied to the optimization of programs. Actual solution methods will be discussed in Section 3.5.

As before, let a program P consisting of exactly one procedure be given, let $STAT$ denote the associated statement set (which does not contain calls), and $G = (N,E,s)$ be its program graph. The nodes of G represent basic blocks of P. We shall formulate and examine data flow problems as flow problems in G; in this context the results of local analysis will be assumed to be available. As we are performing scalar analysis, the set VAR of program variables is supposed to contain only simple variables. Furthermore, we assume that the initial node has no predecessors, that is $pred(s) = \emptyset$.

3.4.1   Use–definition and definition–use chains

Let $v \in VAR$ denote a variable which occurs in a statement $S \in STAT$. S is called a **definition** (of v) iff S is an assignment statement with left-hand side v or a read statement READ(v). If S is a definition of v, then the execution of S results in the assignment of a value to v. S is called a **use** (of v) iff, during execution of S, the value of v is read. A statement S may be both a definition as well as a use of the same variable, as in $v = v + 1$.

Definition 3.16

(1) $S\_DEFS := \{S \in STAT: S$ is a definition$\}$

(2) $S\_USES := \{S \in STAT: S$ is a use$\}$ ∎

Many analysis and optimization problems are closely tied to **use–definition** (UD) and **definition–use** (DU) chains. A UD chain links a use to the set of all definitions that may reach it; a DU chain links a definition to all its possible uses. The notation and terminology introduced below provide a framework for the precise definition of these concepts.

Definition 3.17   Let $S \in STAT$ be an arbitrary statement.

(1) $DEF(S) := \{v \in VAR: S$ is a definition of $v\}$

(2) $USE(S) := \{v \in VAR: S$ is a use of $v\}$ ∎

The sets S_DEFS, S_USES, $USE(S)$, and $DEF(S)$ can all be determined by a simple parse of the program. As we have excluded side effects,

$|DEF(S)| \leq 1$ for all S. We now extend the meaning of USE and DEF to basic blocks and introduce additional local data flow information sets.

A definition S of a variable v in a basic block n is said to be **outward exposed** if it is the last definition of v in n; a use of v is outward exposed if n does not contain a definition of v before this use. Outward exposed definitions and uses are the links that connect a basic block to its environment.

Definition 3.18   Let n ∈ N be an arbitrary basic block.

(1) $DEF(n)$ $:= \{v \in VAR$: there is an outward exposed definition of v in $n\}$

(2) $USE(n)$ $:= \{v \in VAR$: there is an outward exposed use of v in $n\}$

(3) $PRE(n)$ $:= VAR - DEF(n)$

(4) $S\_DEF(n) := \{S \in STAT$: S is an outward exposed definition in $n\}$

(5) $S\_USE(n) := \{S \in STAT$: S is an outward exposed use in $n\}$

(6) $S\_PRE(n) := \{S' \in S\_DEFS$: for all $S \in S\_DEF(n)$: $DEF(S') \neq DEF(S)\}$

The prefix $S\_$ indicates a set of statements rather than variables. PRE stands for 'preserved'.

Example 3.8

We construct some of the sets defined above for the program of Example 3.2:

$$VAR \quad = \{C, K, L, M, N\}$$
$$S\_DEFS = \{S1, S2, S3, S4, S5, S6, S8, S9\}$$
$$S\_USES = \{S5, S6, S7, S8, S9, S11\}$$

	1	2	3	4
$USE(n)$	$\emptyset$	$\{K, L, M\}$	$\{M, N\}$	$\{N\}$
$DEF(n)$	$\{K, L, M, N\}$	$\{C, K\}$	$\{M, N\}$	$\emptyset$
$S\_PRE(n)$	$\{S6\}$	$\{S1, S2, S4, S8, S9\}$	$\{S1, S3, S5, S6\}$	S_DEFS
$PRE(n)$	$\{C\}$	$\{L, M, N\}$	$\{C, K, L\}$	VAR

The sets introduced in Definition 3.18 are strictly local in the sense that they describe the effect of a particular basic block on the data flow problem we are interested in, and they can be derived from an analysis of that block alone.

In the following it will sometimes be convenient to examine the control flow of a program on the basis of statements rather than basic blocks. In order to do so, we define a **statement path** as a sequence of statements that can be executed in the given order. For each path of the flowgraph we obtain a statement path by substituting the associated statement sequences for basic blocks; conversely, each statement path can be mapped to a path of the flowgraph. For example, the path (1,2,4) in the flowgraph of Example 3.2 corresponds to the statement path ($S0$, $S1$, $S2$, $S3$, $S4$, $S5$, $S6$, $S7$, $S11$, $S12$).

We shall now examine how data flow information is propagated through the flowgraph. For example, in order to construct the use–definition chain for a given use we have to find the set of all possible statement paths that link a definition to that use. In the program of Example 3.2, the set of definitions reaching the use of N in the statement $S11$:WRITE(N) is $\{S2, S8\}$ and $S2$ reaches $S11$ along the statement path ($S2$, $S3$, $S4$, $S5$, $S6$, $S7$, $S11$), while $S8$ reaches $S11$ via ($S8$, $S9$, $S10$, $S5$, $S6$, $S7$, $S11$).

As the analysis of each basic block can be done locally, it suffices to consider the propagation of information at the flowgraph level, thinking of basic blocks as 'black boxes' whose effect is described by the sets of Definition 3.18. Data flow information will then be associated with basic blocks. Depending on the direction of propagation, this information will be attached to either the entry or the exit point of the block. Each problem specification that associates data flow information with basic blocks is implicitly assumed to be analogously defined for single statements.

The following example illustrates how data flow information associated with a basic block can be used to derive the corresponding information for the statements within the basic block.

Example 3.9

Let n denote the following basic block:

```
S1: A = B + C
S2: B = A * C
S3: C = A - B
```

Then $USE(n) = \{B,C\}$, where $S1$ contains an outward exposed use of B and C, and $S2$ an outward exposed use of C. All other uses are related to local definitions and therefore not outward exposed. Now assume that we have already determined the set $RD(n)$ of definitions reaching n (this is precisely defined below) as:

$RD(n) = \{S_1', S_2', S_3'\}$ with $DEF(S_1') = \{A\}$, $DEF(S_2') = \{B\}$, and $DEF(S_3') = \{D\}$

For each statement $S \in STAT(n)$, let $RD(S)$ denote the set of definitions reaching S. Then we can obtain the following sets from $RD(n)$ by local analysis:

$$RD(S1) = RD(n) = \{S'_1, S'_2, S'_3\}$$
$$RD(S2) = \{S1, S'_2, S'_3\}$$
$$RD(S3) = \{S1, S2, S'_3\}$$

and the set of definitions leaving n is $\{S1, S2, S3, S'_3\}$.

A path in G is **definition-free** for a variable v iff v is not defined in any of its nodes. Let $n, n' \in N$, and $S \in S\_DEF(n')$ be an outward exposed definition of a variable v. We say that (the definition of v in) S **reaches** n iff there is a path from n' to n, which, except for its endpoints, is definition-free for v. If the definition of v in S reaches n and $v \in USE(n)$, then (the definition of v in) S **reaches a use** of v in n. In the program of Example 3.2, all paths $(2,3)^r$, $r \geqslant 1$, are definition-free for L, but for no other variable. In the path $(1,2,3,2)$, the definition of M in 1 (statement $S4$) reaches uses in 2 and 3 ($S5$ and $S9$, respectively); the definition of M in 3 ($S9$) also reaches a use in 2 ($S5$).

A variable v is called **live** at (the exit of) a basic block n iff there is a path from n to an outward exposed use of v in a node n', which, apart from its end nodes, is definition-free for v. The **live variables problem** is the problem of determining, for each $n \in N$, the set of all variables that are live at the exit of n. In Example 3.2, all variables except C are live at the end of every node $\neq 4$.

We are now ready to state the central definitions of this section.

Definition 3.19

(1)   Let $n \in N$ denote an arbitrary basic block.

$$RD(n) := \{S: S \in S\_DEFS \text{ and } S \text{ reaches } n\}.$$

RD is called the set of **reaching definitions** for n.

(2)   Let $n \in N$ and $v \in USE(n)$:

$$UD(n,v) := \{S': S' \in RD(n) \text{ and } v \in DEF(S')\}$$

$UD(n,v)$ is called the **use–definition** chain for basic block n and variable v.

(3)   Let $n' \in N$ and $S' \in S\_DEF(n')$ with $v \in DEF(S')$:

$$DU(n',v) := \{S: S \in S\_USE(n) \text{ for some } n \in N, v \in USE(S), \text{ and } S' \in UD(n,v)\}$$

$DU(n',v)$ is called the **definition–use** chain for basic block n' and variable v.   ∎

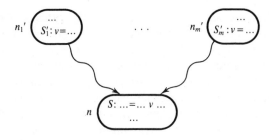

Figure 3.9 A UD chain: $UD(n,v) = \{S'_1, \ldots, S'_m\}$.

The following lemma, which establishes the relationship between UD and DU chains, is an immediate consequence of the definition. It is informally illustrated in Figures 3.9 and 3.10.

Lemma 3.3 For any $n,n' \in N$, $S \in S\_USE(n)$, $S' \in S\_DEF(n')$ and $v \in USE(S) \cap DEF(S')$:

$$S' \in UD(n,v) \Longleftrightarrow S \in DU(n',v) \qquad \blacksquare$$

Let S be an outward exposed use of the variable v in basic block n. Then $UD(n,v)$ is the set of all definitions of v that reach S. Note that $UD(n,v) = \emptyset$ would point to a use of v without proper initialization, and thus expose a programming error.

Similarly, let S' be an outward exposed definition of variable v in basic block n'. Then $DU(n',v)$ is the set of all uses of v that can be reached from S'. If $DU(n',v) \neq \emptyset$, then there is at least one use of this definition of v, and v is live at the exit of n'. If $DU(n',v) = \emptyset$, then we know that the execution of S' has no semantic effect and thus S' can be eliminated as **dead code** (see Algorithm 3.3). This case is not particularly interesting for

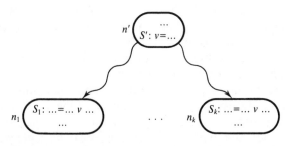

Figure 3.10 A DU chain: $DU(n',v) = \{S_1, \ldots, S_k\}$.

programs written by people (it would probably indicate a programming error), but often occurs when automatic transformations are applied to a program. Such transformations have to make conservative assumptions in order to guarantee that semantic equivalence is maintained. For example, when a new do-variable is created during loop normalization (see Example 1.1 and Section 5.2), the transformation tool must make sure that the old do-variable has an appropriate value when the loop is exited. This forces us to generate an assignment statement immediately after the body of the loop; the probability that this statement is dead code is rather high, in view of common programming practice.

Let S, v, and n be defined as above and assume that we are interested in the value of v when S is executed. If we can show that every S' in $UD(n,v)$ assigns the same constant value c to v, then we can conclude that v always has the value c when used in S. On the other hand, a constant value assigned to v in a statement S' contained in basic block n' can be propagated to all uses connected with that statement: this can be done using $DU(n',v)$. This suggests that we can obtain a solution of the constant propagation problem directly on the basis of the UD and DU chains (Kennedy, 1981). We do not elaborate on this further, but discuss this problem within a more general framework in Section 3.6.4.

Other applications of UD and DU chains will be found in data dependence analysis (Chapter 4) and in standardizing transformations such as scalar forward substitution, induction variable substitution and scalar renaming, all of which are treated in Chapter 5.

UD and DU chains associated with arbitrary statements S (rather than basic blocks) can be immediately derived from the sets defined above by local analysis (see Example 3.9). These sets will be denoted by $UD(S,v)$ and $DU(S,v)$, respectively, and are assumed to be known whenever $UD(n,v)$ and $DU(n,v)$ have been determined for all n and v.

3.4.2   Available expressions and redundant expressions

Let EXP be the set of all expressions contained in a program, let $exp \in EXP$ and $n \in N$ be arbitrarily chosen, and let $ops(exp) \subseteq VAR$ denote the set of all variables on which exp depends, that is the set of **operands** of exp. Expression exp is **available** at n iff every path reaching n from the initial node evaluates exp, and the subpath between the last computation of exp and n is definition-free for all operands of exp.

Now assume that exp is available at n, and n contains an occurrence of exp which is outward exposed, that is, none of the variables in $ops(exp)$ is defined in n before exp is evaluated. Such an occurrence is called **redundant**. Redundant expression occurrences can be replaced by a reference to the value resulting from the last evaluation of the expression.

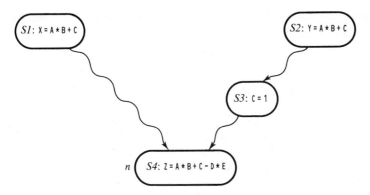

Figure 3.11   An available expression (A * B) in n.

Example 3.10

Consider the program graph sketched in Figure 3.11. Basic block n is reached by two paths in both of which the expression A*B+C, with $ops(A*B+C) = \{A,B,C\}$, is computed. However, the path from definition S2 to n contains a definition of C, and so A*B+C is not available at n. In contrast, the subexpression A*B is preserved on both paths and is therefore available at n. Thus the occurrence of A*B on the right-hand side of the assignment to Z in S4 is redundant. It can be replaced by the temporary variable TEMP, which must be assigned the last value computed for A*B on each path reaching n. The transformed program is shown in Figure 3.12.

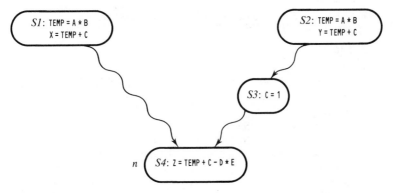

Figure 3.12   The example of Figure 3.11 after the redundant computation is eliminated.

The **available expressions problem** is the problem of determining the set of all available expressions reaching each $n \in N$. It is discussed in Section 3.6.1.

3.4.3 Dead-code elimination

We define a statement as **useful** iff either it is a member of a class of critical statements or it contributes directly or indirectly to one. A statement is **critical** iff no program transformation is ever permitted to eliminate it. In our model, WRITE would be considered to be the only critical statement category but, in a more general model, this set could be larger, including for instance all statements that interact with the program's environment. Dead-code elimination removes all statements that are not useful from a program.

The following algorithm marks the set of all useful statements, starting with the critical statements and proceeding to other useful statements via UD chains.

ALGORITHM 3.3: Mark useful statements

Input (1) Program P with statement set $STAT$.

(2) $CRITICAL$: the set of all critical statements in $STAT$.

(3) The sets $UD(S,v)$ for all $S \in STAT$ and $v \in VAR$ with $v \in USE(S)$.

Output For each statement S, $USEFUL(S) =$ **true** iff S is useful.

Method

```
begin
/* Initialization */
for every S ∈ STAT do USEFUL(S) := false   end for;
STAT_SET := CRITICAL;
/* Iteration */
while STAT_SET ≠ ∅ do
  S := select_and_remove(STAT_SET);   //* S is useful *//
  USEFUL(S) := true;
  for every v ∈ USE(S) do
    for every S' ∈ UD(S,v) do
      /* S depends on S', therefore S' is useful */
      if ¬(USEFUL(S')) then STAT_SET plus {S'} fi
    end for
  end for
end while
end
```
■

3.5   Monotone data flow systems

3.5.1   An informal introduction

Virtually all data flow problems can be modeled and solved in a uniform way by using the concept of **monotone data flow systems**. We shall illustrate the basic ideas for the reaching definitions problem RD (see Definition 3.19).

(1)   *Definition of the data flow information set L*
L is the set of all data flow information items that are relevant for the solution of the given problem.

For every $n \in N$, $RD(n)$ is a subset of S_DEFS. Thus the powerset $\mathcal{P}(S\_DEFS)$ is the data flow information set L in this case.

(2)   *The effect of joining paths*
Assume that $n \in N$ is given, $pred(n) = \{n_1, n_2\}$ and data flow information X_i leaves n_i $(i = 1,2)$. How can we compute the information to be associated with n from X_1 and X_2?

For RD, the question can be answered as follows: any definition that is in X_1 or X_2 reaches n; so we must form the union of X_1 and X_2.

(3)   *The effect of basic blocks*
Each basic block n must be associated with a function f_n, which specifies the effect an execution of n has on the data flow information.

Assume that $X \subseteq S\_DEFS$ is a set of definitions that reaches n. How do we determine the set $X' \subseteq S\_DEFS$ of definitions that leaves n? First, a definition S in X will be passed through n iff S is preserved in n. Secondly, all definitions of n which are outward exposed reach the end of n. Formally, we obtain:

$$X' = f_n(X) = (X \cap S\_PRE(n)) \cup S\_DEF(n)$$
for every $X \subseteq S\_DEFS$

(4)   *Solution of the problem by an iterative algorithm*
Now, after a proper initialization of nodes with data flow information, the problem can be solved by propagating data flow information iteratively through the flowgraph. This process terminates when the propagation does not yield new information for any node of the graph. The iterative algorithm for the reaching definitions problem is given in Algorithm 3.4.

ALGORITHM 3.4: Reaching definitions

Input   (1)   Program P.

(2)   Data flow information set $L = \mathcal{P}(S\_DEFS)$.

(3)   Program graph $G = (N,E,s)$.

(4)   For each $n \in N$: $S\_PRE(n)$ and $S\_DEF(n)$.

Output   For each $n \in N$: $RD(n)$.

Method

/* The algorithm uses the following variables:

   new: a temporary variable, to which elements of L are assigned

   stable: a boolean variable, which is used to test for stabilization of
      the algorithm

   $INF(n)$ for every $n \in N$: a variable that stores the actual data flow information
      associated with node n. The final value of $INF(n)$ specifies the result of
      the algorithm for that node. */

begin

/* Initialization */

for every $n \in N$ **do** $INF(n) := \emptyset$ **end for**;

/* Iteration */

repeat

   stable := **true**;

   for every $n \in N$ **do**

      $new := \bigcup_{n' \in pred(n)} ((INF(n') \cap S\_PRE(n')) \cup S\_DEF(n'))$;

      if $new \neq INF(n)$

      then $INF(n) := new$; *stable* := **false**

         fi

   end for

until *stable*;

for every $n \in N$ **do** $RD(n) := INF(n)$ **end for**

end   ∎

In general, we require the data flow information set L to be a bounded
semilattice, and the functions f_n to be monotone functions on L. The effect
of joining paths is modeled by the meet operation of the semilattice. The
optimum solution of the data flow problem is defined for each $n \in N, n \neq s$,
as the value obtained by (a) determining the effect of every path π from s to n
by propagating data flow information along π, and (b) applying the meet
operation of L to the set of values determined in (a). The iterative algorithm
can be shown to terminate for all instances of the problem, and to yield
either the optimum solution or a conservative approximation thereof.

We now define the concepts needed.

3.5.2   Semilattices

Definition 3.20   A **semilattice** is a set L with a binary **meet** operation $\wedge$ such that for all $a,b,c \in L$:

(1) $a \wedge a = a$ (idempotent)
(2) $a \wedge b = b \wedge a$ (commutative)
(3) $a \wedge (b \wedge c) = (a \wedge b) \wedge c$ (associative)   ∎

If we want to make the association of L with $\wedge$ explicit, we write $(L, \wedge)$ for the semilattice.

A semilattice has a **zero element** 0 iff $a \wedge 0 = 0$ for every $a \in L$. L has a **one element** 1 iff $a \wedge 1 = a$ for every $a \in L$. If 0 or 1 exists, then it is unique.

Definition 3.21   Let $(L, \wedge)$ denote a semilattice, and let a,b be arbitrary elements of L. We define a relation $\leqslant$ in L:

$$a \leqslant b : \Longleftrightarrow a \wedge b = a$$ ∎

Whenever we use the symbol '$\leqslant$' in the context of a semilattice, we will mean the relation defined here. Based on this definition, the relations $<$, $\geqslant$, and $>$ can be obtained in the usual way.

The following lemma can be easily verified.

Lemma 3.4   Let $(L, \wedge)$ denote a semilattice and $\leqslant$ the relation introduced in Definition 3.21. Then $\leqslant$ is a partial order on L.   ∎

Let $a_1, a_2, \ldots$ denote a sequence of elements from a semilattice L. This sequence is called a **chain** iff $a_i > a_{i+1}$ for all $i = 1, 2 \ldots$.

Definition 3.22   A semilattice L is **bounded** iff for every a in L there exists a $c_a \in \mathbb{N}$ such that the length of every chain beginning with a is at most c_a.   ∎

Example 3.11

Let M denote an arbitrary finite set.

(1) $(\mathscr{P}(M), \cap)$ is a bounded semilattice with both 0 and 1 ($\varnothing$ and M, respectively). The relation $\leqslant$ is the set-theoretic inclusion $\subseteq$.

(2) $(\mathcal{P}(M), \cup)$ is a bounded semilattice with 0 and 1 elements, where 0 is
       M and 1 is $\emptyset$. The relation $\leqslant$ corresponds to the inverse inclusion,
       $\subseteq^{-1}$. ∎

The meet operation can be readily extended to an arbitrary number $m \geqslant 1$
of elements by defining:

$$\bigwedge_{1 \leqslant i \leqslant m} a_i := a_1 \wedge a_2 \wedge \ldots a_m$$

If L is bounded, then $\wedge$ can be further extended to countably infinite sets:
Let $M \subseteq L$ denote such a set. Then:

$$\bigwedge_{a \in M} a := \lim_{m \to \infty} \bigwedge_{1 \leqslant i \leqslant m} a_i$$

The limit exists and is equal to

$$\bigwedge_{1 \leqslant i \leqslant q} a_i$$

for some $q \in N$.

   In all of the following we shall assume that $(L, \wedge)$ is a bounded
semilattice with 0 and 1.

3.5.3   Monotonic functions and their largest fixpoint

We have mentioned before that the effect a basic block has on data flow
information will be modeled by a function $f: L \to L$. These functions must
be **monotonic** in the sense defined below. A special subclass of monotonic
functions for which the iterative algorithm produces precise results is the
class of **distributive** functions.

Definition 3.23

(1)   A total function $f: L \to L$ is **monotonic** $:\Longleftrightarrow$ for all $a, b \in L$:
       $f(a \wedge b) \leqslant f(a) \wedge f(b)$.
(2)   A total function $f: L \to L$ is **distributive** $:\Longleftrightarrow$ for all $a, b \in L$:
       $f(a \wedge b) = f(a) \wedge f(b)$. ∎

It can be easily seen that a function is monotonic iff for all $a, b \in L$ $a \leqslant b$
implies $f(a) \leqslant f(b)$.

   A **fixpoint** of a monotonic function $f: L \to L$ is a value $a \in L$ such
that $f(a) = a$. The following theorem provides the foundation for iterative
data flow analysis algorithms.

Theorem 3.2   Let L denote a semilattice and $f: L \to L$ a monotonic function. Then there exists a $t \geq 0$ such that $f^{t+1}(1) = f^t(1)$. $f^t(1)$ is the greatest fixpoint of f.   ■

Proof   Since f is monotonic, the sequence $1, f(1), f(f(1)), \ldots$ is a monotone descending sequence of elements from L. L is bounded, so there is a t such that $f(f^t(1)) = f^t(1)$. Clearly, $fp := f^t(1)$ is a fixpoint of f. Now let a denote an arbitrary fixpoint of f. From $a \leq 1$ and the monotonicity property we obtain $f^r(a) \leq f^r(1)$ for all $r \geq 0$; as $f^r(a) = a$ for all r, we immediately obtain $a \leq f^t(1) = fp$. Therefore, fp is the greatest fixpoint of f.   ■

The fixpoint algorithm to determine the greatest fixpoint of a monotonic function is derived immediately from Theorem 3.2.

ALGORITHM 3.5: Greatest fixpoint of a monotonic function

>*Input*   (1)   Semilattice $(L, \wedge)$.
>   (2) $f: L \to L$, monotonic.
>
>*Output*   The greatest fixpoint, fp, of f.
>
>*Method*

```
begin
   a := 1;
   while f(a) < a do a := f(a) end while;
   fp := a
end
```
■

3.5.4   Monotone data flow systems and their optimal solution

Definition 3.24

(1)   A **monotone function space** for a semilattice L is a set F of monotonic functions which (i) contains the identity function id, (ii) is closed under function composition, and (iii) satisfies the following condition: for each $a \in L$ there is an $f \in F$ such that $f(0) = a$.

(2)   A **distributive function space** is a monotone function space in which all functions are distributive.   ■

The conditions imposed on monotone function spaces are motivated (i) by the need to model basic blocks which do not change data flow information,

(ii) by the necessity of modeling the effect of paths in the flowgraph, and
(iii) by technical considerations.

Definition 3.25   A **monotone data flow system** (MDS) is a tuple $\Omega = (L, \wedge, F, G, FM)$, where:

(1) $(L, \wedge)$ is a bounded semilattice with 0 and 1.
(2) F is a monotone function space for L.
(3) $G = (N, E, s)$ is a program graph.
(4) $FM: N \rightarrow F$ is a total function.

An MDS is **distributive** iff F is a distributive function space for L.   ■

The function FM associates with every node of the flowgraph a function in F. For every $n \in N$ we will use the shorthand f_n instead of $FM(n)$. Let $\pi = (n_1, n_2, \ldots, n_k, n_{k+1})$, $k \geqslant 1$, denote a path in G. Then we define $f_\pi := f_{n_k} \circ f_{n_{k-1}} \circ \ldots \circ f_{n_1}$. Note that the last node, n_{k+1}, has been excluded from the composition. f_π specifies the **effect** of path π in the sense that, for any data flow information $INF \in L$ entering the path, $f_\pi(INF)$ determines the transformation of INF when control passes through the nodes of π (excluding the last node).

Example 3.12: An MDS Ω_{RD} for the problem of reaching definitions

---

Such a system has essentially already been defined in Section 3.5.1. We now specify it formally as an MDS:

(1) $(L, \wedge) = (\mathscr{P}(S\_DEFS), \cup)$

We have already seen (Example 3.11) that $(\mathscr{P}(S\_DEFS), \cup)$ is a bounded semilattice with 0 and 1, where 0 corresponds to S_DEFS and 1 to $\varnothing$.

(2)   The function specifying the effect of a basic block n has the form:

$f_n(X) = (X \cap S\_PRE(n)) \cup S\_DEF(n)$ for every $X \subseteq S\_DEFS$

Clearly, $f_n(X_1 \wedge X_2) = f_n(X_1) \wedge f_n(X_2)$; thus f_n is distributive.

Now let F be the set of all functions $f: L \rightarrow L$ such that $f(X) = (X \cap pre) \cup def$, where pre and def are arbitrary elements of L. Then F is a distributive function space. Note that the definition of F is independent of any particular program graph.

(3)   Let G be the program graph of Example 3.2. From the analysis results given in Example 3.8 we can immediately determine all functions f_i $(1 \leqslant i \leqslant 4, X \subseteq S\_DEFS)$:

$$f_1(X) = (X \cap \{S6\}) \cup \{S1,S2,S3,S4\}$$
$$f_2(X) = (X \cap \{S1,S2,S4,S8,S9\}) \cup \{S5,S6\}$$
$$f_3(X) = (X \cap \{S1,S3,S5,S6\}) \cup \{S8,S9\}$$
$$f_4(X) = X$$

Consider the path $\pi = (1,2,3,2)$ in G. Then $f_\pi = f_3 \circ f_2 \circ f_1$, and $f_\pi(X) = \{S1,S5,S6,S8,S9\}$, independent of X.

We can now introduce the concept of an optimal solution for a data flow system Ω. We have assumed $pred(s) = \emptyset$. Let $NULL \in L$ denote the value to be associated with the initial node. In our intraprocedural setting this value will represent 'no information', which will correspond to 0 or 1 in the semilattice. For example, $RD(s)$ must be defined as the empty set, which corresponds to the 1 element of the lattice. Let $PATH(n)$ for each $n \neq s$ denote the set of all paths from the initial node to n. We can now define the **optimal solution** for node n to be the meet over the effects of all paths reaching n. Because of the way in which this is defined, we also speak of the **meet over all paths** or MOP solution. Formally, this is defined as follows.

Definition 3.26   Let $\Omega = (L, \wedge, F, G, FM)$ be an MDS, where the initial node, s, of G is associated with the value $NULL$, and $pred(s) = \emptyset$. The **optimal solution** of Ω is given by a function $OPT: N \to L$, where:

(1) $OPT(s) = NULL$

(2)   For every $n \in N - \{s\}$: $OPT(n) = \bigwedge_{\pi \in PATH(n)} f_\pi(NULL)$ ∎

It can be shown that the problem of determining the optimal solution of an MDS is undecidable (for a proof see Hecht (1977)):

Theorem 3.3   There is no algorithm that computes OPT for every monotone data flow system Ω.   ∎

Let $X: N \to L$ denote any total function that associates nodes with lattice elements. We shall define such a function as **conservative** or **safe** iff for all

$n \in N$, $X(n) \leqslant OPT(n)$. A conservative function takes into account the effect of all paths from the initial node to n, and thus can safely be used to control optimization transformations. The general iterative algorithm (Algorithm 3.6) determines a conservative approximation to OPT, which will be identical to OPT for the subclass of distributive data flow systems.

Let us conclude this subsection with two remarks concerning Definition 3.26. For any node $n \neq s$, the set $PATH(n)$ may be countably infinite. However, the conditions specified in the definition of the MDS, in particular the boundedness of the semilattice and the monotonicity of the functions $f \in F$, guarantee that $OPT(n)$ is defined for every n.

Finally, we must ask ourselves whether the use of the term 'optimal' is justified here. It is, on the premise that all paths in the program graph are paths that can actually be taken in each program execution. In a particular execution of a real program it may happen that certain paths of the program graph are excluded. In such a case, OPT specifies a suboptimal, but conservative, solution.

3.5.5   The general iterative algorithm

In this section we give the general iterative algorithm, which can be considered to be an adaptation of the fixpoint algorithm (Algorithm 3.5) for MDSs. We have already used a version of this algorithm to solve the reaching definitions problem (Algorithm 3.4). In that case, we did not specify an order for the processing of the nodes in one iteration. Here we impose rPostorder on the nodes of the flowgraph; this will be seen to guarantee the algorithm to be effective.

ALGORITHM 3.6: The general iterative algorithm

> ***Input***   An MDS $\Omega = (L, \wedge, F, G, FM)$ with $G = (N, E, s)$ and N ordered according to rPostorder.
>
> ***Output*** $INF: N \to L$, a total function.
>
> ***Method***
>
> /* The algorithm uses the variables *new*, *stable* and *INF(n)* for every *n* with the same meaning as in Algorithm 3.4 */
> **begin**
> /* Initialization */
> $INF(s) := NULL$;
> **for every** $n \in N - \{s\}$ **do** $INF(n) := 1$ **end for**;

```
/* Iteration */
repeat
    stable := true;
    for every n ∈ N − {s} in rPostorder do
        new :=    ∧    f_n.(INF(n'));
               n' ∈ pred(n)
        if new ≠ INF(n)
            then INF(n) := new; stable := false
        fi
    end for
until stable
end                                                        ■
```

The following results concern the behavior and output of the algorithm. The proofs are to be found in Kam and Ullman (1976, 1977) and Hecht (1977).

Theorem 3.4   Algorithm 3.6 terminates and yields the greatest fixpoint of the following equation system:

(1) $X(s) = NULL$

(2) $X(n) := \bigwedge_{n' \in pred(n)} f_{n'}(X(n'))$ $n \in N - \{s\}$ ■

Theorem 3.5   For every node n: $INF(n) \leq OPT(n)$.   ■

This theorem implies that the solution is conservative. A consequence of this is that all transformations which are based on *INF* rather than *OPT* are semantically safe.

Theorem 3.6

(1)   If Algorithm 3.6 is applied to a distributive MDS, then $INF = OPT$.

(2)   Let $(L, \wedge)$ be a bounded semilattice with 0 and 1, and F a monotone function space for L that is non-distributive. Then there exist G and *FM* such that the application of Algorithm 3.6 to $\Omega = (L, \wedge, F, G, FM)$ yields a suboptimal solution: $INF(n) < OPT(n)$ for an $n \in N$.   ■

In general, the repeat-loop of Algorithm 3.6 needs on the order of $|N|$ iterations, from which we obtain a worst-case complexity of $O(|N|^2)$

operations. In contrast, if Algorithm 3.6 is applied to a reducible flow-graph, then for an important class of data flow systems at most $d + 2$ iterations are needed, where d is the loop-connectedness of the graph (Kam and Ullman, 1976); thus in most cases the algorithm will terminate after at most five iterations. This includes bit vector problems, as discussed below.

3.5.6   Problem classes

The iterative algorithm will execute efficiently when the order in which the nodes of the flowgraph are visited in each iteration coincides with the direction in which data flow information is being propagated. The dominance relation provides us with a simple way to capture this notion of order precisely: we say that any linear order of the nodes which topologically sorts dominance is **top-down**, and the inverse of this is **bottom-up**. The data flow problems of reaching definitions and available expressions are both top-down problems. The condition imposed on the set N in the general iterative algorithm implicitly reflects that assumption, as rPostorder topologically sorts the dominance relation.

There are problems in which the natural order of information propagation is bottom-up. An example is the live variables problem (see Sections 3.4.1 and 3.6.2). In such cases, the numbering of the nodes in the iterative algorithm should be inverted.

Note that for a single-exit flowgraph G a bottom-up problem can be easily converted into a top-down problem for G^{-1}, and vice versa. Thus the two classes of problems are closely related.

There is another, orthogonal, classification which distinguishes between **existence problems** and **all problems**. RD belongs to the former category, because it determines whether a path exists along which a given definition can reach a basic block. The same is true for the live variables problem. Conversely, the available expressions problem is of the latter type, as we consider only those expressions that are computed on all paths reaching a node. The difference between these two classes of problems is reflected in the definition of the join operation on a powerset: for existence problems it is the union, otherwise the intersection.

Finally, some data flow problems can be encoded as **bit vector** problems. Assume that $L = \mathscr{P}(M)$ for some 'small' set M, such as S_DEFS, EXP or the set of scalar variables. Then the elements of L can be represented as bit vectors of length $|M|$, and the meet operation corresponds to a bit vector 'and' or 'or'. The RD, available expressions and live variables problems all belong to this category. These data flow systems can be solved efficiently (see the closing paragraph of Section 3.5.5). A problem that cannot be modeled in this way is constant propagation, which is the subject of Section 3.6.4.

3.6 Examples for data flow systems

Let $\Omega = (L, \wedge, F, G, FM)$ denote an MDS. In the following we sometimes find it convenient to ignore the graph G and the function FM and consider instead systems $\phi = (L, \wedge, F)$. These are known as **monotone data flow analysis frameworks** (MDFs). An MDS can then be interpreted as an **instance** of an MDF, specified by a triple (ϕ, G, FM). Note that our discussion in Section 3.5 was completely independent of a particular choice of G and FM. Concepts such as distributivity can be immediately applied to MDFs.

In this section we shall apply the theory developed thus far to four data flow problems: available expressions, live variables, dominance, and constant propagation. For each of these problems, an MDF will be specified. For RD, we have already done so in Example 3.12.

3.6.1 Available expressions

The **available expressions problem** (AE) is the problem of determining, for each node n of a flowgraph, the set of all available expressions reaching n. Remember that expression $exp \in EXP$ is available at n iff every path reaching n evaluates exp, and the subpath between the last computation of exp and n is definition-free for all operands of the expression (see Section 3.4.2).

An expression exp is said to be **generated** in a basic block n if it is evaluated in n, and n does not contain a definition of any of its operands after the last evaluation of exp. An expression is said to be **preserved** in n if none of its operands is in $DEF(n)$. These relationships are described by two local sets associated with each basic block.

Definition 3.27 Let n denote an arbitrary basic block.

(1) $GEN\_EXP(n) := \{exp \in EXP: exp \text{ is generated in } n\}$
(2) $PRE\_EXP(n) := \{exp \in EXP: exp \text{ is preserved in } n\}$.   ∎

The MDF $\phi_{AE} = (L, \wedge, F)$ for AE can be specified as follows:

(1) $(L, \wedge) = (\mathcal{P}(EXP), \cap)$

This is a bounded semilattice where $0 \equiv \varnothing$, $1 \equiv EXP$, and $\leqslant$ corresponds to set inclusion.

(2)   The effect of a basic block n can be described by a function f_n as follows:

$$f_n(X) = (X \cap PRE\_EXP(n)) \cup GEN\_EXP(n) \text{ for every } X \subseteq EXP.$$

All functions f_n are distributive. Now let F be the set of all functions $f: L \rightarrow L$ such that $f(X) = (X \cap pre) \cup gen$, where pre and gen are arbitrary elements of L. F is a distributive function space.

ϕ_{AE} is a distributive MDF.

3.6.2   Live variables

The **live variables problem** (LV) is the problem of determining, for each node n of a flowgraph, the set of all variables that are live at the end of n. Remember that v is live at the exit of n iff there is a path from n to n' such that there is an outward exposed use of v in n', and the path, except for its endpoints, is definition-free for v.

LV is a bottom-up problem: data flow information is attached to the end of basic blocks and propagated through the flowgraph in an order that topologically sorts the inverse of the dominance relation. The functions f_n associated with basic blocks describe the transformation which data flow information undergoes when it is passed from the exit to the entry of the block. We assume a single-exit flowgraph. The general iterative algorithm must be modified in three places. Firstly, the for-loop is processed in inverse rPostorder. Secondly, in the assignment to the variable new, the meet is taken over all $n' \in succ(n)$. Third, the exit node of the flowgraph (rather than the initial node) is initialized to $NULL$. Everything else remains the same.

The MDF $\phi_{LV} = (L, \wedge, F)$ for LV can be specified as follows:

(1) $(L, \wedge) = (\mathcal{P}(VAR), \cup)$

This is a bounded semilattice where $0 \equiv VAR$, $1 \equiv \emptyset$, and $\leqslant$ corresponds to the inverse of set inclusion.

(2)   The effect of a basic block n can be described by a function f_n as follows:

$$f_n(X) = (X \cap PRE(n)) \cup USE(n) \text{ for every } X \subseteq VAR$$

All functions f_n are distributive, and a distributive function space F can be constructed just as for the other frameworks.

ϕ_{LV} is a distributive MDF.

3.6.3 Dominance

Let $G = (N,E,s)$ be a flowgraph. Then the definition of dominance (Definition 3.7) implies

$$DOM(n) = \bigcap_{\pi \in PATH(n)} \{n' \in N: n' \text{ is a node in } \pi\}.$$

From this, we construct the following MDS:

(1) $(L,\wedge) = (\mathscr{P}(N),\cap)$

This is a bounded semilattice where $0 \equiv \varnothing$, $1 \equiv N$, and $\leq$ corresponds to set inclusion.

(2)   The effect of basic block n can be modeled as follows:

$$f_n(X) = X \cup \{n\} \text{ for every } X \subseteq N$$

The function f_n models the effect of basic block n and is distributive for each n. We can construct a distributive function space F satisfying Definition 3.10 based on the f_n.

The data flow system $\Omega_{DOM} = (L,\wedge,F,G,FM)$ is distributive, and $OPT(n) = DOM(n) - \{n\}$ for every $n \in N$.

3.6.4 Constant propagation

Constant propagation (CP) can be formulated as the problem of determining the value of a variable at a given point of the program whenever this value is constant. We shall model this problem by an MDF ϕ_{CP}; it turns out that ϕ_{CP} is non-distributive, which means that only an approximation can be computed by the iterative algorithm.

When propagating data flow information for CP, for each variable $v \in VAR$

(1)   the value of v is a known constant, c, or

(2)   the value of v is not constant, or

(3)   it is not known whether (1) or (2) applies.

Let $\Gamma' := \Gamma \cup \{nonconst\}$, where Γ is the universal domain introduced in Section 3.2. The 'artificial values' *nonconst* and *undef* are used to model cases (2) and (3), respectively. For the remainder of this section, the concept of 'value' will refer to any element of Γ'. Remember we have defined $\Gamma_r := \Gamma \cup \{undef\}$ as the set of proper values.

Lemma 3.5 Let the binary operation $\wedge$ in Γ' be defined as follows:

(1)   For all $x \in \Gamma'$: $x \wedge nonconst := nonconst$.

(2)   For all $x \in \Gamma'$: $x \wedge undef := x$.

(3)   For all proper values $c,d \in \Gamma_r$:

$$
c \wedge d := \begin{cases} c & \text{if } c = d \\[2em] nonconst & \text{if } c \neq d \end{cases}
$$

Then $(\Gamma', \wedge)$ is a bounded semilattice with $0 \equiv nonconst$ and $1 \equiv undef$. The length of every chain is at most 2.   ∎

Proof The operation $\wedge$ is idempotent, commutative and associative; thus $(\Gamma', \wedge)$ is a semilattice. From (1) and (2) we see that *nonconst* and *undef*, respectively, are the 0 and 1 elements of the semilattice. The associated partial order $\leq$ is defined by:

(4) $nonconst \leq x$ for all $x \in \Gamma'$.

(5) $x \leq undef$ for all $x \in \Gamma'$.

(6)   For all $c,d \in \Gamma_r$ with $c \neq d$: there is no relationship between c and d.

This concludes the proof. A lattice of this type is called **flat**; it can be represented by a Venn diagram as shown in Figure 3.13.

We are now in a position to construct the lattice needed for the constant propagation problem. Let the notion of state, as introduced in Definition 3.5, be extended to include *nonconst*. Then we define L as the set of all states of VAR: $L := \{\beta: \beta \text{ is a total function}, \beta: VAR \rightarrow \Gamma'\}$. Let $\beta, \beta' \in L$. The meet operation in L is defined as follows: for every $v \in VAR$, let $(\beta \wedge \beta')(v) := \beta(v) \wedge \beta'(v)$. It can now easily be shown that $(L, \wedge)$ is a bounded semilattice with 0 element β_{zero} and 1 element β_{one}, where for every $v \in VAR$: $\beta_{zero}(v) = nonconst$ and $\beta_{one}(v) = undef$.

We still have to model the effect of statements on elements of L. We do so by handling assignment statements S: $A = B \sigma C$, where $A, B, C \in VAR$ and σ is a binary operator. σ is assumed to be a total function $\sigma: \Gamma_r \times \Gamma_r \rightarrow \Gamma_r$.[†] Other statements can be treated similarly.

[†] This means that we do not consider operators such as '/' and strategies for handling statements such as $A = 1/0$ at compile time.

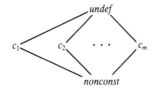

Figure 3.13 The flat lattice $(\Gamma', \wedge)$.

Let $\beta \in L$ be given arbitrarily, and define $\beta' := f_S(\beta)$ as follows:

(1) $\beta'(v) = \beta(v)$ for all $v \in VAR - \{A\}$

(2) $\beta'(A) = $ **if** $(\beta(B) = nonconst) \vee (\beta(C) = nonconst)$ **then** $nonconst$
　　　　orif $(\beta(B) = undef) \vee \beta(C) = undef$ 　　　　　**then** $undef$
　　　　else /* $\beta(B), \beta(C) \in \Gamma_r$: the result of $\beta(B) \, \sigma \, \beta(C)$ can be
　　　　computed in the compiler. Let val denote the value
　　　　yielded by this operation */
　　　　val

　　fi

It remains to be shown that f_S is monotonic, that is

$$\beta_1 \leq \beta_2 \implies f_S(\beta_1) \leq f_S(\beta_2)$$

We must only consider the case for variable A, that is we must verify

$$\beta_1 \leq \beta_2 \implies f_S(\beta_1(A)) \leq f_S(\beta_2(A))$$

We see that this holds by considering all possible values for B and C in β_1 and β_2 and taking into account the fact that $\beta_1(X) < \beta_2(X)$ will only be true, for any variable X, if:

$\beta_2(X) = undef$ and $\beta_1(X) \in \Gamma_r$ or $\beta_1(X) = nonconst$, or
$\beta_2(X) = c \in \Gamma_r$ and $\beta_1(X) = nonconst$

Thus a monotone function space F can be associated with L and we have modeled constant propagation as a data flow system.

However, this system is not distributive: if it were, then $f(\beta_1 \wedge \beta_2) = f(\beta_1) \wedge f(\beta_2)$ would have to hold for all pairs $\beta_1, \beta_2 \in L$. It therefore suffices to construct a counterexample. Let $VAR = \{A, B, C\}$ be linearly ordered, in the order of writing, $\beta_1 = (2, 3, undef)$, $\beta_2 = (3, 2, undef)$ and consider the function f associated with the assignment $C = A + B$. Then

$$f(\beta_1 \wedge \beta_2) = f(nonconst, nonconst, undef) = (nonconst, nonconst, nonconst)$$

but

$$f(\beta_1) \wedge f(\beta_2) = f(2,3,undef) \wedge f(3,2,undef) = (2,3,5) \wedge (3,2,5)$$
$$= (nonconst,nonconst,5).$$

3.7   Interprocedural analysis

3.7.1   Introduction

The purpose of interprocedural analysis is to increase the precision of data flow and dependence analysis by determining the relevant effects of procedure calls. In the absence of interprocedural analysis, worst-case assumptions have to be made.

Interprocedural analysis must begin with the construction of the **call graph**, which is a directed graph representing the calling relationships between the procedures of the program. If formal procedure parameters are used in a program, the call graph can only be built after all possible bindings for such parameters have been found. An algorithm that performs this task is given in Section 3.7.2.

In Section 3.7.3, we discuss in-line expansion, a technique which textually replaces procedure calls by the appropriately modified procedure bodies. Whenever feasible, standard intraprocedural techniques can be applied to the resulting program.

This is followed by a description of several interprocedural data flow problems and solution approaches (Section 3.7.4). Depending on whether or not the set of all control paths inside the procedure is taken into account, problems are respectively classified as **flow-sensitive** (MUST problems) or **flow-insensitive** (MAY problems). Some problems exist in both versions: an example is the set of all global variables and formal reference parameters of a procedure p that MUST/MAY be modified in every activation of p. We emphasize flow-insensitive problems, which are discussed in Section 3.7.4.1; flow-sensitive problems are touched on only briefly in Section 3.7.4.2. Aliasing, the dynamical equivalencing of variables as a result of the argument bindings of formal reference parameters, is then discussed in Section 3.7.4.3. The results of the alias-free analysis and the independent alias analysis can be combined to produce a general solution of a data flow problem.

We base our discussion on the program model introduced in Section 3.2. Only proper procedures (represented by single-entry single-exit flow-graphs) and simple variables will be considered. We further assume that the source code of all procedures is completely accessible for analysis. Remember that the parameter vector of a procedure p, that is, the list of formal parameters in the order of their occurrence in the procedure's declaration, is denoted by pv_p.

3.7.2 Construction of the call graph

Definition 3.28 Let P denote a program. The **call graph** G of P is a directed graph $G = (N,E)$, where there is a one-to-one correspondence between N and P, and $(p,q) \in E$ iff procedure p contains a call whose execution may result in the direct activation of procedure q. ∎

We shall identify the sets N and P for all practical purposes. Note that one or more calls may be mapped to the same edge of the call graph.

Let a program P be given. If none of the procedures in P contains formal procedure parameters, then the construction of the call graph is simple. Otherwise, we must determine all mappings between formal and declared procedures that can arise during program execution before the call graph can be built. We restrict the model here to contain formal procedure parameters as the only formal parameters.

The set of all calls occurring in the program text of a procedure p is denoted by $calls(p)$. Let $c \in calls(p)$. Then we write c in the form $x(\mathbf{y})$, where $x \in P \cup formal(p)$ is a procedure identifier that represents the procedure to be activated, and $\mathbf{y} = (y_1, \ldots, y_m)$ $(m \geq 0)$ is an argument list. If $x \in P$, then we speak of a **direct reference** to x in p, otherwise of a **formal reference**. The subset of direct references in $calls(p)$ is denoted by $direct\_refs(p)$.

Consider an arbitrary time t during the execution of P. Those procedures whose execution has been initiated but not yet terminated are called **active** at time t. The active procedure which was most recently activated is called the **actual** procedure. Recursion has been excluded, so there exists exactly one instantiation of each active procedure. The list $\alpha = (q_1, \ldots, q_k)$ of the currently active procedures in the order of their activation is called an **activation stack**. Clearly, $q_1 = $ MAIN, q_k is the actual procedure, and $q_i \neq q_j$ for all $1 \leq i, j \leq k$ with $i \neq j$. The termination of the actual procedure can be modeled by popping it off the activation stack.

For each procedure p in the activation stack there exists a **binding** that associates every formal parameter of p with a unique value in P. This binding is established at the time p is called and is valid throughout that particular instantiation of p. We can model it by a total function $bind_p \colon formal(p) \rightarrow P$ (note that this function depends on the activation stack α). For any $f \in formal(p)$, we define the **range** of f to be the set of all elements of P that can be bound to f during any program execution.

Let p be the actual procedure and $c = q(\mathbf{y})$ a direct reference to q in p. In order to execute this call, every formal parameter $f \in formal(p)$ that occurs in c has to be substituted by $bind_p(f)$. Let $c' = q(\mathbf{b})$ denote the call resulting from this substitution. The execution of c' activates q, making it the actual procedure, and establishes a binding function $bind_q$ by associating the formal parameters of q with the corresponding elements of $\mathbf{b}$, thus $bind_q(pv_q(i)) := \mathbf{b}(i)$ for all i, $1 \leqslant i \leqslant |\mathbf{b}|$ (see Definition 3.2).

Each list $\mathbf{b}$ that is obtained by this substitution process is called a **procedure vector** of q. Algorithm 3.7, which is due to Ryder (1979), constructs the call graph by propagating this information through the program. It assumes that each element of $calls(p)$ can be executed in each activation of p: in other words, we solve the problem of constructing the call graph as a flow-insensitive problem; the intraprocedural control flow will not be taken into account. We will need to characterize one particular usage of a procedure: if, in the body of a procedure p, a procedure $q \in P$ occurs only as an argument in calls (but not as the procedure to be activated), then we will speak of a **referral**. The set of all referrals in p will be denoted by $referrals(p)$. An example can be found in Example 3.14.

Even if a program does not execute recursive calls, the process of determining the call graph, as sketched above, may lead to a cyclic graph when conditional calls occur.

Example 3.13

```
PROGRAM MAIN
...
CALL SUB1
...
CALL SUB2(0)
...
END

SUBROUTINE SUB1
...
IF ... THEN CALL SUB2(1) FI
...
END

SUBROUTINE SUB2(X)
...
IF X = 0 THEN CALL SUB1 FI
...
END
```

Here $P = \{\text{MAIN},\text{SUB1},\text{SUB2}\}$ and the call graph as shown above is cyclic. The maximum length activation stacks are $\alpha_1 = (\text{MAIN},\text{SUB1},\text{SUB2})$ and $\alpha_2 = (\text{MAIN},\text{SUB2},\text{SUB1})$. Note that, as a consequence of the condition controlling the call of SUB1 in SUB2, $(\text{MAIN},\text{SUB1},(\text{SUB2},\text{SUB1})^k)$, $k \geqslant 1$, is not an activation stack for any k.

The case illustrated by Example 3.13 is called **static recursion**. It will be excluded in the following, that is we assume all call graphs to be acyclic. Let $G = (N,E)$ denote a call graph. Then a sequence $(q_1, \ldots, q_n)$ of all elements of N will be called an **invocation order** if it topologically sorts G. For any invocation order ORD, the reverse sequence ORD^R is a **reverse invocation order**.

We finally exclude 'useless' parameters by assuming that each formal parameter of a procedure p occurs in a call contained in p.

ALGORITHM 3.7: Construction of the call graph

> ***Input***   Program P and for every $p \in P$ the sets $calls(p)$, $direct\_refs(p)$, and $referrals(p)$.

> ***Output***   If the call graph is cyclic, the algorithm stops. Otherwise, it produces the call graph $G = (N,E)$ and, for each $p \in P$, the set $proc\_vectors(p)$ of all procedure vectors for p.

Method

/* The construction of the call graph $G = (N,E)$ starts with $E = \emptyset$. Two kinds of edges are used to construct E: (i) **permanent** edges, which are not removed again, and (ii) **temporary** edges, which are used temporarily to represent paths in G. This distinction is made via a boolean predicate, *permanent*(e), for each $e \in E$. In the final state, E contains only permanent edges.

Three items of information are associated with each $p \in P$:

(1)   *visited*(p) is a boolean value indicating whether or not p has already been processed in the iteration phase.

(2)   *proc_vectors*(p).

(3)   *level*(p) is an integer number $\geqslant 0$. At any time, *level*(p) specifies the length of the longest path leading from MAIN to p in G. Such a path may contain permanent or temporary edges. This attribute respects the invocation order in the sense that for every activation stack $\alpha = (q_1, \ldots, q_k)$ the condition (INV) is satisfied:

(INV) *level*(q_i) < *level*(q_j) for all i,j with $1 \leqslant i < j \leqslant k$. */

/* Auxiliary procedures: */

function substitute(**a,f**,z): P;
/* Here it is assumed that **a** is a procedure vector and **f** is the associated parameter vector of a procedure p. **a** and **f** determine a binding function $bind_p$. If $z \in formal(p)$, then the function yields $bind_p(z)$, otherwise $z \in P$ and z is returned. */

procedure update(p,q);
/* This procedure is called after (p,q) has been added to E as a new permanent or temporary edge. If necessary, update increases the levels of one or more nodes to maintain the validity of the invariant (INV) */

```
            begin
              if in_stack(q)
                then halt("Cycle in call graph")
                else if level(p) ⩾ level(q)
                        then push(q);
                             level(q) := level(p) + 1;
                             for every r ∈ succ(q) do update(q,r) end for;
                             pop
                     fi
              fi
            end update;

        procedure enter_and_update(p,q,x);
        begin
        if (p,q) ∉ E
          then permanent(p,q) := x;
               E plus {(p,q)};
               update(p,q)
          else if x ∧ ¬permanent(p,q)
                  then permanent(p,q) := true
               fi
        fi
        end enter_and_update;

        /* MAIN PROGRAM */

        begin

        /* Initialization */

        init_stack;
        E := ∅;
        N := P;
        for every p ∈ N do
          visited(p) := false;
          level(p) := 0;
          proc_vectors(p) := ∅
        end for;

        proc_vectors(MAIN) := {ε};

        for every p ∈ N do
          for every q(a) ∈ direct_refs(p) do
            enter_and_update(p,q,true);   /* Enter a permanent edge */
            if a ∈ P*
              then   /* a contains no formal parameters */
                proc_vectors(q) plus {a}
            fi
          end for;
          for every q ∈ referrals(p) do
            enter_and_update(p,q,false)   /* Enter a temporary edge */
          end for
        end for;
```

```
/* Iteration */
while ∃p ∈ N: ¬visited(p) do
    p := select({p' ∈ N: ¬visited(p') ∧ level(p') is minimal});
    for every x(y) ∈ calls(p) do
        for every a ∈ proc_vectors(p) do
            /* For each occurrence of a formal procedure in x(y) substitute the
               corresponding argument in a: thus x(y) is mapped to a call q(b) which
               does not contain a formal parameter */
            q := substitute(a,pvₚ,x);
            enter_and_update(p,q,true);   /* Enter a permanent edge */
            for k := 1 to |y| do
                b(k) := substitute(a,pvₚ,y(k));
                enter_and_update(q,b(k),false);   /* Enter a temporary edge */
            end for;
            if b ∉ proc_vectors(q)
                then proc_vectors(q) plus {b}
            fi
        end for
    end for
    E minus {(p,q'): ¬permanent(p,q')};   /* Eliminate all temporary edges
                                              whose source is p */
    visited(p) := true
end while
end                                                              ∎
```

Example 3.14

```
PROGRAM MAIN ... CALL A(B) ... CALL A(C) ... CALL B ... END

SUBROUTINE A(X) ... CALL X ... END

SUBROUTINE B ... END

SUBROUTINE C ... CALL B ... END
```

Here, $P = \{$MAIN,A,B,C$\}$ and

p	$formal(p)$	$calls(p)$	$direct\_refs(p)$	$referrals(p)$
MAIN	$\varnothing$	$\{A(B),A(C),B\}$	$\{A(B),A(C),B\}$	$\{C\}$
A	$\{X\}$	$\{X\}$	$\varnothing$	$\varnothing$
B	$\varnothing$	$\varnothing$	$\varnothing$	$\varnothing$
C	$\varnothing$	$\{B\}$	$\{B\}$	$\varnothing$

After initialization, we have the following situation (a temporary edge in E is marked by the superscript t; in the graphical representation, these edges are shown as dotted lines):

p	$level(p)$	$proc\_vectors(p)$
MAIN	0	$\{\varepsilon\}$
A	1	$\{(B),(C)\}$
B	2	$\{\varepsilon\}$
C	1	$\varnothing$

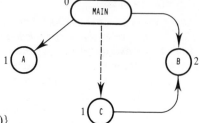

$$E = \{(\mathrm{MAIN},A),(\mathrm{MAIN},B),(\mathrm{MAIN},C)^t,(C,B)\}$$

After MAIN has been processed:

p	$level(p)$	$proc\_vectors(p)$
MAIN	0	$\{\varepsilon\}$
A	1	$\{(B),(C)\}$
B	3	$\{\varepsilon\}$
C	2	$\varnothing$

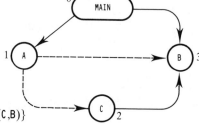

$$E = \{(\mathrm{MAIN},A),(\mathrm{MAIN},B),(A,B)^t,(A,C)^t,(C,B)\}$$

After A has been processed:

p	$level(p)$	$proc\_vectors(p)$
MAIN	0	$\{\varepsilon\}$
A	1	$\{(B),(C)\}$
B	3	$\{\varepsilon\}$
C	2	$\{\varepsilon\}$

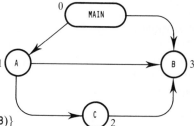

$$E = \{(\mathrm{MAIN},A),(\mathrm{MAIN},B),(A,B),(A,C),(C,B)\}$$

These are the final results of the algorithm.

Note that the input of the algorithm can be computed in one pass over the program, which extracts the required information from the procedures and stores it in appropriate data structures. The algorithm as specified above need only operate on these data structures.

The algorithm processes the procedures of the program in invocation order. Each procedure is analyzed exactly once. The iteration phase could also be formulated as an unordered process that proceeds until stabilization. This would result in a simpler algorithm, as temporary edges would no longer be required, but at the expense of increased run time complexity. The approach above has the additional advantage that it can easily be combined with other analysis algorithms that operate in invocation order, such as ALIAS processing (see Section 3.7.4.3). A detailed analysis of the algorithm can be found in Ryder (1979).

Note that Algorithm 3.7 yields more precise information than could be obtained by separately computing the range of every formal parameter. This is because the sets *proc_vectors*(p) contain context information that is not present in the cross-product of the range sets of the formal parameters of p.

Functions can be treated in the same way as proper procedures. Furthermore, if h is a function and a call $q(h(a))$ occurs in a procedure p, then this is equivalent to the sequence TEMP := $h(a)$; q(TEMP) and leads to the insertion of an edge (p,h) in the call *graph*.[†]

If the algorithm is applied in a situation where a cyclic call graph would result, it terminates (see the auxiliary procedure update). Since procedures are non-recursive, cycles can be broken by eliminating edges and/or splitting nodes of the call graph. This can be integrated into the algorithm. Throughout the following, we assume that the call graph is an acyclic flowgraph. Formal references will no longer be taken into account.

3.7.3   In-line expansion

Let p be a procedure, and $c = q(\mathbf{y}) \in calls(p)$ a direct reference of $q \in P$. Then the occurrence of c in the body of p can be textually replaced by the body of q, after the arguments have been substituted for the formal parameters of q and any necessary syntactic adjustments have been performed. This process is called **in-line expansion**. It can be generally applied, as the call graph is assumed to be acyclic, and requires one pass over P in reverse invocation order.

Let P' denote the modified program after all calls in P have been expanded: $P' = \{\text{MAIN}'\}$, where MAIN' is the modified main program. We can construct an intraprocedural flowgraph for MAIN', to which all algorithms, techniques, and results discussed in Sections 3.3–3.6 can be applied. Thus, at least in principle, more precise results can be obtained with less effort in this manner than with interprocedural analysis.

The drawback of this method is of course the – potentially exponential – growth in program size, which makes it generally infeasible for all but small programs. In-line expansion is a valuable method if applied selectively: for example, if it is controlled by the user within an

---

[†] This is true for the semantics of Fortran 77. A call by name parameter mechanism would instead require the insertion of an edge (r, h), where r is either q or some procedure which may be called from q.

interactive system. However, it cannot replace interprocedural analysis completely.

A detailed description of the method can be found in Huson (1982).

3.7.4   Interprocedural data flow problems and their solution

In interprocedural analysis, information about a global object g may be propagated through a procedure in which g is not visible. In effect, propagation has to proceed as if every object in $GLOBAL$ was accessible in every procedure. This motivates the following definition: for each $p \in P$, the **environment** of p, $env(p)$, is the set $env(p) := GLOBAL \cup visible(p)$.

3.7.4.1 Flow-insensitive problems

We introduce two problems here, MAY_DEF and MAY_USE. For each procedure p, $MAY\_DEF(p)$ is the set of all global variables and formal reference parameters of p that may be defined as a result of an execution of p; $MAY\_USE(p)$ is the set of all global variables and parameters of p whose value may be used in p. MAY_DEF and MAY_USE are both flow-insensitive problems, as the intraprocedural control flow is ignored in their formulation.[†]

We restrict our discussion to MAY_DEF. Procedures are assumed to have reference parameters only, and the effects of aliasing are not taken into account (see Section 3.7.4.3).

The starting point for a computation of the sets $MAY\_DEF(p)$ is a simple, flow-insensitive parsing process that determines the **direct definition set** $DIR\_DEF(p)$ for each p as follows:

$$DIR\_DEF(p) := \{v: v \in (global(p) \cup formal(p)) \wedge p \text{ contains a statement}$$
$$S, \text{ which is not a call, such that } v \in DEF(S)\}$$

In the following algorithm to perform this computation, we assume that p has no formal procedure parameters, so $calls(p)$ contains direct references only.

ALGORITHM 3.8: Computation of the MAY_DEF sets

> **Input**   Program P with call graph $G = (N,E)$, a reverse invocation order RORD, and the sets $calls(p)$ and $DIR\_DEF(p)$ for all $p \in P$.
>
> **Output** $MAY\_DEF(p)$ for each $p \in P$.

[†] Note that $MAY\_USE(p)$ is not defined as the set of variables with an outward exposed use in p, that is with a use in p that is not preceded by a definition inside p (see Section 3.4.1). This would be a flow-sensitive problem formulation (Banning, 1979).

Method

/* The output is computed in a single pass over all procedures, using RORD. */

begin

/* Initialization */

for every $p \in N$ **do** $MAY\_DEF(p) := DIR\_DEF(p)$ **end for**;

/* Iteration */

for every $p \in N$ in order RORD **do**

  for every q such that $(p,q) \in E$ **do**

    /* propagate the effect of definitions of global variables in q (which has been already computed) to procedure p */

    $MAY\_DEF(p)$ **plus** $(GLOBAL \cap MAY\_DEF(q))$;

    if $MAY\_DEF(q) \cap formal(q) \neq \varnothing$

      then /* propagate to procedure p the effects of definitions of formal parameters of q (which have been computed in a previous iteration), using all calls of q in p */

        for every $x(\mathbf{y}) \in calls(p)$ such that $x = q$ **do**

          for every $k := 1$ to $|\mathbf{y}|$ **do**

            if $pv_q(k) \in MAY\_DEF(q) \wedge \mathbf{y}(k) \in (GLOBAL \cup FORMAL)$

              then $MAY\_DEF(p)$ **plus** $\{\mathbf{y}(k)\}$

            fi

          end for

        end for

    fi

  end for

end for

end ■

Note that for any procedure p, $MAY\_DEF(p) \cap GLOBAL$ need not be a subset of $visible(p)$, as a procedure q called in p may change a global variable g that is not visible in p (but may be visible in a procedure that calls p). This is illustrated in the following example.

Example 3.15

```
PROGRAM MAIN
INTEGER I1, I2, I3, I4, I5
COMMON I1, I2
...
CALL A(I3, I5)
...
CALL A(I4, 1)
...
END
```

```
SUBROUTINE A(F1, F2)
INTEGER I1, F1, F2
COMMON I1

...

IF ... THEN CALL B(F1) FI
I1 = ...

...
END


SUBROUTINE B(F3)
INTEGER I1, I2, F3
COMMON I1, I2
...
I2 = ...
F3 = ...
...
END
```

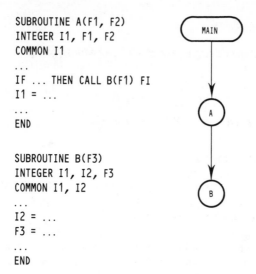

In our program, we have $P = \{\texttt{MAIN},\texttt{A},\texttt{B}\}$, $GLOBAL = \{\texttt{I1},\texttt{I2}\}$, and $G = (N,E)$ with $E = \{(\texttt{MAIN},\texttt{A}), (\texttt{A},\texttt{B})\}$; the only reverse invocation order is RORD = (B,A,MAIN). Initial analysis yields $DIR\_DEF(\texttt{A}) = \{\texttt{I1}\}$ and $DIR\_DEF(\texttt{B}) = \{\texttt{I2},\texttt{F3}\}$, which provides the initialization for $MAY\_DEF(\texttt{A})$ and $MAY\_DEF(\texttt{B})$, respectively. The processing of B in the iteration phase has no effect. The processing of A propagates the definitions of $\texttt{I2}$ and $\texttt{F3}$ in B to A, yielding $MAY\_DEF(\texttt{A}) = \{\texttt{I1},\texttt{I2},\texttt{F1}\}$. As a result, we see that the two calls in MAIN have the following effects: CALL A(I3, I5) may modify $\texttt{I1}, \texttt{I2}$, and $\texttt{I3}$; and CALL A(I4, 1) may modify $\texttt{I1}, \texttt{I2}$, and $\texttt{I4}$.

Let p denote a procedure and $S: q(\mathbf{y})$ a call in p, where all arguments are variables. Then:

$$MAY\_DEF(S) :=$$
$$(MAY\_DEF(q) \cap visible(p)) \cup$$
$$\{v \in local(p): v \text{ occurs in } \mathbf{y} \text{ and the corresponding formal parameter is in}$$
$$MAY\_DEF(q)\}$$

If n is the basic block of p whose only statement is S, then $MAY\_DEF(n) = MAY\_DEF(S)$. These two sets are conservative approximations for the sets $DEF(S)$ and $DEF(n)$ introduced in Section 3.4.1.

If, in the absence of interprocedural analysis, worst-case assumptions must be made, then we would specify:

$$DEF(S) := DEF(n) := global(p) \cup \{v \in local(p): v \text{ occurs in } \mathbf{y}\}$$

3.7.4.2 Flow-sensitive problems

The problem discussed in the previous section can be converted to a flow-sensitive problem if the intraprocedural control flow is taken into account: For each p, let $MUST\_DEF(p)$ denote the set of all global variables and formal reference parameters of p that are modified in every activation of p. In contrast to flow-insensitive problems, the solution of flow-sensitive problems requires that all activations of a procedure and all intra-procedural paths for any such activation be examined.

For general program models which permit recursion, these problems have been shown to be intractable (Myers, 1981). Within our model, a solution can be computed based on an intraprocedural data flow analysis of the program's procedures. We do not go into details.

3.7.4.3 Aliasing

This section defines the concept of aliasing precisely and specifies an algorithm for the computation of the alias sets of a procedure. We assume that all formal parameters of a procedure are reference parameters.

Definition 3.29   Let a,b be variables.

a is an alias of b, $a \equiv b$: $\Longleftrightarrow$ a and b are associated with the same location during program execution.   ∎

Clearly, $\equiv$ is an equivalence relation. If $a \equiv b$, then we speak of a **trivial** alias if $a = b$, otherwise of a **non-trivial** alias. In general, there are two types of aliasing, **static** and **dynamic**. Static aliasing results from explicitly specified storage overlays, such as EQUIVALENCE in Fortran. Dynamic aliasing is in general caused by the effect of the execution of certain statements, such as pointer manipulations or calls with reference parameters. We shall discuss only the latter case here.

The Fortran standard disallows assignments to dynamically aliased variables. Nevertheless, such assignments are common programming practice and tolerated by most compilers. So we ignore this restriction here.

Example 3.16

```
PROGRAM MAIN
INTEGER G
COMMON G
CALL A(G)
...
END
```

```
SUBROUTINE A(F)
INTEGER G, I
COMMON G
S1: G = 2
S2: F = 3
S3: I = F + G
...
END
```

During the execution of procedure A, G and F are aliases. *S2* assigns the value 3 to F and G. Thus the value assigned to I in *S3* is 6.

Example 3.17

```
PROGRAM MAIN
INTEGER I1, I2, I3, G
COMMON G
S1: G = 0
S2: CALL A(I1, I1)
S3: G = G + 3
S4: CALL A(G, I2)
S5: I3 = I1 + I2 + G
END

SUBROUTINE A(F1, F2)
INTEGER F1, F2
S6: F2 = 1
S7: CALL B(F1)
END

SUBROUTINE B(F3)
INTEGER F3
COMMON G
S8: F3 = F3 + 2
S9: G = G + 1
END
```

Table 3.2 summarizes the effect of the execution of this program.

Consider a call $q(\mathbf{y})$ in a procedure p. We want to know what alias relations may possibly hold in $env(q)$ during execution of q. The only way to generate non-trivial aliases in Fortran is via reference parameters in calls. Two cases must be distinguished.

Table 3.2   Effect of the program in Example 3.17.

	Bindings						Values						
p	F1	F2	F3	Stat	Assignment effects	G	I1	I2	I3	F1	F2	F3
MAIN												
MAIN				S1	G = 0	0						
A	I1	I1		S2		0						
A	I1	I1		S6	I1 = F1 = F2 = 1	0	1			1	1	
B	I1	I1	F1	S7		0	1			1	1	
B	I1	I1	F1	S8	I1 = F1 = F2 = F3 = 3	0	3			3	3	3
B	I1	I1	F1	S9	G = 1	1	3			3	3	3
MAIN				S3	G = 4	4	3					
A	G	I2		S2		4	3			4		
A	G	I2		S6	I2 = F2 = 1	4	3	1		4	1	
B	G	I2	F1	S7		4	3	1		4	1	4
B	G	I2	F1	S8	G = F1 = F3 = 6	6	3	1		6	1	6
B	G	I2	F1	S9	G = F1 = F3 = 7	7	3	1		7	1	7
MAIN				S5	I3 = 11	7	3	1	11			

Notation

p. Actual procedure.

Bindings. Valid bindings for formal parameters of the active procedures.

Stat. The most recently executed statement. For assignments, the effect of their execution is given; for calls, the establishment of the bindings between formal parameters of the called procedure and their arguments is specified.

Assignment effects. Specifies all effects of the execution of an assignment, including the effects caused by aliasing.

Values. Current values of variables in $env(q)$ for all active procedures q. An empty space represents an undefined value.

- **Alias 1**   Two different formal parameters of q are bound to alias arguments

  Assume that q is declared with two formal parameters $f1$, $f2$ and that a call $q(y1,y2)$ is executed, where $y1 \equiv y2$. Then $f1$ and $f2$ are bound to $y1$ and $y2$, respectively, and therefore become aliases in that particular execution of q, that is $f1 \equiv f2$. An important special case occurs if $y1 = y2$.

- **Alias 2**   A formal parameter is bound to an argument which is an alias of a global variable

  Assume that q is declared with a formal parameter f, and that a call $q(y)$ is executed, where $y \equiv g$ with $g \in GLOBAL$. Then f is bound to y by the call, and therefore $f \equiv g$ during the execution of q. An important special case is $y = g$.

Note that it is not necessary that $g \in global(q)$: if g is not visible in q, then the association between q and g does not affect q, but may have an effect on a procedure r via a call $r(f)$ in q, if g is visible in r (see Example 3.18).

These are the only two cases that have to be examined; they include the initial introduction of aliases (the special cases associated with trivial aliases) and their propagation via non-trivial aliases.

Whenever a procedure q is called, a specific alias relation $\equiv$ holds for that particular activation of q, and determines a partition of $env(q)$ (for the definition of $env(q)$ see Section 3.7.1). Different calls may produce different partitions.

For the moment, we shall consider one particular call of q and the associated relation $\equiv$. For each $a \in env(q)$, the associated equivalence class $[a]$ will be called the **alias set** associated with a. For all $a \in env(\text{MAIN})$, $[a] = \{a\}$. If $q \neq \text{MAIN}$, then $[a] = \{a\}$ for all $a \in local(q)$, and each alias set of q with more than one element contains one or more formal parameters of q and at most one global variable.

We now formulate our algorithm. It determines, for each procedure p, the set $PARTITIONS(p)$ of all partitions that may be created by calls of p. It is important to note that if $part_1$ and $part_2$ are different partitions of p generated by alias relations $\equiv_1$, and $\equiv_2$, respectively, and if $b \equiv_1 a, c \equiv_2 a$, then it is incorrect to conclude that b and c are aliases.

ALGORITHM 3.9: Computation of alias partitions

> ***Input***   Program P with call graph $G = (N,E)$, an invocation order ORD, and $calls(p)$ for all $p \in P$ (again assuming that p has no formal procedure parameters).

> ***Output*** $PARTITIONS(p)$ for all $p \in P$.

> ***Method***

> /* After initialization, the sets $PARTITIONS(p)$ are computed in a single pass over all procedures in order ORD. */

> /* Auxiliary functions */

> **function** construct($al\_set,q,\mathbf{y}$): **set**;
> /* al_set represents an alias set, q a procedure, and $\mathbf{y}$ an argument list associated with a call of q. The function computes the effect of the call $q(\mathbf{y})$ on al_set. It yields either an alias set for q, or the empty set. */
> **begin**
> $construct := (al\_set \cap GLOBAL) \cup \{pv_q(k): 1 \leqslant k \leqslant |\mathbf{y}| \wedge (\mathbf{y}(k) \in al\_set)\}$
> **end** construct;

> /* MAIN PROGRAM */

> **begin**

/* Initialization */

/* For MAIN, there exists only one partition, which is a set of singletons. The following assignment specifies the final value of *PARTITIONS*(MAIN): */

PARTITIONS(MAIN) := {{{v}: $v \in env$(MAIN)}};

for every $p \in P - $ {MAIN} **do** *PARTITIONS*(p) := $\varnothing$ **end for**;

/* Iteration */

for every $p \in P$ in order ORD **do**
  for every q such that $(p,q) \in E$ **do**
    /* propagate to procedure q the (previously computed) partitions for p */
    for every $q(\mathbf{y}) \in calls(p)$ **do**
      for every *part* $\in$ *PARTITIONS*(p) **do**
        /* Construct a partition, *new_part*, for q by evaluating the effect of the call $q(\mathbf{y})$ on the partition *part* */
        new_part := $\varnothing$;
        for every *al_set* $\in$ *part* **do**
          TEMP := *construct*(*al_set*,q,$\mathbf{y}$);
          if |*TEMP*| $\geqslant 2$ **then** *new_part* **plus** *TEMP* **fi**
        end for;
        /* Now we have to determine those variables in $env(q)$ which do not occur in any alias set contained in *new_part*. For each of these variables, a singleton has to be included in *new_part*. */
        unprocessed_variables := {v: $v \in env(q) - \cup$ *new_part*};
        PARTITIONS(q) **plus** (*new_part* $\cup$ {{v}: $v \in$ *unprocessed_variables*})
      end for
    end for
  end for
end for;
end   ■

Example 3.18

We now apply Algorithm 3.9 to the program of Example 3.17. The variable sets required for the analysis and the call graph are given as follows:

$GLOBAL = $ {G}
env(MAIN) $= $ {I1,I2,I3,G}
env(A) $= $ {F1,F2,G}
env(B) $= $ {F3,G}

The only invocation order is (MAIN,A,B). The partitions are now obtained as follows:

$PARTITIONS$(MAIN) $= $ { {{I1},{I2},{I3},{G}} }
$PARTITIONS$(A) $\quad = $ { {{F1,F2},{G}}, {{G,F1},{F2}} }
$PARTITIONS$(B) $\quad = $ { {{F3},{G}}, {{G,F3}} }

The first and second partition of A are obtained by applying the calls *S2* and *S4*, respectively, to the single partition of MAIN. The first and second partition of B are produced by the application of the call *S7* to the first and second partition, respectively, of A.

BIBLIOGRAPHICAL NOTES

There is a large body of literature on flow analysis and optimization. Books by Schaefer (1973), Hecht (1977), Muchnick and Jones (1981) and Zima (1983) discuss a broad range of subjects; Chapter 10 in Aho *et al.* (1986) is an extensive, well-readable introduction; Kennedy (1981) is a survey on data flow analysis techniques.

Early work on data flow analysis and optimization was carried out by F. Allen, Cocke and Schwartz. Optimizations in basic blocks and loops are described in Cocke and Schwartz (1970), Allen and Cocke developed a catalog of optimization transformations (Allen, 1969; Allen and Cocke, 1972), and one of the first systematic studies of data flow techniques (originally published in 1970) is Allen and Cocke (1976).

The iterative algorithm was first used by Vyssotsky in a Fortran II compiler developed in 1962. Kildall (1973) developed the lattice-theoretic approach to data flow analysis, which was later clarified and generalized by Kam and Ullman (1976, 1977) among others. The method discussed in this book is usually referred to as the 'round-robin' strategy; alternative techniques have been proposed with the objective of improving the run-time efficiency – by constructing data structures (such as work lists and node lists) which attempt to reduce the number of visits to a node, and by using information about the structure of the flowgraph and the actual changes made in an iteration (Ullman 1973; Hecht and Ullman, 1975; Kennedy, 1975, 1976).

An important alternative approach to data flow analysis is based on reductions of reducible graphs. Interval analysis and T1/T2 transformations belong to this category. A reducible flowgraph is transformed via a number of graph transformation steps into a trivial flowgraph; data flow analysis is performed by first collecting information on successively larger program sections, beginning with basic blocks and ending with the whole program, and then distributing the information in an inverse pass back to the individual basic blocks. A method found by Tarjan achieves a complexity of $O[|N|\alpha(|N|)]$.

Data flow analysis has also been used for detecting program anomalies (Fosdick and Osterweil, 1976).

The above refers to intraprocedural analysis only. Early work in the area of interprocedural analysis was done by Spillman and F. Allen (Spillman, 1972; Allen, 1974).

The algorithm for the construction of the call graph (Algorithm 3.7) is based on work by B. Ryder (Ryder, 1979). The call graph is often modeled as a multigraph, with a separate edge for each call of a procedure (this is hidden in our model in the set *calls(p)*). Our algorithm for the solution of flow-insensitive problems (Algorithm 3.8) is largely based on F. Allen's work (Allen, 1974), while the treatment of the alias problem (Algorithm 3.9) is due to Banning (1979). The major restriction made in Section 3.7 is the exclusion of recursive procedures. In many cases, efficient solutions for general interprocedural problems (including recursion) can be found by modeling the problems as monotone data flow systems on the call flowgraph, and applying the iterative algorithm. The discussion below refers to the general case.

Barth (1978) includes aliasing in his solution algorithms for interprocedural data flow problems; his method is based on forming transitive closures of some basic relationships underlying these problems. Banning (1979) finds independent solutions for alias-free analysis and alias analysis, and combines these solutions to solve the general problem. This general strategy has been used by Cooper and Kennedy (1988, 1989) in a flow-insensitive algorithm for determining the side effects of reference parameters that takes time $O(|N| + |E|)$, where $G = (N,E)$ is the call graph.

Interprocedural constant propagation can be carried out as a generalization of the intraprocedural approach by modeling the mappings from formal parameters of a procedure to arguments in call sites occurring in that procedure (Callahan *et al.*, 1986). This may significantly improve the precision of analysis for library routines, whose calls often contain constant arguments that are used to select a specific version of the routine.

Chapter 4

Data Dependence

4.1 Introduction

The semantics of sequential languages such as Fortran, Algol 60, or Pascal specifies a linear order on statement executions. This order is in general more restrictive than is necessary to guarantee the desired output of a program. For example, two consecutive statements which access disjoint sets of variables – such as $A = B + C * D; E = F - G/H$ – can be interchanged without affecting the program's result. Moreover, in a loop, the order of iterations may be semantically irrelevant, as in:

```
DO I = N, M
  A(I) = 0
END DO
```

where all iterations can be executed concurrently, for example as a vector statement $A(N:M) = 0$.

This leads us to the question: how can we relax the linear order of statement executions so that parts of the program may be executed concurrently, while retaining the semantics of the program? The answer is provided by the **dependence relation**, which essentially specifies the semantically relevant constraints on statement order. In this chapter, we formally introduce the concept of data dependence as a relation on the set of statements and describe methods for its computation (control dependence was discussed in Section 3.3.5).

Let us take a closer look at data dependence, beginning with a simple example that involves only straight-line code and scalar variables:

S_1:   A = 1.0
S_2:   B = A + 3.1415271828
S_3:   A = 1/3 * (C - D)
      . . .
S_4:   A = (B * 3.8) / 2.7182831415

Consider statement S_2: the value of A that is used in the evaluation of the expression A + 3.1415271828 is the value assigned to A by S_1, that is 1.0. We call this a **true dependence** from S_1 to S_2, or, alternatively, say that S_2 is true dependent on S_1. The relative textual order of S_1 and S_2 must be maintained: an interchange of S_1 and S_2 would result in S_2 accessing the 'old' value of A (that is, the value that A had before the execution of S_1, which may be undefined). Since this would potentially modify the effect of the program, such a transformation would be semantically invalid.

Now consider S_2 and S_3. While S_2 uses the current value of A, S_3 performs an assignment to A. We call this an **anti dependence** from S_2 to S_3. An interchange of S_2 and S_3 would again result in S_2 using a potentially wrong value. Finally, the relationship between S_3 and S_4 is called an **output dependence** from S_3 to S_4: as with true and anti dependence, the relative order of S_3 and S_4 has to be maintained to preserve the semantics of the program.

The concept of data dependence always implies a direction: there is a dependence from a statement S to a statement S' if S may be executed before S' and both statements access the same variable, with at least one of them assigning a value to the variable. If S' depends on S, then it may or may not be that S depends on S'. If we are not interested in the direction of a dependence, and either S' depends on S, or vice versa, then we simply say that S and S' are dependent.

There is a subtle difference between true dependence and the other two types of dependences. While true dependence expresses a fundamental relationship that also exists in functional and data flow languages, anti and output dependences are inherently related to the imperative, sequential nature of Fortran and similar languages, which permit the programmer to express use and re-use of memory via accesses to variables. These dependences can, at least in principle, always be eliminated in a semantically valid way by the introduction of new variables. As a consequence, they are sometimes called **artificial dependences**.

We shall represent data dependences in a set of statements by the graph of the dependence relation[†], which is called the **dependence graph**.

[†] Whenever we use the term 'dependence' without further qualification in this chapter, we will mean data dependence.

Its arcs are often labeled with the symbols δ^t, δ^a, and δ^o, which respectively denote true, anti and output dependence. The dependence graph for the example is given below:

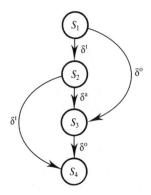

It is obvious that scalar data flow analysis suffices to determine the dependences occurring in the example. However, if we want to decide whether or not the iterations of a loop can be executed concurrently, we must analyze subscripted variables. While data flow analysis can recognize subscripted variables only as accesses to the whole array – which is not sufficient for our purposes – dependence analysis examines them individually, taking into account their subscript expressions. Consider for example the loop

```
DO I = 1, 100
  S:    A(2 * I) = B(I) + 1
  S':   D(I) = A(2 * I + 1)
END DO
```

If $A(2*I)$ and $A(2*I+1)$ were only recognized as references to array A, then we would have to assume the existence of a dependence from S to S' and vice versa, which would inhibit vectorization as well as parallelization. On the other hand, a simple analysis of the subscript expressions $2*I$ and $2*I+1$ reveals that they can never assume the same value; thus S and S' are not dependent and we know that the iterations of the loop can be executed concurrently.

We shall discuss methods for dependence analysis that can handle arbitrarily nested do-loops with subscripted variables whose subscript expressions are linear functions in the do-variables. Testing for dependence essentially amounts to examining whether a diophantine equation can be solved in a certain region which is defined by the bounds of the loop. For example, in order to perform a dependence test for the above loop, we have to determine whether or not the diophantine equation $2x = 2y + 1$ can be solved in the region $1 \leqslant x, y \leqslant 100$. Here, x and y represent independent values of the do-variable I, which are associated with the respective occurrences of I in the subscripted variables A(2*I) and A(2*I+1). The equation $2x = 2y + 1$ cannot be solved in any region, thus there is no dependence between S and S'. In contrast, an examination of the two references to A in the loop

```
DO I = 2, 10
    S:    A(I) = B(I) + 1
    S':   D(I) = A(I - 1)
END DO
```

shows that the diophantine equation $x = y - 1$ must be solved in the region $R: 2 \leqslant x, y \leqslant 10$. If we let $y = x + 1$, then for each pair (x,y) with $2 \leqslant x \leqslant 9$ we obtain a solution of the equation in R. As S is executed in iteration x before S' is executed in iteration $x + 1$, we have found a true dependence from S to S'.

We shall discuss one exact test, which is applicable to an important class of problems (the separability test), and two approximate tests, which are based on necessary conditions for dependence (the gcd test and the Banerjee test) and provide a conservative solution to the dependence problem.

Chapter 4 consists of eight sections. After introducing the basic loop model (Section 4.2), we formally define the concept of data dependence in Section 4.3. Section 4.4 precisely formulates the problem of dependence analysis and provides the mathematical background required for the treatment of the fundamental methods – separability, gcd and Banerjee tests – which are discussed in Section 4.5. In Section 4.6, we describe a general algorithm for dependence testing. The chapter closes with a number of remarks (Section 4.7) and bibliographical notes.

4.2 Basic concepts

4.2.1 Vectors

If M is a non-empty set and $n \in \mathbb{N}$, then M^n denotes the set of all tuples of length n whose elements are in M (see Appendix C, Section C.3). We shall assume here $M = \mathbb{R}$ or $M = \mathbb{Z}$; M^n is then a **vector space**, and its elements are **vectors** of length n. The notation introduced in Section C.3 will be applied to vector spaces; in addition, for any $\mathbf{a} \in M^n$, we use a_j synonymously with $\mathbf{a}(j)$ to denote the jth element of $\mathbf{a}$ ($1 \leqslant j \leqslant n$).

For all $\mathbf{x}, \mathbf{y} \in M^n$, $\mathbf{z} = \mathbf{x} + \mathbf{y}$ and $\mathbf{z} = \mathbf{x} - \mathbf{y}$, defined respectively by $z_j := x_j + y_j$ and $z_j := x_j - y_j$ for all j with $1 \leqslant j \leqslant n$, are in M^n. Furthermore, for any $\mathbf{x} \in M^n$ and $a \in M$, $\mathbf{w} = a \cdot \mathbf{x}$, where $w_j := a \cdot x_j$ for all j, is also in M^n.

The following discussion will be based on $\mathbb{Z}^n$, where $n \geq 1$ is arbitrary. All definitions and results are also valid for $\mathbb{R}^n$.

Definition 4.1   Let $c \in [1:n]$. Then for any two vectors $\mathbf{x}, \mathbf{y} \in \mathbb{Z}^n$:

$$\mathbf{x} <_c \mathbf{y} : \Longleftrightarrow (\forall j \in [1:c-1]: x_j = y_j) \wedge x_c < y_c \qquad \blacksquare$$

Example 4.1

Let $n = 3$. Then the following relations $<_c$ ($c = 1,2,3$) hold in $\mathbb{Z}^3$:

$$(1,2,3) <_1 (2,1,0)$$
$$(1,2,3) <_1 (3,4,5)$$
$$(5,5,1) <_2 (5,8,9)$$
$$(2,2,2) <_3 (2,2,4)$$

For any pair of the above elements of $\mathbb{Z}^3$, exactly one of the relations $<_c$ holds. For instance, $(1,2,3) <_2 (3,4,5)$ does not hold.

The following lemma is an immediate consequence of the definition:

Lemma 4.1

(1)   For every $c \in [1:n]$, $<_c$ is an irreflexive partial order on $\mathbb{Z}^n$.

(2)   For every pair $\mathbf{x}, \mathbf{y} \in \mathbb{Z}^n$: either $\mathbf{x} = \mathbf{y}$, or there exists a unique $c \in [1:n]$, such that either $\mathbf{x} <_c \mathbf{y}$, or $\mathbf{y} <_c \mathbf{x}$.

(3)   For every $\mathbf{x}, \mathbf{y}, \mathbf{z} \in \mathbb{Z}^n$, and $c, c' \in [1:n]$:

$$\mathbf{x} <_c \mathbf{y} \wedge \mathbf{y} <_{c'} \mathbf{z} \implies \mathbf{x} <_{c''} \mathbf{z}, \text{ where } c'' = min(c, c') \qquad \blacksquare$$

Definition 4.2: Lexicographical order

For all $\mathbf{x}, \mathbf{y} \in \mathbb{Z}^n$: $\mathbf{x} < \mathbf{y} : \Longleftrightarrow \exists c \in [1:n]: \mathbf{x} <_c \mathbf{y}$

The relation $<$ on $\mathbb{Z}^n$ is called the **lexicographical order**. $\qquad \blacksquare$

Lemma 4.2   The lexicographical order on $\mathbb{Z}^n$ is an irreflexive linear order. ∎

We shall use lexicographical order to characterize the sequential execution of nested loops.

4.2.2 Loops

We refer to the program model described in Section 3.2, and assume that a program consists of a single procedure MAIN. The set of statements is modified as shown in Table 4.1: it includes only assignment statements and the do-loop to allow us to concentrate on the essential aspects of data dependence (extensions will be discussed in Section 4.7).

The semantics of the do-loop are the same as in Fortran. However, we impose some restrictions: the do-variable is an integer variable which is local to the loop and may not be defined in the body. The bounds are expressions of the type of integer, the loop increment is 1.

The syntax of the do-control is restrictive, compared with Fortran. However, in Chapter 5 we shall see that any Fortran do-loop with an integer do-variable and increment can be transformed automatically into a semantically equivalent and even more tightly constrained loop, which is called normalized.

Definition 4.3   A do-loop as defined in Table 4.1 is **normalized** iff its lower bound is the constant 1. ∎

Thus, in a normalized loop both the lower bound and the increment are constant and equal to +1. Normalized loops will dominate much of our discussion, but data dependence and dependence tests will be discussed for the more general case.

Table 4.1   Syntax of the do-loop.

statement	$\rightarrow$	assignment | do
do	$\rightarrow$	"DO" do-control body "END DO" [do-variable]
do-control	$\rightarrow$	do-variable "=" lower-bound "," upper-bound
lower-bound	$\rightarrow$	expression
upper-bound	$\rightarrow$	expression
body	$\rightarrow$	statement*

Example 4.2

Consider the do-loop

```
DO I = T, U
  S:  A(I) = B(I) + 1
END DO
```

where T and U are integer constants. If $T > U$, the effect of the loop is empty. Otherwise, the loop executes $U - T + 1$ iterations by consecutively assigning the values $T, T+1, \ldots, U$ to I and executing the body (that is, in our case, the statement S) exactly once in each iteration. The net effect of the loop execution is then the ordered execution of the statements:

```
A(T)     = B(T) + 1
A(T + 1) = B(T + 1) + 1
...
A(U)     = B(U) + 1
```

We shall generally use the terms introduced in the next definition to describe loops. Note that the whole program can be considered to be a loop (if necessary, this can be enforced by enclosing it into an implicit trivial loop with one iteration).

Definition 4.4   Let L denote a loop, S a statement within L, and $L = L_1, L_2, \ldots, L_n$ ($n \geq 1$) be the sequence of all do-loops enclosing S, numbered successively from the outermost to the innermost loop (Program 4.1).

(1) L_j ($1 \leq j \leq n$) is the loop at **level** j, and $(L_1, \ldots, L_n)$ the **(loop) nest** enclosing S. $DOVARS := \{I_j: 1 \leq j \leq n\}$ is the associated set of do-variables, and $\mathbf{I} := (I_1, \ldots, I_n)$ the vector of do-variables. The level of S is n.

(2)   The do-control for every loop L_j has the form $I_j = t_j, u_j$, where t_j and u_j are integer expressions.

(3)   For any particular execution of S, let T_j, U_j and i_j respectively denote the values of t_j, u_j, and I_j, where $i_j \in [T_j : U_j]$ ($1 \leq j \leq n$). The vector $\mathbf{i} = (i_1, \ldots, i_n) \in \mathbb{Z}^n$ is called an **iteration vector**; it identifies an **iteration** of L. The associated state of $DOVARS$ is an **iteration state**. The set of all iteration vectors is the **execution index set** of S, denoted by $[S]$.

Program 4.1   A loop nest.

$$L:L_1: \quad \text{DO } I_1 = t_1, \, u_1$$

$$\cdots$$

$$L_2: \quad \text{DO } I_2 = t_2, \, u_2$$

$$\cdots$$

$$L_n: \quad \text{DO } I_n = t_n, \, u_n$$

$$\cdots$$

$$S$$

$$\cdots$$

$$\text{END DO } I_n$$

$$\cdots$$

$$\text{END DO } I_2$$

$$\cdots$$

$$\text{END DO } I_1$$

Remark   The above terms only make sense when we have a well-defined point of reference (for example S). When it is clear within the context of our discussion what this is, we will not refer to it explicitly. If the execution index set of a statement identifies all iterations of the loop (or all iterations we are interested in), then we speak of the **iteration space** of the loop. The iteration space can be thought of as a region in n-dimensional discrete cartesian space whose points correspond one-to-one to the iteration vectors.   ■

Example 4.3

Program 4.2 illustrates a nest of normalized loops, where S and S' are statements, and the ellipses represent zero or more assignment statements. Statement S is at level 3, where (IL,JL,KL) is the loop nest enclosing S; these loops are at levels 1, 2, and 3, respectively. The execution index set $[S]$ is $[1:10] \times [1:20] \times [1:30]$. Every vector $\mathbf{i} = (i_1, i_2, i_3)$ with $1 \leq i_1 \leq 10$, $1 \leq i_2 \leq 20$, and $1 \leq i_3 \leq 30$ is an iteration vector. Finally, $DOVARS = \{I, J, K\}$.

S' is at level 5. Its loop nest is (IL,JL,LL,ML,NL); the loops in the nest have levels 1–5. $[S'] = [1:10] \times [1:20] \times [1:10] \times [1:100] \times [1:20]$, and $DOVARS = \{I, J, L, M, N\}$.

Note that S and S' have only the loops IL and JL in common.

Definition 4.5   The nest of Definition 4.4 is called **perfect** iff for each j with $1 \leq j < n$ the body of L_j is L_{j+1}.   ■

Program 4.2   A nest of normalized loops.

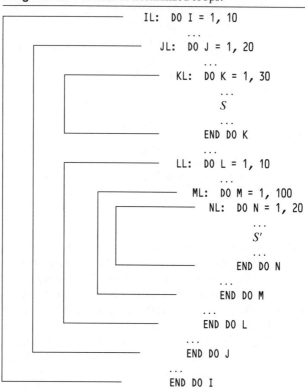

```
IL:  DO I = 1, 10
        ...
    JL:  DO J = 1, 20
            ...
        KL:  DO K = 1, 30
                ...
                S
                ...
            END DO K
            ...
        LL:  DO L = 1, 10
                ...
            ML:  DO M = 1, 100
                NL:  DO N = 1, 20
                        ...
                        S'
                        ...
                    END DO N
                ...
                END DO M
            ...
            END DO L
        ...
        END DO J
    ...
    END DO I
```

4.2.3   Statement instances and execution orders

Whenever we talk about a loop L and a statement S contained in L in the following, then we always implicitly refer to Definition 4.4. We now introduce the concept of a statement instance, which allows us to identify the specific execution of S for a given iteration vector in $[S]$.

Definition 4.6   Let $i \in [S]$. The execution of S in iteration i is called the **instance** of S associated with i, and is denoted by $S(i)$.   ∎

Whenever we talk of the relative order of statement executions, we will include do-loops as well as assignment statements, but assume that for any pair of statements within the scope of our discussion neither of them is nested in the other. The concept of an execution order in a set of statement executions, as defined in the following, models the linear order associated with sequential languages as well as the partial orders that belong to concurrent programs.

Definition 4.7   Let an arbitrary loop L be given. An **execution order** for L is an irreflexive partial order in the set of statement instances associated with L.   ∎

Example 4.4

Consider the following perfect nest

```
L₁:  DO J = 1, 100
   L₂:  DO I = 1, 100
      L₃:  DO K = 1, 100
            S:  C(I, J) = C(I, J) + A(I, K) * B(K, J)
          END DO K
        END DO I
      END DO J
```

We see that S is a statement at level 3, with associated loop nest (L_1, L_2, L_3). The set of all instances of S is given by $\{S(j,i,k): (j,i,k) \in [S]\}$, where $[S] = [1{:}100]^3$. $S(j,i,k)$ is executed before $S(j',i',k')$ iff $(j,i,k) < (j',i',k')$, where the relation $<$ denotes lexicographic ordering in the set of iteration vectors. So in our example the instances of S are executed in the order:

$S(1,1,1), S(1,1,2), \ldots, S(1,1,100),$
$S(1,2,1), S(1,2,2), \ldots, S(1,2,100),$
$\ldots$
$S(1,100,1), S(1,100,2), \ldots, S(1,100,100),$
$\ldots$
$\ldots$
$S(100,100,1), S(100,100,2), \ldots, S(100,100,100).$

4.2.4   The standard execution order

Definition 4.8   The **standard execution order** is the execution order defined by the Fortran standard. It is denoted by the symbol '≪'.   ∎

Example 4.5

Consider statement S in Example 4.4. The standard execution order for the instances of this statement is given by:

$S(j,i,k) \ll S(j',i',k')$ iff $(j,i,k) < (j',i',k')$

We shall give a general characterization of the standard execution order in the following. The first step is the definition of the control set and a specification of the textual relationship between two statements.

Definition 4.9   Let S and S' denote arbitrary statements in a loop. The **control set** of S and S', denoted by $[S,S']$, is defined by: $[S,S'] := \{(\mathbf{i},\mathbf{i}') \in [S] \times [S']: S(\mathbf{i}) \ll S'(\mathbf{i}')\}$. A pair $(\mathbf{i},\mathbf{i}')$ of iteration vectors for S and S' is called **plausible** if it is in $[S,S']$, otherwise **implausible**.   ∎

Definition 4.10   Let S and S' be arbitrary statements. Then $S \text{ bef } S' :\Longleftrightarrow S$ occurs textually before S'.   ∎

The control set of S and S' specifies the set of all pairs of iteration vectors $\mathbf{i}$ and $\mathbf{i}'$ for S and S', respectively, that cause the relationship $S(\mathbf{i}) \ll S'(\mathbf{i}')$ to be satisfied. For any pair of statements, exactly one of the following holds: $S = S'$, $S \text{ bef } S'$, or $S' \text{ bef } S$.

We now extend our notation so that we can consider statement pairs. Terms used in connection with a statement S' will be qualified by a prime $(')$ where applicable. In particular, n and n' will denote the levels of statements S and S', respectively, and $(L = L_1, \ldots, L_n)$, $(L = L'_1, \ldots, L'_{n'})$ will be their associated loop nests. This is illustrated in Program 4.3.

Definition 4.11   Let L be a loop containing two statements S and S' as in Program 4.3. Then the **maximum common loop index**, m, of S and S' is given by $m := max\{j: L_j = L'_j\}$ ∎

The maximum common loop index is the level of the innermost loop enclosing both S and S'. Thus, $1 \leq m \leq min(n,n')$. We can represent the loop as shown in Program 4.4, where the statements S_r, $1 \leq r \leq s$, constitute the body of L_m. Each S_r is either a loop or an assignment statement. For some $h \in [1:s]$, S is either equal to S_h (iff $n = m$), or S_h is a loop properly containing S. Similarly, there is an $h' \in [1:s]$ such that either $S' = S_{h'}$, or S' is properly contained in $S_{h'}$. We shall frequently need access to the vector $\mathbf{i}(1:m)$, where $\mathbf{i}$ is an iteration vector. This will be abbreviated, using the notation $\backslash \mathbf{i}$.

We can now proceed to the characterization of the standard execution order. We formulate first a lemma that states an obvious relationship for statements in the body of L_m. Based on this result, we shall prove a theorem for the general case.

Lemma 4.3   We assume the loop of Program 4.4. Let S_h and $S_{h'}$ be statements at level m $(1 \leq h, h' \leq s)$, with associated iteration vectors $\mathbf{j}$ and $\mathbf{j}'$. Then:

Program 4.3 A loop with two statements S and S'.

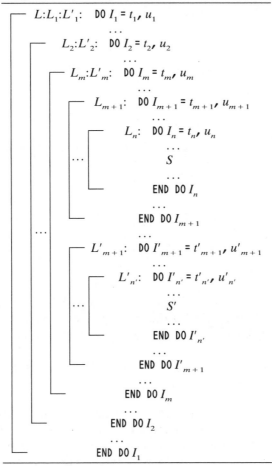

$S_h(\mathbf{j}) \ll S_{h'}(\mathbf{j'}) \Longleftrightarrow (\mathbf{j} < \mathbf{j'}) \vee (\mathbf{j} = \mathbf{j'} \wedge h < h')$ ∎

Corollary For $h = h'$ we obtain: $S_h(\mathbf{j}) \ll S_h(\mathbf{j'}) \Longleftrightarrow \mathbf{j} < \mathbf{j'}$. ∎

Theorem 4.1 Assume that S and S' are two statements with associated iteration vectors $\mathbf{i}$ and $\mathbf{i'}$, respectively. Then:

$S(\mathbf{i}) \ll S'(\mathbf{i'}) \Longleftrightarrow (\backslash \mathbf{i} < \backslash \mathbf{i'}) \vee (\backslash \mathbf{i} = \backslash \mathbf{i'} \wedge S \text{ bef } S')$ ∎

Proof Let the indices of S and S' in the statement sequence of the body of L_m be h and h', respectively, and let $\mathbf{i} \in [S]$ and $\mathbf{i'} \in [S']$ be

Program 4.4   A view of the loop of Program 4.3.

$L:L_1:L_1':$ DO $I_1 = t_1,\, u_1$

    . . .

    $L_2:L_2':$ DO $I_2 = t_2,\, u_2$

       . . .

       $L_m:L_m':$ DO $I_m = t_m,\, u_m$

          S_1

          . . .

          S_h ← contains S or is equal to S

          . . .

          $S_{h'}$ ← contains S' or is equal to S'

          . . .

          S_s

       END DO I_m

       . . .

    END DO I_2

    . . .

  END DO I_1

arbitrarily selected. Then $\backslash i \in [S_h]$ and $\backslash i' \in [S_{h'}]$, and $S_h(\backslash i) \ll S_{h'}(\backslash i')$ iff $S(\mathbf{i}) \ll S'(\mathbf{i'})$. The application of Lemma 4.3 (with $\mathbf{j} = \backslash i$, $\mathbf{j'} = \backslash i'$) yields:

$$S(\mathbf{i}) \ll S'(\mathbf{i'}) \Longleftrightarrow (\backslash i < \backslash i') \vee (\backslash i = \backslash i' \wedge h < h') \qquad \blacksquare$$

Note that this theorem completely characterizes the control set $[S,S']$, using only the first m components of iteration vectors. The remaining components are irrelevant for the relative order of $S(\mathbf{i})$ and $S'(\mathbf{i'})$.

Whenever we refer to loops L and statements S and S' in the following, we will implicitly refer to Programs 4.3 and 4.4 and the associated definitions.

4.2.5   Abstractions of the control set

Control sets will play an important role in the definition and analysis of data dependence. In most cases, however, either they are too large to be explicitly used in a transformation system, or they are not completely known at compile time. Thus the control set must be replaced by some abstracted version. We define a hierarchy of abstractions: in each step we obtain sets that are smaller and easier to manage, at the cost of giving up some information previously known. We discuss three steps, which take us from a control set to a set of distance vectors, then to a set of direction vectors, and finally to a set of relations $<_c$ in $[S,S']$.

Definition 4.12   Let S and S' be two statements in a loop, and assume that $(\mathbf{i},\mathbf{i}') \in [S] \times [S']$. The **distance vector** of $\mathbf{i}$ and $\mathbf{i}'$, denoted by $dist(\mathbf{i},\mathbf{i}')$, is defined by $dist(\mathbf{i},\mathbf{i}') := \backslash\mathbf{i}' - \backslash\mathbf{i}$.   ∎

Note that the length of $dist(\mathbf{i},\mathbf{i}')$ is m, the maximum common loop index of S and S'. We extend this notion to sets.

Definition 4.13   Let S and S' be two statements in a loop and let $M \subseteq [S] \times [S']$. Then $dist(M) := \{dist(\mathbf{i},\mathbf{i}'): (\mathbf{i},\mathbf{i}') \in M\}$.   ∎

In the next step we introduce direction vectors:

Definition 4.14   A **direction vector** is a vector $\boldsymbol{\theta} \in \{<,=,>,*\}^k$ for some $k \geqslant 1$.   ∎

We use direction vectors to specify the relationship between a pair of iteration vectors. In particular, we have the following.

Definition 4.15   Let S and S' be two statements in a loop, let $(\mathbf{i},\mathbf{i}') \in [S] \times [S']$, and $\boldsymbol{\mu} = dist(\mathbf{i},\mathbf{i}')$. The **direction vector** $\boldsymbol{\theta}$ of $\mathbf{i}$ and $\mathbf{i}'$, denoted by $dir(\mathbf{i},\mathbf{i}')$, is of length m, and for all j ($1 \leqslant j \leqslant m$) defined by

$$
\theta_j = \begin{cases} \text{`<'}, \text{ if } \mu_j > 0 \\ \text{`='}, \text{ if } \mu_j = 0 \\ \text{`>'}, \text{ if } \mu_j < 0 \end{cases}
$$

$dir(\mathbf{i},\mathbf{i}')$ is called **plausible** iff $(\mathbf{i},\mathbf{i}')$ is plausible.   ∎

We now define the direction vector of a set.

Definition 4.16   Let S and S' be two statements in a loop and let $M \subseteq [S] \times [S']$. Then $dir(M) := \{dir(\mathbf{i},\mathbf{i}'): (\mathbf{i},\mathbf{i}') \in M\}$.   ∎

A direction vector $\boldsymbol{\theta}$ will be called **proper** or **extended**, depending on whether or not it only contains '<', '=', and '>'. The symbol '*' stands for an arbitrary relationship between corresponding components of two iteration vectors; it can be used to define classes of direction vectors. Thus

$(*, \ldots, *)$ represents the set of all direction vectors of a given length and $(=,<,*)$ stands for the set $\{(=,<,<), (=,<,=), (=,<,>)\}$.

Example 4.6

Let us take another look at the loop in Example 4.4. We have $[\textbf{S},S] = \{(\textbf{i},\textbf{i}'): \textbf{i} < \textbf{i}'\}$. Now let $\textbf{i} = (10,20,30)$ and $\textbf{i}' = (20,20,2)$. Then $\textbf{i} < \textbf{i}'$ holds, $dist(\textbf{i},\textbf{i}') = (10,0,-28)$, and $dir(\textbf{i},\textbf{i}') = (<,=,>)$. Furthermore, $dir([S,S]) = \{(<,*,*)\} \cup \{(=,<,*)\} \cup \{(=,=,<)\}$.

We can now easily see what plausible direction vectors must look like in general (see Theorem 4.1).

Theorem 4.2 Let S and S' be two statements in a loop. Then

$$dir([S,S']) = \{(<,*,*, \ldots, *)\} \cup$$
$$\{(=,<,*, \ldots, *)\} \cup$$
$$\{(=,=, \ldots, =,<)\} \cup CEQ$$

where $CEQ = \{(=, \ldots, =)\}$ if S bef S', $\varnothing$ otherwise. All vectors are of length m. ∎

The classes of plausible direction vectors that occur here lead us to the third step of abstraction. If we extend the relations $<_c$ (see Definition 4.1) to pairs of iteration vectors in an obvious way, then we see that these relations identify the first m classes that occur in the above theorem.

Definition 4.17 Let S and S' be two statements in a loop with associated iteration vectors $\textbf{i}$ and $\textbf{i}'$, respectively, and let $c \in [1:m]$. Then:

$$\textbf{i} <_c \textbf{i}' :\Longleftrightarrow \backslash\textbf{i} <_c \backslash\textbf{i}'$$ ∎

We can immediately see that for each $c \in [1:m]$:

$$dir(<_c) = dir(\{(\textbf{i},\textbf{i}') \in [S] \times [S']: \textbf{i} <_c \textbf{i}'\}) = (=^{c-1},<,*, \ldots, *)$$

This allows us to rewrite Theorem 4.2 in the form:

$$dir([S,S']) = \bigcup_{1 \le c \le m} dir(<_c) \cup CEQ$$

where CEQ is defined as above.

4.3   The definition of data dependence

In this section we define the concept of data dependence. Whenever the term 'statement' is used, it refers to an assignment statement contained in a loop nest.

4.3.1   Input and output sets

Suppose that statements S and S' in a loop are given, and we want to decide whether or not there is a data dependence from S to S'. Then we have to find the control set $[S,S']$ (or some set derived from it), and determine whether or not there exists a pair $(i,i') \in [S,S']$ such that the statement instances $S(i)$ and $S'(i')$ access a common variable, and at least one of them writes it.

Let us suppose that the control set is already known. Our subsequent tests begin by finding out which variables the statements access. As we want to analyze subscripted variables, we have to extend the notion of the sets USE and DEF, as introduced in Chapter 3 (see Definition 3.17). We shall refer to these sets as **input** and **output** sets, respectively.

The input and output sets of a statement S are extended in two steps. First we include subscripted variables with symbolic subscript expressions that occur in the program text (see Definitions 3.4 and 3.17):

$$DEF(S) := \{v \in VARX: S \text{ is a definition of } v\}$$
$$USE(S) := \{v \in VARX: S \text{ is a use of } v\}$$

These sets can be determined by a simple parse of the program.

Assume that $v \equiv A(exp_1, \ldots, exp_d)$ is a subscripted variable in $USE(S)$ or $DEF(S)$. Then any variable occurring in an expression exp_j $(1 \leq j \leq d)$ will be included in $USE(S)$, independent of whether $v \in USE(S)$ or $v \in DEF(S)$.

Example 4.7

We return to the loop

```
DO I = 1, 100
  S:    A(2 * I) = B(I) + 1
  S':   D(I) = A(2 * I + 1)
END DO
```

discussed in the introduction. The input and output sets associated with the statements S and S' are:

$$USE(S) = \{B(I),I\} \qquad\qquad DEF(S) = \{A(2 * I)\}$$
$$USE(S') = \{A(2 * I + 1),I\} \qquad DEF(S') = \{D(I)\}$$

If we were to base our dependence analysis directly on input and output sets for statements, then the results would be much too weak to help us make the program transformations we want. What we must do is find out which values the subscript expressions may take on during the execution of the loop; that is, we must map the sets defined above to subsets of VAR (the set of declared variables), by replacing subscript expressions by their values. If no restrictions are imposed, then this problem is undecidable. So we restrict subscript expressions to contain variables in $DOVARS$ only and exclude function references altogether.

Definition 4.18 A variable v is **admissible** in a loop iff either $v \in DOVARS$, or v is a subscripted variable whose subscript expressions contain no function reference and depend only on variables in $DOVARS$. A set of variables $V \subseteq VARX$ is **admissible** iff each variable in V is admissible. ∎

Now when we discuss dependence tests, we also need a notation which allows us to map an admissible input or output set to a corresponding execution set.

Definition 4.19 Let S be a statement in a loop, $\mathbf{i} \in [S]$, β the iteration state associated with $\mathbf{i}$, and assume that $USE(S)$ and $DEF(S)$ are admissible:

(1)
$$DEF(S(\mathbf{i})) := \{v : v \in DEF(S) \wedge v \text{ is simple}\} \cup$$
$$\{A(\beta(exp_1), \ldots, \beta(exp_d)) :$$
$$A(exp_1, \ldots, exp_d) \in DEF(S)\}$$

$DEF(S(\mathbf{i}))$ is called the **output execution set** of instance $S(\mathbf{i})$.

(2)
$$USE(S(\mathbf{i})) := \{v : v \in USE(S) \wedge v \text{ is simple}\} \cup$$
$$\{A(\beta(exp_1), \ldots, \beta(exp_d)) :$$
$$A(exp_1, \ldots, exp_d) \in USE(S)\}$$

$USE(S(\mathbf{i}))$ is called the **input execution set** of instance $S(\mathbf{i})$. ∎

Example 4.8

The input and output sets for statement S in

```
DO I = 1, 100
  S:  X(I + 1) = X(I) + Y(I)
END DO
```

are $USE(S) = \{X(I), Y(I), I\}$ and $DEF(S) = \{X(I+1)\}$. For an iteration vector $\mathbf{i} = (i)$, $1 \leqslant i \leqslant 100$, $USE(S(\mathbf{i})) = \{X(i), Y(i), I\}$, and $DEF(S(\mathbf{i})) = \{X(i+1)\}$.

4.3.2 Dependences

We formally define data dependence as a relation between statement instances below. We assume that all input and output sets are admissible.

Definition 4.20   Let S and S' be statements in a loop with associated iteration vectors $\mathbf{i}$ and $\mathbf{i}'$, respectively. Then $S(\mathbf{i}) \, \delta \, S'(\mathbf{i}') : \Longleftrightarrow$

(DEP-1) $S(\mathbf{i}) \ll S'(\mathbf{i}')$ and

(DEP-2) $\exists \, v \in VAR$:
$\quad v \in DEF(S(\mathbf{i})) \cap USE(S'(\mathbf{i}')) \; \vee$
$\quad v \in USE(S(\mathbf{i})) \cap DEF(S'(\mathbf{i}')) \; \vee$
$\quad v \in DEF(S(\mathbf{i})) \cap DEF(S'(\mathbf{i}'))$ and

(DEP-3)   There is no statement instance SI such that:

$\quad$ (C) $S(\mathbf{i}) \ll SI \ll S'(\mathbf{i}')$ and $v \in DEF(SI)$

If $S(\mathbf{i}) \, \delta \, S'(\mathbf{i}')$ then we say that $S'(\mathbf{i}')$ is **data dependent** on $S(\mathbf{i})$.   ■

Whenever it is clear from the context that we are not talking about control dependence, we will simply call this 'dependence'.

Definition 4.21   Suppose that S and S' are statements as above and that $S(\mathbf{i}) \, \delta \, S'(\mathbf{i}')$ holds. We distinguish between three **types** of data dependence, depending on which of the three possible conditions in (DEP-2) is satisfied:

(i) $S(\mathbf{i}) \, \delta^t \, S'(\mathbf{i}') :\Longleftrightarrow v \in DEF(S(\mathbf{i})) \cap USE(S'(\mathbf{i}'))$

(ii) $S(\mathbf{i}) \, \delta^a \, S'(\mathbf{i}') :\Longleftrightarrow v \in USE(S(\mathbf{i})) \cap DEF(S'(\mathbf{i}'))$

(iii) $S(\mathbf{i}) \, \delta^o \, S'(\mathbf{i}') :\Longleftrightarrow v \in DEF(S(\mathbf{i})) \cap DEF(S'(\mathbf{i}'))$

The relations δ^t, δ^a, and δ^o are known as **true**, **anti** and **output** dependence respectively.   ∎

Whenever there is a dependence $S(\mathbf{i}) \, \delta \, S'(\mathbf{i}')$, then the three conditions of Definition 4.20 hold. Let us take a look at these one by one.

(DEP-1)   This condition imposes a constraint upon the order in which the two statement instances involved are carried out: $S(\mathbf{i})$ must be executed before $S'(\mathbf{i}')$. We have already described the related sets $[S,S']$ and $dir([S,S'])$ (see Theorems 4.1 and 4.2).

(DEP-2)   The second condition tells us that there must be a variable v which is accessed in both statement instances and defined in at least one of them. We then have three possible cases, corresponding to the three types of dependence: true, anti, and output dependence.

A fourth conceivable type of dependence would be **input dependence**, with the corresponding condition formulated as:

(iv) $v \in USE(S(\mathbf{i})) \cap USE(S'(\mathbf{i}'))$

This type of dependence would not be related to statement ordering (see our discussion in the introduction): program semantics are not modified if we change the relative order of statements that are input dependent. We shall thus not consider it when we discuss our program transformations. Input dependence does, however, play an important role in algorithms that deal with memory allocation.

(DEP-3)   If there is a statement instance SI satisfying condition (C), then it is said to **cover** the dependence. What would happen if there were such a statement and (DEP-1) and, say, the first line of (DEP-2) were fulfilled? Then SI would assign a value to the variable v after $S(\mathbf{i})$ has performed its assignment; so the value for v which is read in $S'(\mathbf{i}')$ will in general not be the one which was assigned in $S(\mathbf{i})$. SI will similarly destroy the other two types of dependence.

Example 4.9

The input and output sets for statement S in

```
DO I = 1, 100
   S:  X(I) = X(I) + Y(I)
END DO
```

are $USE(S) = \{X(I),Y(I),I\}$ and $DEF(S) = \{X(I)\}$. For an iteration vector $\mathbf{i} = (i)$, where $i \in [1:100]$, we thus have the execution sets $USE(S(i)) = \{X(i),Y(i),I\}$ and $DEF(S(i)) = \{X(i)\}$.

   To establish a dependence, it is necessary to find iteration vectors $\mathbf{i} = (i)$ and $\mathbf{i}' = (i')$ satisfying conditions (DEP-1) and (DEP-2). Since $S = S'$, (DEP-1) and Theorem 4.1 imply $\mathbf{i} < \mathbf{i}'$, and thus $1 \leqslant i < i' \leqslant 100$.

   From (DEP-2), we must look for a variable v such that:

$$
\begin{array}{lll}
v \in \{X(i)\} & \cap \{X(i'),Y(i'),I\} & \vee \\
v \in \{X(i),Y(i),I\} \cap & \{X(i')\} & \vee \\
v \in \{X(i)\} & \cap \{X(i')\} &
\end{array}
$$

Since this obviously cannot be satisfied, there are no dependences between statement instances of S.

Example 4.10

We now modify our loop slightly:

```
DO I = 1, 100
   S:  X(I + 1) = X(I) + Y(I)
END DO
```

As above, (DEP-1) requires that $1 \leqslant i < i' \leqslant 100$. (DEP-2) becomes

$$
\begin{array}{lll}
v \in \{X(i + 1)\} & \cap \{X(i'),Y(i'),I\} & \vee \\
v \in \{X(i),Y(i),I\} \cap \{X(i' + 1)\} & & \vee \\
v \in \{X(i + 1)\} & \cap \{X(i' + 1)\} &
\end{array}
$$

If we let $i' = i + 1$, then for each $i \in [1:99]$ the first line will be satisfied. Also, since (DEP-3) obviously holds, $S(\mathbf{i}) \; \delta^t \; S(\mathbf{i}')$ for all such pairs.

We can easily see that the reason for this true dependence is that $S(\mathbf{i})$ assigns the value to $X(i + 1)$ which is used in the next iteration. Since, in a sense, the value causing the dependence is 'carried' from one iteration of the loop to the next, we call it a **loop-carried dependence** (see Definition 4.22).

Example 4.11

We look for dependences in the following loop:

```
DO J = 1, 100
  DO I = 1, 100
    S:  C(I, J) = 0.0
      DO K = 1, 100
        S':  C(I, J) = C(I, J) + A(I, K) * B(K, J)
      END DO K
  END DO I
END DO J
```

The input and output sets are:

$USE(S) = \{I,J\}$ $DEF(S) = \{C(I,J)\}$

$USE(S') = \{C(I,J), A(I,K), B(K,J), I, J, K\}$ $DEF(S') = \{C(I,J)\}$

Here, S is a statement at level 2 and S' is at level 3. The execution index sets are $[S] = [1{:}100]^2$ and $[S'] = [1{:}100]^3$. The maximum common loop index of S and S' is 2, and the control sets are:

$[S,S] = \{((j,i),(j',i')) \in [S] \times [S]: (j,i) < (j',i')\}$

$[S,S'] = \{((j,i),(j',i',k')) \in [S] \times [S']: (j,i) \leq (j',i')\}$

$[S',S] = \{((j',i',k'),(j,i)) \in [S'] \times [S]: (j';i') < (j,i)\}$

$[S',S'] = \{((j,i,k),(j',i',k')) \in [S'] \times [S']: (j,i,k) < (j',i',k')\}.$

Clearly, $S(j,i) \,\delta\, S(j',i')$ and $S'(j,i,k) \,\delta\, S(j',i')$ cannot hold, but is there a dependence of the form $S(j,i) \,\delta\, S'(j',i',k')$? We must consider the set of all pairs in $[S,S']$, and distinguish two cases:

Case 1: $((j,i),(j',i',k')) \in [S,S']$ with $(j,i) < (j',i')$

Since such a pair of iteration vectors cannot satisfy (DEP-2), there are no dependences here.

Case 2: $((j,i),(j',i',k')) \in [S,S']$ with $(j,i) = (j',i')$, that is $j = j' \wedge i = i'$

This does satisfy (DEP-2); and, for $k' = 1$, (DEP-3) is satisfied also.

Thus for all j,i:

$$S(j,i)\ \delta^t\ S'(j,i,1)\ \text{and}\ S(j,i)\ \delta^o\ S'(j,i,1)$$

Note that the dependence here is simply a result of the textual order of S and S'. Thus it is 'loop-independent' (see Definition 4.22).

Is there also a dependence $S'(j,i,k)\ \delta\ S'(j',i',k')$? If so, there must be a pair of iteration vectors such that $(j,i,k) < (j',i',k')$ holds and (DEP-2) and (DEP-3) are both satisfied. Let $j = j'$, $i = i'$, $k < k'$, and $v = C(i,j)$: (DEP-2) is satisfied. (DEP-3) is also fulfilled if we let $k' = k + 1$.

Suppose that $S(\mathbf{i})\ \delta\ S'(\mathbf{i}')$. Then we say that the iteration vectors $\mathbf{i}$ and $\mathbf{i}'$ are **associated** with the dependence. Each variable v that satisfies (DEP-2) is said to **cause** the dependence. A variable may cause more than one dependence for the same pair of statements and iteration vectors, as can be seen in

```
S:    A(I) = B(I) + 1
      ...
S':   A(I) = A(I) - 1
```

We can then pinpoint the instances of the variable that cause a specific dependence to hold. If $S,S',\mathbf{i},\mathbf{i}',v$, and the instances of v causing (DEP-2) to hold are all known, then we speak of an **instance** of the dependence. For each instance of a dependence, the dependence type is uniquely determined.

The above classification of dependences – true, anti, and output – was based on the relationships between the input and output sets of statement instances. In the following, we shall qualify dependences by characterizing the associated pairs of iteration vectors. We shall use the concepts developed in Section 4.2, in particular distance vectors, direction vectors, and the relations $<_c$, to do so.

Let us first introduce the following notation. If S and S' are statements in a loop with associated iteration vectors $\mathbf{i}$ and $\mathbf{i}'$, respectively, and if $S(\mathbf{i}) \ll S'(\mathbf{i}')$ holds, then we allow the relational symbol '$\ll$' to be qualified as follows:

$$S(\mathbf{i}) \ll_\mu S'(\mathbf{i}') \quad \text{iff} \quad \mu = dist(\mathbf{i},\mathbf{i}')$$
$$S(\mathbf{i}) \ll_\theta S'(\mathbf{i}') \quad \text{iff} \quad \theta = dir(\mathbf{i},\mathbf{i}')$$
$$S(\mathbf{i}) \ll_c S'(\mathbf{i}') \quad \text{iff} \quad \mathbf{i} <_c \mathbf{i}'$$
$$S(\mathbf{i}) \ll_\infty S'(\mathbf{i}') \quad \text{iff} \quad \backslash\mathbf{i} = \backslash\mathbf{i}' \text{ and } S \text{ bef } S'$$

This notation can now be applied in the same way to dependences. Suppose that $S(i) \delta S'(i')$. Then we can write:

$$
\begin{aligned}
S(i)\, \delta\mu\, S'(i') \quad &\text{iff} \quad S(i) \ll_\mu S'(i') \\
S(i)\, \delta\theta\, S'(i') \quad &\text{iff} \quad S(i) \ll_\theta S'(i') \\
S(i)\, \delta_c\, S'(i') \quad &\text{iff} \quad S(i) \ll_c S'(i') \\
S(i)\, \delta_\infty\, S'(i') \quad &\text{iff} \quad S(i) \ll_\infty S'(i')
\end{aligned}
$$

We can then speak of a **dependence distance**, **dependence direction**, etcetera. The dependence classes characterized by δ_c and δ_∞ will play a dominating role in our discussion of restructuring transformations. We introduce the following terminology.

Definition 4.22

(1)   If $S(i)\, \delta_c\, S'(i')$, then we say that there is a **loop-carried** dependence at level c of $S'(i')$ on $S(i)$. The loop at level c is called the **carrier** of the dependence.

(2)   If $S(i)\, \delta_\infty\, S'(i')$ holds, then we say that there is a **loop-independent** dependence of $S'(i')$ on $S(i)$.

(3)   Whenever $S(i)\, \delta_k\, S'(i')$ holds for a $k \in [1{:}m] \cup \{\infty\}$, then we say that k is a **level** of the dependence.   ■

For each instance of a dependence, the level is uniquely determined.

The notation introduced above can be combined freely with a specification of a dependence type.

The concepts defined above to describe execution orders and dependences all refer to particular statement instances. However, in general, we need to work with relationships between statements themselves. The first two appropriate extensions of a definition are given explicitly; all others are implicitly generalized in a similar manner.

Definition 4.23   Let S, S' be statements in a loop. Then:

(1) $S \ll S' :\Longleftrightarrow \exists i, i' : S(i) \ll S'(i')$

(2) $S \delta S' :\Longleftrightarrow \exists i, i' : S(i) \delta S'(i')$

$S \delta S'$ is expressed as: S' is **(data) dependent** on S.   ■

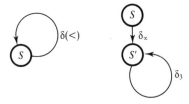

Figure 4.1 Dependence graphs.

Dependences can be represented by directed labelled graphs, as defined below.

Definition 4.24 Suppose we have a loop L, and $STAT(L)$ is the set of assignment statements in L. The **dependence graph** of L, denoted by $DG(L)$, is the graph of the relation δ on $STAT(L)$. ∎

The edges of the dependence graph may be labeled with any attributes of the related dependences that are relevant in a given context. This may include distance vectors, direction vectors, and dependence levels.

Frequently, we are interested in subgraphs or partial graphs of the dependence graph. For example, we may examine a graph $DG(L)|STAT'$, where $STAT' \subseteq STAT(L)$, or we may want to consider only particular types or levels of dependences. We apply the notion 'dependence graph' to all graphs obtained in such a way from $DG(L)$.

Example 4.12

Consider again the program in Example 4.10. The dependences in it can be equivalently characterized either by $S\,\delta(<)\,S$, or by $S\,\delta_1\,S$: this is a (cyclic) loop-carried dependence at level 1. The first of the diagrams in Figure 4.1 displays its dependence graph.

The dependences in the program of Example 4.11 can be described by $S\,\delta(=,=)\,S'$ or $S\,\delta_\infty\,S'$, and $S'\,\delta(=,=,<)\,S'$ or $S'\,\delta_3\,S'$. Its dependence graph is given in the second diagram of Figure 4.1.

A dependence between two statements can be associated with more than one level. This is illustrated in the following.

Example 4.13

In the following program, $S \delta_k S'$ for $k = 1, 2$, and ∞.

```
DO I = -100, 100
  DO J = 0, 200
    S:   A(I, J) = ...
    S':  B(I, J) = 1/3 * (A(I, J) + A(I - 1, J) + A(I, J - 1))
    ...
  END DO J
END DO I
```

Lemma 4.4   The dependence relation is in general not transitive. ■

Proof   Consider the following example:

S_1:   A = B + 1
S_2:   B = A * 2
S_3:   C = B - 1

Here, $S_1 \delta S_2$ and $S_2 \delta S_3$, but not $S_1 \delta S_3$.   ■

The dependence relation is not transitive because, for statements S, S' and S'', the reason why $S \delta S'$ is valid may be quite different from the reason why $S' \delta S''$ holds: perhaps the dependences are caused by incompatible pairs of iteration vectors or by different variables, or perhaps the first is an anti dependence and the second a true dependence. In all these cases we cannot expect that $S \delta S''$.

In the introduction to this chapter we said that dependences between statements imply restrictions on the order in which they are executed. These restrictions, in contrast, are inherently transitive. When discussing restructuring transformations we shall need to enforce transitivity on our dependence relation also; this will be done in a natural way by using the transitive closure δ^+ of δ.

4.4   Dependence testing: a mathematical problem formulation

4.4.1   The dependence system

Assume that S and S' are statements in a loop. Our main objective is to prove that no dependence between S and S' exists; if this is not feasible, we want to characterize the set of dependences between the two statements as precisely as possible. Starting from the definition of dependence, we shall narrow the scope of the problem to be solved step by step, until we arrive at a linear diophantine equation which we test for the existence of solutions in a certain region.

We begin by taking a look at (DEP-3). This condition disallows covering. Now assume that for $S(\mathbf{i})$ and $S'(\mathbf{i}')$ (DEP-1) and (DEP-2) are fulfilled, but that there are one or more statement instances that cover the dependence. Then a dependence test that ignores covering will compute a (possibly proper) superset of the dependence relation. This is the approach taken here: it will provide a conservative, but not necessarily precise, solution to the dependence problem.

Now consider (DEP-1). When developing algorithms for dependence testing, we have to keep in mind that control sets may be too large to handle or be not completely known at compile time. As a consequence, we shall use extended direction vectors instead of the control sets. Furthermore, we shall combine dependence tests for both directions, that is try to disprove $S \delta S'$ and $S' \delta S$ at the same time by considering plausible as well as implausible direction vectors for S, S'.

Condition (DEP-2) holds if the intersection of certain input and output execution sets of S and S' is non-empty; the specific pair of sets for which this is the case determines the type of the dependence. The actual tests can be easily combined for all three types of dependence by parameterizing them with the pair of subscripted variables for which (DEP-2) is to be examined. Thus the dependence type is not relevant, and we can restrict our discussion to a specific case without loss of generality.

The dependence problem for simple variables can be solved with methods that were developed in Chapter 3, so we restrict our discussion further by only considering subscripted variables which are admissible. Let v and v' denote such a pair of variables, which are associated with the same array:

$$v: A(f_1(\mathbf{I}), \ldots, f_d(\mathbf{I})) \in DEF(S)$$
$$v': A(f'_1(\mathbf{I}'), \ldots, f'_d(\mathbf{I}')) \in USE(S')$$

where $\mathbf{I} = (I_1, \ldots, I_n)$ and $\mathbf{I}' = (I'_1, \ldots, I'_{n'})$ $d \geqslant 1$, $f_r: [S] \to \mathbb{Z}$ and $f'_r: [S'] \to \mathbb{Z}$ for all $r \in [1:d]$.

The problem can now be stated as follows:

Are there $\mathbf{i}, \mathbf{i}'$, such that $(\mathbf{i}, \mathbf{i}') \in [S, S']$ or $(\mathbf{i}', \mathbf{i}) \in [S', S]$ and $f_r(\mathbf{i}) = f'_r(\mathbf{i}')$ for all $r \in [1:d]$?

This is still too general. One of the reasons for this is that we still allow arbitrary subscript expressions in the do-variables. Another reason is the occurrence of the control sets in the problem formulation. Furthermore, we shall only consider one-dimensional arrays for the time being (multi-dimensional arrays are treated in Section 4.6). In the following we therefore:

(1)   restrict subscript expressions to be linear functions in the do-variables,

(2)   assume $d = 1$, and

(3)   examine the existence of solutions for the equation under the constraints of a region – which is determined by the loop bounds – and a given direction vector θ.

This leads us to the final formulation of our problem. Remember that our notation and terminology are chiefly based on Definition 4.4 and Program 4.3. Let $v \equiv A(f(\mathbf{I}))$ and $v' \equiv A(f'(\mathbf{I}'))$. The functions f and f' are admissible and moreover satisfy the **linearity condition** (LIN):

$$(\text{LIN}) \begin{cases} f(\mathbf{I}) = a_0 + \sum_{1 \leq j \leq n} a_j I_j \\ f'(\mathbf{I}') = b_0 + \sum_{1 \leq j \leq n'} b_j I'_j \end{cases}$$

where all a_j $(0 \leq j \leq n)$ and all b_j $(0 \leq j \leq n')$ are integer constants.

The **dependence system** for S, S', v, v' and a direction vector $\theta \in dir([S] \times [S'])$ consists of the **dependence equation** (DEQ), the **region** (REG), and the **constraint** (CST), as given by:

(DEQ) $a_0 + \sum_{1 \leq j \leq n} a_j i_j - (b_0 + \sum_{1 \leq j \leq n'} b_j i'_j) = 0$

(REG) $i_j \in [T_j : U_j]$ $(1 \leq j \leq n)$
$\quad\quad\quad i'_j \in [T'_j : U'_j]$ $(1 \leq j \leq n')$

(CST) $i_j \, \theta_j \, i'_j$ $(1 \leq j \leq m)$

Our problem is then to determine whether there exist i_j $(1 \leq j \leq n)$ and i'_j $(1 \leq j \leq n')$ such that (DEQ), (REG), and (CST) are all satisfied.

We conclude this section by returning to a point discussed above: that we combine dependence tests for both directions. We begin with a definition.

Definition 4.25   Let θ denote a proper direction vector. Then the **inverse** of θ, denoted by θ^{-1}, is defined as $\theta^{-1} := (\theta_1^{-1}, \ldots, \theta_m^{-1})$, where '$<$'$^{-1}$:= '$>$', '$>$'$^{-1}$:= '$<$', and '$=$'$^{-1}$:= '$=$'. If M is a set of direction vectors, then $M^{-1} := \{\theta^{-1} : \theta \in M\}$.   ∎

Lemma 4.5   Assume that $S' \, \delta\theta \, S$ with $\theta \neq (=^m)$. Then (DEQ) can be solved in (REG) for S and S' under the constraint θ^{-1}.   ∎

Proof   Let $S'(i') \, \delta \, S(i)$, and $\theta = dir(i',i)$. Then the equation $f'(i') - f(i) = 0$ can be solved in the region (REG) with constraint θ, where θ is plausible for (S',S). However, then clearly $f(i) - f'(i') = 0$ in the same region and under the constraint θ^{-1}. This completes the proof.   ∎

The lemma shows that we can test for a dependence from S' to S by examining a dependence equation (DEQ) associated with (S,S') in a region (REG) under a constraint θ^{-1}, where θ is plausible for (S',S) and therefore θ^{-1} is implausible for (S,S'). This will be utilized in the dependence tests discussed later.

We shall develop three tests that examine the dependence of one-dimensional subscripted variables. The first test – the separability test – is only applicable if at most one do-variable occurs in the dependence equation (see Section 4.5.1). The separability test is **exact**, that is it yields a sufficient and necessary condition for dependence. If it cannot be applied, then the gcd test is attempted (Section 4.5.2). The gcd test provides a sufficient and necessary condition for the existence of a solution to the dependence equation. If no solution exists, then there can be no dependence. Otherwise, we know that the equation can be solved, but not whether it can be solved in the region (REG) under the constraint (CST). So we do not assume dependence in this case, but instead execute a third test, the Banerjee test (Section 4.5.3). This test provides a sufficient and necessary condition for the existence of a real solution of the dependence equation in the region (REG) under the constraint (CST). If there is no solution, no dependence can exist. Otherwise, we know that a real solution exists, but we do not know whether there is an integer solution. In the absence of additional information, we must assume dependence. The gcd test and the Banerjee test are **approximate** tests, since they yield only a necessary condition for dependence.

These tests will subsequently be applied to multidimensional subscripted variables by performing a separate test in each dimension (Section 4.6).

In order to develop dependence tests, we need a number of mathematical results involving linear diophantine equations and bounds of linear functions. Readers familiar with this material may proceed directly to Section 4.5.

4.4.2   Linear diophantine equations

The purpose of this section is to determine conditions under which linear diophantine equations can be solved. We begin by defining the greatest common divisor, characterizing its properties, and describing Euclid's algorithm.

Let a, b be integer numbers ($b \neq 0$). We say that b **divides** a, written $b|a$, iff there is an integer x such that $a = bx$. The **greatest common divisor** (gcd) of $n \geqslant 1$ integer numbers $a_1, \ldots, a_n$, which are not all 0, is defined as: $gcd(a_1, \ldots, a_n) := max\{b: b|a_j$ for all $j \in [1{:}n]\}$. So $gcd(4,6) = 2$, $gcd(12,-18) = 6$, and $gcd(15031,32768) = 1$. The two lemmata below specify elementary properties of the gcd.

Lemma 4.6 Let a, b, and q be integer numbers (a,b not both 0). Then:

(1) $gcd(a) = gcd(a,0) = a$ $(a \neq 0)$
(2) $gcd(a,1) = 1$
(3) $gcd(a,b) = gcd(b,a)$
(4) $gcd(a,b) = gcd(a,-b)$
(5) $gcd(a,b) = gcd(a,b + aq)$
(6) $gcd(qa,qb) = |q|.gcd(a,b)$ $(q \neq 0)$
(7) $gcd(a/g,b/g) = 1$, where $g = gcd(a,b)$ ■

Lemma 4.7 Let $n \geqslant 2$ and $a_1, \ldots, a_n$ be integer numbers, not all of which are 0. $gcd(a_1, \ldots, a_n) = gcd(a_1, gcd(a_2, \ldots, a_n))$.   ■

Theorem 4.3 Let $n \geqslant 2$ and $a_1, \ldots, a_n$ be integer numbers, not all of which are 0, and let $g := gcd(a_1, \ldots, a_n)$. Then there exist integers $v_1, \ldots, v_n$, such that

$$g = min\{z: z = \sum_{1 \leqslant j \leqslant n \atop v_j \in \mathbb{Z}} a_j v_j \wedge z > 0\}$$

■

Proof We shall consider only $n = 2$: the general case will follow easily via an inductive argument. Assume that a, b are two integer numbers which are not both 0.

Let $M := \{ax + by: \quad x,y \in \mathbb{Z}\}$,   and $z_0 := min\{z: z \in M \wedge z > 0\}$. z_0 clearly exists; let $z_0 = au + bv$. We now show that z_0 is a common divisor of a and b.

If z_0 does not divide a, then there are integers q and r with $a = z_0 q + r$ and $0 < r < z_0$. However, then $r = a - z_0 q = a(1 - uq) + b(-vq)$, and thus $r \in M$. This contradicts the definition of z_0. Similarly, we can see that $z_0|b$, and therefore z_0 is a common divisor of a and b.

Let $g := gcd(a,b)$ denote the greatest common divisor of a and b. By definition g divides a and b; thus $g|z_0$. As g cannot be less than z_0, we obtain $g = z_0$, which concludes the proof.   ■

Corollary

(1)   The gcd of $a_1, \ldots, a_n$ can be represented in the form

$$g = \sum_{1 \leqslant j \leqslant n} a_j v_j$$

(2) g is uniquely determined by the a_j $(1 \leqslant j \leqslant n)$.

(3)   If $t|a_j$ for all j, then $t|g$.   ■

Note that the factors v_j in the representation of g specified in Corollary (1) are not determined uniquely by the a_j $(1 \leqslant j \leqslant n)$: for example, $gcd(2,3) = 1$, and $1 = 2 \cdot (-1) + 3 \cdot 1 = 2 \cdot 2 + 3 \cdot (-1)$.

We now describe Euclid's algorithm for the computation of the greatest common divisor of two natural numbers a and b $(b \neq 0)$. The algorithm constructs the **remainder sequence** $(a_0, a_1, \ldots, a_m)$, where $m \geqslant 1$, $a_0 = a$, $a_1 = b$, a_{j+1} $(1 \leqslant j \leqslant m-1)$ is the remainder of the division a_{j-1}/a_j $(a_j \neq 0)$, and $a_m|a_{m-1}$. Then $gcd(a,b) = a_m$. In the extended form given below, the algorithm also yields the coefficients for a representation of the gcd as given in Theorem 4.3.

ALGORITHM 4.1: Euclid's algorithm – extended version

Input $a,b \in \mathbb{N}_0$, $b \neq 0$.

Output $g,x,y \in \mathbb{Z}$, where $g = gcd(a,b)$, and $g = ax + by$.

Method

```
begin x₀ := y₁ := 1; x₁ := y₀ := 0; a₀ := a; a₁ := b; j := 1;  /* Initialization */
    while ¬(aⱼ|aⱼ₋₁) do
        q := aⱼ₋₁ div aⱼ;  /* q is the (truncated) quotient of aⱼ₋₁ and aⱼ */
        aⱼ₊₁ := aⱼ₋₁ mod aⱼ;    //* A₁: ⊢aⱼ₋₁ = aⱼq + aⱼ₊₁, with 0 < aⱼ₊₁ < aⱼ *//
        xⱼ₊₁ := xⱼ₋₁ - q * xⱼ;
        yⱼ₊₁ := yⱼ₋₁ - q * yⱼ;
        j := j + 1    //* A₂: ⊢axⱼ + byⱼ = aⱼ *//
    end while;
    //* aⱼ|aⱼ₋₁ *//
    g := aⱼ;
    x := xⱼ;
    y := yⱼ
end
```
    ■

Example 4.14

We apply the algorithm to the numbers $a = 4235$, $b = 728$. The table below shows the value sequences computed by the algorithm; the value given for q is the value computed in iteration j. We obtain $g = 7$, $x = -11$, and $y = 64$.

j	a_j	q	x_j	y_j
0	4235	–	1	0
1	728	5	0	1
2	595	1	1	-5
3	133	4	-1	6
4	63	2	5	-29
5	7	–	-11	64

In order to prove the correctness of the algorithm, we have to examine the assertions A_1 and A_2. While A_1 is obvious, the correctness of A_2 can be shown by induction: A_2 is trivially true for $j = 0,1$; if we assume that it is true for $j - 1$ and j ($j \geqslant 1$), then the correctness for $j + 1$ follows easily from the assignments in the while-loop.

Assertion A_1 implies that the remainder sequence a_j ($j \geqslant 0$) is finite, and thus the algorithm terminates. Let m denote the final value of j. From $gcd(a_j, a_{j+1}) = gcd(a_{j+1}, a_{j+2})$ for all j with $0 \leqslant j \leqslant m - 2$ and $gcd(a_{m-1}, a_m) = a_m$ we obtain $a_m = gcd(a,b)$; and A_2, applied to $j = m$, yields $ax_m + by_m = a_m$.

Definition 4.26   A **linear diophantine equation** is an equation of the form

$$\sum_{1 \leqslant j \leqslant n} a_j x_j = c$$

where $n \geqslant 1$, $c \in \mathbb{Z}$, $a_j \in \mathbb{Z}$ for all j, not all a_j are equal to 0, and the x_j are integer variables ($1 \leqslant j \leqslant n$). ∎

A diophantine equation may or may not have solutions. Consider for example $x + 4y = 1$. This is a linear diophantine equation in the two variables x and y; it can be solved with $x = 5$, $y = -1$. Actually, infinitely many solutions exist for this equation. On the other hand, the equation $5x - 10y = 2$ has no solution, as every substitution of integer values for x and y yields a multiple of 5 at the left-hand side.

The criterion for the existence of a solution is very simple: a solution exists iff the gcd of the coefficients on the left-hand side divides the right-hand side. For our first equation, we have $gcd(1,4) = 1|1$; for the second equation, we obtain $gcd(5,-10) = 5$, which does not divide 2. Furthermore, if one solution exists, then there are infinitely many. We prove this for $n = 2$ and specify the set of all solutions explicitly in this case.

The following theorem gives a sufficient and necessary condition for the existence of solutions.

Theorem 4.4   Let

$$\sum_{1 \le j \le n} a_j x_j = c$$

be a linear diophantine equation, and $g = gcd(a_1, \ldots, a_n)$. The equation has a solution iff $g|c$.   ∎

> ***Proof***   We consider only the case $n = 2$: the general case can be shown by induction. Let $ax + by = c$ denote a linear diophantine equation, and $g = gcd(a,b)$.
>
> Assume first that $g|c$. Then there are integers u,v,c' such that $g = au + bv$ and $gc' = c$. This yields $gc' = c = a(uc') + b(vc')$: the diophantine equation has a solution $(uc',vc') = (uc/g,vc/g)$.
>
> If the equation has a solution (x_0,y_0), then $ax_0 + by_0 = c$. From $g|a$ and $g|b$ we can then immediately conclude $g|c$.   ∎

The proof of the theorem for $n = 2$ has shown us that we can use the extended Euclidean algorithm to find a solution for a diophantine equation. We will see below that the knowledge of a single solution suffices to determine the set of all solutions. In order to prove this, we need the following simple lemma.

Lemma 4.8   Let a, b, c, d be integer numbers such that $ab = cd$ and $gcd(a,c) = 1$. Then $a|d$ and $c|b$.   ∎

Theorem 4.5   Let $ax + by = c$ denote a linear diophantine equation, assume that $g := gcd(a,b)|c$, and that u, v are integer numbers with $g = au + bv$. Then the set of all solutions (x_t,y_t), $t \in \mathbb{Z}$, of the equation is given as follows:

$$x_t = uc/g + tb/g$$
$$y_t = vc/g - ta/g$$ ∎

Proof From the proof of Theorem 4.4 we know that $(x_0, y_0) = (uc/g, vc/g)$ is a solution, that is $auc/g + bvc/g = c$. So we can see immediately that each pair (x_t, y_t), $t \in \mathbb{Z}$, is also a solution of the equation.

Now let (x', y') denote any solution. Then $ax' + by' = ax_0 + by_0$, which yields (E) $(a/g)(x' - x_0) = (-b/g)(y' - y_0)$. From $gcd(a/g, b/g) = 1$ and Lemma 4.8 we obtain $(a/g)|(y' - y_0)$ and $(b/g)|(x' - x_0)$. Now define the integer $t := -(y' - y_0)/(a/g)$. Then from (E) we obtain $x' = x_0 + tb/g$ and $y' = y_0 - ta/g$, that is $(x', y') = (x_t, y_t)$. Thus every solution of the equation can be represented in the form specified in the theorem. ∎

The following example illustrates an application of the theory developed above to the solution of dependence problems.

Example 4.15

We want to examine the loop

```
DO I = 10, 20
  S:    A(2 * I - 1) = ...
        ...
  S':   ...            = A(4 * I - 7)
END DO
```

for dependences between S and S'. If dependences exist, then there must be values x, y of I, such that the variable accessed by statement instance $S(x)$ is the same as the one accessed by $S'(y)$. This means that there must exist a solution to the dependence equation $2x - 1 = 4y - 7$.

Let us first ask whether $S\,\delta_\infty\,S'$ can hold: if so, then $x = y$, for which $x = y = 3$ is the only solution. As this value is outside the region $10 \leqslant x, y \leqslant 20$, there is no loop-independent dependence.

Let us now consider the general case. If we write the equation in the form $2x - 4y = -6$ we see that $g := gcd(2, -4) = 2 | -6$; so there exist solutions. Furthermore, the equation $2u - 4v = g$ can be solved by $(u, v) = (3, 1)$; and by Theorem 4.5 the set of all solutions is $(x_t, y_t) = (-9 - 2t, -3 - t)$. However, the existence of a solution for the linear diophantine equation is not sufficient for the existence of a dependence: we need a solution that satisfies additional criteria. In our case, this means the following:

(1)   For $S\,\delta\,S'$ to hold, we must have $10 \leqslant x < y \leqslant 20$. A simple analysis shows that this cannot be satisfied.

(2)   For $S' \delta S$ to hold, x and y must satisfy $10 \leq y < x \leq 20$. There are actually two solutions that meet this additional condition, namely $(x,y) = (17,10)$ and $(x,y) = (19,11)$. Thus we have $S'(10) \delta^a S(17)$, caused by a common access to A(33), and $S'(11) \delta^a S(19)$, caused by an access to A(37).

These are all the dependences that exist in the loop.

Example 4.16

Now consider the loop

```
DO I = 30, 100
  S:    A(3 * I - 5) = ...
        ...
  S':   ...          = A(6 * I)
END DO
```

The dependence equation is $3x - 6y = 5$. As $gcd(3,6) = 3$ does not divide 5, there cannot be a dependence between S and S'.

We have seen that the methods developed above give us a necessary condition for the existence of a dependence: if we can show that the dependence equation has no solution, then we know that there cannot be a dependence. This is the basis of the gcd test described in Section 4.5.2. On the other hand, the existence of a solution does not automatically imply a dependence, as we require the solution to satisfy additional criteria.

   The above approach can be generalized to one diophantine equation in more than two variables and to systems of such equations. We do not discuss this here; for details see Banerjee (1988).

4.4.3   Bounds of linear functions

In this section we deal with another aspect of the dependence problem by determining lower und upper bounds for linear functions in a connected region of $\mathbb{R}^n$. The bounds will be expressed in terms of the positive and negative parts of a real number, which are defined as follows.

Definition 4.27   Let $z \in \mathbb{R}$ be arbitrarily chosen. Then:

(1) $z^+ := \textbf{if } z > 0 \textbf{ then } z \textbf{ else } 0 \textbf{ fi}$

(2) $z^- := $ **if** $z < 0$ **then** $-z$ **else** 0 **fi**

z^+ and z^- are respectively called the **positive** and the **negative part** of z.   ∎

The following lemma characterizes some important properties of z^+ and z^-.

Lemma 4.9   Let z be a real number.

(1) $z^+ \geqslant 0$ and $z^- \geqslant 0$
(2) $z^+ - z^- = z$
(3) $(-z)^+ = z^-$
(4) $(-z)^- = z^+$ ∎

We now proceed by determining lower and upper bounds for linear functions in rectangular regions. In the first step, we find bounds for the function ax in the interval $[T,U]$; this can then be immediately generalized to arbitrary linear functions in n-dimensional rectangular regions. Although we are eventually interested in functions with integer coefficients that are defined on regions of $\mathbb{Z}^n$ (only such functions can be derived from a dependence equation), the theory developed here relates to real-valued functions on regions of $\mathbb{R}^n$.

Lemma 4.10   Let T,U be numbers such that $T \leqslant U$.

(1)   *min* $\{ax : T \leqslant x \leqslant U\} = a^+ T - a^- U$
(2)   *max* $\{ax : T \leqslant x \leqslant U\} = a^+ U - a^- T$

> **Proof**   We prove (1); (2) is similar. Note that $a^+ T \leqslant a^+ x$, since $a^+ \geqslant 0$ and $T \leqslant x$. Similarly, $-a^- U \leqslant -a^- x$, as $-a^- \leqslant 0$ and $x \leqslant U$. From these inequalities and (2) in Lemma 4.9 we obtain: $a^+ T - a^- U \leqslant a^+ x - a^- x = (a^+ - a^-)x = ax$.
>   Furthermore, if $a \geqslant 0$, then $a^+ T = a^+ T - a^- U = aT$, that is the function ax assumes the lower bound for $x = T$. Similarly, if $a < 0$, then $a^+ T - a^- U = aU$; that is, the function assumes the lower bound for $x = U$. This concludes the proof.   ∎

The following theorem is a straightforward generalization of the lemma.

Theorem 4.6   Let $n \geqslant 1$, a_j, T_j, U_j be numbers with $T_j \leqslant U_j$ for all $j \in [1:n]$, and

$$\sum_{1 \leqslant j \leqslant n} a_j x_j$$

denote a linear function in n variables. Then:

(1) $min\{ \sum_{1 \leqslant j \leqslant n} a_j x_j \colon (x_1, \ldots, x_n) \in \underset{1 \leqslant j \leqslant n}{\text{\Large$\times$}} [T_j \colon U_j]\} = \sum_{1 \leqslant j \leqslant n} (a_j^+ T_j - a_j^- U_j)$

(2) $max\{ \sum_{1 \leqslant j \leqslant n} a_j x_j \colon (x_1, \ldots, x_n) \in \underset{1 \leqslant j \leqslant n}{\text{\Large$\times$}} [T_j \colon U_j]\} = \sum_{1 \leqslant j \leqslant n} (a_j^+ U_j - a_j^- T_j)$ ∎

Let us now look at an example that applies this theorem to a dependence problem.

Example 4.17

Consider the loop

```
DO I = 0, 10
  S:   A(3 * I - 30) = ...
       ...
  S':  A(4 * I + 1) = ...
END DO
```

We want to test for an output dependence involving S and S'. The dependence equation is $3x - 4y = 31$, which can be solved, as $gcd(3,4) = 1|31$. If we want to rule out dependence, we could determine the set of all solutions and examine it under the constraints $0 \leqslant x,y \leqslant 10$ as in Example 4.15. Here, we adopt a different method. The application of Theorem 4.6 to the function $3x - 4y$ yields ($a_1 = 3, a_2 = -4, T_1 = T_2 = 0, U_1 = U_2 = 10$):

$$-40 \leqslant 3x - 4y \leqslant 30 \qquad \text{for } 0 \leqslant x,y \leqslant 10.$$

From this we can immediately conclude that the dependence equation cannot be solved.

Example 4.18

Now consider the loop

```
DO I = 0, 10
  S:    A(7 * I + 20) = ...
        ...
  S':   A(2 * I + 3)  = ...
END DO
```

We want to solve the same problem as above. The dependence equation is $7x - 2y = -17$, and, as before, the computation of the $gcd(7,2)$ does not exclude dependence. If we now apply Theorem 4.6, we obtain:

$$-20 \leqslant 7x - 2y \leqslant 70 \text{ for } 0 \leqslant x,y \leqslant 10.$$

This means that the equation can be solved in the region. Nevertheless, there is no dependence between S and S', as only real solutions (for example $(x,y) = (0,8.5)$) but no integer solutions exist in the region.

The examples have shown how we can utilize the knowledge of the bounds of a linear function to disprove dependence. Note that we have derived only a necessary condition for dependence, as we do not know whether a solution that exists within a given region is an integer solution. This technique will be used to develop the Banerjee test (see Section 4.5.3). We need one more lemma for the proof of this test.

Lemma 4.11 Let $f(x,y) = ax + by$ denote a linear function, and $U \geqslant 0$ a number.

(1) $min\{ax + by: 0 \leqslant y \leqslant x \leqslant U\} = -(a - b^-)^- U$

(2) $max\{ax + by: 0 \leqslant y \leqslant x \leqslant U\} = (a + b^+)^+ U$ ∎

Proof We prove (1) and leave (2) to the reader. The application of Lemma 4.10 to the function, letting $T = 0$, $U = x$, yields $by \geqslant -b^- x$, from which we obtain $ax + by \geqslant (a - b^-)x$. Now we distinguish three cases and prove the inequality separately for each case. Let MIN denote the value of $-(a - b^-)^- U$.

- Case 1: $b \geqslant 0$
  $b \geqslant 0$ implies $b^- = 0$, yielding $(a - b^-)x = ax \geqslant -a^- U = -(a - b^-)^- U$. If $a > 0$, then $MIN = f(0,0)$, otherwise $MIN = f(U,0)$.
- Case 2: $b < 0$ and $a \geqslant |b|$
  Here, we have $a - b^- \geqslant 0$, from which we obtain $(a - b^-)x \geqslant 0 = -(a - b^-)^- U$. Furthermore, $MIN = f(0,0)$.

- Case 3: $b < 0$ and $a < |b|$

  In this case, $a - b^- < 0$. Then, $(a - b^-)x \geqslant (a - b^-)U =$ $-(a - b^-)^- U$. Here, $MIN = f(U,U)$.

This completes the proof of the lemma.   ■

We have considered the bounds of linear functions in rectangular regions. These results can be used to analyze dependences in loops whose bounds are constant. In order to handle loop bounds that are functions in the do-variables of enclosing loops, we would have to examine triangular and trapezoidal regions. We do not pursue this topic further. Note, however, that Lemma 4.11 handles the case of a triangular region; this is used by Banerjee (1988) as a starting point for an elimination algorithm that determines bounds for arbitrary n-dimensional trapezoidal regions. In the general case, these bounds are, however, no longer values that the function may assume.

4.5   Dependence tests

We consider below the dependence system described in Section 4.4.1 for statements S and S_1' and use the notation introduced there. In particular, we assume that the functions f and f' satisfy the linearity condition:

$$(\text{LIN})\begin{cases} f(\mathbf{I}) = a_0 + \sum_{1 \leqslant j \leqslant n} a_j I_j \\ f'(\mathbf{I}') = b_0 + \sum_{1 \leqslant j \leqslant n'} b_j I_j' \end{cases}$$

4.5.1   The separability test

The separability test is an exact test that can be applied iff the dependence equation contains at most one do-variable. For example, the test is applicable if $f(\mathrm{I},\mathrm{J}) = 3*\mathrm{J}-2$ and $f'(\mathrm{I},\mathrm{J}) = 5*\mathrm{J}-7$, or if $f(\mathrm{I},\mathrm{J}) = \mathrm{I} + 1$ and $f'(\mathrm{I},\mathrm{J}) = 2*\mathrm{I} + 9$. It would, however, not be applicable in the case $f(\mathrm{I},\mathrm{J}) = \mathrm{I} + 1, f'(\mathrm{I},\mathrm{J}) = \mathrm{J} - 1$.

As well as yielding a necessary and sufficient condition for dependence, the separability test also computes the minimum and maximum dependence distances, if a dependence exists. The restriction for the applicability of the test, although it may seem severe, is frequently satisfied in real programs; thus its practical relevance is very high.

The separability test can be applied iff the separability condition, as defined below, is fulfilled:

Definition 4.28: Separability condition

$$(\text{SEP})\quad \exists k \in [1{:}m]: \forall j \in [1{:}n]: \ j \neq k \implies a_j = 0 \ \wedge$$
$$\forall j \in [1{:}n']: j \neq k \implies b_j = 0 \qquad ■$$

Assume that (SEP) is fulfilled. Then:

$$f(\mathbf{I}) = a_0 + a_k I_k \text{ and}$$
$$f'(\mathbf{I}') = b_0 + b_k I'_k$$

If we set $a := a_k$, $b := b_k$, $T_k := T$, and $U_k := U$, then we have to solve the following dependence system:

$$(\text{SEP–SYS}) \begin{cases} (\text{SEP–DEQ}) & ax - by = b_0 - a_0 \\ (\text{SEP–REG}) & x, y \in [T{:}U] \\ (\text{SEP–CST}) & x \, \theta \, y \end{cases}$$

where θ is a direction vector element $\theta \in \{<,=,>,*\}$ (see Section 4.4.1).

Theorem 4.7: Separability test   Assume that the separability condition (SEP) holds and T,U are constants ($T < U$). Then S and S' are dependent iff the value of *DEPENDENCE*, as specified below, is **true**. If S and S' are dependent, then *SOLUTION_SET* := $\{(x,y)|(x,y)$ satisfy (SEP–SYS)$\}$ and *MIN_DIST*, *MAX_DIST*, which respectively represent the minimum and maximum dependence distance, are as given below:

(1)   If $a = b$ or $a = 0$ or $b = 0$, then we speak of **strong separability**. Table 4.2 summarizes the relevant information as follows:

   (i)   *Existence of a dependence*

   DEPENDENCE is true iff a, b and θ satisfy any one of the pairs of equations $p_1(a,b)$ and $p_2(a,b)$ in Table 4.2.

   (ii)   *Characterization of a dependence*

   Assume that S and S' are dependent. Then:
   SOLUTION_SET := $\{(x,y)| \quad T \leqslant x,y \leqslant U \quad \wedge \quad p_3(x,y)\}$.
   MIN_DIST and *MAX_DIST* are given explicitly.

(2)   Let $a \neq b$, $a \neq 0$, and $b \neq 0$ (we call this case **weak separability**). Then S and S' are dependent iff $\gcd(a,b)|(b_0 - a_0)$ and Algorithm 4.2 yields *DEPENDENCE* = **true**. If a dependence exists, then *SOLUTION_SET*, *MIN_DIST* and *MAX_DIST* are determined by Algorithm 4.2.   ∎

Proof   The conditions under (1) and (2) cover all possible different cases for a and b.

Table 4.2 Test for strong separability.

Assertion $p_1(a,b)$	θ	Dependence condition $p_2(a,b)$	Solution condition $p_3(x,y)$	MIN_DIST	MAX_DIST
I: $a = b = 0$					
	<	$a_0 = b_0$	true	1	$U - T$
	=	$a_0 = b_0$	true	0	0
	>	$a_0 = b_0$	true	1	$U - T$
	*	$a_0 = b_0$	true	0	$U - T$
II: $a = b \neq 0 \wedge$ $a\|(b_0 - a_0)$					
	<	$1 \leq w \leq U - T$	$y - x = w$	w	w
	=	$a_0 = b_0$	$y - x = w$	0	0
	>	$1 \leq -w \leq U - T$	$y - x = w$	$-w$	$-w$
	*	$0 \leq \|w\| \leq U - T$	$y - x = w$	$\|w\|$	$\|w\|$
III: $a \neq 0, b = 0 \wedge$ $a\|(b_0 - a_0)$					
	<	$T \leq -w \leq U - 1$	$x = -w$	1	$U + w$
	=	$T \leq -w \leq U$	$x = -w$	0	0
	>	$T + 1 \leq -w \leq U$	$x = -w$	1	$-w - T$
	*	$T \leq -w \leq U$	$x = -w$	0	$max(U + w, -w - T)$
IV: $a = 0, b \neq 0 \wedge$ $b\|(b_0 - a_0)$					
	<	$T + 1 \leq s \leq U$	$y = s$	1	$s - T$
	=	$T \leq s \leq U$	$y = s$	0	0
	>	$T \leq s \leq U - 1$	$y = s$	1	$U - s$
	*	$T \leq s \leq U$	$y = s$	0	$max(s - T, U - s)$

Notation: $w = -(b_0 - a_0)/a$ $(a \neq 0)$; $s = -(b_0 - a_0)/b$ $(b \neq 0)$.

The information in Table 4.2 can be easily obtained by analyzing the four possible cases (I through IV) for $p_1(a,b)$ under the condition of strong separability.

Now consider (2), and let $g = gcd(a,b)$. From Theorem 4.4 we know that $g\|(b_0 - a_0)$ is a sufficient and necessary condition for the solution of (SEP-DEQ). If $g\|(b_0 - a_0)$, then Algorithm 4.2 determines a sufficient and necessary condition for the existence of a solution to (SEP-SYS) within the region (SEP-REG) under the constraint (SEP-CST). The reason why is explained in the comments given in the algorithm. ∎

ALGORITHM 4.2: Test for weak separability

Input (1) Integer numbers a and b such that $a \neq b$, $a \neq 0$, $b \neq 0$, and $g | (b_0 - a_0)$, where $g = gcd(a, -b)$.

(2) Integers u and v such that $g = au - bv$.

(3) Direction vector element $\theta \in \{<, =, >, *\}$.

Output (1) A sufficient and necessary condition for dependence between S and S', expressed by the value of the boolean variable *DEPENDENCE*.

(2) If S and S' are dependent, then *SOLUTION_SET*, *MIN_DIST*, and *MAX_DIST*.

Method

```
/* Auxiliary function */
function diff(t): integer;
begin
diff := v * (b₀ - a₀)/g - u * (b₀ - a₀)/g + t * (a - b)/g
end diff;
/* MAIN PROGRAM */
begin
```
$x_0 := u * (b_0 - a_0)/g;$
$y_0 := v * (b_0 - a_0)/g;$

/* By Theorem 4.5, (x_0, y_0) is a solution of the dependence equation. The general solution is the set of all pairs $(x_t = x_0 + tb/g, y_t = y_0 + ta/g)$, where $t \in \mathbb{Z}$. We now construct lower and upper bounds for t from $T \leqslant x_t, y_t \leqslant U$ */

$X_1 := (T - x_0) * g/b;$ /* derived from $x_t \geqslant T$ */
$X_2 := (U - x_0) * g/b;$ /* derived from $x_t \leqslant U$ */
$Y_1 := (T - y_0) * g/a;$ /* derived from $y_t \geqslant T$ */
$Y_2 := (U - y_0) * g/a;$ /* derived from $y_t \leqslant U$ */

if $b > 0$ **then** $LWB := X_1;$ $UPB := X_2$ **else** $LWB := X_2;$ $UPB := X_1$ **fi**;
if $a > 0$ **then** $LWB := max(LWB, Y_1);$ $UPB := min(UPB, Y_2)$
         else $LWB := max(LWB, Y_2);$ $UPB := min(UPB, Y_1)$
fi;

/* Construction of bounds from the direction vector */

if $\theta = '<'$
   then $Z := (y_0 - x_0 - 1) * g/(b - a);$ /* derived from $x_t \leqslant y_t - 1$ */
      if $b > a$ **then** $UPB := min(UPB, Z)$ **else** $LWB := max(LWB, Z)$ **fi**
orif $\theta = '='$
   then $Z := (y_0 - x_0) * g/(b - a);$ /* derived from $x_t = y_t$ */
     $UPB := min(UPB, Z);$ $LWB := max(LWB, Z)$
orif $\theta = '>'$
   then $Z := (y_0 - x_0 + 1) * g/(b - a);$ /* derived from $x_t \geqslant y_t + 1$ */
      if $a > b$ **then** $UPB := min(UPB, Z)$ **else** $LWB := max(LWB, Z)$ **fi**
fi;

$LWB := CEIL(LWB)$;
$UPB := FLOOR(UPB)$;
$DEPENDENCE := (UPB - LWB) \geq 0$;   /* This is a necessary and sufficient
condition for the existence of a
dependence between S and S' */

if $DEPENDENCE$
   then $SOLUTION\_SET := \{(x_t, y_t): x_t = x_0 + t * b/g, \, y_t = y_0 + t * a/g,$
        $LWB \leq t \leq UPB\}$;

/* We now compute the minimum and maximum dependence distances: let
$diff(t) := y_t - x_t = y_0 - x_0 + t(a - b)/g$ for all y_t, x_t in the solution set. $diff(t)$ is
a linear function in t, and the lower and upper bounds of t are given by LWB
and UPB, respectively. Let $diff(t) = At + B$, where $A = (a - b)/g$, and
$B = y_0 - x_0$. Now we can apply Lemma 4.10 and obtain:
$A^+ LWB - A^- UPB + B \leq diff(t) \leq A^+ UPB - A^- LWB + B$. If $A > 0$, that is
$a > b$, then we obtain $A \cdot LWB + B = diff(LWB) \leq diff(t) \leq A \cdot UPB + B =$
$diff(UPB)$. If $A < 0$, then $A \cdot UPB + B = diff(UPB) \leq diff(t) \leq A \cdot LWB + B =$
$diff(LWB)$. The rest of the algorithm is then obvious. */

if $\theta = '='$
   then $MIN\_DIST := MAX\_DIST := 0$
   else
      $W_1 := diff(LWB)$;
      $W_2 := diff(UPB)$;
      if $(a > b \wedge \theta = '<') \vee (a < b \wedge \theta = '>')$
         then $MIN\_DIST := |W_1|$; $MAX\_DIST := |W_2|$
      orif $(a > b \wedge \theta = '>') \vee (a < b \wedge \theta = '<')$
         then $MIN\_DIST := |W_2|$; $MAX\_DIST := |W_1|$
      else /* $\theta = '*'$ */
         $MIN\_DIST := MIN(|W_1|, |W_2|)$;
         $MAX\_DIST := MAX(|W_1|, |W_2|)$
      fi
  fi
fi
end
■

Lemma 4.12   Suppose that S, S' are statements such that the separability condition is satisfied for $k \in [1:m]$, and the separability test yields $DEPENDENCE =$ **true** when applied to S and S' and a direction vector element $\theta \in \{<, =, >\}$. Then:

(1)   If $\theta = \,'<'$, then

   (i) $S \, \delta_r \, S'$ for all $r \in [1:k]$, and

   (ii) $S' \, \delta_r \, S$ for all $r \in [1:k - 1]$

(2)   If $\theta = $ '=', then

   (i) $S \, \delta_r \, S'$ for all $r \in [1:m] - \{k\}$
   (ii) $S' \, \delta_r \, S$ for all $r \in [1:m] - \{k\}$, and
   (iii) $S \, \delta_\infty \, S'$ if S bef S'
       $S' \, \delta_\infty \, S$ if S' bef S

(3)   If $\theta = $ '>', then

   (i) $S \, \delta_r \, S'$ for all $r \in [1:k - 1]$, and
   (ii) $S' \, \delta_r \, S$ for all $r \in [1:k]$ ∎

Proof   We prove the lemma for (3); in all other cases it can be shown similarly.

   If dependence holds for $\theta = $ '>', then every pair of iteration vectors $\mathbf{i} \in [S]$, $\mathbf{i}' \in [S']$ where (i_k, i'_k), with $i_k > i'_k$, are arbitrarily selected from $SOLUTION\_SET$, solves the dependence equation. In particular, we can choose for $r = 1, \ldots, k - 1$ iteration vectors $\mathbf{i}_r \in [S]$, $\mathbf{i}'_r \in [S']$ such that $dir(\mathbf{i}_r, \mathbf{i}'_r) = (=, \ldots, =, <, *, \ldots, > \ldots, *)$, where the symbol '<' appears in position r, and the symbol '>' in position k. We have $\mathbf{i}_r <_r \mathbf{i}'_r$ for all $r \in [1:k - 1]$, from which we can immediately conclude $S \, \delta_r \, S'$. Thus, (i) is correct. Similarly, we can construct iteration vectors $\mathbf{i}_r \in [S]$, $\mathbf{i}'_r \in [S']$ for all $r \in [1:k]$, such that $dir(\mathbf{i}_r, \mathbf{i}'_r) = (=, \ldots, =, >, *, \ldots, *)$, where the symbol '>' appears in position r. We have $\mathbf{i}'_r <_r \mathbf{i}_r$ for all $r \in [1:k]$, from which (ii) follows.   ∎

In the following examples – and in the general algorithm for dependence testing – the separability test will also be applied to the dimensions of a multidimensional array if the separability condition is satisfied for the subscript functions in this dimension. We will then say that dependence or independence has been found 'in a dimension'. If independence is found in any dimension, then there cannot be a dependence at all.

Example 4.19

```
DO I = -100, 100
   S:   A(3) = ...
        ...
   S':  ... = A(3)
        ...
   S'': A(4) = ...
END DO
```

The separability condition is satisfied for any pair of statements and $k = 1$. For (S,S), (S,S'), (S',S), (S',S'), and (S'',S'') the dependence equation satisfies case (I) in Table 4.2 ($a = b = 0$, $b_0 - a_0 = 0$). Thus all dependences allowed by plausible direction vectors actually occur between these statement pairs; the minimum and maximum dependence distances are 0 (or 1) and 200, respectively. In contrast, there is no dependence involving S'' and any of S,S', as the dependence equation is $3 = 4$ in this case.

Example 4.20

```
DO I = 1, 100
  DO J = -1, 199
    S:    B(K - 2 * I, 3 * J) = ...
         ...
    S':   ... = B(K + M * (I - 1) - 2, 3 * J + 2)
  END DO J
END DO I
```

The subscript expressions in the first dimension are inadmissible and cannot be analyzed with our methods. Now consider the second dimension. The dependence equation is $3x - 3y = 2$, that is the separability condition is satisfied ($k = 2$) with $a = b = 3 \neq 0$ and $b_0 - a_0 = 2$. This is strong separability, but none of the cases in Table 4.2 applies; thus we have independence in dimension 2, and therefore independence between S and S'.

Example 4.21

```
DO I = 1, 100
  S:    A(2 * I + 1) = ...
       ...
  S':   ... = ... A(3 * I - 2)
END DO I
```

The separability condition is satisfied ($k = 1$), the dependence equation is $2x - 3y = -3$, and $T = 1$, $U = 100$, $a_1 = 2$, $b_1 = 3$, $b_0 - a_0 = -3$. This is weak separability. As $gcd(a_1, -b_1) = 1 | (b_0 - a_0)$, a dependence between S and S' exists iff Algorithm 4.2 yields $DEPENDENCE = $ **true**. We can choose $u = 2$ and $v = 1$ for representing the gcd. This gives us a solution $(x_0, y_0) = (-6, -3)$ to the dependence equation. The set of all solutions is (x_t, y_t) with $x_t = -6 + 3t$, and $y_t = -3 + 2t$. Algorithm 4.2 computes the values of the X_i, Y_i as $X_1 = 7/3$, $X_2 = 106/3$, $Y_1 = 2$, and $Y_2 = 103/2$. X_1 and Y_1 are lower, X_2 and Y_2 upper bounds. We now examine separately the cases $\theta = $ '<', '=', and '>'.

If $\theta = \text{'}<\text{'}$, then $Z = 2$ is an upper bound, and we obtain $LWB = 3$, $UPB = 2$. There is no t that can satisfy $LWB \leq t \leq UPB$; therefore there is no dependence in this case.

If $\theta = \text{'}=\text{'}$, then $Z = 3$ yields a solution $x_3 = 3, y_3 = 3$, and thus $S(3) \, \delta_\infty S'(3)$ is a true dependence.

If $\theta = \text{'}>\text{'}$, then $Z = 4$ is a lower bound, which yields $LWB = 4$, $UPB = 35$. For all t with $4 \leq t \leq 35$, the corresponding solutions (x_t, y_t) cause an anti dependence $S'(y_t) \, \delta \, S(x_t)$. In particular, $x_4 = 6$, $y_4 = 5$, and $x_{35} = 99$, $y_{35} = 67$ are the solutions associated with the lower and upper bounds of t, respectively. The minimum dependence distance is 1, the maximum distance is 32.

We add one final remark. The method upon which the separability test is based – the explicit representation of the solution space of a diophantine equation – can be generalized to systems of diophantine equations in arbitrarily many variables (Banerjee, 1988). Thus, this approach can in principle be extended to multidimensional arrays in arbitrarily nested loops. However, the problem of matching the solution space with the given bounds is in general computationally too expensive to be applicable to real programs.

4.5.2 The gcd test

Theorem 4.8: gcd test. For the coefficients in the dependence equation (DEQ) and a direction vector θ let $eq := \{ j \in [1{:}m] : \theta_j = \text{'}=\text{'} \}$, and $g := gcd(\{ a_j - b_j : j \in eq \}, \{ a_j : j \in [1{:}n] - eq \}, \{ b_j : j \in [1{:}n'] - eq \})$.

If $S \, \delta\theta \, S'$ or $S' \, \delta\theta^{-1} \, S$, then either g is defined and $g | (b_0 - a_0)$, or $b_0 = a_0$. ∎

Proof If $S \, \delta\theta \, S'$ or $S' \, \delta\theta^{-1} \, S$, then (DEQ) can be solved under the constraint θ, that is there exist iteration vectors $\mathbf{i} \in [S]$, $\mathbf{i}' \in [S']$ such that:

$$a_0 + \sum_{1 \leq j \leq n} a_j i_j = b_0 + \sum_{1 \leq j \leq n'} b_j i'_j$$

where $i_j = i'_j$ iff $j \in eq$. From this we obtain:

(E) $\displaystyle \sum \{ (a_j - b_j) i_j : j \in eq \} + \sum \{ a_j i_j : j \in [1{:}n] - eq \}$
$\displaystyle \qquad - \sum \{ b_j i'_j : j \in [1{:}n'] - eq \} = b_0 - a_0$

This is a diophantine equation in the $n + n' - |eq|$ variables i_j $(1 \leq j \leq n)$ and i'_j ($j \in [1:n'] - eq$). If g is defined, then the application of Theorem 4.4 to (E) yields $g|(b_0 - a_0)$. Otherwise all arguments of gcd are 0, which reduces the dependence equation to the form $a_0 = b_0$. ∎

The gcd test ignores the region associated with the dependence system; therefore, unlike the separability test, it yields only a necessary condition for dependence. The following example illustrates this.

Example 4.22

```
DO I = 0, 10
  DO J = 0, 10
  S:    A(2 * I + J) = ...
    ...
  S':   ... = A(-I + 2 * J - 21)
  END DO J
END DO I
```

We test for dependences between S and S'. The dependence equation is $2x_1 + x_2 + y_1 - 2y_2 = -21$. For an arbitrary choice of the direction vector, we obtain $g = 1|21$. However, there is no solution to the dependence equation in the region $\{0 \leq x_1, x_2, y_1, y_2 \leq 10\}$.

In Example 4.23, the gcd test is able to disprove dependence between S and S'.

Example 4.23

```
DO I = 1, N
  DO J = 2, M
  S:    A(2 * I + 2 * J) = ...
    ...
  S':   ... = A(4 * I - 6 * J + 3)
  END DO J
END DO I
```

The dependence equation is $2x_1 + 2x_2 - 4y_1 + 6y_2 = 3$. For any choice of a dependence vector, we obtain $g = 2$, which does not divide 3. Thus, no dependence can exist between S and S'.

The following lemmata are immediate consequences of Theorem 4.8, and can be used to improve the efficiency of the gcd test when testing for loop-carried and loop-independent dependencies. We first introduce some notation.

Definition 4.29   Let $c \in [1{:}m]$ be arbitrarily chosen, and assume that a_j, b_j are the coefficients of the dependence equation:

(1) $g_c := gcd(\{a_j - b_j : 1 \leqslant j < c\}, \{a_j : c \leqslant j \leqslant n\}, \{b_j : c \leqslant j \leqslant n'\})$

(2) $g_\infty := gcd(\{a_j - b_j : 1 \leqslant j \leqslant m\}, \{a_j : m < j \leqslant n\},$
$\{b_j : m < j \leqslant n'\})$.   ∎

Lemma 4.13   Let $k \in [1{:}m] \cup \{\infty\}$.

$$S \, \delta_k \, S' \text{ or } S' \, \delta_k \, S \implies g_k | (b_0 - a_0), \text{ if } g_k \text{ is defined};$$
$$\text{else } b_0 = a_0.$$
   ∎

Lemma 4.14   Let $c \in [1{:}m]$.

$$g_c | (b_0 - a_0) \implies \text{for all } r, c < r \leqslant m: g_r | (b_0 - a_0) \text{ and}$$
$$g_\infty | (b_0 - a_0).$$
   ∎

Proof   Let $c < m$. We prove the lemma for $r = c + 1$; the rest can be shown by induction. The proof for g_∞ is similar.

Let d denote any integer, and suppose that $g_c | d$ and $g_{c+1} | d$. From $g_c | a_c$, $g_c | b_c$ we obtain $g_c | (a_c - b_c)$; thus $g_c | g_{c+1}$ by Corollary (3) to Theorem 4.3 and therefore $g_c | d$, a contradiction to the assumption.   ∎

We conclude with a few pragmatic notes. Lemma 4.14 suggests we test for dependence at level k in the order $k = 1, \ldots, m, \infty$. Then, as soon as independence has been determined for k, $1 \leqslant k \leqslant m$, it follows for all r, $k < r \leqslant m$, and $r = \infty$.

If $b_0 = a_0$, then every number is a divisor of $b_0 - a_0$; the gcd test cannot establish independence in this case. The same is true if the gcd is 1: thus, if the gcd has to be determined for more than two arguments, then the process can be aborted as soon as a value of 1 is found: for example, if $gcd(a,b) = 1$, then $gcd(a,b,c) = gcd(gcd(a,b),c) = 1$. Since this occurs quite frequently, the practical applicability of the gcd test is limited.

4.5.3   The Banerjee test

Definition 4.30   Let θ denote a direction vector of length m. Then:

$$lt := \{j: j \in [1{:}m] \wedge \theta_j = \text{`<'}\}$$
$$eq := \{j: j \in [1{:}m] \wedge \theta_j = \text{`='}\}$$
$$gt := \{j: j \in [1{:}m] \wedge \theta_j = \text{`>'}\}$$
$$st := \{j: j \in [1{:}m] \wedge \theta_j = \text{`*'} \}$$ ∎

Note that each element $j \in [1{:}m]$ is in exactly one of the four sets, and $lt \cup eq \cup gt \cup st = [1{:}m]$. This subdivision will help us to formulate and prove the Banerjee test in a more manageable way.

Theorem 4.9: Banerjee test   Consider a dependence system, where all bounds T_j, U_j, T'_j, and U'_j are constant. Then $S \,\delta\theta\, S'$ or $S' \,\delta\theta^{-1}\, S$ implies:

$$\sum_{1 \leqslant j \leqslant m} LC_j + \sum_{m < j \leqslant n} LA_j + \sum_{m < j \leqslant n'} LB_j \;\leqslant\; b_0 - a_0 \;\leqslant$$
$$\sum_{1 \leqslant j \leqslant m} UC_j + \sum_{m < j \leqslant n} UA_j + \sum_{m < j \leqslant n'} UB_j$$

where:

(1) $LC_j = \begin{cases} -(a_j^- + b_j)^+ (U_j - T_j - 1) + (a_j - b_j)T_j - b_j & \text{for } j \in lt \\ -(a_j - b_j)^- (U_j - T_j) + (a_j - b_j)T_j & \text{for } j \in eq \\ -(b_j^+ - a_j)^+ (U_j - T_j - 1) + (a_j - b_j)T_j + a_j & \text{for } j \in gt \\ -(a_j^- + b_j^+)(U_j - T_j) + (a_j - b_j)T_j & \text{for } j \in st \end{cases}$

(2) $LA_j = -a_j^- (U_j - T_j) + a_j T_j \quad \text{for } m < j \leqslant n$

(3) $LB_j = -b_j^+ (U'_j - T'_j) - b_j T'_j \quad \text{for } m < j \leqslant n'$

(4) $UC_j = \begin{cases} (a_j^+ - b_j)^+ (U_j - T_j - 1) + (a_j - b_j)T_j - b_j & \text{for } j \in lt \\ (a_j - b_j)^+ (U_j - T_j) + (a_j - b_j)T_j & \text{for } j \in eq \\ (b_j^- + a_j)^+ (U_j - T_j - 1) + (a_j - b_j)T_j + a_j & \text{for } j \in gt \\ (a_j^+ + b_j^-)(U_j - T_j) + (a_j - b_j)T_j & \text{for } j \in st \end{cases}$

(5) $UA_j = a_j^+ (U_j - T_j) + a_j T_j \quad \text{for } m < j \leqslant n$

(6) $UB_j = b_j^- (U'_j - T'_j) - b_j T'_j \quad \text{for } m < j \leqslant n'$ ∎

Proof   see Appendix B.

Corollary 1   Let $c \in [1:m]$. Then $S \, \delta_c \, S'$ implies:

$$\sum_{1 \leqslant j \leqslant c-1} (-(a_j - b_j)^-(U_j - T_j) + (a_j - b_j)T_j) -$$

$$(a_c^- + b_c)^+(U_c - T_c - 1) + (a_c - b_c)T_c - b_c +$$

$$\sum_{c < j \leqslant m} (-(a_j^- + b_j^+)(U_j - T_j) + (a_j - b_j)T_j) +$$

$$\sum_{m < j \leqslant n} (-a_j^-(U_j - T_j) + a_j T_j) +$$

$$\sum_{m < j \leqslant n'} (-b_j^+(U_j' - T_j') - b_j T_j')$$

$$\leqslant b_0 - a_0 \leqslant$$

$$\sum_{1 \leqslant j \leqslant c-1} ((a_j - b_j)^+(U_j - T_j) + (a_j - b_j)T_j) +$$

$$(a_c^+ - b_c)^+(U_c - T_c - 1) + (a_c - b_c)T_c - b_c +$$

$$\sum_{c < j \leqslant m} ((a_j^+ + b_j^-)(U_j - T_j) + (a_j - b_j)T_j) +$$

$$\sum_{m < j \leqslant n} (a_j^+(U_j - T_j) + a_j T_j) +$$

$$\sum_{m < j \leqslant n'} (b_j^-(U_j' - T_j') - b_j T_j')$$

∎

Corollary 2 $S \, \delta_\infty \, S'$ implies:

$$\sum_{1 \leqslant j \leqslant m} (-(a_j - b_j)^-(U_j - T_j) + (a_j - b_j)T_j) +$$

$$\sum_{m < j \leqslant n} (-a_j^-(U_j - T_j) + a_j T_j) +$$

$$\sum_{m < j \leqslant n'} (-b_j^+(U_j' - T_j') - b_j T_j')$$

$$\leqslant b_0 - a_0 \leqslant$$

$$\sum_{1 \leqslant j \leqslant m} ((a_j - b_j)^+(U_j - T_j) + (a_j - b_j)T_j) +$$

$$\sum_{m < j \leqslant n} (a_j^+(U_j - T_j) + a_j T_j) +$$

$$\sum_{m < j \leqslant n'} (b_j^-(U_j' - T_j') - b_j T_j')$$

∎

Proof The corollaries follow immediately from the theorem and the direction vectors associated with δ_c and δ_∞, respectively: the direction vector for δ_c is $(=^{c-1},<,*^{m-c})$, and the associated sets are $lt = \{c\}$, $eq = [1:c-1]$, $gt = \varnothing$, and $st = [c+1:m]$. The direction vector for δ_∞ is $(=^m)$, and thus $eq = [1:m]$ and $lt = gt = st = \varnothing$. ∎

By applying the intermediate value theorem from analysis to the condition specified in the Banerjee test, one can show that this condition is also sufficient for the dependence equation to have a solution in the given region. However, a solution may be integer or real. As we are only interested in integer solutions, we can use the test only as a necessary condition, that is for disproving dependence.

For any specific application of the test, the expressions occurring in the inequalities may become significantly simpler: whenever two corresponding coefficients have the same value – which happens often in practice – a number of terms will drop out. This also qualifies our assumption that all loop bounds must be constant – not all bounds may occur in an actual test. For example, if $a_j = b_j$ and $j \in eq$, then $LC_j = UC_j = 0$. Furthermore, sometimes we shall only need to know the difference of the loop bounds: for example, if $a_j = b_j > 0$ and $j \in st$, then $T = LC_j$ (that is, $LC_j = -b_j^+(U_j - T_j)I$, $UC_j = -LC_j$) and we can perform the test even if we do not know the value of N in L_j: DO $I_j = N, N + 1000$.

4.6 A general algorithm for dependence testing

4.6.1 Introduction

In the previous section we developed dependence tests for one-dimensional arrays in arbitrarily nested loops. We use these methods here to formulate a general algorithm for dependence testing. In this context, we will say that the gcd test or the Banerjee test is 'satisfied' if the necessary condition related to the test is **true**.

Multidimensional arrays will be handled by performing the test in each dimension separately, and then combining the results. In this context, we speak of a 'dependence in dimension r'. A dependence exists only if there is at least one direction vector for which a dependence exists in every dimension.

Let us review the problem specification that led to the formulation of a dependence system in Section 4.4.1. Everything that was said there still holds, with the exception that now the dimension $d \geq 1$ can be arbitrary: let

S, S' denote statements and v and v' subscripted variables

$$v: A(f_1(\mathbf{I}), \ldots, f_d(\mathbf{I})) \in DEF(S)$$
$$v': A(f_1'(\mathbf{I}'), \ldots, f_d'(\mathbf{I}')) \in USE(S')$$

where $d \geq 1$, $f_r: [S] \rightarrow \mathbb{Z}$ and $f_r': [S'] \rightarrow \mathbb{Z}$ for all $r \in [1:d]$. We have to determine whether there exist $\mathbf{i} \in [S]$, $\mathbf{i}' \in [S']$ such that the system (DEQS) with d equations can be solved in region (REG) under the constraint of an arbitrary direction vector $\boldsymbol{\theta}$:

(DEQS)	$f_r(\mathbf{i}) = f'_r(\mathbf{i}')$	$(1 \leq r \leq d)$
(REG)	$i_j \in [T_j : U_j]$	$(1 \leq j \leq n)$
	$i_j' \in [T_j' : U_j']$	$(1 \leq j \leq n')$
(CST)	$i_j \, \theta_j \, i_j'$	$(1 \leq j \leq m)$

Let $r \in [1:d]$. The subscript functions f_r and f_r' $(1 \leq r \leq d)$ may or may not be admissible and satisfy the linearity condition. If they do not, we assume dependence in dimension r. Otherwise, we substitute f for f_r and f' for f_r' and assume the linearity condition as defined in Section 4.4.1.

$$\text{(LIN)} \begin{cases} f(\mathbf{I}) & = a_0 + \sum_{1 \leq j \leq n} a_j I_j \\[2mm] f'(\mathbf{I}') = b_0 + \sum_{1 \leq j \leq n'} b_j I_j' \end{cases}$$

4.6.2   The basic algorithm

ALGORITHM 4.3: Dependence test

Input   Loop L, S, S', v and v' as specified above.

Output   Sets $DEPS(S,S')$ and $DEPS(S',S)$ that contain the set of all direction vectors associated with dependences from S to S' or S' to S, respectively.

Method

/* We shall use the following notation:
   DIRV: the set of all proper direction vectors of length m

EDIRV: the set of all extended direction vectors of length *m*

starred(θ): a predicate that yields **true** for θ ∈ *EDIRV* iff θ contains a position with a '*'

subst_leftmost_star(θ,dve): if θ ∈ EDIRV such that *starred*(θ) is satisfied and dve ∈ {'<','=','>'}, then this yields a direction vector θ' that is identical to θ, except that the leftmost occurrence of '*' in θ has been replaced by dve. */

function proper(θ): $\mathcal{P}$(*DIRV*);

/* θ is a direction vector. The function yields the set of all proper direction vectors associated with θ: for example, *proper*((<,>)) = {(<,>)} and *proper*((<,*)) = {(<,<),(<,=),(<,>)} */

function separability_test: $\mathcal{P}$(*DIRV*);

/* The function yields the set of all proper direction vectors for which the dependence equation (DEQ) can be solved in region (REG) */

function GCD_test(θ): **boolean**;

/* θ is a direction vector. The function yields **true** iff the gcd test applied to (DEQ), can be solved for θ: that is, dependence cannot be disproved by an application of the test */

function Banerjee_test(θ): **boolean**;

/* θ is a direction vector. The function yields **true** iff the Banerjee test applied to (DEQ) in the region (REG) can be solved for θ: that is, dependence cannot be disproved by an application of the test */

function TEST(θ): $\mathcal{P}$(DIRV);

/* θ is a direction vector. The function yields the set of all direction vectors in *proper*(θ) for which dependences cannot be disproved by first applying the gcd test and then the Banerjee test.

TEST is a recursive function: if θ is proper, it yields either ∅ or {θ}, depending on whether or not the gcd test or the Banerjee test can disprove dependence. If θ contains a '*', then let θ = α||(*)||β, where α is empty or proper and β is a direction vector. The result of TEST(θ) is the union of all sets TEST(α||β'), where β' ∈ *proper*((*)||β). TEST(θ) is computed by recursively calling TEST(α||(<)||β), TEST(α||(=)||β), and TEST(α||(>)||β), and forming the union of these partial results. Each activation of TEST has its own instance of the variable *L_SET*.

This algorithm is called a **hierarchical dependence test**. */

begin
    L_SET := ∅;
    if *GCD_test*(θ)
        then
            if *Banerjee_test*(θ)
                then   /* Dependence cannot be disproved for θ. If θ is proper, this
                            result is final; otherwise *TEST* is recursively called with
                            direction vectors, in which the leftmost '*' of θ is
                            successively replaced by '<','=', and '>'. */

```
                    if starred(θ)
                        then
                            L_SET := TEST(subst_leftmost_star(θ,'<'));
                            L_SET plus TEST(subst_leftmost_star(θ,'='));
                            L_SET plus TEST(subst_leftmost_star(θ,'>'))
                        else L_SET := {θ}
                    fi
                fi
        fi;
        TEST := L_SET
    end TEST;
```

function DIM_TEST(r): $\mathcal{P}(DIRV)$;

/* DIM_TEST(r) yields the set of all proper direction vectors for which dependence in dimension r can either be positively proven (if the separability test can be applied) or not disproved */

begin
    if either f_r or f'_r does not satisfy the linearity condition (LIN)
        then DIM_TEST := DIRV   /* No test performed –
                                          worst-case assumption */
    orif f_r and f'_r satisfy the separability condition
        then DIM_TEST := separability_test
    else DIM_TEST := TEST((*^{m}));   /* Hierarchical test */
    fi
end DIM_TEST;

/* MAIN PROGRAM */

begin

/* Looping over the dimensions of the subscripted variables: */

AD := DIRV;

for r := 1 **to** d **do**
    AD := AD ∩ DIM_TEST(r);
    //* AD is the set of all direction vectors that may cause a dependence in
        each dimension between 1 and r *///
    if AD = ∅
        then DEPS(S,S') := DEPS(S',S) := ∅; **halt**   /* No dependence */
    fi;
end for;

//* ⊧AD ≠ ∅ *///

DEPS(S,S') := AD ∩ dir([S,S']);
DEPS(S',S) := AD^{-1} ∩ dir([S',S])
end ∎

We discuss a few aspects of the algorithm in the following, in particular the hierarchical test. Possible extensions and improvements will then be treated in the next two subsections.

Consider the main program of the algorithm. The for-loop is executed for $r = 1, 2, \ldots$; iteration r tests for dependence in dimension r.

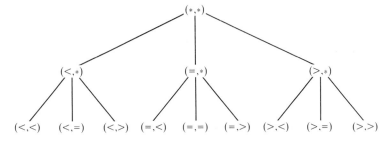

Figure 4.2   Dependence tree for $m = 2$.

The call to $DIM\_TEST(r)$ yields the set of all direction vectors causing a dependence in this dimension. (The use of 'cause' in this discussion is convenient, but imprecise: what is actually meant is that the direction vector is yielded by the dependence test. This may only mean that dependence cannot be excluded.) Remember that a dependence between S and S' exists only if there is a simultaneous solution of the equation system (DEQS). Therefore, any direction vector that can cause a dependence between S and S' must cause it in all dimensions $r = 1, \ldots, d$. This justifies the intersection performed in each iteration: the variable AD is initialized to the set of all direction vectors; after the intersection of AD with $DIM\_TEST(r)$ it contains the set of all direction vectors causing dependences in all dimensions 1 through r. We can stop the test with the result 'No dependence', if this set is empty. For example, if we find the set $\{(<,<,=),(=,=,=)\}$ in iteration 1, and $\{(<,<,<), (<,=,=), (>,=,<)\}$ in iteration 2, then there can be no dependence, and we can terminate.

The value of AD at the end of the for-loop specifies the set of all direction vectors that can cause a dependence in every dimension. If AD is empty, then there can be no dependence, and we are finished. Otherwise, AD has to be intersected with $dir([S,S'])$ to find the set of all direction vectors that are associated with a dependence from S to S'; and similarly for the inverse of AD and $dir([S',S])$.

The call $DIM\_TEST(r)$ performs a **hierarchical dependence test** if both subscript functions satisfy the linearity condition and the separability condition is not fulfilled. This test is initiated by a call to the function $TEST$ with the argument $(*, \ldots, *)$. We can think of all direction vectors as organized in a ternary tree of height m, which we call the **dependence tree**. There are 3^m possible proper direction vectors; they are associated with the leaves of the tree. A tree for $m = 2$ is shown in Figure 4.2. We also use the case $m = 2$ in the discussion below.

Our objective in the hierarchical test is to establish independence as fast as possible. Therefore the first call performs the dependence test for $(*,*)$. If we find no dependence for this direction vector, we are finished. If there is a dependence, then we step down one level in the tree, replace

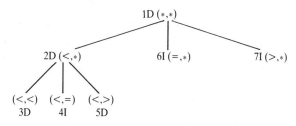

Figure 4.3 Tree walk for $m = 2$ and dependences $(<,<)$ and $(<,>)$.

successively the leftmost '*' with '<', '=', and '>', and perform the dependence tests for the direction vectors thus modified. This process is repeated recursively. Note that whenever independence has been established in a particular position, the subtrees at that position are cut off by the algorithm.

Assume that the only proper direction vectors for which a dependence is finally found are $(<,<)$ and $(<,>)$. Then the sequence of tests is indicated by the numbers attached to the nodes in Figure 4.3. The letter beside each number indicates that the test has found dependence (D) or no dependence (I).

Let us conclude with a few general remarks. Our algorithm has been applied to a specific pair of statements and a specific pair of variables in the input and output sets of these statements. In general, if we want to determine the set of all dependences in a region of the program, then all statement pairs and all related pairs v,v' of variables must be considered. Assume that S,S' is an arbitrarily selected pair of statements. The algorithm determines the dependences in both directions, so we do not have to apply it separately to (S,S') and (S',S). Furthermore, it can be easily extended to deal with all pairs (v,v') of subscripted variables occurring in S and S' that are candidates for causing a dependence. Thus, all dependence types in both directions will then be computed. Note that tests for different dependence types are combined: for example, if $v \in DEF(S)$ and $v' \in USE(S')$, then we test simultaneously for $S \, \delta^t \, S'$ and $S' \, \delta^a \, S$.

If there are q statements in the program, then we have to apply the algorithm to $O(q^2)$ statement pairs; in the worst case, $p \cdot 3^m$ dependence tests have to be performed for each pair, where p is the number of variable pairs to be examined. The number of tests can be significantly reduced by combining sets of direction vectors into single vectors. For example, the symbols '$\leq$', '$\geq$', and '$\neq$' can be included in direction vectors, and we could modify $DIM\_TEST(r)$ to yield just one direction vector of this kind. Such an approach saves space and time at the cost of precision. Details are discussed in Wolfe's thesis (Wolfe, 1982) and in Wolfe and Banerjee (1987).

Sometimes we are interested only in one specific type of dependence or in a subset of all direction vectors. The algorithm can be readily adapted to such requirements.

In a given implementation, the efficiency of dependence testing is strongly related to a number of design parameters, such as (1) the internal organization of the program, in particular with respect to loops and their relevant parameters, (2) the representation of statements, (3) the efficient accessibility of input and output sets, and (4) the representation of coefficients of subscript expressions, and of important terms in the expressions that occur in dependence tests.

Let us finally take a look at another example involving inadmissible subscript expressions:

Example 4.24

```
DO I = 1, 100
  S:   A(Y - I ** 2, I + 100) = ...
  S':  ...        = A(3 * K * I ** 2 + X, I)
END DO
```

In both subscripted variables, the expressions in the first dimension are not admissible (K,X,Y are assumed to be arbitrary variables) and the algorithm makes worst-case assumptions: all direction vectors are assumed to cause a dependence in this dimension. However, the separability test, when applied to the second dimension, reveals independence in that dimension and, as a consequence, independence of S and S'.

4.6.3   Linearization

The method of dependence testing in Algorithm 4.3, which is characterized by a separate and independent test in each dimension, will be called the **dimensional** approach. Another approach is to **linearize** a subscripted variable as follows. Let A denote an array of dimension d, declared with bounds LB_j, UB_j $(1 \leq j \leq d, LB_j \leq UB_j$ for all $j)$. Then, assuming that each element occupies e storage locations, the memory address $A(x_1, \ldots, x_d)$ is determined as follows†:

$$adr(A(x_1, \ldots, x_d)) = a_0 + e \cdot \sum_{1 \leq j \leq d} x_j D_j$$

† Here, we assume the mapping specified in Fortran 77, that is column-major order. For row-major order, only the role of the D_j changes.

where

$$D_1 = 1, D_j = \prod_{1 \leq k < j} (UB_k - LB_k + 1) \qquad \text{for } j \geq 2, \text{ and}$$

$$a_0 = adr(A(LB_1, \ldots, LB_d)) - e \cdot \sum_{1 \leq j \leq d} LB_j \cdot D_j$$

Note that $adr(A(LB_1, \ldots, LB_d))$ is the location of the first element of the array. The D_j and a_0 are constants determined by the array declaration: thus we have represented the d-dimensional subscripted variable by one linear expression in the subscripts $x_1, \ldots, x_d$, and effectively transformed it into a one-dimensional variable. Using this mapping, all dependence tests can be performed for the linearized variable instead of the original subscripted variable. The tradeoffs between the two approaches can be summarized as follows:

(1)   The dimensional approach can be applied to subscripted variables with subscript expressions that are inadmissible and/or non-linear. The linearized approach fails in this case (see Example 4.24).

(2)   An exact test – such as the separability test – may be applicable in the dimensional approach, but not after linearization (if different subscript positions use different do-variables, as in A(I + 1, 2 * J - 3)).

(3)   The gcd test is potentially – but not necessarily – better when applied to the linearized version. We illustrate this by an example (Example 4.25).

(4)   If subscript bounds are violated, or in certain cases of aliasing, the linearized test may be necessary to detect a dependence (Burke and Cytron, 1986; Wolfe and Banerjee, 1987).

Example 4.25

Let A be declared as A(1:20, 1:10), and consider the do-loop

```
DO I = 1, 100
  S:    A(I, I + 1) = ...
  S':   ... = A(I - 1, I - 2)
END DO
```

Algorithm 4.3 determines a true dependence from S to S', associated with the direction vector ($<$). If we linearize the array, we obtain ($e = 1$):

$$adr(A(x_1, x_2)) = a_0 + x_1 + 20x_2, \text{ where } a_0 = adr(A(1,1)) - 21$$

Let A' denote the linearized version of A: then the loop can be rewritten as

```
DO I = 1, 100
  S:    A'(a₀ + 21 * I + 20) = ...
  S':   ... = A'(a₀ + 21 * I - 41)
END DO
```

The dependence equation becomes $a_0 + 21x + 20 = a_0 + 21y - 41$, which is equivalent to $21x - 21y = -61$. The gcd test can now determine independence.

In order to achieve the best possible dependence information, it may be appropriate to combine both tests.

4.7   Concluding remarks

The methods for dependence testing described in this chapter include one exact test – the separability test – and two tests that examine a necessary condition for dependence – the gcd test and the Banerjee test.

In general, the range of exact tests can be significantly extended by applying, for example, linear programming techniques or exhaustive searches of solution spaces. Most of these methods are, however, computationally too expensive to be usable in a practical environment (Kuhn, 1980; Shostak, 1981; Triolet, 1984).

Our basic model contains only assignments and do-loops; however, several features can be added within the framework developed in this chapter. One possible extension is the inclusion of conditionals and gotos, if the direction of branches is **forward**, that is their target occurs textually after the branch at the same loop level. As a consequence, a statement may not be executed in certain iterations of the loop. The sets $[S]$ and the control sets $[S,S']$ have to be adjusted correspondingly: for example, in

```
DO I = T, U
...
IF cond(I)   THEN GOTO L FI
S: ...
L:
...
END DO
```

(*i*) may not be in [*S*] for some values of $i \in$ [T:U]. Similarly, in

```
DO I = T, U
...
IF cond(I)
   THEN S
   ELSE S'
FI
...
END DO
```

$S \ll (=) S'$ is not possible; thus there can be no loop-independent dependence from *S* to *S'*. The model can be also extended to deal with **exit branches**, which jump out of a loop (see Chapter 6). We cannot, however, handle **backward** branches: these create implicit loops, with the consequence that statements may be executed arbitrarily often within a single iteration. Then, our concept of statement instance loses its intended meaning. Allen and Kennedy (Allen, 1983; Allen *et al.*, 1983) have developed methods for the conversion of control dependences into data dependences. To a limited extent, the methods of Chapter 3 can be used to transform implicit loops automatically into while or repeat-loops, sometimes even into do-loops.

Additional statements such as read or write can be included in the model without problems. For calls, it is essential that interprocedural side effect analysis has been performed to determine the sets *DEF* and *USE* as precisely as possible and to avoid worst-case assumptions (see Section 3.7). In some cases, this is not sufficient to rule out cyclic dependences: for example, in

```
DO I = ...
   S:    CALL P1(A, I)
         ...
   S':   A(I + 1) = B(I) - 1
END DO
```

the call to P1 may result in a cyclic dependence involving *S* and *S'*, which inhibits the concurrent execution of loop iterations. In order to rule out dependences in such a context, the effects of calls on subscripted variables must be determined by an interprocedural dependence analysis. The objective is to provide the calling program (via the *DEF* and *USE* sets associated with the call statement) with a specification of the array regions accessed in the procedure (such as rectangular subarrays, rows, columns, or diagonals), together with the type of access. This is a difficult problem and still very much an area of research. Significant work in this field has been done by Triolet (1984), Burke and Cytron (1986), Callahan and Kennedy (1988a), and Balasundaram (1989).

We have discussed concepts and techniques for dependence analysis at the level of assignment statements. This can be easily extended to either a lower or a higher level of abstraction. For example, if dependences are analyzed at an intermediate language level, where each operation (such as add or multiply) is considered a separate node, it may be possible to break a dependence cycle between statements (Wolfe, 1982). On the other hand, compound statements – such as whole loops – may be considered as elementary units to which dependence analysis is applied (see for example Midkiff and Padua (1986)). Often, it is advantageous to build a dependence graph, and then to form an abstraction by condensing several nodes into a single node. A special case of this technique is the construction of PI-graphs, and the related set of vectorization and parallelization transformations (see Chapters 6 and 7).

We did not discuss dependence tests involving symbolic quantities. Symbolic quantities may occur in the loop bounds and in subscript expressions. While the gcd test is independent of loop bounds – and thus can be applied if the loop bounds are arbitrary expressions – the separability test and the Banerjee test require the bounds to be constant. (Banerjee specifies an extension of the Banerjee test for trapezoidal regions, in which the loop bounds may depend on do-variables (Banerjee, 1988).) Under certain circumstances, this condition can be relaxed (see the last paragraph of Section 4.5.3). If the Banerjee test is used in an interactive environment, it can compute assertions involving symbolic quantities which may be approved or rejected by the user. In general, no systematic approach is known for handling symbolic quantities in dependence analysis; a set of useful heuristics has been developed in Allen's thesis (Allen (1983); see also Lichnewsky and Thomasset (1988)). However, even in a simple case such as that illustrated in Example 4.26, worst-case assumptions are necessary if nothing is known about the value of variable K.

Example 4.26

```
DO I = 1, 100
  S:    A(I) = B(I) + 1
        ...
  S':   C(I) = A(I + K) - 1
END DO
```

The existence of a dependence between S and S', and the direction as well as the type of dependence, if any, is determined by the value of K:

- if $K = 0$, then $S\, \delta^t(=)\, S'$
- if $-99 \leqslant K \leqslant -1$, then $S\, \delta^t(<)\, S'$

- if $1 \leqslant K \leqslant 99$, then $S'\, \delta^a(<)\, S$
- if $|K| \geqslant 100$, then S and S' are independent

We shall discuss the application of dependence analysis to restructuring in Chapters 6 and 7. It can be applied in a variety of other contexts, such as vector register allocation, cache optimization, and memory management in a hierarchical memory structure, which are beyond the scope of this book.

Finally, dependence analysis as discussed in this chapter is restricted to sequential languages. Extensions to Fortran 90-type vector constructs are treated by Wolfe and Banerjee (1987), and Allen and Kennedy (1988).

BIBLIOGRAPHICAL NOTES

The theory of data dependence and related analysis methods were originally developed by Kuck, Lamport and coworkers, based on work by Bernstein (Bernstein, 1966; Lamport, 1974; Kuck *et al.*, 1984a; Towle, 1976; Banerjee, 1979; Kuhn, 1980). Direction vectors are introduced in Wolfe's thesis (Wolfe, 1982). The δ_k notation was proposed by Allen and Kennedy (Allen, 1983; Allen and Kennedy, 1987). The separability test is due to Lamport (unpublished work), and was later described by Wolfe and Banerjee (Wolfe, 1982; Wolfe and Banerjee, 1987; Banerjee, 1988). The Banerjee test was first introduced in Banerjee's M.S. thesis (Banerjee, 1976), and was further developed by Wolfe, Allen and Kennedy (Wolfe, 1982; Allen, 1983; Allen and Kennedy, 1987; Wolfe and Banerjee, 1987). The hierarchical test is due to Burke and Cytron (1986) and was improved by Wolfe and Banerjee (1987). Wolfe and Banerjee (1987) formulate their dependence tests for arbitrary loops (that is, including loops with an increment $\neq 1$). The relationships between dependences and aliasing are explored in Burke and Cytron (1986). Li's Ph.D. dissertation (Li, 1989) introduces a new algorithm for testing dependences between multi-dimensional array references and proposes a novel approach to inter-procedural dependence analysis.

The methods described in this chapter have been implemented in many systems, including Parafrase (Kuck *et al.*, 1984a), PFC (Allen and Kennedy, 1987), PTRAN (Burke and Cytron, 1986) and SUPERB (Zima *et al.*, 1988). They have also been applied in several commercial systems.

Banerjee has published a comprehensive text on dependence analysis (Banerjee, 1988). His book, the dissertations of Wolfe (1982) and Allen (1983), and the work presented in Allen and Kennedy (1987) and Wolfe and Banerjee (1987) have contributed much to the organization and presentation of the material in this chapter.

Further material on diophantine equations can be found in Griffin (1954).

Chapter 5

Standard Transformations

5.1 Introduction

The theory developed in the last two chapters provides the basis for our discussion of program restructuring transformations, which begins here and extends through Chapter 8. In this chapter we shall deal with a set of **standard transformations** whose primary task is to normalize programs, which serves as a suitable starting point for dependence analysis and further processing.

All transformations discussed here are part of the front end of the transformation system (see Figure 1.1). Whenever a standard transformation is carried out, scanning, parsing and semantic analysis have already been applied to the program, an intermediate representation has been created, and the required control flow and scalar data flow information has been provided in an appropriate form as discussed in Chapter 3.

Not all standard transformations that can, in principle, be included into the front end are the subject of consideration here: those transformations which are oriented specifically towards a particular class of architectures, and a number of additional, more complex transformations (such as loop interchange) will be treated in Chapters 6 and 7.

Chapter 5 consists of six sections and is organized as follows.

Section 5.2 discusses the normalization of do-loops. This transformation converts every do-loop with an integer do-variable into an equivalent normalized loop, that is, a do-loop with lower bound and increment 1.

Section 5.3 deals with subscript normalization. The objective is to transform a subscripted variable in such a way that each subscript expression satisfies the linearity condition, which is necessary to avoid worst-case assumptions in dependence analysis. Important transformations related to subscript normalization are scalar forward substitution and induction variable substitution. Scalar forward substitution replaces an applied occurrence of a scalar integer variable by the expression on the right-hand side of an assignment to that variable. Induction variables of a loop are essentially scalar integer variables that are only incremented or decremented in the loop, using constant increments. The right-hand side of an assignment to such a variable can be represented as a linear function of the do-variables, and this function can be substituted for applied occurrences of the variable.

Section 5.4 discusses a method to eliminate dependences in a semantically valid way. If a scalar variable is used in disjoint program regions for distinct purposes (as a means to re-use memory), then scalar renaming creates a different name in each region, thus eliminating the anti and output dependences caused by this use of the variable.

Section 5.5 illustrates the combined use of standardization transformations and relates them to program manipulations discussed in the context of scalar data flow analysis, such as dead-code elimination and constant propagation.

The chapter closes with bibliographical notes.

A final remark is in order here. To avoid unnecessary technical detail, we specify most transformations in a more restricted form than is really necessary. Furthermore, we describe only the input/output mapping realized by the transformations, but not the compiling techniques required for its implementation. More general descriptions of the transformations and details of implementation techniques can be found in the standard compiler literature, for example Aho *et al.* (1986). Our discussion is based upon the program model introduced in Section 3.2, extended by do-loops. Apart from Section 5.2, we will only consider normalized loops.

5.2   Do-loop normalization

A do-loop is normalized when both its lower bound and increment are equal to one (see Table 4.1 and Definition 4.3). To normalize a Fortran do-loop with an integer do-variable, the compiler first generates a new do-variable and then replaces each occurrence of the original do-variable in the body of the loop by an appropriate linear function of the new variable.

This transformation is specified precisely below. Its correctness, that is the semantic equivalence of L and L_{norm}, follows from the semantic specification of do-loops in ANSI (1978), pp10–11.

We distinguish the identifiers of all compiler-generated variables by prefixing them with a '%'.

TRANSFORMATION 5.1: Do-loop normalization

Input   Unnormalized Fortran do-loop

L: DO I = e_1, e_2, e_3 $BODY$ END DO

---

where I is of type integer and e_j $(1 \leqslant j \leqslant 3)$ are expressions.

Output   A statement sequence L_{norm} of the following form:

L_{norm}:

$\%m_1 = \text{INT}(e_1)$
$\%m_2 = \text{INT}(e_2)$ Prelude
$\%m_3 = \text{INT}(e_3)$

DO %I = 1, $(\%m_2 - \%m_1 + \%m_3)/\%m_3$, 1   Normalized
   $BODY_{norm}$ loop
END DO

I = $\%m_1 + \text{MAX}((\%m_2 - \%m_1 + \%m_3)/\%m_3, 0) * \%m_3$ Postlude

---

where we obtain $BODY_{norm}$ from $BODY$ by replacing each use of I
by $\%m_1 + (\%I - 1) * \%m_3$.   ■

Remarks

(1)   We can make the following simple modifications to L_{norm}:

   (i)   If an e_j is of type integer, then we replace each occur-
         rence of $\text{INT}(e_j)$ by e_j $(1 \leqslant j \leqslant 3)$. Similarly, $\text{MAX}(exp, 0)$ is
         appropriately replaced by either exp or 0, whenever the
         sign of exp is known.

   (ii) If an $\text{INT}(e_j)$ is a known constant, then we suppress
         generation of the corresponding $\%m_j$ and its assign-
         ment in the prelude. It is substituted in L_{norm} by the
         value of $\text{INT}(e_j)$ $(1 \leqslant j \leqslant 3)$.

(2)   The upper bound of the normalized loop specifies the number
      of times the original loop is executed.

(3)   The postlude guarantees that I will be assigned the value it
      would have after execution of the original loop. This is a
      candidate for dead-code elimination (see Example 5.12).

(4)   We must generate an appropriate assignment to I whenever
      control is transferred out of the loop.   ■

Example 5.1

Our first example shows how we normalize a simple loop.

```
L:  DO I=1000,1,-1        L_norm:  DO %I=1,((1-1000+(-1))/(-1)
        A(I)= ...                      A(1000+(%I-1)*(-1))= ...
        ...            ⟹             ...
    END DO                         END DO
                                   I=1000+MAX((1-1000+(-1))/(-1)),0)*(-1)
```

This can be simplified to:

```
L_norm:  DO %I = 1, 1000
             A(1001 - %I) = ...

             ...
         END DO
         I=0
```

In the following, we assume that whenever all operands of an expression are constants, the expression has been evaluated and replaced by its value in the generated code, and that all other expressions have been simplified as far as possible. We take all scalar variables to be of type integer.

Example 5.2

```
L:  DO I=4,N,4              L_norm:  %M2=N
        IF MOD(I,100) .EQ. 0         DO %I=1, %M2/4
        ...                              IF MOD(4*%I,100) .EQ. 0
        A(I+4)=A(I-4)+N*M  ⟹             ...
        ...                              A(4+4*%I)=A(-4+4*%I)+N*M
    END DO                               ...
                                     END DO
                                     I=4+MAX(%M2/4,0)*4
```

Example 5.3

```
                              L_norm:   %MI1=N
                                        %MI2=M
 L:   DO I=N,M                          DO %I=1,%MI2-%MI1+1
         D(I)=A(I,I)                       D(%MI1+%I-1)=A(%MI1+%I-1,%MI1+%I-1)
         DO J=I,M                          %MJ1=%MI1+%I-1
            X=X+3*A(I,J)                    %MJ2=M
            ...                 ⟹          DO %J=1,%MJ2-%MJ1+1
         END DO J                             X=X+3*A(%MI1+%I-1,%MJ1+%J-1)
         X=X-A(I,I)                           ...
         ...                             END DO %J
      END DO I                           J=%MJ1+MAX(%MJ2-%MJ1+1,0)
                                         X=X-A(%MI1+%I-1,%MI1+%I-1)

                                         ...
                                      END DO %I
                                      I=%MI1+MAX(%MI2-%MI1+1,0)
```

The above example also illustrates an unfortunate aspect of normalization. While normalization provides an interface which generally makes the manipulation of do-loops simpler for an automatic system, the generated code may be virtually unintelligible for a human reader: this may cause serious problems in an interactive environment. It may sometimes even be more difficult for an automatic transformation system to verify some properties of a loop once it has been normalized – properties which would perhaps allow us to apply special optimization algorithms. It is, for example, easy to see that the original loop in Example 5.3 operates in a triangular iteration space, but this fact is not at all apparent once it is normalized.

5.3 Subscript normalization

In this section we deal with a number of techniques to normalize subscript expressions in loops. Our objective is to enforce the linearity condition (LIN), as defined in Section 4.4.1, whenever possible.

We discuss the following transformations: scalar forward substitution (Section 5.3.1), induction variable detection and substitution (Section 5.3.2), wrap-around variable substitution (Section 5.3.3), and standardization of subscript expressions (Section 5.3.4).

5.3.1   Scalar forward substitution

Programmers often reduce the number of redundant computations by using a scalar variable v as a temporary variable to store the value of a common subexpression. For example:

```
DO I = ...
   ...
   v = -5 + 2 * I
   ...
   A(v) = B(v,v + 1) + 7
   ...
END DO
```

However, subscript expressions containing such a variable are inadmissible, enforcing worst-case assumptions in dependence analysis. In contrast, the subscripted variables in the equivalent loop below satisfy the linearity condition and can be subjected to the standard dependence tests:

```
DO I = ...
   ...
   v = -5 + 2 * I
   ...
   A(-5 + 2 * I) = B(-5 + 2 * I, -4 + 2 * I) + 7
   ...
END DO
```

Scalar forward substitution replaces – under appropriate conditions – every applied occurrence of a variable v by the expression that occurs at the right-hand side of an assignment to v. Note that this transformation is the inverse of redundant expression elimination, a transformation which is important in optimization (see Section 3.4.2).

Definition 5.1   The **scope** of a definition $S: v = exp$, is given by: $SCOPE(S) := \{S': UD(S',v) = \{S\}\}$.   ∎

$SCOPE(S)$ is the set of all uses S' of v that can be reached from S, such that S is the only definition of v reaching S'. It can be computed using techniques developed in Chapter 3 (see Section 3.4.1).

We need to extend the concept of a definition-free path, as introduced in Section 3.4.1, to subscripted variables. Such a variable is interpreted as a representative of the whole array (remember that scalar forward substitution is applied in the front end, before dependence analysis): a path is definition-free with respect to a subscripted variable $A(exp_1, \ldots, exp_d)$ if no statement in that path changes the value of a subscripted variable $A(u_1, \ldots, u_d)$ for arbitrary $u_1, \ldots, u_d$.

TRANSFORMATION 5.2: Scalar forward substitution

> ***Input*** (1)   An assignment statement S: $v = exp$, where v is a scalar variable of type integer, and exp is an expression of type integer containing no function reference.
>
> (2) $SCOPE(S)$
>
> ***Output***   An equivalent program that is generated as follows. Let $S' \in SCOPE(S)$ be chosen arbitrarily. If every path from S to S' (excluding S') is definition free for all operands of exp, then each use of v in S' is replaced by exp.   ∎

Example 5.4

If S' is not the target of a branch which enables another definition of J to reach S', then we can apply the following transformation:

```
S:   J=K+1              S:   J=K+1
S':  A(J)=L*M-2  ⟹    S':  A(K+1)=L*M-2
     ...                     ...
```

Example 5.5

However, here we cannot transform at all:

```
S:    J = K + 1
      ...
S'':  K = 0
      ...
S':   A(J) = L * M - 2
```

In this case, the condition for scalar forward substitution is not satisfied, since an assignment is made to K in S''.

Example 5.6

Here, too, the assignment to B(M) in statement S''

```
S:    J = B(K) - 2
      ...
S'':  B(M) = ...
      ...
S':   A(J) = L * M - 2
```

will prevent scalar forward substitution.

5.3.2   Induction variable substitution

This transformation also deals with a kind of variable which is sometimes introduced to improve program performance on a sequential computer, but which can seriously weaken the precision of dependence tests. Induction variables are scalar integer variables which are used in a loop to simulate do-variables: they are incremented or decremented by a constant amount in each iteration and are mostly employed to get around the restrictions imposed upon permissible subscript expressions in early Fortran standards.

To illustrate this, we consider the following loop:

```
K = 1
DO I = 1, N
  K = K - 2
  A(K) = ...
...
END DO
```

K is an induction variable which assumes the sequence of values described by the arithmetic progression $1 - 2r$, $r = 0, 1, \ldots, N$. Thus, A(K) can be replaced by A(1-2*I) without changing the meaning of the program. While A(K) is inadmissible, the subscript expression in A(1-2*I) satisfies the linearity condition. We can generalize this observation: every induction variable can be replaced by a linear function in the loop's do-variable. The transformation which does so is called induction variable substitution.

Note that, in the above loop, the assignment statement K=K-2 results in an elementary loop in the dependence graph involving all three types of dependences.

We shall assume here that the body of the loop is a basic block. Induction variable substitution will be specified for basic induction variables, which are defined as follows.

Definition 5.2   A variable v is a **basic induction variable** of a loop L if it is a simple integer variable that is defined by one or more assignment statements in L, all of which have the form $v = v + c$, where c is a (positive or negative) constant. ∎

TRANSFORMATION 5.3: Induction variable substitution

Input   A normalized loop L, whose body is a basic block:

L: DO I = 1,u
　　...
　　S: $v = v + c$
　　...

S':   ... v ...

...

END DO

where v is a basic induction variable of L, and S is the only definition of v in L.

Output   A loop $L1$, equivalent to L, preceded by an assignment to a compiler-generated variable:

$$\%v\_init = v$$
$L1$:   DO I = 1,u

...

    $S1$: $v = \%v\_init + c * I$

...

    $S1'$:   ... $\%v\_init + c * I$ ...

...

END DO   ∎

Remark   If the initial value of v is known, then the generation of $\%v\_init$ and the associated assignment can be suppressed and each occurrence of $\%v\_init$ replaced by this value.   ∎

The following is a more general definition of induction variables:

Definition 5.3   A variable v is an **induction variable** of a loop L if it is (i) a basic induction variable, or (ii) the target of exactly one assignment in the loop, this having the form $v = c_1 * v_1 + c_2$, where c_1 and c_2 are constants, and v_1 is a basic induction variable.   ∎

We can similarly define induction variable substitution for general induction variables. Details on how to detect induction variables are to be found in Algorithm 10.9 in Aho *et al.* (1986).

Example 5.7

We apply the transformation to the basic induction variable K, whose initial value is known.

```
K=1                         K=1
DO I=1,N                    DO I=1,N
  K=K+3                       K=-1+5*I
  A(K)=A(K-1)+1  ⟹           A(-1+5*I)=A(-2+5*I)+1
  ...                         ...
  K=K+2                       K=1+5*I
  B(K)=K-1                    B(1+5*I)=5*I
  ...                         ...
END DO                      END DO
```

If there are no occurrences of K except those explicitly shown above, dead-code elimination can further transform this loop into:

```
DO I = 1, N
  A(-1 + 5 * I) = A(-2 + 5 * I) + 1
  ...
  B(1 + 5 * I) = 5 * I
  ...
END DO
```

Example 5.8

The loop below can be transformed as follows:

```
K=1                         K=1
DO I=1,100                  DO I=1,100
  K=K-2                       K=1-2*I+(I-1)*10
  A(K+3)= ...                 A(4-2*I+(I-1)*10)= ...
  DO J=1,10      ⟹           DO J=1,10
    K=K+1                       K=1-2*I+(I-1)*10+J
    B(K)= ...                   B(1-2*I+(I-1)*10+J)= ...
  END DO J                    END DO J
  ...                         ...
END DO I                    END DO I
```

If we again apply dead-code elimination wherever possible, and simplify the subscript expressions, we will obtain the following loop:

```
DO I = 1, 100
  A(-6 + 8 * I) = ...
  DO J = 1, 10
    B(-9 + 8 * I + J) = ...
  END DO J
  ...
END DO I
```

Note that induction variable substitution is the inverse of strength reduction, an optimization transformation which reduces complex operations to simpler ones (for example ** to *, or * to +).

5.3.3 Wrap-around variable substitution

We can perform wrap-around variable substitution when a variable that is essentially an induction variable is used in a loop before it is defined. This may occur, for example, if the elements of a one-dimensional array are cyclically connected. The transformation 'unrolls' one iteration of the loop. We illustrate it in the following (Padua and Wolfe, 1986).

Example 5.9

```
REAL A(0:99)
...
K = 99
DO I = 1, 100
  B(I) = F(A(K), A(I - 1))
  K = I - 1
END DO
```

Here, the elements of array A are cyclically connected in such a way that $A((i + 1) \bmod 100)$ is the neighbor of $A(i)$ for all i, $0 \leq i \leq 99$. In each iteration of the loop, F is applied to a pair of neighbors, starting with $(A(99), A(0))$, and finishing with $(A(98), A(99))$.

Neither scalar forward substitution nor induction variable substitution is of any use in this situation. However, by unrolling the first iteration and performing the appropriate substitutions for K, we obtain the equivalent program:

```
B(1) = F(A(99), A(0))
DO I = 2, 100
  K = I - 2
  B(I) = F(A(-2 + I), A(-1 + I))
END DO
K = 99
```

If K is not used elsewhere, this can be further reduced to:

```
B(1) = F(A(99), A(0))
DO I = 2, 100
  B(I) = F(A(-2 + I), A(-1 + I))
END DO
```

5.3.4   **Standardization of subscript expressions**

We need to standardize subscript expressions so that we have a well-defined interface for transformations operating on subscripted variables in loops: such a standard form will not only make the job of implementing the transformations easier, it will also help us to understand the code afterwards. Thus this transformation is primarily of technical significance.

   To standardize a subscript expression, we must perform two separate tasks: we first test it for linearity and then we transform it into an appropriate canonical form.

(1)   *Test for linearity*
   Let L denote a loop and $f(\mathbf{I})$ a subscript expression in L, where $\mathbf{I}$ is the vector of do-variables. We must first test whether $f(\mathbf{I})$ is admissible (see Definition 4.18). If not, then it cannot satisfy the linearity condition either and we terminate the test. Otherwise, we examine it for linearity in the do-variables (only constant integer coefficients are allowed). If this is satisfied, we proceed with step (2); otherwise we terminate.

(2)   *Transformation into a canonical form*
   We convert $f(\mathbf{I})$ according to the syntax specified in the linearity condition (LIN) so that it has the form (see Section 4.4.1):

$$f(\mathbf{I}) = a_0 + \sum_{1 \leq j \leq n} a_j I_j$$

   where all a_j $(0 \leq j \leq n)$ are integer constants.
   We can always obtain this representation by using the basic laws of algebra and evaluating all constant subexpressions.

Examples for subscript standardization can be found throughout this section.

5.4   **Scalar renaming**

Scalar renaming is a transformation that gives a variable a different name in each region of the program in which it serves a locally distinct purpose. It will simplify the dependence graph by eliminating anti and output dependences. This transformation was already used in some of the early restructuring systems (see Section 1.3).

   Let v denote a local scalar variable, and S: $v = exp$ an assignment to v. In many cases of interest, $DU(S,v)$ will be equal to $SCOPE(S)$: then the occurrence of v on the left-hand side of S and every occurrence of v in $SCOPE(S)$ can be validly replaced by a unique, compiler-generated name. The following example illustrates this simple case.

Example 5.10

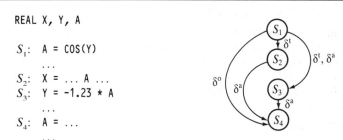

```
REAL X, Y, A

S₁:  A = COS(Y)
     ...
S₂:  X = ... A ...
S₃:  Y = -1.23 * A
     ...
S₄:  A = ...
     ...
```

Assume $SCOPE(S_1) = DU(S_1,A) = \{S_2,S_3\}$. The dependence graph for the statements we are interested in is given on the right-hand side above. If we apply scalar renaming to A, the program and its dependence graph will be transformed to:

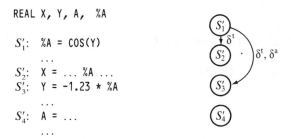

```
REAL X, Y, A,  %A

S'₁:  %A = COS(Y)
      ...
S'₂:  X = ... %A ...
S'₃:  Y = -1.23 * %A
      ...
S'₄:  A = ...
      ...
```

The above condition is too restrictive: we want to define scalar renaming for a more general case, where uses of v in $DU(S,v)$ may be reached from other definitions as well. This is described in detail in Transformation 5.4.

TRANSFORMATION 5.4: Scalar renaming

Input   (1)   An assignment $S: v = exp$, where v is a local scalar variable.

        (2)   For statements S', the sets $UD(S',v)$ and $DU(S',v)$ as required.

Output   An equivalent program which is generated as follows: A new identifier $\%v$ is created, and statement sets *DEFSET* and *USESET* are determined as specified below. All occurrences of v at the left-hand side of a statement in *DEFSET*, and all occurrences of v at the right-hand side of a statement in *USESET* are replaced by $\%v$.

Method

/* The sets *DEFSET* and *USESET* are computed */

procedure no_substitution;
/* This procedure is called if the algorithm terminates unsuccessfully, that is,
without performing a substitution. */
begin
DEFSET := *USESET* := ∅; **halt**
end   /* no_substitution */

/* MAIN PROGRAM */

begin

DEFSET := {*S*}; *USESET* := ∅; *U* := *DU*(*S*,*v*);

while *U* ≠ ∅ **do**
   u := select_and_remove (*U*);
   if *u* ∈ *DEFSET* **then** no_substitution **fi**;
   USESET **plus** {*u*};
   D := *UD*(*u*,*v*) − *DEFSET*;
   for every *d* ∈ *D* **do**
     if *d* ∈ *USESET* **then** no_substitution **fi**;
     DEFSET **plus** {*d*};
     U **plus** (*DU*(*d*,*v*) − *USESET*)
   end for
end while

end   ∎

Example 5.11

Suppose that there are statements S_i: $v = exp_i$ ($i = 1,2,3$), $DU(S_1,v) = \{S'_1, S'_2, S'_3\}$, $DU(S_2,v) = \{S'_3, S'_4\}$, $DU(S_3,v) = \{S'_1, S'_4, S'_5\}$ and $DU(S'_j,v) = \varnothing$ for all $j \in [1:5]$ (see Figure 5.1). Then $DEFSET = \{S_i: 1 \leqslant i \leqslant 3\}$ and $USESET = \{S'_j: 1 \leqslant j \leqslant 5\}$, but $SCOPE(S_1) = \{S_2\}$. Every occurrence of v on the left-hand side of an S_i and on the right-hand side of an S'_j is replaced by a new variable %v.

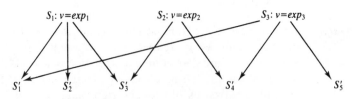

Figure 5.1   Scalar renaming for Example 5.11.

5.5 Concluding remarks

Certain problems may arise in connection with the standard transformations discussed in this chapter. We referred to one of them above: the resulting program could be unintelligible for a human reader. This can be a problem in an interactive environment where the user may often be requested to provide additional information on his program (for example, so that an intelligent choice can be made from a number of possible transformation strategies – see Chapter 8).

Sometimes the performance of a program may actually deteriorate when transformations are applied. Scalar forward substitution, for example, increases the number of computations in a program. If, for some reason, these cannot subsequently be performed concurrently, then execution time will be increased as a result. This means that we sometimes have to 'undo' our transformations: we apply redundant expression elimination, for example, to cancel the effects of scalar forward substitution.

The following example illustrates some of the transformations in this chapter and the effect they have upon each other.

Example 5.12

The following loop

```
K = 0
DO I = 100, 1, -1
  DO J = 0, 100, 4
    K = K + 1
    A(J - 1) = B(J) + C(K)
    E(I, J) = F(J)/E(I, J)
  END DO J
END DO I
```

is normalized to

```
K = 0
DO %I = 1, (1 - 100 + (-1))/(-1)
  DO %J = 1, (100 - 0 + 4)/4
    K = K + 1
    A(0 + (%J - 1) * 4 - 1) = B(0 + (%J - 1) * 4) + C(K)
    E(100 + (%I - 1) * (-1), 0 + (%J - 1) * 4) =
      F(0 + (%J - 1) * 4)/E(100 + (%I - 1) * (-1), 0 + (%J - 1) * 4)
  END DO %J
  J = 0 + MAX((100 - 0 + 4)/4, 0) * 4
END DO %I
I = 100 + MAX((1 - 100 + (-1))/(-1), 0) * (-1)
```

We apply induction variable substitution to obtain

```
K = 0
DO %I = 1, (1 - 100 + (-1))/(-1)
  DO %J = 1, (100 - 0 + 4)/4
    K = 0 + (%I - 1) * ((100 - 0 + 4)/4) * 1 + %J
    A(0 + (%J - 1) * 4 - 1) = B(0 + (%J - 1) * 4) +
      C(0 + (%I - 1) * ((100 - 0 + 4)/4) * 1 + %J)
    E(100 + (%I - 1) * (-1), 0 + (%J - 1) * 4) =
      F(0 + (%J - 1) * 4)/E(100 + (%I - 1) * (-1), 0 + (%J - 1) * 4)
  END DO %J
  ·J = 0 + MAX((100 - 0 + 4)/4, 0) * 4
END DO %I
I = 100 + MAX((1 - 100 + (-1))/(-1), 0) * (-1)
```

and then transform it via dead-code elimination to

```
DO %I = 1, (1 - 100 + (-1))/(-1)
  DO %J = 1, (100 - 0 + 4)/4
    A(0 + (%J - 1) * 4 - 1) = B(0 + (%J - 1) * 4) +
      C(0 + (%I - 1) * ((100 - 0 + 4)/4) * 1 + %J)
    E(100 + (%I - 1) * (-1), 0 + (%J - 1) * 4) =
      F(0 + (%J - 1) * 4)/E(100 + (%I - 1) * (-1), 0 + (%J - 1) * 4)
  END DO %J
END DO %I
```

which, after further simplification and subscript standardization, becomes

```
DO %I = 1, 100
  DO %J = 1, 26
    A(-5 + 4 * %J) = B(-4 + 4 * %J) + C(-26 + 26 * %I + %J)
    E(101 - %I, - 4 + 4 * %J) =
    F(-4 + 4 * %J)/E(101 - %I, -4 + 4 * %J)
  END DO %J
END DO %I
```

Note: To carry out dead-code elimination, we assumed that the values assigned to I, J, and K in the original loop are not used outside the loop.

BIBLIOGRAPHICAL NOTES

The standard transformations are described in much of the general literature on vectorization and parallelization (Allen and Kennedy, 1984a, 1987; Kuck *et al.*, 1984a; Padua and Wolfe, 1986). More detailed specifications can be found in a number of theses (Allen, 1983; Wolfe, 1978, 1982), and in particular in the Parafrase documentation (Leasure, 1985), from which much of the material presented in this chapter has been derived. The problem of finding induction variables is treated in Aho *et al.* (1986).

Chapter 6

Vectorization

6.1 Introduction

In this chapter we consider how sequential programs are automatically transformed into vector code. We focus our attention on do-loops and learn when we can validly rewrite a do-loop as a sequence of vector statements and which transformations are required to do so. This process is referred to as **vectorization**.

Some notation is needed to specify array processing in our output language VP-Fortran (see Section 1.4). We use the appropriate features of Fortran 90 (ANSI, 1989); for their semantics the reader is referred to our discussion of vector instructions in Section 2.2.3.

Fortran operators, most intrinsic functions and the assignment statement are extended so that they can be applied to arrays, in the sense that the operations are to be performed componentwise, subject to FS-semantics (see ANSI (1989) and Section 2.2.3). For example: let A, B, C be declared by

```
DIMENSION A(1:N, 1:M), B(1:N, 1:M), C(1:N, 1:M)
```

Then, the statement A = B * C is functionally equivalent[†] to the loop

---

[†] We emphasize here that the equivalence does not extend to execution order. The details of the mapping from vector statements to the vector instructions of a particular machine are implementation dependent. Some aspects of the mapping are discussed in Section 6.8.

```
DO J = 1, M
  DO I = 1, N
    A(I, J) = B(I, J) * C(I, J)
  END DO I
END DO J
```

Rectangular **array sections** can be defined in triplet notation. Let x_i ($1 \leq i \leq 3$) be expressions: then the triplet ($x_1 : x_2$ [$:x_3$]) specifies the first and last subscript, and the stride for a given dimension (for simplicity, we assume $x_3 | (x_2 - x_1)$). The default value for x_3 is 1. A triplet may be specified for one or more dimensions of a multi-dimensional array.

For example, A(I,1:M) denotes the Ith row, and A(1:N,J) the Jth column of A; A($T_1 : U_1, T_2 : U_2$) is the subarray consisting of all elements A(I,J) such that $T_1 \leq I \leq U_1$, and $T_2 \leq J \leq U_2$.

The assignment A(I,1:M:2) = B(I-1,M:1:-2) is equivalent to the loop

```
DO J = 1, M, 2
  A(I, J) = B(I - 1, M + 1 - J)
END DO
```

If only the identifier of an array occurs in a statement, then it represents the entire array, that is an occurrence of A is equivalent to A(1:N:1,1:M:1).

Sometimes we want to access elements of an array at random. Assume D(1:N) and X(1:LG) are one-dimensional arrays, and the elements of X are arbitrary values in the interval [1:N] (replication is permitted): then D(X) defines the sequence of elements of D given by D(X(1)), D(X(2)), ..., D(X(LG)). X is called an **index vector**.

In contrast to the static allocation scheme of Fortran 77, we provide executable statements for the dynamic allocation and deallocation of memory for arrays; for example:

```
ALLOCATE X(0:K, 0:K)   /* Memory allocation for X */
...
/* Here X can be accessed */
...
DEALLOCATE X           /* Memory deallocation for X */
```

Scalars that occur in the context of an array operation are always implicitly expanded to matching arrays, whose elements are all identical to the scalar operand. For example, A = A + 1 is equivalent to

```
DO J = 1, M
  DO I = 1, N
    A(I, J) = A(I, J) + 1
  END DO I
END DO J
```

The where-statement allows the specification of masked assignment statements in the form WHERE (*mask*) A = *exp*, where *mask* is an expression whose value is a boolean array. For example:

```
WHERE (B ≠ 0) A = A/B
```

is equivalent to

```
DO J = 1, M
  DO I = 1, N
    IF B(I, J) ≠ 0
      THEN A(I, J) = A(I, J)/B(I, J)
    FI
  END DO I
END DO J
```

Syntactically, more than one assignment statement can be associated with the same mask, for example

```
WHERE (A < 0) A = A + 1
             B = B * C
END WHERE
```

This completes our discussion of array features in VP-Fortran. Further extensions are added where required.

We now proceed with an overview of our basic approach to vectorization. Except where otherwise noted, the discussion will be based on loops satisfying the model of Chapter 4 (see Section 4.2.2), where the bounds of all loops at levels ≥ 2 are constant; that is we deal with loops whose body contains assignment statements and do-loops, and for which the increment is equal to 1. All arrays occurring in examples are assumed to be suitably declared.

Example 6.1

Take the following loop:

```
DO I = 1, 100
  S:  A(I) = 0
END DO
```

When this loop is executed sequentially, we know that $S(1)$ is executed before $S(2)$, and so on. In contrast, if we rewrite the loop as a vector statement, all $S(i)$ are executed concurrently $(1 \leq i \leq 100)$: this is expressed as S(1:100) or A(1:100) = 0.

Vectorization is semantically valid if all dependences of the original program are retained. This is satisfied for the above example.

Example 6.2

Statement S below, on the other hand:

```
DO I = 1, N
  S:  A(I + 1) = A(I) * B(I)
END DO
```

is contained in a cyclic true dependence. The statement instances are executed in standard order as follows:

```
S(1):  A(2) = A(1) * B(1)
S(2):  A(3) = A(2) * B(2)
       ...
S(N):  A(N + 1) = A(N) * B(N)
```

As we see when we unroll the loop, the values of all $A(i)$, $2 \leqslant i \leqslant N$, are determined in the loop and subsequently used in it. If we were to vectorize S, then the products $A(i) * B(i)$ would be computed using the values $A(i)$ held prior to entering the loop. Since this would generally produce different results, vectorization is invalid.

However, an existing dependence need not always prevent vectorization, as the next example shows.

Example 6.3

In this loop,

```
L:  DO I = 1, 100
      S:   D(I) = A(I - 1) * D(I)
      S':  A(I) = B(I) + C(I)
    END DO
```

S depends on S'. By applying two simple transformations we can vectorize both S and S'; in the first step, we exchange the textual order of S and S': this reordering transformation, which does not modify the program semantics in our example, yields the loop:

```
L1:  DO I = 1, 100
       S':  A(I) = B(I) + C(I)
       S:   D(I) = A(I - 1) * D(I)
     END DO
```

The dependence arc for this loop points downwards and we can perform **loop distribution** as shown below:

```
L21:  DO I = 1, 100
        S':  A(I) = B(I) + C(I)
      END DO
```

```
L22:  DO I = 1, 100
        S:  D(I) = A(I - 1) * D(I)
      END DO
```

Loop distribution has converted the loop-carried dependence from S' to S in $L1$ into a loop-independent dependence. There are no dependences within $L21$ and $L22$, and hence vectorization is possible:

```
A(1:100) = B(1:100) + C(1:100)
D(1:100) = A(0: 99) * D(1:100)
```

Roughly speaking, we can vectorize a statement S if it is not contained in a cycle of the dependence graph. On the other hand, if S is contained in a dependence cycle, then an order must be retained for certain instances of S, which makes vectorization in general invalid (as Example 6.2 shows).

A vectorizing compiler could be based on this principle; that is, rule out vectorization when a dependence cycle has been found. However, this is unnecessarily restrictive. Consider the following:

Example 6.4

This loop has a cyclic loop-carried dependence at level 1 involving S, but no dependences in the inner loop:

```
DO I = 1, N
  DO J = 1, N
    S:  C(I, J) = C(I - 1, J) - D(I - 1, J + 1)
  END DO J
END DO I
```

If we do not modify the outer loop, then the dependence is satisfied and the inner loop may be executed as a vector statement. The loop may thus be transformed into:

```
DO I = 1, N
  C(I, 1:N) = C(I - 1, 1:N) - D(I - 1, 2:N + 1)
END DO I
```

Thus even cyclic dependences may not altogether prevent vectorization when the level at which the dependence occurs is taken into account.[†] Our approach to vector code generation is based on this concept.

Chapter 6 consists of nine sections.

Section 6.2 introduces the fundamental transformations required for vectorization, and derives conditions for their semantic validity. These transformations are statement reordering, loop distribution, and vector statement generation. Statement reordering changes the textual position of two adjacent statements; it can be validly applied if no loop-independent dependences exist between these statements. Loop distribution splits a loop with two or more statements into a sequence of loops by distributing the loop control over single statements or statement groups. It can be applied validly if there are no loop-carried dependences pointing backward. Vector statement generation rewrites a perfectly nested loop with just one statement as a vector statement.

Section 6.3 derives a condition under which the concurrent execution of all statement instances at a given loop level is semantically valid. Applied to vectorization, this provides the basis of the Allen–Kennedy algorithm for vector code generation which is presented in Section 6.4. Suppose that S is a statement at level n of a loop L. If S is not contained in a dependence cycle, then the algorithm generates vector code for S at all levels. Otherwise, it determines the smallest number c_0 such that the serial execution of the c_0 outermost loops suffices to break the dependence cycle; the innermost $n-c_0$ loops, if any, can then be executed in vector mode. The algorithm operates on the dependence graph and uses its strongly connected components to distinguish between sequential and vectorizable regions.

Section 6.5 presents an assortment of transformations that can remove obstacles to vectorization. Loop interchange, for example, swaps the control statements of two adjacent loops in a loop nest: this can be used in vectorization to move a dependence cycle outward. Another transformation, scalar expansion, converts a temporary scalar variable of a loop into an array and thus may eliminate a dependence cycle.

[†] Certain kinds of cyclic dependences do not rule out vectorization altogether (see Section 6.5.3). This will be ignored for the time being.

The discussion up to Section 6.5 is based upon the loop model of Section 4.2. Section 6.6 introduces a way to deal with control structures in the context of vectorization. We transform them by a method known as if-conversion, which essentially converts control dependences caused by if-statements and branches into data dependences. Put simply, it turns each assignment statement S within the scope of a control dependence into a conditional statement, which uses a mask to control the execution of S. Then an attempt is made to vectorize such statements by converting them to where-statements.

In Section 6.7, we discuss how to deal with procedure calls in the context of vectorization.

Section 6.8 addresses various aspects of implementation-dependent code generation. We consider how to write code for a particular vector register length, in what way vector length affects performance, and how access to memory can be improved.

The chapter ends with a discussion of selected issues and biblio-graphical references.

A final note: much of the discussion in this chapter is not only relevant for vectorization, but can be directly applied to parallelization as well. This is in particular true for Sections 6.2, 6.3, and 6.5.

6.2   Fundamental transformations

6.2.1   Statement reordering

Statement reordering exchanges the textual position of two adjacent statements. We show this transformation to be valid iff there is no loop-independent dependence between them. Example 6.3 illustrated how statement reordering can be applied when a loop is being vectorized.

TRANSFORMATION 6.1: Statement reordering

> **Input**   A loop L containing adjacent assignment statements S and S' (S bef S').
>
> **Output**   A modified loop L', which is obtained from L by reversing the textual order of S and S'.   ∎

In Example 6.5, the reordering is valid (the loop-carried dependence from S to S' is not affected), and in Example 6.6 it is not, since there is a loop-independent true dependence from S to S', which is 'reversed' into an anti-dependence from S' to S by the transformation.

Example 6.5

Valid reordering is illustrated by

```
DO I=1,N                    DO I=1,N
  S:  A(I)=B(I)*2             S': C(I)=A(I-1)-4
  S': C(I)=A(I-1)-4   ⟹       S:  A(I)=B(I)*2
END DO                      END DO
```

Example 6.6

This reordering is not valid:

```
DO I=1,N                    DO I=1,N
  S:  A(I)=B(I)*2             S': C(I)=A(I)-4
  S': C(I)=A(I)-4    ⟹        S:  A(I)=B(I)*2
END DO                      END DO
```

Lemma 6.1 Let L be a loop and S, S' adjacent statements within L such that S bef S' and not $S\,\delta_\infty\,S'$. Let L' be the loop obtained by reordering S and S'. Then for any pair of assignment statements S_1, S_2 in L, dependence type $x \in \{t,a,o\}$, and level $k \in \mathbb{N} \cup \{\infty\}$:

$$S_1\,\delta_k^x\,S_2 \text{ in } L' \text{ iff } S_1\,\delta_k^x\,S_2 \text{ in } L. \qquad \blacksquare$$

Proof Suppose that $S_1\,\delta_k^x\,S_2$ in L. Then there exist $\mathbf{i}_1 \in [S_1]$ and $\mathbf{i}_2 \in [S_2]$ such that $S_1(\mathbf{i}_1) \lessdot_k S_2(\mathbf{i}_2)$, and x determines a pair of input/output sets related to $S_1(\mathbf{i}_1)$ and $S_2(\mathbf{i}_2)$, which have a non-empty intersection. From our assumption, $k = \infty$ implies $\{S_1,S_2\} \neq \{S,S'\}$. Reordering of S and S' does not modify the contents of input or output sets and does retain the order in which the statement instances $S_1(\mathbf{i}_1)$ and $S_2(\mathbf{i}_2)$ are executed. Moreover, only a loop-independent output dependence from S to S' could destroy the covering condition. Thus we can conclude that $S_1\,\delta_k^x\,S_2$ holds in L' as well. Since no new dependences are introduced by the transformation, the correctness of the lemma has been established. $\blacksquare$

In Example 6.6 we saw that reordering, when applied to a pair of statements between which a loop-independent dependence exists, may be invalid. This observation can be generalized by showing that in such a case a dependence $S\,\delta_\infty^x\,S'$ is reversed to a dependence $S'\,\delta_\infty^{x'}\,S$, where x' and x are related as follows: $x' = a$, if $x = t$; $x' = t$, if $x = a$; and $x' = x$ otherwise. Other (loop-carried and loop-independent) dependences between statements of the loop may be affected as well. This immediately yields a criterion for valid reordering.[†]

Theorem 6.1   Statement reordering, applied to a loop L and statements S and S', is valid iff there is no loop-independent dependence from S to S'. ■

6.2.2 Loop distribution: basic version

Loop distribution is a transformation that distributes the control of a do-loop over groups of statements in its body; it precedes vector code generation. In its basic version – which is discussed here – control is distributed over single statements.

In the following, $D := DG(L)$ denotes the dependence graph of a loop L. A set of statements in L that is contained in a cycle of D is called a **recurrence**. Statement S in Example 6.4 is an example of a (single-statement) recurrence.

TRANSFORMATION 6.2: Loop distribution – basic version

Input   A loop L, where $S_1, \ldots, S_p$ are the assignment statements of L in their textual order $(p \geqslant 1)$.

Output $DISTR(L)$: this is a sequence of loops $DISTR(S_1)$; $\ldots$; $DISTR(S_p)$, where for every $r \in [1{:}p]$, $DISTR(S_r)$ is defined as follows: Let $S = S_r$ be characterized as in Program 4.1. Then $DISTR(S_r)$ is a perfectly nested loop containing S_r as the only statement in its body:

$DISTR(S_r)$: DO $I_1 = t_1$, u_1
            DO $I_2 = t_2$, u_2
            $\ldots$
            DO $I_n = t_n$, u_n
                S_r
            END DO I_n
            $\ldots$
            END DO I_2
            END DO I_1 ■

[†] The condition 'there is no loop-independent dependence between S and S'' is necessary for the correctness of statement reordering in the sense that the existence of a dependence $S \, \delta_\infty \, S'$ implies *in general* (without taking into account the specific effect of S and S') that reordering is not valid. For special (mostly pathological) cases such as, for example, $S: A = exp$ and $S': A = exp$, reordering may be valid although $S \, \delta_\infty \, S'$ holds. The correctness criterion for loop distribution (see Theorem 6.2) must be interpreted analogously.

Distribution essentially rearranges statement instances in such a way that each statement is executed for all elements of its execution index set before any statement that textually follows.

Example 6.7

Consider Example 4.11

```
DO J = 1, 100
  DO I = 1, 100
    S:  C(I, J) = 0.0
        DO K = 1, 100
          S':  C(I, J) = C(I, J) + A(I, K) * B(K, J)
        END DO K
  END DO I
END DO J
```

Loop distribution yields:

```
DO J = 1, 100
  DO I = 1, 100
    S:  C(I, J) = 0.0
  END DO I
END DO J


DO J = 1, 100
  DO I = 1, 100
    DO K = 1, 100
      S':  C(I, J) = C(I, J) + A(I, K) * B(K, J)
    END DO K
  END DO I
END DO J
```

Definition 6.1   A loop L is **distributive** iff loop distribution (basic version), applied to L, is semantically valid.   ∎

While the loop of Example 6.7 is distributive, as the reader can easily verify, the following loop is not.

Example 6.8

```
L:  DO I = 1, N
      S:   C(I) = A(I - 2)
      S':  A(I) = ...
    END DO
```

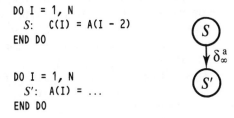

Distribution of L destroys the loop-carried dependence from S' to S:

```
DO I = 1, N
  S:   C(I) = A(I - 2)
END DO

DO I = 1, N
  S':  A(I) = ...
END DO
```

and is therefore invalid.

In the following, we make precise the conditions under which a loop is distributive. The generalization of the above example yields a sufficient and necessary criterion.

Definition 6.2   Let S and S' denote statements in a loop. A dependence $S' \delta S$ is said to be **backward** iff S bef S'. Any dependence that is not backward is called a **forward** dependence.   ∎

The loop-carried dependence from S' to S in Example 6.8 is an example for a backward dependence. Obviously then we have the following.

Lemma 6.2   Every backward dependence is loop-carried.   ∎

Theorem 6.2   A loop is distributive iff all its dependences are forward.   ∎

Proof Assume first that L is a loop with a backward dependence. Then there exist statements S and S', iteration vectors $\mathbf{i} \in [S]$ and $\mathbf{i}' \in [S']$, and $c \in \mathbb{N}$ such that:

(1) S bef S'

(2) $S'(\mathbf{i}') \, \delta_c \, S(\mathbf{i})$.

A valid transformation must preserve the order of the statement instances implied by (2). However, from (1), after distribution of L, all instances of S are executed before all instances of S'. Thus, the backward dependence is destroyed by the transformation, and L is not distributive. (See footnote on page 197.)

Suppose now that L is a loop that contains only forward dependences. Then each dependence is of the form $S \, \delta \, S'$, where either $S = S'$ or S bef S'. A single-statement recurrence is preserved by loop distribution, so it suffices to examine the case $S \, \delta \, S'$, where S bef S'. Then there exist iteration vectors $\mathbf{i} \in [S]$, $\mathbf{i}' \in [S']$ such that $S(\mathbf{i}) \, \delta \, S'(\mathbf{i}')$, and there is a non-empty intersection between certain input and/or output execution sets of S and S' associated with these instances. After distribution, all instances of S are executed before all instances of S'; thus the relative order of the statement instances involved in the dependence is not changed.

It remains to show that a dependence cannot be covered as a result of loop distribution. Assume that $v \in VARX$ is the variable occurrence that causes the dependence, and $v(\mathbf{i}) \in DEF(S(\mathbf{i}))$. If v were scalar, then $v(\mathbf{j})$ would be the same variable for all iteration vectors $\mathbf{j} \in [S]$, and a backward dependence would exist, contrary to our assumptions. More generally, we can conclude that v must be a subscripted variable which is mapped into pairwise disjoint array elements for different iteration vectors of S. A similar conclusion can be drawn for S', if $v(\mathbf{i}') \in DEF(S')$. Thus covering cannot occur, and since the input and output execution sets of statements are not modified by distribution, the dependence is preserved. ∎

The following example illustrates a (rather pathological) case in which loop distribution would cover a dependence, but since a backward dependence exists, the premises for a valid application of loop distribution are not satisfied.

Example 6.9

The distribution of the loop

```
DO I = 1, N
  DO J = 1, M
   S:   A(I, I) = J + 1
   S':  B(I, J) = A(I, I)
  END DO J
END DO I
```

would cover all dependences $S(i,j)\ \delta_\infty\ S'(i,j)$ with $i \in [1:N]$ and $j \in [1:M-1]$, and change the effect of the loop.

Lemma 6.3   Assume that L is a distributive loop and L' is obtained by distributing L. Then the type of all dependences in L remains the same after distribution; the level is affected as follows ($c \in \mathbb{N}$):

(1)   If $S\ \delta_\infty\ S'$ in L, then $S\ \delta_\infty\ S'$ in L'.
(2)   If $S\ \delta_c\ S$ in L, then $S\ \delta_c\ S$ in L'.
(3)   If $S\ \delta_c\ S'$ in L and $S \neq S'$, then $S\ \delta_\infty\ S'$ in L'.   ∎

The following is our most important result for the use of loop distribution.

Theorem 6.3   A loop can be made distributive by a sequence of valid statement reordering transformations iff its dependence graph D is either acyclic or contains only elementary loops.   ∎

Proof   Suppose that D contains a cycle which is not an elementary loop. Assume first that the cycle is of length 2 and involves the adjacent statements S and S', where S bef S'. Then the dependence from S' to S is backward: $S'\ \delta_c\ S$ for some $c \in \mathbb{N}$, and L is not distributive. If there is a loop-independent dependence from S to S', then S and S' cannot be validly reordered. Otherwise, $S\ \delta_{c'}\ S'$ for some $c' \in \mathbb{N}$, and reordering is valid, converting the backward dependence from S' to S into a forward dependence, and the forward dependence from S to S' into a backward dependence. In both cases, we cannot eliminate all backward dependences, and therefore never obtain a distributive loop.

   This argument can be easily generalized to cycles of arbitrary length and to arbitrary statement positions.

Now suppose that D either is acyclic or contains only elementary loops. According to Theorem 6.2 it is sufficient to show that all backward dependences can be converted to forward dependences by a sequence of valid statement reordering transformations. We prove this for the case in which S and S' are both contained in the same loop environment. This can be generalized to cover the remaining cases.

First, note that elementary loops play no role with respect to distributivity: therefore we may assume without loss of generality that D is acyclic, with its nodes $S_1, \ldots, S_N$ sorted topologically: thus $S_{j_1} \delta S_{j_2}$ implies $j_1 < j_2$. We now proceed with an inductive argument as follows.

Let $L_0 := L$, and for each i, $1 \leq i \leq N$, define L_i such that:

(1)   The first i assignment statements in L_i are $S_1, \ldots, S_i$.

(2) L_i is obtained from L_{i-1} by a valid reordering sequence.

If we succeed in constructing the loops L_i in this way, then L_N cannot contain any backward edges and is obtained from L by a valid reordering sequence; this would prove the correctness of the theorem.

(I)   *Basis of induction: $i = 1$*
We have to show that S_1 can be made the first statement of L_1. If this is already true, then we set $L_1 := L$ and are finished. Otherwise, note that there is no statement S such that $S \delta S_1$ holds: in particular, if S is any statement textually before S_1 in L, then $S \delta_\infty S_1$. Thus, by Theorem 6.1, S_1 can be moved upward by a sequence of valid statement reorderings until it has reached the first position.

(II)   *Induction step: $i - 1 \to i$ $(2 \leq i \leq N)$*
Assume that a valid reordering sequence has been found that transforms L into L_{i-1}, which has $S_1, \ldots, S_{i-1}$ in the first $i - 1$ positions. We have to find a valid reordering sequence that transforms L_{i-1} into L_i, moving S_i into position i.
     If S_i is already in that position, we set $L_i := L_{i-1}$, and are finished. Otherwise, let S be the statement immediately preceding S_i in L_{i-1}:

L_{i-1}: S_1
         S_2
         ...
         S_{i-1}
         ...
         S
         S_i
         ...

We have $S \phi_\infty S_i$, and thus by Theorem 6.1, S and S_i can be validly reordered. The same argument applies to every statement between S_{i-1} and S_i, so S_i may be validly moved in a finite number of steps into position i. The resulting loop is defined as L_i. It satisfies criteria (1) and (2). ∎

6.2.3 Loop distribution: general version

The basic version of loop distribution cannot handle loops with non-elementary cycles correctly. However, as the following example illustrates, there can be useful concurrency in such loops as well.

Example 6.10

The loop L

```
L:  DO I = 1, N
      S₁:  C(I) = A(I - 2) * B(I)
      S₂:  D(I) = B(I) + B(I - 1)/2
      S₃:  A(I) = C(I) + 2
    END DO
```

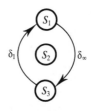

is not distributive. However, after reordering S_2 and S_3, it can be split into two loops L_1 and L_2, where L_1 is non-distributive, but L_2 is distributive and can be vectorized. This transformation preserves the semantics of the program:

```
L₁:  DO I = 1, N
       S₁:  C(I) = A(I - 2) * B(I)
       S₃:  A(I) = C(I) + 2
     END DO

L₂:  DO I = 1, N
       S₂:  D(I) = B(I) + B(I - 1)/2
     END DO
```

We extend loop distribution to handle cases like the one above. The generalization consists of applying distribution of the loop control not only to single assignment statements, but to groups of such statements (which may be cyclically connected in the dependence graph). This transformation is frequently called **loop fission** (Wolfe, 1982).

TRANSFORMATION 6.3: Loop distribution – general version

Input   A loop L, where $S_1, \ldots, S_p$ are the assignment statements of L in their textual order $(p \geqslant 1)$. These are partitioned into blocks $B_1, \ldots, B_q$, such that each block consists of one or more adjacent assignment statements, and the first statement of a block B_s $(1 < s \leqslant q)$ is the successor of the last statement of B_{s-1}.

Output $DISTR(L)$: this is a sequence of loops $DISTR(B_1); \ldots, DISTR(B_q)$, where for every $s \in [1:q]$, $DISTR(B_s)$ is $DISTR(S)$ as defined in Transformation 6.2, if B_s consists of a single statement S; otherwise $DISTR(B_s)$ is the loop nest enclosing precisely the statements of B_s.   ∎

Example 6.11

Consider the nested loop

```
L:  DO I = 1, N
      DO J = 1, N
        S₁:  A(I, J) = ...
        S₂:  A(I, J + 1) = A(I, J) - 1
      END DO J
      S₃:  B(I) = 2 * D(I) + 3
      S₄:  C(I) = B(I) - 4
    END DO I
```

S_1 and S_2 are contained in a cyclic region of the dependence graph. We can isolate this region from the other two statements (which may be vectorized) by validly applying loop distribution, with blocks defined by: $B_1 = \{S_1, S_2\}$, $B_2 = \{S_3\}$, and $B_3 = \{S_4\}$. This yields:

```
DO I = 1, N
  DO J = 1, N
    S₁:  A(I, J) = ...
    S₂:  A(I, J + 1) = A(I, J) - 1
  END DO J
END DO I

DO I = 1, N
  S₃:  B(I) = 2 * D(I) + 3
END DO I

DO I = 1, N
  S₄:  C(I) = B(I) - 4
END DO I
```

If we consider the dependence relationships between groups of statements (the blocks in the sense of Transformation 6.3), then the definition of distributivity and related results for the basic version of loop distribution (in particular Theorem 6.3) can be generalized. We do not elaborate this in detail.

6.2.4 Vector statement generation

The last thing we must do when vectorizing code is generate the actual vector statements. Transformation 6.4 rewrites a perfectly nested loop with exactly one statement S in its body as a vector statement, in which the iterations of all loops enclosing S are executed concurrently. This is semantically valid if S is not part of a recurrence $S \, \delta \, S$.

TRANSFORMATION 6.4: Vector statement generation

Input A perfectly nested loop L with exactly one assignment statement S at level n:

$$L: \quad \text{DO } I_1 = t_1, u_1$$
$$\text{DO } I_2 = t_2, u_2$$
$$\ldots$$
$$\text{DO } I_n = t_n, u_n$$
$$S$$
$$\text{END DO } I_n$$
$$\ldots$$
$$\text{END DO } I_2$$
$$\text{END DO } I_1$$

Output The vector statement $S(T_1:U_1, T_2:U_2, \ldots, T_n:U_n)$, where the T_j and U_j are the values of t_j and u_j, respectively $(1 \le j \le n)$. ∎

Theorem 6.4 Vector statement generation is valid if $S \, \phi \, S$.

Proof If $S \, \phi \, S$, then there is no restriction on the order in which the statement instances $S(\mathbf{i})$, $\mathbf{i} \in [S]$, can be executed. Since we can compute the values of all t_j and u_j $(1 \le j \le n)$, the output of the transformation is a well-defined vector statement which is equivalent to the original loop. ∎

If $S \, \delta \, S$, then we cannot conclude that vector statement generation is valid, since the recurrence implies in general that there are iteration vectors

$i,i' \in [S]$ such that $S(i)$ must be executed before $S(i')$. Nevertheless, certain special recurrences (see Sections 6.5.3 and 6.5.7) can be correctly rewritten as vector statements. Whenever we do not deal explicitly with these cases, we will assume in the following that vector code generation is not possible if $S \delta S$ holds.

6.2.5 Vectorization: the basic approach

Let L denote a loop and $D = DG(L)$ its dependence graph. L can be vectorized as follows:

- *Step 1*
  Construct the strongly connected components (SCCs) of the dependence graph D, and its acyclic condensation $G = AC(D)$ (see Appendix A and Appendix C, Section C.6). Each SCC is either a trivial graph – representing an assignment statement not involved in a recurrence – or a cyclic graph that represents a set of one or more assignment statements which form a recurrence. In the literature, G is often called the **PI-graph**, and the SCCs are known as **PI-blocks**.

- *Step 2*
  Sort the SCCs topologically.

- *Step 3*
  Perform a sequence of valid statement reordering transformations such that:

  (i)   all statements belonging to an SCC are adjacent, and
  (ii) the relative order of statements belonging to different SCCs is determined by the topological order of the SCCs to which they belong.

- *Step 4*
  The loop resulting from Step 3 is distributive, and loop distribution (general version) can be validly applied.

- *Step 5*
  Define the blocks B_s $(1 \leq s \leq q)$ corresponding to the SCCs, in their topological order. Consider each loop $DISTR(B_s)$ separately. If B_s corresponds to an SCC $(\{S\}, \emptyset)$, then vector code generation is possible (Transformation 6.4). Otherwise, B_s is not modified, and the sequential loop control is retained.

The following example illustrates this transformation in detail.

Example 6.12

```
L:L₁:  DO I = 1, N
   L₂:   DO J = 1, M
       S₁:  C(I, J) = A(I, J) * B(I, J)
       S₂:  A(I + 1, J + 1) = C(I, J - 2)/2 + C(I - 1, J) * 3
       S₃:  D(I, J) = D(I - 1, J - 1) + 1
       S₄:  B(I, J + 4) = D(I, J) - 1
       END DO J
     END DO I
```

- *Step 1*
  The dependence graph $D := DG(L)$ is specified in Figure 6.1. Its SCCs are given by $G_1 = (\{S_3\}, \{(S_3, S_3)\})$, $G_2 = (\{S_4\}, \varnothing)$, and $G_3 = (\{S_1, S_2\}, \{(S_1, S_2), (S_2, S_1)\})$. G_1 and G_3 are cyclic SCCs, while G_2 is a trivial graph. $AC(D)$ is shown in Figure 6.2.

- *Step 2*
  Topological sorting of $AC(D)$ yields the order G_1, G_2, G_3.

- *Step 3*
  The statements in each SCC are already adjacent. Reordering them in accordance with the topological order of the SCCs yields:

```
DO I = 1, N
  DO J = 1, M
    S₃:  D(I, J) = D(I - 1, J - 1) + 1
    S₄:  B(I, J + 4) = D(I, J) - 1
    S₁:  C(I, J) = A(I, J) * B(I, J)
    S₂:  A(I + 1, J + 1) = C(I, J - 2)/2 + C(I - 1, J) * 3
  END DO J
END DO I
```

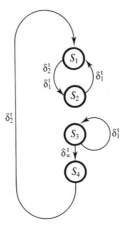

Figure 6.1   Dependence graph D for the loop of Example 6.12.

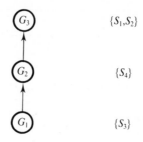

Figure 6.2 $AC(D)$ for the loop of Example 6.12.

- *Step 4*

  By applying loop distribution (general version) to the above loop, with blocks $B_1 = \{S_3\}$, $B_2 = \{S_4\}$, and $B_3 = \{S_1, S_2\}$, we obtain:

```
DO I = 1, N
  DO J = 1, M
    S₃:  D(I, J) = D(I - 1, J - 1) + 1
  END DO J
END DO I

DO I = 1, N
  DO J = 1, M
    S₄:  B(I, J + 4) = D(I, J) - 1
  END DO J
END DO I

DO I = 1, N
  DO J = 1, M
    S₁:  C(I, J) = A(I, J) * B(I, J)
    S₂:  A(I + 1, J + 1) = C(I, J - 2)/2 + C(I - 1, J) * 3
  END DO J
END DO I
```

- *Step 5*

  Vector code can be generated for the second loop, while the other two loops (both of which produce recurrences) are left sequential. This yields the following final code:

```
DO I = 1, N
  DO J = 1, M
    S₃:  D(I, J) = D(I - 1, J - 1) + 1
  END DO J
END DO I

B(1:N, 5:M + 4) = D(1:N, 1:M) - 1
```

```
DO I = 1, N
  DO J = 1, M
    S₁:  C(I, J) = A(I, J) * B(I, J)
    S₂:  A(I + 1, J + 1) = C(I, J - 2)/2 + C(I - 1, J) * 3
  END DO J
END DO I
```

The basic method of vectorization as outlined above does not fully exploit the concurrency present in a loop. In particular, in a loop nest we want to vectorize inner levels even if there is a recurrence at some outer level.

For example, the statements S_1, S_2, and S_3 above can all be vectorized in the J loop, as the recurrence which they are part of exists only in the I loop.

The next section examines concurrency at arbitrary levels of a loop nest. This will provide us with the theoretical background for a more general approach to vectorization as well as parallelization.

6.3   Concurrency in loops

Suppose that L is an arbitrarily nested loop and $D = (N,E)$ is an associated dependence graph.

Our first definition is related to the fact that a single edge of the dependence graph may represent one or more dependences, which may be at different levels. An example is the edge (S_1,S_2) in the dependence graph of Figure 6.1. This graph will be used throughout this section – in conjunction with the program of Example 6.12 – to illustrate the newly defined concepts.

Definition 6.3   For each edge $e \in E$:

(1)   *levels*(e) is the set of all levels $k \in \mathbb{N} \cup \{\infty\}$ associated with e.

(2)   *minlevel*$(e) := min(levels(e))$.

(3)   *maxlevel*$(e) := max(levels(e))$.   ∎

For each $e \in E$, *levels*(e) is well-defined and non-empty. When we increment and compare levels below, we assume that $\infty + 1 = \infty$ and, for all $c \in \mathbb{N}$, $c < \infty$.

We now introduce **layered** dependence graphs:

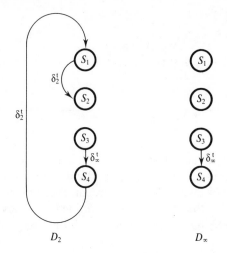

Figure 6.3 Layered graphs D_2 and D_∞ for the dependence graph of Figure 6.1.

Definition 6.4 Let $k \in \mathbb{N} \cup \{\infty\}$ denote a level. Then the **level** k **dependence graph** of D, denoted by $constrain(D,k)$, is given as follows:

$$constrain(D,k) := (N,E_k), \text{ where } E_k := \{e \in E: maxlevel(e) \ge k\}. \qquad \blacksquare$$

In the following, we will usually denote the level k dependence graph of D by D_k. D_k is a directed graph, which contains all nodes of D, but only those edges that are at level k or deeper.

The following lemma states some basic facts about layered dependence graphs.

Lemma 6.4

(1) $constrain(D,1) = D$.

(2) $constrain(D,\infty)$ is an acyclic graph.

(3) $constrain(D,k) = constrain(D,\infty)$ for all levels k, where k is larger than the maximum depth of L. $\blacksquare$

We attach the same levels to the edges in a layered dependence graph as in the original graph. Consider the loop in Example 6.12 and its dependence graph $D = DG(L)$ in Figure 6.1. Figure 6.3 specifies D_2 and D_∞.

We now extend Definition 6.3 to arbitrary paths in D. Each such path has the form $\pi = S_0, \ldots, S_t$, where the S_r are assignment statements ($0 \le r \le t$), and, for every r with $1 \le r \le t$, $S_{r-1} \delta S_r$ holds.

Definition 6.5   Let π be a path in D.

(1) $levels(\pi) := \{k \in \mathbb{N} \cup \{\infty\}:$
$$\forall e \text{ in } \pi: maxlevel(e) \geq k \text{ and } \exists e \text{ in } \pi: k \in levels(e)\}.$$

(2) $minlevel(\pi) := min(levels(\pi)).$

(3) $maxlevel(\pi) := max(levels(\pi)).$ ∎

As in Definition 6.3 we see easily that, for each path π, $levels(\pi)$ is well defined and non-empty. Let π and $k \in levels(\pi)$ be arbitrarily chosen. Then there exists at least one edge in π with a level k, and all other edges have levels that are at least k. We can think of k as a level that can be 'maintained' along π. $minlevel(\pi)$ and $maxlevel(\pi)$ are the minimum and maximum levels, respectively, that can be maintained along π.

Consider for example the path $\pi = (e_1, e_2, e_3)$, where $levels(e_1) = \{1,3\}$, $levels(e_2) = \{\infty\}$, and $levels(e_3) = \{1,4\}$. Then $levels(\pi) = \{1,3\}$.

The example shows that, if we choose k' arbitrarily such that $minlevel(\pi) \leq k' \leq maxlevel(\pi)$, then we cannot conclude that $k' \in levels(\pi)$. The following simple lemma relates $minlevel$ and $maxlevel$ for paths to the corresponding attributes of their edges.

Lemma 6.5   For each path π:

(1) $minlevel(\pi) = min\{minlevel(e): e \text{ is an edge in } \pi\}.$

(2) $maxlevel(\pi) = min\{maxlevel(e): e \text{ is an edge in } \pi\}.$ ∎

Cyclic paths and their levels play an important role when we investigate the applicability of vectorization and parallelization transformations. In the following, assume that S is an arbitrary statement at level n of loop L, and $D = DG(L)$. $CP(S)$ is the set of all cyclic paths from S to S in D.

Definition 6.6 $CP(S) := \{\pi: \pi \text{ is a path } S_0, \ldots, S_t \text{ in } D, \text{ where } t \geq 1$ and $S_0 = S_t = S\}.$ ∎

Example 6.13

We refer to the loop in Example 6.12 (see also Figures 6.1 and 6.3).

$$CP(S_1) = (S_1, S_2, S_1)(S_2, S_1)^*$$

Thus $CP(S_1)$ is the set of all paths:

(S_1,S_2,S_1)
(S_1,S_2,S_1,S_2,S_1)
$(S_1,S_2,S_1,S_2,S_1,S_2,S_1)$
. . .

Furthermore:

$CP(S_2) = (S_2,S_1,S_2)(S_1,S_2)^*$
$CP(S_3) = \{(S_3)^r: r \geqslant 2\}$
$CP(S_4) = \varnothing$

We finally note: for every path $\pi \in CP(S_1) \cup CP(S_2) \cup CP(S_3)$: $maxlevel(\pi) = 1$.

Lemma 6.6   For each cycle $\pi \in CP(S)$, where S is a statement at level n, $1 \leqslant maxlevel(\pi) \leqslant min(j: j$ is the level of a statement in $\pi)$.   ∎

Proof   This follows immediately from (1) and (2) below.

(1)   If $e = (S_1,S_2) \in E$, with S_i at level n_i ($i = 1,2$), then every $c \in levels(e) - \{\infty\}$ (if such a c exists) satisfies $c \leqslant m \leqslant min(n_1,n_2)$, where m is the maximum common loop index of S_1 and S_2.

(2)   In a cyclic path, not all edges may have a level ∞.   ∎

Consider a cycle π at level c in D. π is mapped to a cycle at level c in every $D_{c'}$ ($1 \leqslant c' \leqslant c$), but it is 'broken' in D_{c+1}. For example, the cycle (S_1,S_2,S_1) in the dependence graph D of Figure 6.1 exists only at level 1; it is broken in D_2, where the edge (S_2,S_1) disappears (see Figure 6.3).

Definition 6.7   Let S denote a statement at level n, and $c \in \mathbb{N}$. S is **serial** at level c iff either $c > n$ or there exists a path $\pi \in CP(S)$ such that $c \in levels(\pi)$; otherwise S is called **concurrent** at level c.   ∎

A statement which is serial as a result of the validity of the condition $c > n$ is called **scalar**; this will be of no relevance until we discuss parallelization in the next chapter.

The following theorem formulates an important property of the classification introduced in Definition 6.7.

Theorem 6.5   Let $c \in [1:n]$ and L_j $(1 \leqslant j \leqslant n)$ be the loop at level j enclosing S. If S is concurrent at level c, then the instances of S in L_c can be executed concurrently. ■

Proof   Assume that S is concurrent at level c. It suffices to show that dependences do not enforce an order on the execution of any two instances of S in L_c. We prove this indirectly. Suppose that there are iteration vectors $\mathbf{i}$, $\mathbf{i}' \in [S]$ such that $S(\mathbf{i}) \ll_c S(\mathbf{i}')$, and this order must be retained because of the presence of dependences. This implies that there exists a statement sequence $S_0, \ldots, S_t$ $(t \geqslant 1)$ such that $S_0 = S_t = S$, a sequence of levels c_r $(1 \leqslant r \leqslant t)$, and a sequence of iteration vectors $\mathbf{i}_r \in [S_r]$ $(0 \leqslant r \leqslant t)$ such that the following holds for all r with $1 \leqslant r \leqslant t$:

(1) $\mathbf{i} = \mathbf{i}_0$ and $\mathbf{i}' = \mathbf{i}_t$.
(2) $S_{r-1}(\mathbf{i}_{r-1}) \, \delta_{c_r} \, S_r(\mathbf{i}_r)$, where $c_r \in levels(S_{r-1}, S_r)$.
(3) $c_r \geqslant c$.
(4)   There is at least one r', $1 \leqslant r' \leqslant t$, such that $c_{r'} = c$.

However, then $\pi = S_0, \ldots, S_t$ is a path in $CP(S)$ at level c, contrary to our assumption that S is concurrent at that level. ■

If S is serial at level c, then the existence of a dependence cycle enforces an order on two different instances of S at that level. We then cannot conclude that the instances of S in L_c can be executed concurrently in general. The required ordering can always be enforced by executing all iterations of L_c for S in standard order.

This completes the general part of the theory, which is relevant for parallelization as well as vectorization. We now turn to the specific problem of vectorization. Our goal is to vectorize a statement S, which is contained at level n of a loop nest, in as many inner loops as possible. If S is the single statement of a perfectly nested loop, and not part of a recurrence, then it can be validly rewritten as a vector statement at all n levels (Theorem 6.4). In general, we determine the largest number c_0 such that S is part of a dependence cycle at level c_0 ($c_0 = 0$ if S is not contained in any recurrence); S can then be validly vectorized in the inner $n - c_0$ levels. We discuss this in more detail below.

Definition 6.8   Let L denote a loop, and S an assignment statement at level n.

(1) $maxcycle(S) := \begin{cases} max\{maxlevel(\pi) : \pi \in CP(S)\} & \text{if } CP(S) \neq \varnothing \\ \\ 0, \text{ otherwise} \end{cases}$

(2) $\alpha(S) := n\text{-}maxcycle(S)$.
       $\alpha(S)$ is called the **vectorization index** of S.   ∎

$maxcycle(S)$ is the c_0 of the above discussion. We can immediately conclude the following lemma.

Lemma 6.

$0 \leqslant \alpha(S) \leqslant n$ ∎

Example 6.14

In Example 6.12, $n = 2$ for all assignment statements; thus we obtain $maxcycle(S_i) = \alpha(S_i) = 1$ for $i = 1,2,3$ and $maxcycle(S_4) = 0$, $\alpha(S_4) = 2$.

We now arrive at the central theorem of vectorization, which follows immediately from Theorem 6.5, and is a generalization of Theorem 6.4.

Theorem 6.6   Let S be an assignment statement at level n of a loop L, and let L_j $(1 \leqslant j \leqslant n)$ denote the level j loop enclosing S, with loop variable I_j and bounds t_j, u_j. The instances of S in L can be validly rearranged as described by the following loop:

```
DO I₁ = t₁, u₁
  DO I₂ = t₂, u₂
  ...
    DO I_c₀ = t_c₀, u_c₀
      S(I₁, ..., I_c₀, T_c₀+₁:U_c₀+₁, ..., Tₙ:Uₙ)
    END DO I_c₀
  ...
  END DO I₂
END DO I₁
```

where $c_0 = maxcycle(S)$.   ∎

The transformation described in Theorem 6.6 is called **partial vectorization** (at $n - c_0$ levels); it can be performed by valid statement reordering, loop distribution, and vector code generation. This will be apparent from the algorithm presented in the next section.

Note that the theorem says nothing about transformations that either eliminate or reduce the level of dependences. The vectorization index of statements may increase when such transformations are applied to a loop (see Chapter 5 and Section 6.5).

6.4   Vector code generation

ALGORITHM 6.1: Allen–Kennedy vector code generation

Input   Loop L with dependence graph $D = DG(L)$ and statement set $STAT$.

Output   A program L', equivalent to L, where each statement S in L is rewritten as specified by Theorem 6.6.

Method

procedure vectorize(R,c);

/* R is a set of assignment statements in L, and $c \in \mathbb{N}$ is a level. This procedure (excluding recursive calls) generates code for the statements of R at level c of the loop. If $c > 1$, then R represents a cyclic SCC of $constrain(D, c-1)$, and sequential code has already been generated for the outermost $c - 1$ loops enclosing $R^\dagger$.

For the output of a VP-Fortran statement ST, the algorithm uses a call to the built-in procedure generate ("ST"). */

begin

$DD := constrain(D,c) | R$;

$G' = (N',E') := AC(DD)$;

for every $n' \in N'$ in topological order **do**

   if n' corresponds to a cyclic SCC $G_i = (N_i, E_i)$ of DD

   then

   /* There is a cyclic path π in DD that contains all nodes of N_i, such that $maxlevel(\pi) \geq c$ (S may be concurrent at level c, but there is a level $c' \geq c$ where it is serial). In this case, the level c loop is executed in standard order for all statements of N_i. Let I_c, T_c, and U_c be the do-variable, the lower and the upper bound of that loop. */

   generate (" DO $I_c = T_c, U_c$ ");

   vectorize ($N_i, c + 1$);

   generate (" END DO I_c ")

   else

   /* n' corresponds to a SCC $G_i = (\{S\}, \emptyset)$ of DD, where S is an assignment statement. Then $c = maxcycle(S) + 1$, $\alpha(S) = n - (c - 1)$, and S can be rewritten as a vector statement S_{vect}, which is executed sequentially at levels $1, \ldots, c - 1$, and concurrently at the remaining levels. Assume that the do-variables and bounds of the loops enclosing S are given by I_j, T_j and U_j, respectively ($1 \leq j \leq n$). */

   generate(" $S(I_1, \ldots, I_{c-1}, T_c:U_c, \ldots, T_n:U_n)$ ")

---

† For $c > 1$, $constrain(D,c)|R$ can be efficiently constructed using a previously computed graph $constrain(D, c-1)|R'$. This is not reflected in the algorithm.

```
    fi
  end for
  end;  /* vectorize */
  /* MAIN PROGRAM */
  begin vectorize(STAT,1) end
```
∎

The algorithm terminates, since the number of recursive invocations of vectorize is limited by the maximum level of L. Its correctness can then be derived from the results of the last section. We do not elaborate the details.

The time complexity can be established as follows: let p,q denote the number of nodes and edges in $DG(L)$, respectively, and let r be the depth of L. At each single level c (excluding recursive calls, but including all calls vectorize(R,c) for statement sets R), we need at most:

(1) $O(max(p,q))$ steps to construct the acyclic condensation $AC(DD)$, using Tarjan's algorithm (see Appendix A),

(2) $O(p + q)$ steps to topologically sort the AC(DD), and

(3) $O(p)$ steps to execute the body of the for-loop.

Thus, a single level can be executed in $O(p + q)$ steps. The total effort involved in vectorizing L is therefore bounded above by $O(r(p + q))$.

Example 6.15

We now apply the algorithm to the program of Example 6.12 (see also Figures 6.1, 6.2 and 6.3). Dependence graphs and the associated acyclic condensations will be combined into one figure, whereby the nodes and edges of SCCs are represented by dotted lines. The numbers in the column on the left indicate the actual invocation of vectorize. All local variables are implicitly qualified by this number. We mark the position at which an invocation terminates by its number and an asterisk.

1   $vectorize(\{S_1,S_2,S_3,S_4\},1)$

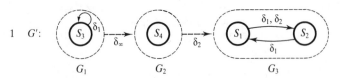

1   first n': $G_1 = (\{S_3\},\{(S_3,S_3)\})$ is cyclic

1   $\boxed{generate("\ \texttt{DO I = 1, N}\ ")}$

   2   $vectorize(\{S_3\},2)$

   2   G':   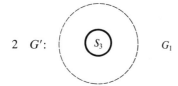 G_1

   2   first n': $G_1 = (\{S_3\},\varnothing)$ is acyclic, $\alpha(S_3) = 1$

   2   $\boxed{generate("\ S_3\texttt{(I, 1:M)}\ ")}$

   2*

1   $\boxed{generate("\ \texttt{END DO I}\ ")}$

1   second n': $G_2 = (\{S_4\},\varnothing)$ is acyclic, $\alpha(S_4) = 2$

1   $\boxed{generate("\ S_4\texttt{(1:N, 1:M)}\ ")}$

1   third n': $G_3 = (\{S_1,S_2\},\{(S_1,S_2),(S_2,S_1)\})$ is cyclic

1   $\boxed{generate("\ \texttt{DO I = 1, N}\ ")}$

   3   $vectorize(\{S_1,S_2\},2)$

   3   G':   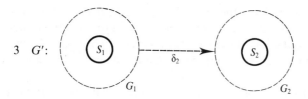

   3   first n': $G_1 = (\{S_1\},\varnothing)$ is acyclic, $\alpha(S_1) = 1$

   3   $\boxed{generate("\ S_1\texttt{(I, 1:M)}\ ")}$

3   second n': $G_2 = (\{S_2\}, \varnothing)$ is acyclic, $\alpha(S_2) = 1$

3 | *generate*(" $S_2(I, 1:M)$ ") |

3*

1 | *generate*(" END DO I ") |

1*

The complete sequence of VP-Fortran statements generated for the loop is given in Program 6.1.

Program 6.1   Vector code for the program of Example 6.12.

```
DO I = 1, N
   S₃vect:  D(I, 1:M) = D(I - 1, 0:M - 1) + 1
END DO I

S₄vect:  B(1:N, 5:M + 4) = D(1:N, 1:M) - 1

DO I = 1, N
   S₁vect:  C(I, 1:M) = A(I, 1:M) * B(I, 1:M)
   S₂vect:  A(I + 1, 2:M + 1) = C(I, -1:M - 2)/2 + C(I - 1, 1:M) * 3
END DO I
```

6.5   An assortment of loop transformations

In this section, we describe a set of transformations that can be used by a restructurer to improve the target program with respect to a variety of criteria. Although the demands of vectorization provide the motivation for much of our discussion, these transformations can be applied to parallelization, reduction of traffic in a memory hierarchy and many other problems as well.

Most transformations discussed here (such as loop interchange, scalar expansion and variable copying) have the purpose of eliminating dependences in a semantically valid way. Another set of transformations – summarized by the term **idiom recognition** – detects program patterns (in particular recurrences, such as the dot product) that can be efficiently realized on many machines.

6.5.1   Loop interchange

Loop interchange is a transformation that exchanges two levels of a nested loop. The following examples illustrate what can be achieved by this.

Example 6.16

In the do-loop

```
DO I = 1, 100
  DO J = 1, 100
    S: A(I, J + 1) = A(I, J) * B(I, J)
  END DO J
END DO I
```

$\overset{\frown}{S} \, \big)\delta_2$

there is a cyclic dependence at level 2. Algorithm 6.1 generates sequential code for this loop. However, if we take note of the fact that there is no dependence at level 1 and exchange the two levels of the loop, we obtain:

```
DO J = 1, 100
  DO I = 1, 100
    S: A(I, J + 1) = A(I, J) * B(I, J)
  END DO I
END DO J
```

$\overset{\frown}{S} \, \big)\delta_1$

We have now constructed a loop that is equivalent to the original one, has a cyclic dependence at level 1 and no dependence at level 2. Vectorization in the inner loop has been made possible, yielding:

```
DO J = 1, 100
  A(1:100, J + 1) = A(1:100, J) * B(1:100, J)
END DO J
```

Example 6.17

The following program illustrates the conventional method for multiplying matrices (the initialization of C has been omitted):

```
DO J = 1, 100
  DO I = 1, 100
    DO K = 1, 100
      S: C(I, J) = C(I, J) + A(I, K) * B(K, J)
    END DO K
  END DO I
END DO J
```

$\overset{\frown}{S} \, \big)\delta_3$

This loop has a cyclic dependence involving S at level 3; hence only serial code can be generated by Algorithm 6.1. However, if we interchange the loops at levels 1 and 3 we obtain:

```
DO K = 1, 100
  DO I = 1, 100
    DO J = 1, 100
      S:  C(I, J) = C(I, J) + A(I, K) * B(K, J)
    END DO J
  END DO I
END DO K
```

$$\left(\ S\ \right) \circlearrowright \ \big)\,\delta_1$$

This transformation has moved the cyclic dependence to level 1, and there are now no dependences in the innermost two levels. As can be easily seen, the transformation is valid, that is no dependences of the original loop have been destroyed and vector code can be generated at levels 2 and 3, yielding:

```
DO K = 1, 100
  S:  C(1:100, 1:100) = C(1:100, 1:100) +
                        SPREAD(A(1:100, K), 2, 100) *
                        SPREAD(B(K, 1:100), 1, 100)

END DO K
```

(SPREAD(X,DIM,NC) replicates an array X by generating NC copies in the new dimension DIM (ANSI, 1989)).

Loop interchange can also be applied when parallelizing a program. In this case, we will wish to move a dependence cycle inward.

Loop interchange is not always semantically valid. Assume that (in the course of parallelization) we want to apply it to the following loop.

Example 6.18

```
DO I = 1, 100
  DO J = 1, 100
    S:  A(I + 1, J) = A(I, J + 1) * B(I, J)
  END DO J
END DO I
```

Here we have a cyclic true dependence involving S at level 1: $S\,\delta(<,>)\,S$. For example, $S(1,2)\,\delta^t\,S(2,1)$, that is $S(2,1)$ reads the value of A(2,2) previously defined by $S(1,2)$. By interchanging the two levels (in an attempt to move the dependence to the inner level) we obtain:

```
DO J = 1, 100
  DO I = 1, 100
    S:  A(I + 1, J) = A(I, J + 1) * B(I, J)
  END DO I
END DO J
```

Now the dependence has disappeared, in particular the instance of S where $I = 2, J = 1$ is executed *before* the instance with $I = 1, J = 2$. Thus the transformation is invalid.

Loop interchange is one of the most powerful restructuring transformations. Some of the important ways in which it may be used are as follows.

(1) *Vectorization* When vectorizing, we want to move loops with cyclic dependences outwards and loops without dependences inwards. We will frequently wish to access arrays with stride 1, either because this is the only way we can create vector instructions for a particular target machine (such as the Cyber-205), or because it improves efficiency. Loop interchange may permit us to modify array access correspondingly. Finally, vector pipelines deal most efficiently with long vectors: loop interchange can help us put the 'longest loop' in the most appropriate place, as for example if only the innermost level of

```
DO I = 1, 10000
  DO J = 1, 5
    A(J, I) = B(J, I) * C(J - 1, I + 1)
  END DO J
END DO I
```

is going to be vectorized (for more details see Section 6.8).

(2) *Parallelization* When parallelizing, we aim to move parallelizable loops outwards and dependence cycles inwards where possible. As in the case of vectorization, it is usually most advantageous to parallelize the longest loops.

(3) *Memory access* Loop interchange can be used to reduce bank conflicts, to enhance cache efficiency, and to decrease the number of page faults in a virtual memory system by improving the locality of programs.

We now need to define loop interchange precisely. We shall do this for perfectly nested loops and the interchanging of adjacent loops.

Loop interchange rearranges the execution order of the statement instances associated with a loop. The transformation is valid iff the new execution order preserves all dependences of the old order.

TRANSFORMATION 6.5: Loop interchange at level c

Input   (1)   A perfectly nested loop L of depth $n \geqslant 2$. L_j denotes the loop at level j $(1 \leqslant j \leqslant n)$.

        (2)   A level c with $1 \leqslant c < n$ *(c* is called the **interchange level**).

Output   A loop, denoted by L/c, which is constructed by exchanging the order of the do-control associated with loops L_c and L_{c+1}. ∎

In the following, we use $\ll/c$ to denote the standard execution order of L/c, and δ/c for its dependence relation. For an arbitrary vector $\mathbf{x}$ of length n, $\mathbf{x}/c$ is the vector obtained from $\mathbf{x}$ by swapping components x_c and x_{c+1}. Note that $(L/c)/c = L$.

We now seek a criterion for the validity of loop interchange, by characterizing those cases in which the standard execution order is reversed. We recall Example 6.18 and use Theorem 4.1 to prove the following.

Lemma 6.8   Assume that S,S' are statements in L, $\mathbf{i}$ and $\mathbf{i}'$ are iteration vectors associated with S and S', respectively, $\boldsymbol{\theta} = dir(\mathbf{i},\mathbf{i}')$, c is an interchange level, and $S(\mathbf{i}) \ll S'(\mathbf{i}')$. Then:

$$S'(\mathbf{i}'/c) \ll/c\ S(\mathbf{i}/c) \text{ iff } \boldsymbol{\theta} = (=^{c-1},<,>,*\ldots*)$$ ∎

Proof   Let the assumptions of the lemma hold. We apply Theorem 4.1 twice to obtain:

(1) $S(\mathbf{i}) \ll S'(\mathbf{i}')$ $\Longleftrightarrow$ $\mathbf{i} < \mathbf{i}'$ or $(\mathbf{i} = \mathbf{i}'$ and S bef $S')$

(2) $S'(\mathbf{i}'/c) \ll/c\ S(\mathbf{i}/c)$ $\Longleftrightarrow$ $\mathbf{i}'/c < \mathbf{i}/c$ or $(\mathbf{i}'/c = \mathbf{i}/c$ and S' bef $S)$

Now suppose $S'(\mathbf{i}'/c) \ll/c\ S(\mathbf{i}/c)$. Then $\mathbf{i}'/c < \mathbf{i}/c$, $\mathbf{i} = \mathbf{i}'$ cannot hold, and there is a $k \in [1{:}n]$ such that $\mathbf{i} <_k \mathbf{i}'$. Clearly, the condition cannot be satisfied for any $k \neq c$. For $k = c$, we have:

$$\mathbf{i} = (i_1, \ldots, i_{c-1}, i_c, i_{c+1}, \ldots, i_n)$$
$$\mathbf{i}' = (i_1, \ldots, i_{c-1}, i'_c, i'_{c+1}, \ldots, i_n)$$

with $i_c < i'_c$. In $\mathbf{i}/c$ and $\mathbf{i}'/c$, the components c and $c+1$ are switched. From $S'(\mathbf{i}'/c) \ll/c\ S(\mathbf{i}/c)$ we obtain immediately $i_{c+1} > i'_{c+1}$, that is the direction vector has the form $\boldsymbol{\theta} = (=^{c-1},<,>,*\ldots*)$.

    Conversely, $\boldsymbol{\theta} = (=^{c-1},<,>,*\ldots*)$ implies $S'(\mathbf{i}'/c) \ll/c\ S(\mathbf{i}/c)$, which concludes the proof of the lemma. ∎

Definition 6.9 A dependence $S(i) \, \delta \, S'(i')$ in loop L is c-**interchange preventing** iff $S(i/c) \, \delta/c \, S'(i'/c)$ does not hold. ∎

From Lemma 6.8 we obtain the following.

Theorem 6.7 A dependence $S \, \delta\theta \, S'$ in L is c-interchange preventing iff $\theta = (=^{c-1},<,>,*\ldots*)$. ∎

Theorem 6.8 Loop interchange at level c is valid iff there exists no c-interchange preventing dependence. ∎

Note that loop-independent dependences can never prevent valid interchange. Now that we have a criterion to determine the validity of loop interchange at level c, we can see what the effects of such a transformation are.

Example 6.19

Let L be the loop:

```
DO I = 1, 100
   DO J = 1, 100
      S:  A(I, J + 1) = A(I, J) * A(I - 1, J + 1)
   END DO J
END DO I
```

Here, $S \, \delta(=,<) \, S$ and $S \, \delta(<,=) \, S$. Interchange at level 1 is valid, and yields $L/1$:

```
DO J = 1, 100
   DO I = 1, 100
      S:  A(I, J + 1) = A(I, J) * A(I - 1, J + 1)
   END DO I
END DO J
```

This has transformed the dependences to $S \, (\delta/1)(<,=) \, S$ and $S \, (\delta/1)(=,<) \, S$, respectively. So the dependence at level 2 in L has moved outward and the dependence at level 1 has moved inward. In consequence, neither of these loops can be vectorized.

Whereas loop-carried dependences at level $c + 1$ always move outward as a result of an interchange at level c, a loop-carried dependence at level c may (as in Example 6.19) or may not move inward. Loop-carried dependences at other levels and loop-independent dependences are not modified. We formulate this precisely in the following theorem.

Theorem 6.9 Let L be a perfectly nested loop of depth n, S and S' statements in L with iteration vectors $\mathbf{i}$ and $\mathbf{i}'$, c an interchange level, and L/c the loop resulting from a valid interchange at level c. Then the interchange does not modify the type of a dependence. Moreover:

(1)   For all k with $1 \leqslant k < c$, $c + 2 \leqslant k \leqslant n$, or $k = \infty$:

$$S(\mathbf{i}) \, \delta_k \, S'(\mathbf{i}') \implies S(\mathbf{i}/c) \, (\delta/c)_k \, S'(\mathbf{i}'/c)$$

(2)   For all $\mathbf{i},\mathbf{i}'$ with $S(\mathbf{i}) \, \delta_c \, S'(\mathbf{i}')$ and $dir(\mathbf{i},\mathbf{i}') = (=^{c-1},<,=,*\ldots*)$, the dependence moves inward, from level c to level $c + 1$:

$$S(\mathbf{i}/c) \, (\delta/c)_{c+1} \, S'(\mathbf{i}'/c)$$

(3)   For all $\mathbf{i},\mathbf{i}'$ with $S(\mathbf{i}) \, \delta_c \, S'(\mathbf{i}')$ and $dir(\mathbf{i},\mathbf{i}') = (=^{c-1},<,<,*\ldots*)$, the dependence remains at level c:

$$S(\mathbf{i}/c) \, (\delta/c)_c \, S'(\mathbf{i}'/c)$$

(4)   For all $\mathbf{i},\mathbf{i}'$:

$$S(\mathbf{i}) \, \delta_{c+1} \, S'(\mathbf{i}') \implies S(\mathbf{i}/c) \, (\delta/c)_c \, S'(\mathbf{i}'/c) \qquad \blacksquare$$

Proof If we examine the direction vectors which cause a specific kind of dependence and consider the effect of exchanging the components at positions c and $c + 1$, then it is easy to see that the above holds. For (4): $S(\mathbf{i}) \, \delta_{c+1} \, S(\mathbf{i}')$ implies $dir(\mathbf{i},\mathbf{i}') = (=^c,<,*\ldots*)$. After the loop interchange, $dir(\mathbf{i}/c,\mathbf{i}'/c) = (=^{c-1},<,=,*\ldots*)$, which implies $S(\mathbf{i}/c) \, (\delta/c)_c \, S'(\mathbf{i}'/c)$. $\qquad \blacksquare$

Corollary All loop-carried dependences at level $c + 1$ in L/c correspond to loop-carried dependences at level c in L. $\qquad \blacksquare$

The above theorem provides us with two general rules ((1) and (4)) about the behavior of dependences if a valid interchange at level c is made. In contrast, we must test the direction vector of each loop-carried dependence at level c individually to determine whether or not the dependence moves inward. We call a dependence satisfying (2) an **inward moving** dependence. Clearly, such a dependence may prevent loop interchange for vectorization.

If, for a loop L, there is a level c at which no loop-carried dependence exists, then we can move L_c right to the innermost loop via the transformation sequence $(\ldots(L/c)/c + 1)/\ldots)/n - 1$. Algorithm 6.1 can be easily generalized to include this transformation. Allen (1983) has inserted a test into the algorithm to evaluate the effect of validly interchanging the innermost two loops, and, depending on the outcome, decides whether or not to perform this transformation.

We can easily derive a test for the dependence property 'c-interchange preventing' from the Banerjee test (see Section 4.5.3). The reader may wish to verify this as an exercise; details are given in Allen (1983) and Allen and Kennedy (1987). It is similarly possible to devise a test to decide whether a dependence would be moved inward or not, that is whether it satisfies case (2) or (3) of Theorem 6.9. To implement this, we can label the edges of the dependence graph with information which will tell the code generation algorithm whether or not a c-interchange preventing dependence and/or an inward moving dependence exists.

6.5.2 Scalar expansion

Scalar expansion is a transformation we may apply to a scalar variable that occurs in a loop. It creates a copy of the variable for each iteration of the loop nest in which it is used by replacing the variable with an appropriately dimensioned array. This eliminates dependences associated with the variable in a manner which preserves the semantics and thus may help to permit vectorization by breaking a dependence cycle.

Example 6.20

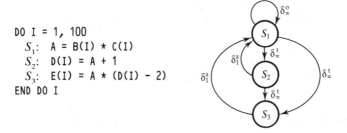

```
DO I = 1, 100
    S₁:  A = B(I) * C(I)
    S₂:  D(I) = A + 1
    S₃:  E(I) = A * (D(I) - 2)
END DO I
```

Since all statements in this loop are part of a dependence cycle, none of them can be vectorized. If we apply scalar expansion to A, then we have a new implicitly declared compiler-generated array %A(1:100). We can subsequently transform the loop as follows:

```
DO I = 1, 100
  S₁':  %A(I) = B(I) * C(I)
  S₂':  D(I) = %A(I) + 1
  S₃':  E(I) = %A(I) * (D(I) - 2)
END DO I
```

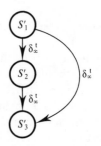

Since the transformed loop is equivalent to the original loop and none of its statements is involved in a dependence cycle, it can be vectorized by Algorithm 6.1.

TRANSFORMATION 6.6: Scalar expansion

    Input   A perfect nest $L = (L_1, \ldots, L_n)$ of loops, whose loop variables are I_j, and whose lower and upper bounds have the values T_j, U_j $(1 \leqslant j \leqslant n)$, respectively. In L, a scalar variable A occurs which satisfies the following conditions:

    (1) A is the target of at least one assignment in L
    (2) A is not any of the following:

        (a)   a formal parameter
        (b)   a COMMON variable
        (c)   an induction variable
        (d)   the target of an assignment which is a single-statement recurrence that can be replaced by a single operation (the dot product, for example).

  Output Case I – The first occurrence of A in L is a definition

    (1)   An n-dimensional temporary array $\%A(T_1:U_1, \ldots, T_n:U_n)$ with the same element type as A is generated.
    (2)   All occurrences of A in L are replaced by $\%A(I_1,I_2, \ldots, I_n)$.
    (3)   Immediately after the transformed loop, an assignment $A = \%A(U_1,U_2, \ldots, U_n)$ is generated.

  Output Case II – The first occurrence of A in L is a use

    (1)   An n-dimensional temporary array $\%A$ with the same element type as A, and with lower and upper bounds LWB_j and UPB_j, respectively $(1 \leqslant j \leqslant n)$, is defined as follows:

(a) $LWB_j = T_j$ $(1 \leqslant j < n)$

(b) $LWB_n = T_n - 1$

(c) $UPB_j = U_j$ $(1 \leqslant j \leqslant n)$

(2)   The assignment $\%A(T_1, \ldots, T_{n-1}, T_n - 1) = A$ is generated immediately before L.

(3)   All uses of A before the first definition in L are replaced by $\%A(I_1, \ldots, I_{n-1}, I_n - 1)$.

(4)   All other occurrences of A in L are replaced by $\%A(I_1, I_2, \ldots, I_n)$.

(5)   After each END DO I_j $(1 \leqslant j < n)$ a conditional assignment is generated as shown in Program 6.3.

(6)   Immediately after the transformed loop, an assignment $A = \%A(U_1, U_2, \ldots, U_n)$ is generated.

The effect of the transformation is schematically illustrated in Programs 6.2 and 6.3.   ∎

Remark   The restriction which requires L to be perfectly nested can be easily removed. Wolfe (1978) gives the details of this more general transformation.   ∎

Program 6.2   Scalar expansion (first occurrence of A is a definition).

$\langle type \rangle$ A	$\langle type \rangle$ A
	$\langle type \rangle$ %A$(T_1 : U_1, \ldots, T_n : U_n)$
...	...
DO $I_1 = T_1,\ U_1$	DO $I_1 = T_1,\ U_1$
...	...
DO $I_n = T_n,\ U_n$	DO $I_n = T_n,\ U_n$
...	...
...	...
A = ... $\Longrightarrow$	%A$(I_1, \ldots, I_{n-1}, I_n) = \ldots$
...	...
... = ... A ...	... = ... %A$(I_1, \ldots, I_{n-1}, I_n)$ ...
...	...
END DO I_n	END DO I_n
...	...
END DO I_1	END DO I_1
	A = %A$(U_1, \ldots, U_n)$

Program 6.3 Scalar expansion (first occurrence of A is a use).

$\langle type \rangle$ A	$\langle type \rangle$ A
	$\langle type \rangle$ %A$(T_1:U_1, \ldots, T_n - 1:U_n)$
$\ldots$	$\ldots$
	%A$(T_1, \ldots, T_{n-1}, T_n - 1) = $ A
DO $I_1 = T_1, U_1$	DO $I_1 = T_1, U_1$
$\ldots$	$\ldots$
DO $I_n = T_n, U_n$	DO $I_n = T_n, U_n$
$\ldots$	$\ldots$
$\ldots = \ldots$ A $\ldots$	$\ldots = \ldots$ %A$(I_1, \ldots, I_{n-1}, I_n - 1) \ldots$
$\ldots$	$\ldots$
$\ldots = \ldots$ A $\ldots$ $\Longrightarrow$	$\ldots = \ldots$ %A$(I_1, \ldots, I_{n-1}, I_n - 1) \ldots$
$\ldots$	$\ldots$
A $= \ldots$	%A$(I_1, \ldots, I_{n-1}, I_n) = \ldots$
$\ldots$	$\ldots$
$\ldots = \ldots$ A $\ldots$	$\ldots = \ldots$ %A$(I_1, \ldots, I_{n-1}, I_n) \ldots$
$\ldots$	$\ldots$
END DO I_n	END DO I_n
$\ldots$	IF $I_{n-1} < U_{n-1}$
END DO I_1	THEN %A$(I_1, \ldots, I_{n-1} + 1, T_n - 1) = $
	%A$(I_1, \ldots, I_{n-1}, U_n)$
	FI
	END DO I_{n-1}
	$\ldots$
	IF $I_1 < U_1$
	THEN %A$(I_1 + 1, T_2, \ldots, T_{n-1}, T_n - 1) = $
	%A$(I_1, U_2, \ldots, U_n)$
	FI
	END DO I_1
	A $= $ %A$(U_1, \ldots, U_n)$

Example 6.21

```
REAL A                      REAL A
                            REAL %A(1:10,0:20)

...                         ...
A=F(0,0)                    A=F(0,0)
                            %A(1,0):=A
DO I=1,10                   DO I=1,10
  DO J=1,20                   DO J=1,20
    B(I,J)=A*B(I+1,J-1)  ⟹     B(I,J)=%A(I,J-1)*B(I+1,J-1)
    A=F(I,J)                   %A(I,J)=F(I,J)
  END DO J                   END DO J
END DO I                    IF I<10 THEN %A(I+1,0)=%A(I,20) FI
                            END DO I
                            A=%A(10,20)
```

Scalar expansion is a transformation that must be applied with great care. If sufficient information on the loop bounds is not available, or if the range is too large, then we should either refrain from applying the transformation altogether or restrict its application to the innermost level(s) of the loop; otherwise we may end up with an unjustifiable increase in the program's memory requirements. A transformation system providing scalar expansion will also have to include the inverse transformation, **array shrinking**, so that we can undo it if it has had undesirable effects that could not be recognized at the time it was performed (Leasure, 1985).

6.5.3 Variable copying

Assume that L is a loop, S and S' are statements in L and that there exist iteration vectors $\mathbf{i}$ and $\mathbf{i}'$ such that $S(\mathbf{i}) \, \delta^a \, S'(\mathbf{i}')$, and $USE(S(\mathbf{i})) \cap DEF(S'(\mathbf{i}')) = \{v\}$.

We transform the program as follows:

(1)   Allocate a new temporary variable $\%v$ and generate an assignment $\%v = v$ that assigns to $\%v$ the value of v read in $S(\mathbf{i})$, and which is executed before $S(\mathbf{i})$ and $S'(\mathbf{i}')$.

(2)   Change S such that $S(\mathbf{i})$ reads $\%v$ instead of v.

It can be seen easily that the transformation eliminates the anti dependence (at the cost of additional memory) in a semantically valid way.

Example 6.22

The two statements in the loop

```
DO I = 1, N
  S:   A(I) = B(I) * C(I)
  S':  D(I) = A(I) + A(I + 1)
END DO
```

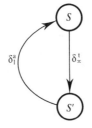

cannot be vectorized since there exists a dependence cycle containing both S and S': $S(i) \, \delta_\infty \, S'(i)$ for all i, and for each i with $1 \leqslant i < N$ there is an anti dependence $S(i) \, \delta^a \, S'(i + 1)$. After the loop is transformed into:

```
ALLOCATE %A(N)
%A(1:N) = A(2:N + 1)
```

```
DO I = 1, N
  A(I) = B(I) * C(I)
  D(I) = A(I) + %A(I)
END DO
DEALLOCATE %A
```

vectorization is possible, yielding:

```
ALLOCATE %A(N)
%A(1:N) = A(2:N + 1)
A(1:N)  = B(1:N) * C(1:N)
D(1:N)  = A(1:N) + %A(1:N)
DEALLOCATE %A
```

Assume now that $S \, \delta^a \, S$ is a single-statement recurrence, and no other dependence exists. In this case, the FS-semantics of vector statements renders the generation of the temporary variable superfluous.

Theorem 6.10   A single-statement recurrence based only on anti dependence may be vectorized.   ∎

Example 6.23

The do-loop

```
DO I = 1, N
  A(I) = A(I + 2) + 1
END DO
```

can be vectorized, yielding:

```
A(1:N) = A(3:N + 2) + 1
```

6.5.4   Index set splitting

Assume that L is a loop with statements S and S', such that $S \, \delta^t \, S'$ and $S' \, \delta^a S$, or vice versa, holds. If the iteration range of L can be partitioned into two disjoint sets, one of which causes the true and the other the anti dependence, then the dependence cycle may be broken by splitting the original loop into two loops. This transformation is referred to as **index set splitting**.

In order to apply this transformation, the index value where the dependence 'changes direction' must be determined. This is related to the algorithms for dependence testing discussed in Chapter 4. We illustrate the transformation by an example.

Example 6.24

Consider the loop

```
L:  DO I = 1, 200
    S:   B(I) = A(201 - I) + C(I)
    S':  A(I) = C(I - 1) * 2
    END DO
```

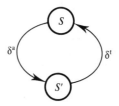

The set of all dependences in L can be found by determining all pairs i, i' $(1 \le i, i' \le 200)$, which satisfy the dependence equation $201 - i = i'$:

(1) $S(i) \, \delta^a \, S'(i')$ for all $1 \le i \le 100 < i' \le 200$ with $i + i' = 201$.

(2) $S'(i') \, \delta^t \, S(i)$ for all $1 \le i' \le 100 < i \le 200$ with $i + i' = 201$.

Since this establishes a cyclic dependence relationship involving S and S', neither statement can be vectorized.

We now split S into two statements S_1 and S_2 such that S_1 and S_2 execute the instances $S(1:100)$ and $S(101:200)$, respectively. Similarly, S' is split into S'_1 and S'_2 (for the instances $S'(1:100)$ and $S'(101:200)$, respectively). This yields the following program, which is equivalent to L:

```
DO I = 1, 100
    S₁:   B(I) = A(201 - I) + C(I)
    S'₁:  A(I) = C(I - 1) * 2
    END DO

DO I = 101, 200
    S₂:   B(I) = A(201 - I) + C(I)
    S'₂:  A(I) = C(I - 1) * 2
    END DO
```

Now the following dependences exist: $S_1 \, \delta^a \, S'_2$ and $S'_1 \, \delta^t \, S_2$. Both loops can be vectorized, yielding:

```
B(1:100)   = A(200:101: - 1) + C(1:100)
A(1:100)   = C(0:99) * 2
B(101:200) = A(100:1: - 1) + C(101:200)
A(101:200) = C(100:199) * 2
```

6.5.5 Node splitting

Assume that a statement S in a loop is involved in a dependence cycle. We usually treat statements as atomic units, with the consequence that a variable occurrence in S that contributes to a dependence cycle makes the whole statement non-vectorizable, independent of its other components. **Node splitting** is a transformation that uses a lower level dependence graph, whose nodes represent terms occurring in statements. Then, operations that are not involved in a cycle may be isolated and vectorized. We discuss an example.

Example 6.25

The loop

```
L:  DO I = 1, N
     S:   B(I) = A(I) + C(I) * D(I)
     S':  A(I + 1) = B(I) * (D(I) - C(I))
    END DO
```

cannot be vectorized owing to the cycle of true dependences involving S and S'. This cycle is exclusively caused by the variables $B(I)$ and $A(I)$ in S, and $A(I+1)$ and $B(I)$ in S'. The computations $C(I) * D(I)$ and $D(I) - C(I)$ can be separated and individually vectorized, as shown in loop L', which is equivalent to L:

```
L':  DO I = 1, N
      S₁:  T1(I)    = C(I) * D(I)
      S₂:  T2(I)    = D(I) - C(I)
      S₃:  B(I)     = A(I) + T1(I)
      S₄:  A(I + 1) = B(I) * T2(I)
     END DO
```

After loop distribution and vectorization, applied to S_1 and S_2, we obtain:

```
T1(1:N) = C(1:N) * D(1:N)
T2(1:N) = D(1:N) - C(1:N)
DO I = 1, N
  S₃:  B(I)     = A(I) + T1(I)
  S₄:  A(I + 1) = B(I) * T2(I)
END DO
```

6.5.6 Loop peeling, unrolling, and rerolling

If there are anomalies in the control flow of a loop, it may be advantageous to peel off the first and/or last iteration(s), and to transform the loop accordingly. An example for loop peeling (wrap-around variable) was discussed in Chapter 5 (Example 5.9). Below, we show how loop peeling can be used to eliminate a dependence cycle from a loop to make it vectorizable.

Example 6.26

```
DO J = 1, N
  DO I = 1, N
    S₁: F(I, J) = G(I, J) + 3 * G(I - 1, J)
        IF J < 2 THEN GOTO S₄ FI
        IF J < N THEN GOTO S₃ FI
    S₂: G(I, J) = F(I, J)
    S₃: G(I - 1, J) = F_OLD(I, J)
    S₄: F_OLD(I, J) = F(I, J)
  END DO I
END DO J
```

The dependence graph of this loop is given below:

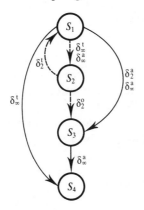

The dotted lines represent dependences that are caused by the last iteration of the J loop (J = N) only; without these dependences, the graph would be acyclic. We now peel off iterations J = 1 and J = N, which results in:

```
DO I = 1, N
  F(I, 1) = G(I, 1) + 3 * G(I - 1, 1)
  F_OLD(I, 1) = F(I, 1)
END DO I
```

```
DO J = 2, N - 1
  DO I = 1, N
    F(I, J) = G(I, J) + 3 * G(I - 1, J)
    G(I - 1, J) = F_OLD(I, J)
    F_OLD(I, J) = F(I, J)
  END DO I
END DO J

DO I = 1, N
  F(I, N) = G(I, N) + 3 * G(I - 1, N)
  G(I, N) = F(I, N)
  G(I - 1, N) = F_OLD(I, N)
  F_OLD(I, N) = F(I, N)
END DO I
```

Loop distribution and vectorization yield the final program:

```
F(1:N, 1) = G(1:N, 1) + 3 * G(0:N - 1, 1)
F_OLD(1:N, 1) = F(1:N, 1)
F(1:N, 2:N - 1) = G(1:N, 2:N - 1) + 3 * G(0:N - 1, 2:N - 1)
G(0:N - 1, 2:N - 1) = F_OLD(1:N, 2:N - 1)
F_OLD(1:N, 2:N - 1) = F(1:N, 2:N - 1)
DO I = 1, N
  F(I, N) = G(I, N) + 3 * G(I - 1, N)
  G(I, N) = F(I, N)
END DO
G(0:N - 1, N) = F_OLD(1:N, N)
F_OLD(1:N, N) = F(1:N, N)
```

Unrolling of a loop refers to the process of making one or more copies of the loop body, whereby the loop control must be suitably modified. This can be used to reduce the control overhead for the sequential execution of the loop (see below) or to decrease the amount of data movement in a memory hierarchy (see Section 6.8.5).

Example 6.27: Loop unrolling

The following transformation

```
DO I=1,1000                DO I=1,999,2
  A(I)=B(I+2)*C(I-1)   ⟹     A(I)  =B(I+2)*C(I-1)
END DO                       A(I+1)=B(I+3)*C(I)
                           END DO
```

reduces the loop control overhead during sequential execution by 50%.

The inverse transformation, **loop rerolling**, may be even more important for restructuring. The effect of loop rerolling consists of undoing a loop unrolling transformation that was done to improve the sequential code. The Livermore Kernels described in Arnold (1982) include three programs (2, 5, and 6) which contain unrolled code optimized for scalar execution. For example, kernel 2 is a camouflaged version of a dot product, unrolled into a loop summing five partial products. This loop and its transformation are described below:

Example 6.28: Livermore loops — loop 2 (outer loop omitted)

```
Q = 0.0
DO K = 1, 996, 5
  Q = Q + Z(K) * X(K) + Z(K + 1) * X(K + 1) + Z(K + 2) * X(K + 2) +
        Z(K + 3) * X(K + 3) + Z(K + 4) * X(K + 4)
END DO K
```

Rerolling of the inner loop yields:

```
Q = 0.0
DO K = 1, 1000
  Q = Q + Z(K) * X(K)
END DO K
```

If DOTPRODUCT(A,B) is a function that computes the inner product of two vectors A and B, then we obtain the final form (see also Section 6.5.7):

```
Q = DOTPRODUCT(Z, X)
```

A detailed specification of loop rerolling can be found in Leasure (1985).

6.5.7 Idiom recognition

Idiom recognition refers to the detection of program sections realizing particular functions for which an efficient special implementation exists.

A **reduction** is a function that computes a scalar value from an array. Table 6.1 describes a number of reductions which are defined in Fortran 90, and explains their mathematical meaning (for a complete specification see ANSI (1989)).

Table 6.2 specifies a mapping between Fortran code segments and the reductions they represent. The detection of such code segments in a program, and their replacement by the associated reductions, characterizes

Table 6.1 Fortran 90 target functions for reductions.

```
REAL ARRAY     A(1:N), B(1:N)
LOGICAL ARRAY C(1:N)
```

Fortran function	Meaning
SUM(A)	$\sum\limits_{i=1}^{N} A(i)$
PRODUCT(A)	$\prod\limits_{i=1}^{N} A(i)$
DOTPRODUCT(A)	$\sum\limits_{i=1}^{N} (A(i) * B(i))$
MAXVAL(A)	$\underset{i=1}{\overset{N}{MAX}}\, A(i)$
MINVAL(A)	$\underset{i=1}{\overset{N}{MIN}}\, A(i)$
MAXLOC(A)	i such that $A(i) = $ MAXVAL(A)[a]
MINLOC(A)	i such that $A(i) = $ MINVAL(A)[a]
ANY(C)	$\bigvee\limits_{i=1}^{N} C(i)$
ALL(C)	$\bigwedge\limits_{i=1}^{N} C(i)$
COUNT(C)	$|\{i: C(i) = \mathbf{true}\}|$

[a] If there is more than one subscript i satisfying this condition, one of those subscripts is arbitrarily chosen.

a typical application of idiom recognition. I and J are integer variables, S and T are real, and L is a logical variable. N is assumed to have a value ≥ 1.

SUM, PRODUCT, and DOTPRODUCT, as discussed above, are special cases of **linear recurrence systems**, for which efficient hardware support exists on some computers. A survey of time and processor bounds for the parallel solution of such systems is given in Kuck (1977), while the dissertation of Wolfe (1982) contains an elaborate discussion of various solution methods. Many of these methods have been implemented in the Parafrase system (Leasure, 1985).

Table 6.2   Reductions.

```
DO I = 1, N
  S = S + A(I)                          S = S + SUM(A)
END DO

S = 1
DO I = 1, N
  S = S * A(I)                          S = PRODUCT(A)
END DO

S = 0
DO I = 1, N
  S = S + A(I) * B(I)                   S = DOTPRODUCT(A, B)
END DO

DO I = 1, N
  S = AMAX1(A(I), S)                    S = AMAX1(MAXVAL(A), S)
END DO

S = A(1)
DO I = 2, N
  IF (A(I) > S)                         S = MAXVAL(A)
    THEN S = A(I)
  FI
END DO

DO I = 1, N
  S = AMIN1(A(I), S)                    S = AMIN1(MINVAL(A), S)
END DO

DO I = 1, N
  L = L OR C(I)                         L = L OR ANY(C)
END DO

L = TRUE
DO I = 1, N
  L = L AND (A(I) ≤ 0)                  L = ALL(A ≤ 0)
END DO

J = 0
DO I = 1, N
  IF C(I) THEN J = J + 1 FI             J = COUNT(C)
END DO

S = A(1)
J = 1
DO I = 2, N
  IF (A(I) > S)                         J = MAXLOC(A) [a]
    THEN S = A(I)                       S = A(J)
        J = I
  FI
END DO
```

[a] The transformed program is equivalent to the original one iff MAXLOC(A) determines the minimum subscript associated with a maximal element of A.

6.6 Control dependence and vectorization

6.6.1 Introduction

Up to now our discussion has been based on the model of Section 4.2, which includes only assignment statements and loops. In this section, we examine how the control dependences caused by branches and if-statements can be dealt with in the context of vectorization. We present in Section 6.6.2 a systematic approach – called **if-conversion** – which essentially converts control dependences into data dependences by computing for each statement the precise condition for its execution (the **mask** of the statement). The program can then be rewritten as a sequence of assignment statements whose execution depends on the mask; all other if-statements and goto-statements are eliminated. If the transformed program can be vectorized, then it allows us to exploit the capability of vector computers to execute masked vector instructions directly (see Section 2.2.3).

If-conversion will be defined for programs with if-statements and goto-statements, whose branches are in a forward direction. It can be generalized to deal with branches that exit from a loop and backward branches; we shall, however, discuss these two cases only informally (Section 6.6.3). Note that the special control patterns related to idioms have been already dealt with in Section 6.5.7 and will not be mentioned here further. Machine-dependent aspects of code generation will be treated in Section 6.8.

We include in our loop model goto-statements and if-statements of the form

$$if \quad \rightarrow \quad \text{"IF"} \; cond \; \text{"THEN"} \; statement^* \; [\text{"ELSE"} \; statement^*] \; \text{"FI"}$$
$$cond \quad \rightarrow \quad expression$$

A **branch** is either a goto statement or a conditional statement in the sense of Table 3.1. The **source** of a branch is the statement causing the control transfer, the **target** is the statement to which control is transferred. We introduce a classification of branches that depends on the relative positions of source and target in the program text, and on their respective levels (see Program 6.4).

Definition 6.10 A branch with source S and target S' in a loop L, where n, n' are the respective levels of S and S', is classified as forward, backward, or exit according to the following criteria:

Program 6.4 Branch categories.

Forward branch	Backward branch	Exit branches
| ```
DO I = ...

  ...
  S:   GOTO S'
  ...
  S':  ...


  ...
END DO
``` | ```
DO I = ...

  ...
  S:   ...
  ...
  S':  IF K < 0
         THEN GOTO S
       FI

  ...
END DO
``` | ```
DO I = ...
  S₁:
  DO J = ...

    ...
    S₂:  IF K < EPS
           THEN GOTO S₁
         FI
    S₃:  IF L > UPB
           THEN GOTO S₄
         FI

  END DO J
END DO I
S₄: ...
``` |

(1)   **forward:** S bef S' and $n = n'$.

(2)   **backward:** S' bef S and $n = n'$.

(3)   **exit:** $n' < n$.   ∎

Each branch belongs to exactly one of these three categories (note that branches into the interior of a loop are not permitted). The source and target of a forward or backward branch are both contained in the same loop nest. An exit branch terminates $n - n'$ levels of the loop. This classification is important for our treatment of if-conversion: while forward branches can be converted together with if-statements in a straightforward way, exit and backward branches pose more difficult problems. In this and the following subsection (until Section 6.6.3), we shall assume that all branches in a program are forward.

The principle of if-conversion depends on the concept of a statement mask.

Definition 6.11 Let S denote a statement. Then $mask(S)$ is a logical expression whose value at execution time specifies whether or not S is to be executed. The **masked statement** associated with S is given by IF ($mask(S)$) THEN S FI.   ∎

We illustrate the concept of if-conversion by an example:
```

Example 6.29

```
                                              mask(S_i)

DO I=1,N
  S_1:  A(I)=A(I)+B(I)                        TRUE
  S_2:  IF A(I)=0                             TRUE
          THEN S_3:  GOTO S_7 FI              A(I)=0
  S_4:  IF A(I)>C(I)                          NOT(A(I)=0)
          THEN S_5:  A(I)=A(I)-2              NOT(A(I)=0) AND (A(I)>C(I))
          ELSE S_6:  A(I)=A(I)+1              NOT(A(I)=0) AND NOT(A(I)>C(I))
        FI
  S_7:  ᵇD(I)=A(I)*2                          TRUE
END DO
```

The first line at the right-hand side specifies $mask(S_1)$ as the constant TRUE, meaning that S_1 is to be executed unconditionally in the loop. To S_3, the mask A(I) = 0 is attached, implying that S_3 will be executed iff the value of A(I) = 0 is true in an iteration. The meaning of the other masks can be interpreted similarly.

The loop can be transformed as follows. First, for each conditional expression *cond* which is not a single variable, an auxiliary variable %C and an assignment %C = *cond* are generated. The if-statements are transformed so that they refer to these variables:

```
                                              mask(S_i)

DO I=1,N
  S_1:   A(I)=A(I)+B(I)                       TRUE
  S_2':  %C2=(A(I)=0)                         TRUE
  S_2:   IF %C2                               TRUE
           THEN S_3:  GOTO S_7 FI             %C2
  S_4':  %C4=(A(I)>C(I))                      NOT(%C2)
  S_4:   IF %C4                               NOT(%C2)
           THEN S_5:  A(I)=A(I)-2             NOT(%C2) AND %C4
           ELSE S_6:  A(I)=A(I)+1             NOT(%C2) AND NOT(%C4)
         FI
  S_7:   D(I)=A(I)*2                          TRUE
END DO
```

In a second step, the program is rewritten in such a way that the effects of if-statements and forward branches are combined to determine a sequence of masked assignment statements; all if-statements of the original program and all branches are eliminated in this process:

```
DO I=1,N
  S₁:   A(I)=A(I)+B(I)
  S₂':  %C2=(A(I)=0)
  S₄'': IF (NOT(%C2))                   THEN %C4=(A(I)>C(I)) FI
  S₅'': IF (NOT(%C2) AND %C4)           THEN A(I)=A(I)-2 FI
  S₆'': IF (NOT(%C2) AND NOT(%C4))      THEN A(I)=A(I)+1 FI
  S₇:   D(I)=A(I)*2
END DO
```

We apply scalar expansion to %C2 and %C4, converting these variables into arrays %C2A and %C4A, respectively. Now the dependence graph can be computed (all variables occurring in the mask of a statement S belong to the input set $USE(S)$): it reveals that no recurrences exist, and thus all statements can be vectorized, using masks where necessary. The final code is given below:

```
A(1:N)=A(1:N)+B(1:N)
%C2A(1:N)=(A(1:N)=0)
WHERE (NOT(%C2A(1:N)))                        %C4A(1:N)=(A(1:N)>C(1:N))
WHERE (NOT(%C2A(1:N)) AND %C4A(1:N))          A(1:N)=A(1:N)-2
WHERE (NOT(%C2A(1:N)) AND NOT(%C4A(1:N)))     A(1:N)=A(1:N)+1
D(1:N)=A(1:N)*2
```

6.6.2   If-conversion for loops with forward branches

ALGORITHM 6.2: If-conversion

Input   A statement sequence $SEQ \equiv S_1, \ldots, S_p$ ($p \geq 1$), satisfying the following properties:

(1)   Each S_r ($1 \leq r \leq p$) is an arbitrary statement, which is not a backward or exit branch.

(2)   All statements are contained in the same loop nest L.

(3) $mask(S_1) \equiv C_1$ (the initial condition for executing SEQ).

(4)   If any S_r is the target of a branch, then the source is another statement in the same sequence.

Output   A sequence of masked assignment statements, equivalent to SEQ.

Method

```
/*
```
   – The **current condition** is a boolean expression specifying the condition
     for the execution of a statement.
   – For each statement S, *source_conds*(S) is a global variable attached to
     S. If S is the target of a branch, then the value of *source_conds*(S),
     upon reaching S, is the set of all current conditions associated
     with sources of branches to S. For all other statements S,
     source_conds(S) $= \emptyset$.
   – *code*(*exp*) specifies the output code for expression *exp*.
```
*/
```

function generate_masked_statement(S,AC): boolean;
   /* S is an arbitrary statement, AC the condition for its execution, not taking
      into account branches to S. *curr_cond* is a local variable whose value
      (after the initial assignment) represents the current condition for the
      execution of S. The value returned by the function is the condition for the
      execution of the statement following S. */

begin
/* The effect of branches (join) is modeled by the disjunction of AC with all
   conditions associated with branch sources whose target is S: */

curr_cond $:= AC \vee \bigvee \{ sc : sc \in source\_conds(S) \}$;

case S **in**

IF *cond* THEN SEQ1 ELSE SEQ2 FI:
   begin
      c_true $:=$ generate_masked_sequence(SEQ1,*curr_cond* $\wedge$ *cond*);
      c_false $:=$ generate_masked_sequence(SEQ2,*curr_cond* $\wedge \neg$*cond*));
      curr_cond $:= c\_true \vee c\_false$
   end;

IF *cond* THEN SEQ1 FI:
   begin
      c_true $:=$ generate_masked_sequence(SEQ1,*curr_cond* $\wedge$ *cond*);
      curr_cond $:= c\_true \vee \neg$*cond*
   end;

GOTO S':
   begin
      source_conds(S') **plus** $\{ curr\_cond \}$;
      curr_cond $:=$ **false**
   end;

else   /* assignment statement */
   generate(" IF (*code*(*curr_cond*)) THEN S FI ")

end case;

generate_masked_statement $:= curr\_cond$

end;   /* generate_masked_statement */

function generate_masked_sequence(*SQ*,*AC*): boolean;

/* *SQ* is a statement sequence, *AC* and *curr_cond* play an analogous role as in generate_masked_statement. The value returned by the function is the condition for the execution of the statement following *SQ*. */

begin
curr_cond := *AC*;
for every *S* in *SQ* **do** *source_conds*(*S*) := ∅ **end for**;
for every *S* in *SQ* in textual order **do**
  curr_cond := generate_masked_statement(*S*,*curr_cond*)
end for
end   /* generate_masked_sequence */

/* MAIN PROGRAM */

begin generate_masked_sequence(SEQ,C_1) **end**   ∎

Algorithm 6.2 represents a very basic form of if-conversion. In particular, the boolean expressions manipulated in the algorithm, which may become highly complex and redundant, must be simplified, using methods such as those developed by Quine (1952) and McCluskey (1956). Furthermore, a mask which is **true** should be suppressed when a masked assignment statement is being generated. The reader may want to look in more detail at the operation of the algorithm by applying it to Example 6.29: this yields a program which is equivalent to the third version of the example program (with %C2 and %C4 substituted by the corresponding expressions, and their assignments omitted).

   We now apply if-conversion to kernel 15 of the Livermore loops. Few compilers are able to vectorize this loop (Levesque and Williamson, 1989). By applying if-conversion, we will see that it can easily be handled with our tools.

Example 6.30

The original program of kernel 15, rewritten in our syntax, is given as follows:

```
DO J = 2, NR
  DO K = 2, NZ
    IF (J - NR < 0)
      THEN GOTO S1
    FI
    VY(K, J) = 0.0
    GOTO END_K
```

```
      S1:IF (VH(K, J + 1) - VH(K, J) ≤ 0)
          THEN GOTO S2
        FI
        T = AR
        GOTO S3
      S2:T = BR
      S3:IF (VF(K, J) - VF(K - 1, J) ≥ 0)
          THEN GOTO S4
        FI
        R = AMAX1(VH(K - 1, J), VH(K - 1, J + 1))
        S = VF(K - 1, J)
        GOTO S5
      S4:R = AMAX1(VH(K, J), VH(K, J + 1))
        S = VF(K, J)
      S5:VY(K, J) = SQRT(VG(K, J)**2 + R * R) * T/S
        IF (K - NZ < 0)
          THEN GOTO S6
        FI
        VS(K, J) = 0.
        GOTO END_K
      S6:IF (VF(K, J) - VF(K, J - 1) ≥ 0)
          THEN GOTO S7
        FI
        R = AMAX1(VG(K, J - 1), VG(K + 1, J - 1))
        S = VF(K, J - 1)
        T = BR
        GOTO S8
      S7:R = AMAX1(VG(K, J), VG(K + 1, J))
        S = VF(K, J)
        T = AR
      S8:VS(K, J) = SQRT(VH(K, J)**2 + R * R) * T/S
   END_K:END DO K
        END DO J
```

Note that the only dependences in this loop are caused by scalar variables. After peeling off the last iteration of the J and K loops, reordering, and applying if-conversion, we obtain:

```
DO J = 2, NR - 1
  DO K = 2, NZ - 1
    %C1 = (VH(K, J + 1) - VH(K, J) ≤ 0)
    IF NOT(%C1) THEN T = AR FI
    IF %C1      THEN T = BR FI
    %C2 = (VF(K, J) - VF(K - 1, J) < 0)
    IF %C2      THEN R = AMAX1(VH(K - 1, J), VH(K - 1, J + 1))
                     S = VF(K - 1, J)
    FI
    IF NOT(%C2) THEN R = AMAX1(VH(K, J), VH(K, J + 1))
                     S = VF(K, J)
```

```
   FI
   VY(K, J) = SQRT(VG(K, J)**2 + R * R) * T/S
   %C3 = (VF(K, J) - VF(K, J - 1) < 0)
   IF %C3      THEN R = AMAX1(VG(K, J - 1), VG(K + 1, J - 1))
                     S = VF(K, J - 1)
                     T = BR
   FI
   IF NOT(%C3) THEN R = AMAX1(VG(K, J), VG(K + 1, J))
                     S = VF(K, J)
                     T = AR
   FI
   VS(K, J) = SQRT(VH(K, J)**2 + R * R) * T/S
  END DO K
END DO J


DO J = 2, NR - 1
  %D1 = (VH(NZ, J + 1) - VH(NZ, J) ≤ 0)
  IF NOT(%D1) THEN T = AR FI
  IF %D1      THEN T = BR FI
  %D2 = (VF(NZ, J) - VF(NZ - 1, J) < 0)
  IF %D2      THEN R = AMAX1(VH(NZ - 1, J), VH(NZ - 1, J + 1))
                   S = VF(NZ - 1, J)
  FI
  IF NOT(%D2) THEN R = AMAX1(VH(NZ, J), VH(NZ, J + 1))
                   S = VF(NZ, J)
  FI
  VY(NZ, J) = SQRT(VG(NZ, J)**2 + R * R) * T/S
  VS(NZ, J) = 0.
END DO J


DO K = 2, NZ
  VY(K, NR) = 0.0
END DO K
```

Appropriate scalar expansion of C1, C2, C3, D1, D2, R, S, and T eliminates all cycles from the dependence graph, and the loops can be vectorized:

```
ALLOCATE
%C1A(2:NR - 1, 2:NZ - 1)
%C2A(2:NR - 1, 2:NZ - 1)
%C3A(2:NR - 1, 2:NZ - 1)
%D1A(2:NR - 1)
%D2A(2:NR - 1)
%RA(2:NR - 1, 2:NZ - 1)
%SA(2:NR - 1, 2:NZ - 1)
%TA(2:NR - 1, 2:NZ - 1)
```

```
%C1A = (VH(2:NZ - 1, 3:NR) - VH(2:NZ - 1, 2:NR - 1) ≤ 0)
WHERE (NOT(%C1A)) %TA = AR
WHERE (%C1A)      %TA = BR
%C2A = (VF(2:NZ - 1, 2:NR - 1) - VF(1:NZ - 2, 2:NR - 1) < 0)
WHERE (%C2A)      %RA = AMAX1(VH(1:NZ - 2, 2:NR - 1),
                              VH(1:NZ - 2, 3:NR))
                  %SA = VF(1:NZ - 2, 2:NR - 1)
END WHERE
WHERE (NOT(%C2A)) %RA = AMAX1(VH(2:NZ - 1, 2:NR - 1),
                              VH(2:NZ - 1, 3:NR))
                  %SA = VF(2:NZ - 1, 2:NR - 1)
END WHERE
VY(2:NZ - 1, 2:NR - 1) = SQRT(VG(2:NZ - 1, 2:NR - 1)**2 +
                         %RA * %RA) * %TA/%SA
%C3A = (VF(2:NZ - 1, 2:NR - 1) - VF(2:NZ - 1, 1:NR - 2) < 0)
WHERE (%C3A)      %RA = AMAX1(VG(2:NZ - 1, 1:NR - 2),
                              VG(3:NZ, 1:NR - 2))
                  %SA = VF(2:NZ - 1, 1:NR - 2)
                  %TA = BR
END WHERE
WHERE (NOT(%C3A)) %RA = AMAX1(VG(2:NZ - 1, 1:NR - 1),
                              VG(3:NZ, 2:NR - 1))
                  %SA = VF(2:NZ - 1, 2:NR - 1)
                  %TA = AR
END WHERE
VS(2:NZ - 1, 2:NR - 1) = SQRT(VH(2:NZ - 1, 2:NR - 1)**2 +
                         %RA * %RA) * %TA/%SA


%D1A = (VH(NZ, 3:NR) - VH(NZ, 2:NR - 1) ≤ 0)
WHERE (NOT(%D1A)) %TA = AR
WHERE (%D1A)      %TA = BR
%D2A = (VF(NZ, 2:NR - 1) - VF(NZ, 2:NR - 1) < 0)
WHERE (%D2A)      %RA = AMAX1(VH(1:NZ - 2, 2:NR - 1),
                              VH(1:NZ - 2, 3:NR))
                  %SA = VF(1:NZ - 2, 2:NR - 1)
END WHERE
WHERE (NOT(%D2A)) %RA = AMAX1(VH(2:NZ - 1, 2:NR - 1),
                              VH(2:NZ - 1, 3:NR))
                  %SA = VF(2:NZ - 1, 2:NR - 1)
END WHERE
VY(2:NZ - 1, 2:NR - 1) = SQRT(VG(2:NZ - 1, 2:NR - 1)**2 +
                         %RA * %RA) * %TA/%SA
VS(NZ, 2:NR - 1) = 0.


VY(2:NZ, NR) = 0.0


DEALLOCATE %C1A, %C2A, %C3A, %D1A, %D2A, %RA, %SA, %TA
```

We have seen in the example above that relational expressions involving only the loop variable (such as $J - NR < 0$ and $K - NZ < 0$) can often be treated in a special way, leading to an improvement of the standard pattern of if-conversion. Similarly, loop-invariant expressions, and in particular conditions, can be pulled out of the loop.

Example 6.31

```
DO I = 1, N
  IF Q ≤ M * N THEN A(I) = B(I + 1) * C(I - 2) FI
END DO
```

The expression $Q \le M * N$ is loop invariant. The loop can be transformed as follows:

```
IF Q ≤ M * N
  THEN
    DO I = 1, N
      A(I) = B(I + 1) * C(I - 2)
    END DO
FI
```

and vectorization yields:

```
IF Q ≤ M * N THEN A(1:N) = B(2:N + 1) * C( - 1:N - 2) FI
```

If e_1 is the time required for the computation of the condition $Q \le M * N$ and e_2 the time for one component assignment, then the total time T for the execution of the above if-statement (ignoring pipeline setup) is $T = e_1 + Ne_2$, if the value of the condition is **true**, and $T = e_1$ otherwise. In contrast, the code generation based on masking without movement of the expression would produce:

```
WHERE (Q ≤ M * N) A(1:N) = B(2:N + 1) * C(-1:N - 2)
```

The execution time for this statement is Ne_2, independent of the value of the conditional expression (whose computation is assumed to be overlapped with the assignment).

6.6.3   Backward and exit branches

Both backward and exit branches represent a difficult problem for vectorization. Although some methods have been proposed for their elimination, the outcome of these transformations is sometimes questionable.

The method of Allen and Kennedy (Allen, 1983; Allen *et al.*, 1983) associates a new logical variable *v* with each exit branch of a loop; the value of *v* is defined in such a way that it remains **true** as long as the exit has not been taken, and is set to **false** afterwards. By *and*-ing *v* with the mask of each statement at each level left by the exit, *v* can control the execution of these statements with respect to the branch.

Example 6.32

```
DO I = 1, N
   A(I) = B(I) * (C(I - 1) + 1)
   DO J = 1, M
     D(I, J) = D(I, J - 1)/A(I)
     IF D(I, J) < 0 THEN GOTO S FI
   END DO J
   B(I) = B(I)/C(I + 1)
 S:A(I) = A(I) * B(I)
END DO I
```

We call the variable associated with the exit branch GOTO S %INJ; the loop can be transformed as follows:

```
DO I = 1, N
   %INJ = TRUE
   A(I) = B(I) * (C(I - 1) + 1)
   DO J = 1, M
     IF %INJ THEN D(I, J) = D(I, J - 1)/A(I)
     IF %INJ THEN %INJ = NOT(D(I, J) < 0)
   END DO J
   IF NOT(%INJ) THEN GOTO S
   B(I) = B(I)/C(I + 1)
 S:A(I) = A(I) * B(I)
END DO I
```

This loop is equivalent to the original one if J is not live at the end of the inner loop. Note that the exit branch has been converted into a forward branch.

The problem with this transformation lies in the fact that the loop to be exited is executed for its whole iteration range, regardless of the iteration in which the exit condition becomes true. This may imply a severe run-time overhead even if vectorization is possible after the transformation.

The elimination of exit branches generates either forward or backward branches. Backward branches normally create an implicit loop. Allen eliminates them with a complex algorithm (Allen, 1983; Allen *et al.*, 1983), which essentially converts an implicit iterative region into a DO WHILE loop. This algorithm has been included in the PFC system.

In some cases, an implicit loop may be converted into a do-loop. This can be handled using techniques that were discussed in Chapter 3. As well as detecting a single-entry strongly connected region in the program graph, the exit conditions, the single controlling variable (if it exists) and its increment must be analyzed. Precise conditions are given in Leasure (1985).

Example 6.33

The program on the left-hand side describes an implicit do-loop and can be transformed into the program at the right:

```
     IND=1                              IND=1
S:  A(IND-1)=A(IND)+1              S:  A(IND-1)=A(IND)+1
     IND=IND+2              ⟹          DO IND=3, TP, 2
     IF IND≤TP THEN GOTO S FI             A(IND-1)=A(IND)+1
                                        END DO
```

which can be normalized as described in Section 5.2.

The completely automatic elimination of exit and backward branches does not seem to be a viable course of action for a restructuring system. We should rather view these transformations as tools that can be applied by the programmer to optimize the program selectively in a judicious way. As a last resort, a loop can always be executed in standard order.

6.7 Procedure calls

When discussing procedure calls, we distinguish between intrinsics and statement functions on the one hand – whose effect is known precisely without an elaborate analysis – and external functions and subroutines on the other hand.

If a reference to an intrinsic function occurs in a do-loop without being involved in a dependence cycle, then it can be replaced by a reference to the corresponding vector version if the function is elemental (ANSI, 1989). A similar transformation can be applied to statement function references under appropriate conditions.

Example 6.34

```
SQADD(X,Y)=X+SQRT(X+Y*1.2)


DO I=1,N
  A(I)=SIN(B(I))+COS(C(I))      ⟹   A(1:N)=SIN(B(1:N))+COS(C(1:N))
  D(I)=SQADD(B(I+1),C(I-1))           D(1:N)=SQADD(B(2:N+1),C(0:N-1))
END DO
```

If the compiler provides no facilities for the analysis of external procedures, then the occurrence of a call in a loop may enforce the sequential execution of the whole loop. For example, if the effect of procedure SUB in

```
DO I = 1, 1000
  S₁:  CALL SUB(A, B, I)
  S₂:  B(I) = A(I) + 1
END DO
```

is not known, then S_2 cannot be vectorized, since the procedure could be potentially declared as (for instance)

```
SUBROUTINE SUB(X, Y, I)
  X(I) = Y(I - 1)**2 - 1
END
```

in which case a cyclic dependence involving S_1 and S_2 would be created by the call.

Depending on what information is available about a procedure, a compiler may improve the execution of a loop containing a call in a variety of ways. One possible strategy is in-line expansion (see Section 3.7.3). It replaces a call by the body of the called procedure – after the necessary adjustments – so that subsequently the whole range of intraprocedural techniques for data flow analysis, dependence analysis and restructuring can be applied. Consider the following example.

Example 6.35

Let L denote the loop

```
L:  DO I = 1, N
        CALL Q(A(I), B(I), H)
    END DO I
```

and let Q be declared by

```
SUBROUTINE Q(X, Y, Z)
  T = Z * Y * Y
  X = T + COS(X)
END
```

In-line expansion yields

```
L:  DO I = 1, N
        T = H * B(I) * B(I)
        A(I) = T + COS(A(I))
    END DO I
```

This reduces (sequential) execution time by eliminating the time required for the call and return sequences, and for the parameter transfer. Furthermore, after scalar forward substitution (for T) and dead-code elimination, vectorization is possible, resulting in the statement A(1:N) = H * B(1:N) * B(1:N) + COS(A(1:N)).

In-line expansion has a number of drawbacks and limitations (see Section 3.7.3), so it is not universally applicable. If it is not used, interprocedural analysis is required to avoid worst-case assumptions. Such an analysis might derive the access pattern of Q in Example 6.35 and recognize that the loop could be 'pushed' into the subroutine. In general, interprocedural analysis provides us with summary information about the effect of a procedure (Section 3.7), and thus allows a more precise specification of the *DEF* and *USE* sets related to the call than is possible under worst-case assumptions. Given these sets, the call can be subjected to the same analysis as an assignment statement (for example, it can be included in the dependence graph), and the results of analysis can be used to determine the validity of transformations such as statement reordering or loop distribution. For example, if we know that the occurrence of a call in a loop cannot cause a backward dependence to occur, then loop distribution is possible (assuming no other condition prevents it); this allows the isolation of the call and opens up the way for a potential vectorization of the other statements in the loop. Special transformations – such as pushing a loop into a call – can then possibly be applied. We illustrate this with an example.

Example 6.36

```
L:  DO I = 1, N
      S₁:  T = A(I)
      S₂:  A(I) = F(T)
      S₃:  B(I) = T * A(I) - 2
    END DO

FUNCTION F(X)
  IF X < 5
    THEN F = 0.
    ELSE F = SQRT(X * X + 27)
  FI
END
```

We now transform L in the following steps: First, scalar expansion is applied to T. After that, only loop-independent dependences exist in L and loop distribution can be performed:

```
ALLOCATE %TA(1:N)

DO I = 1, N
  %TA(I) = A(I)
END DO

DO I = 1, N
  A(I) = F(%TA(I))
END DO

DO I = 1, N
  B(I) = %TA(I) * A(I) - 2
END DO

DEALLOCATE %TA
```

Now we can push the loop into the body of F and transform F into a vector subroutine VF:

```
ALLOCATE %TA(1:N)

DO I = 1, N
  %TA(I) = A(I)
END DO

CALL VF(%TA, A, N)

DO I = 1, N
  B(I) = %TA(I) * A(I) - 2
END DO

DEALLOCATE %TA

SUBROUTINE VF(TX, AX, N)
  DIMENSION TX(*), AX(*)
  DO I = 1, N
    IF TX(I) < 5
      THEN AX(I) = 0.
      ELSE AX(I) = SQRT(TX(I) * TX(I) + 27)
    FI
  END DO
END
```

Finally, if-conversion and vectorization yield:

```
ALLOCATE %TA(1:N)
%TA(1:N) = A(1:N)
CALL VF(%TA, A, N)
B(1:N) = %TA(1:N) * A(1:N) - 2
DEALLOCATE %TA

SUBROUTINE VF(TX, AX, N)
  DIMENSION TX(*), AX(*), C(N)
  C(1:N) = TX(1:N) < 5
  WHERE (C(1:N))        AX(1:N) = 0.
  WHERE (NOT(C(1:N))) AX(1:N) = SQRT(TX(1:N) * TX(1:N) + 27)
END
```

The discussion in this section illustrated a number of ways in which loops with procedure calls can be handled in a compiler. We should keep in mind, however, that at present not much systematic knowledge about these transformations exists, and, in general, user interaction is necessary to determine a suitable restructuring strategy in the presence of calls. Some of the heuristics outlined above are described more broadly in Levesque and Williamson (1989).

6.8   Machine-dependent code generation

In this section, we examine a few aspects of machine-dependent vector code generation. These problems can, in principle, be taken care of by the VP-Fortran compiler. We discuss them here primarily to illustrate some facets of the translation from vector statements in VP-Fortran to the vector instructions of an actual computer such as the Cray-1, the Fujitsu VP-200, or the Cyber-205.

6.8.1   Loop sectioning (strip mining)

The loop

```
L:  DO I = 1, N
      S:  A(I) = B(I) + C(I)
    END DO
```

can be vectorized, yielding the vector statement

$$S_{vect}: \quad A(1:N) = B(1:N) + C(1:N)$$

On the Cyber-205, which is a memory-to-memory vector architecture with a maximum vector length of 64K, S_{vect} can be directly mapped to the vector instruction A(1:N) ←B(1:N) + C(1:N), if N < 65536. For a register-to-register vector architecture such as the Cray-1 or the Fujitsu VP-200, this simple mapping is only feasible if N is not greater than the length of the vector registers. Otherwise, a transformation known as **loop sectioning** or **strip mining** must be performed (as it must on the Cyber-205 if the vector length is ≥64K). We illustrate this for the Cray-1 with register length $s = 64$.

Suppose that $N = 64q + r$, where q and r are integers with $q \geq 0$ and $0 \leq r < 64$. Then, rather than producing S_{vect} from L, the loop is split into an outer **sectioning loop** and a **blocked vector operation** (**strip loop**) as follows:

```
DO %SEC = 1, q + 1
  DO %BL = 1, MIN(64, N - (%SEC - 1) * 64)
    I = (%SEC - 1) * 64 + %BL
    A(I) = B(I) + C(I)
  END DO %BL
END DO %SEC
```

The sectioning loop is executed q times with the range %BL = 1,64 for the inner loop, which uses the full register length. For %SEC = $q + 1$, a cleanup operation is executed, with the inner loop in the range %BL = 1,r. Suppose that I is not live at the end of the loop. Then, forward substitution, standardization of the subscript expressions, elimination of the assignment to I, and the separation of the cleanup loop yield:

```
DO %SEC = 1, q
  DO %BL = 1, 64
    A(-64 + 64 * %SEC + %BL) = B(-64 + 64 * %SEC + %BL) +
                                C(-64 + 64 * %SEC + %BL)
  END DO %BL
END DO %SEC
IF r ≠ 0
  THEN
  DO %BL = 1, r
    A(64 * q + %BL) = B(64 * q + %BL) + C(64 * q + %BL)
  END DO %BL
FI
```

After vectorization, we finally obtain:

```
DO %SEC = 1, q
  S₁:  A(-63 + 64 * %SEC:64 * %SEC) = B(-63 + 64 * %SEC:64 * %SEC) +
                                       C(-63 + 64 * %SEC:64 * %SEC)
END DO
IF r ≠ 0
  THEN S₂:  A(64 * q + 1:64 * q + r) = B(64 * q + 1:64 * q + r) +
                                        C(64 * q + 1:64 * q + r)
FI
```

In contrast to S_{vect}, S_1 and S_2 can be directly mapped to vector instructions on the Cray-1. If the value of r is known, then the if-statement can be omitted for $r = 0$, and reduced to S_2 otherwise. We conclude the discussion by illustrating the generated code under the assumption that N is known and has the value N $= 8192$ or N $= 1000$:

- *Case 1:* N $= 8192$ $(q = 128, r = 0)$

```
DO %SEC = 1, 128
  A(-63+64*%SEC:64*%SEC) = B(-63+64*%SEC:64*%SEC) +
                            C(-63+64*%SEC:64*%SEC)
END DO
```

- *Case 2:* N $= 1000$ $(q = 15, r = 40)$

```
DO %SEC = 1, 15
  A(-63+64*%SEC:64*%SEC) = B(-63+64*%SEC:64*%SEC) +
                            C(-63+64*%SEC:64*%SEC)
END DO
A(64*q+1:64*q+40) = B(64*q+1:64*q+40) + C(64*q+1:64*q+40)
```

6.8.2   Vector processing: lengths and strides

The length of vectors is not only relevant in the context of sectioning, but also must be considered when comparing the efficiency of a vector operation with the equivalent sequence of scalar instructions. We have defined the vector breakeven length as the minimum vector length that makes vector mode more efficient than scalar mode (see Section 2.2.5). It is about 4 for the Cray-1, but one order of magnitude higher for the Cyber-205. Thus, the decision whether to create vector or scalar code for a 'short' loop is to a large extent machine dependent.

In a system which vectorizes only the innermost level of loop nests, loop interchange, if applicable, may be used to move the vectorizable loop with the largest iteration range to the innermost position. **Loop collapsing** combines two loop levels into one and thus increases the vector length for the resulting vector operations, as shown in the example below.

Example 6.37

```
DIMENSION A(100, 100), B(100, 100), C(100, 100)

DO I = 1, 100
  DO J = 1, 100
    A(I, J) = B(I, J) * C(I, J)
  END DO
END DO
```

The vectorization system VAST-2 (Pacific Sierra Research, 1986a) recognizes that the nested loop can be executed as one vector instruction on one-dimensional interpretations of A, B, and C. It transforms the loop into the statement A(1:10000,1) = B(1:10000,1) + C(1:10000,1).

Another important parameter of vector processing is the **stride** (see Section 2.2.3). Some vector computers (for example, the Cyber-205) allow only a stride of 1, that is all vectors must be contiguously stored before a vector instruction can be applied to them. Consider the loop

```
L:  DO I = 2, 10000, 2
      C(I) = A(I) * B(I)
    END DO
```

L can be vectorized, resulting in the vector statement C(2:10000:2) = A(2:10000:2) + B(2:10000:2). In order to map this statement to the Cyber-205 architecture, we must create temporary arrays, using 'gather periodic' and 'scatter periodic' instructions which, when expressed in Fortran, essentially amount to the following transformation:

```
ALLOCATE %TEMPA(1:5000), %TEMPB(1:5000), %TEMPC(1:5000)

DO J = 1, 5000                           /* Gather A */
  %TEMPA(J) = A(2 * J)
END DO

DO J = 1, 5000                           /* Gather B */
  %TEMPB(J) = B(2 * J)
END DO

%TEMPC(1:5000) = %TEMPA(1:5000) * %TEMPB(1:5000) /* Operation */

DO J = 1, 5000                           /* Scatter %TEMPC */
  C(2 * J) = %TEMPC(J)
END DO

DEALLOCATE %TEMPA, %TEMPB, %TEMPC
```

Most vector computers can process vector operands with a stride $\neq 1$, but, because of the address calculation required and the possibility of bank conflicts, this may result in a run-time penalty. For example, a memory bank on an eight-bank Cray-1 requires four cycles to handle one access, and adjacent addresses are cyclically associated with banks $0, 1, \ldots, 7$. Stride 1 or 2 yields one operand per cycle, stride 4 one operand every other cycle, and stride 8 one operand every four cycles. Loop interchange may be used to adjust the stride to the machine characteristics.

Example 6.38

The following program computes the product of a matrix A with a vector B:

```
DIMENSION A(64, N), B(64), C(64)

DO I = 1, 64
  DO J = 1, N
    S:  C(I) = C(I) + A(I, J) * B(J)
  END DO
END DO
```

Statement S accesses the elements of A with stride 64 as a result of the column-major order for storing arrays in Fortran. Loop interchange – which is valid – results in stride 1:

```
DO J = 1, N
  DO I = 1, 64
    S:  C(I) = C(I) + A(I, J) * B(J)
  END DO
END DO
```

6.8.3 Pipeline parallelization and chaining

Vector computers contain a set of pipelines which can operate in parallel and may allow chaining (see Section 2.2.4). Furthermore, scalar operations can often be overlapped with vector computations. We discuss an example that illustrates the application of pipeline scheduling to an already vectorized program, requiring the reordering of operations. Note that optimizations related to scalar program analysis, such as redundant subexpression elimination and dead-code elimination, can be easily generalized to apply to vector statements.

Example 6.39

Consider the loop

```
L:  DO I = 1, N
      A(I) = C(I) + D(I) + E(I) + F(I)
      B(I) = C(I) * D(I) * E(I) * F(I)
    END DO
```

We examine the optimization of this loop for the Fujitsu VP-200 system (Amdahl, 1984). Suppose that vectors of length N can be directly processed by the machine, and that R_i $(i = 0, 1, \ldots)$ denote vector registers. Then, L can essentially be translated into the following vector code VC_1:

$$
\begin{array}{lll}
VC_1: & S_1: & R_0 = C(1{:}N) \\
      & S_2: & R_1 = D(1{:}N) \\
      & S_3: & R_2 = R_0 + R_1 \\
      & S_4: & R_3 = E(1{:}N) \\
      & S_5: & R_4 = R_2 + R_3 \\
      & S_6: & R_5 = F(1{:}N) \\
      & S_7: & R_6 = R_4 + R_5 \\
      & S_8: & A(1{:}N) = R_6 \\
      & S_9: & R_6 = R_0 * R_1 \\
      & S_{10}: & R_7 = R_6 * R_3 \\
      & S_{11}: & R_8 = R_7 * R_5 \\
      & S_{12}: & B(1{:}N) = R_8
\end{array}
$$

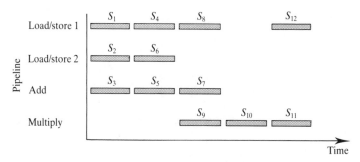

Figure 6.4 Timing chart for vector code VC_1.

The machine contains two load/store, one add, and one multiply pipeline which can all operate in parallel and be linked by chaining. The timing chart for the execution of VC_1 is given in Figure 6.4. It reveals that, because of the occurrence of idle times, the pipelines are not scheduled optimally.

We now attempt to achieve a better pipeline utilization by reordering VC_1 subject to the constraints of the dependence relation. This yields the vector code VC_2:

$$
\begin{array}{lll}
VC_2: & S_1: & R_0 = C(1:N) \\
& S_2: & R_1 = D(1:N) \\
& S_3: & R_2 = R_0 + R_1 \\
& S_9: & R_6 = R_0 * R_1 \\
& S_4: & R_3 = E(1:N) \\
& S_6: & R_5 = F(1:N) \\
& S_5: & R_4 = R_2 + R_3 \\
& S_{10}: & R_7 = R_6 * R_3 \\
& S_7: & R_6 = R_4 + R_5 \\
& S_{11}: & R_8 = R_7 * R_5 \\
& S_8: & A(1:N) = R_6 \\
& S_{12}: & B(1:N) = R_8
\end{array}
$$

The timing chart for VC_2 is given in Figure 6.5. It shows that now all pipelines are fully occupied, resulting in a significant reduction of execution time.

6.8.4 Control statement processing

If-conversion (see Section 6.6.2) generates where-statements, which can be directly mapped to masked vector instructions. The execution of masked and unmasked vector instructions takes the same time: thus, this approach

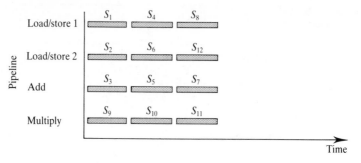

Figure 6.5   Timing chart for vector code VC_2.

is appropriate only when the **true ratio** of a mask, that is the percentage of iterations for which its evaluation yields **true**, is sufficiently large. When the true ratio of a mask is small, as for example in sparse matrix computations, the use of gather/scatter and/or indirect loading is preferable (see also Section 2.2.3). Note that, in many cases, the compiler cannot determine a condition's true ratio; in an interactive system, this information can be provided by the user. We discuss two examples.

Example 6.40: Gather/Scatter

```
DO I = 1,N
  IF A(I) < 0 THEN D(I) = D(I) + B(I) * 2 FI
END DO
```

Assume that the condition $A(I) < 0$ is satisfied only for a few values of I. We can then proceed as follows. The elements to be processed are gathered in temporary arrays, %TEMPB and %TEMPD, to which the vector instruction is applied; subsequently, the resulting temporary vector is scattered back to the original array (see Figure 6.6). This yields the following program (after vectorization):

```
ALLOCATE %TEMPD(1:N), %TEMPB(1:N), %C(1:N)  /* Allocation of temporary arrays */
%C(1:N) = A(1:N) < 0   /* Computation of the mask */
LG = COUNT(%C(1:N))    /* Number of elements for which %C(I) is true */
GATHER(%C,D,%TEMPD)    /* Gather the elements of D for which the corresponding
                          element of C is true, in %TEMPD. This procedure is supported
                          by hardware in many vector computers† */
GATHER(%C,B,%TEMPB)    /* Gather the elements of B in %TEMPB */
%TEMPD(1:%LG) = %TEMPD(1:%LG) + %TEMPB(1:%LG) * 2  /* Execute the vector
                          statement */
SCATTER(%C,D,%TEMPD)   /* Scatter the elements of %TEMPD back to D */
```

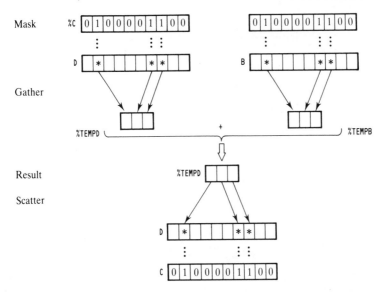

Figure 6.6   Gather/scatter (assumptions: $N = 10$, $LG = 3$, and (2,7,8) is the set of subscripts for which $A(I) < 0$).

Let $t(j)$, $j \in [1:\%LG]$, denote the subscript of the jth element of A such that $A(t(j)) < 0$. Then the mask %C can be replaced by an index vector X of length %LG, where for each j with $1 \leq j \leq \%LG$, $X(j)$ is set to $t(j)$. The loop can be rewritten as follows:

```
J = 0
DO I = 1, N
  IF A(I) < 0 THEN J = J + 1
                   X(J) = I
  FI
END DO I

D(X) = D(X) + B(X) * 2
```

This method can also be used to optimize a loop that accesses data at random locations, as shown in the next example.

† GATHER(%C,D,%TEMPD) can be expressed in Fortran as follows:

```
J = 0
DO I = 1, N
  IF %C(I) THEN J = J + 1; %TEMPD(J) = D(I) FI
END DO
```

Example 6.41: Indirect access

The loop

```
DO I = 1, N
  INDEX = F(I)
  A(I) = A(I) * B(INDEX)
END DO
```

can be transformed into

```
INDEX_VECTOR = F(1:N)
A(1:N) = A(1:N) * B(INDEX_VECTOR)
```

6.8.5 Improving data locality

We apply loop unrolling (see Section 6.5.6) to reduce register/memory traffic for a register-to-register vector architecture. The example below is based on work by Cowell and Thompson (1986).

Suppose that we want to improve the loop of Example 6.38 (second version) for execution on the Cray-1:

```
DO J = 1, N
  DO I = 1, 64
    S:  C(I) = C(I) + A(I, J) * B(J)
  END DO
END DO
```

A direct translation may result in the following vector code VC_1 (the outer loop will not be translated; the T_j ($j = 0,1$) denote scalar registers):

$$VC_1: \quad \text{DO J = 1, N}$$
$$S_1: R_0 = C(1:64)$$
$$S_2: R_1 = A(1:64, J)$$
$$S_3: T_0 = B(J)$$
$$S_4: R_1 = R_1 * T_0$$
$$S_5: R_0 = R_0 + R_1$$
$$S_6: C(1:64) = R_0$$
$$\text{END DO}$$

The execution time of this loop is dominated by the data movement between memory and the vector registers. In VC_1, $3 \cdot 64 \cdot N = 192N$ words (in S_1, S_2, and S_6) have to be moved by vector loads and stores. Now observe the effect obtained by unrolling one level of the outer loop (we assume N to be even):

```
DO J = 1, N - 1, 2
  DO I = 1, 64
    S': C(I) = C(I) + A(I, J) * B(J) + A(I, J + 1) * B(J + 1)
  END DO
END DO
```

The code resulting from this loop nest is:

```
VC₂:  DO J = 1, N - 1, 2
        S'₁:  R₀ = C(1:64)
        S'₂:  R₁ = A(1:64, J)
        S'₃:  T₀ = B(J)
        S'₄:  R₁ = R₁ * T₀
        S'₅:  R₀ = R₀ + R₁
        S'₆:  R₂ = A(1:64, J + 1)
        S'₇:  T₁ = B(J + 1)
        S'₈:  R₂ = R₂ * T₁
        S'₉:  R₀ = R₀ + R₂
        S'₁₀: C(1:64) = R₀
      END DO
```

Here, R_0 is used twice, thus reducing the total data movement between memory and vector registers to 128N words, that is by one-third. In addition, the transformed code contains more parallelism than the original code because of the independence of the statement pairs (S_2, S_6), (S_3, S_7), and (S_4, S_8).

Loop unrolling has been applied by Dongarra and Eisenstat (1984) to matrix multiplication, Cholesky decomposition, and LU decomposition. They varied the depth of unrolling up to 16, achieving for Cray computers a performance improvement of up to 2.8.

BIBLIOGRAPHICAL NOTES

The pioneering work in vectorization was carried out by D. Kuck and associates at the University of Illinois when they developed the Parafrase system (Kuck *et al.*, 1984a; Wolfe, 1982; Padua and Wolfe, 1986; Leasure, 1985). K. Kennedy and his group at Rice University generalized and extended Kuck's methods in the PFC, PTOOL and ParaScope systems (Allen and Kennedy, 1982, 1987; Allen *et al.*, 1986). The SUPERB system (Zima *et al.*, 1988) is an integrated parallelization/vectorization system for the SUPRENUM computer (see also Section 7.5). Commercial compilers with vectorization capabilities have been developed for a broad range of machines (including Texas Instruments ASC (Cohagan, 1973; Wedel,

1975), Cray (Higbee, 1979; Cray Research, 1980), Cyber-205 (Arnold, 1983, Huson *et al.*, 1986), Fujitsu VP-200 (Amdahl, 1984), IBM 3090/VF (Scarborough and Kolsky, 1986), Star Technology's ST-100 attached array processor (Macke *et al.*, 1986), Alliant FX/8, ETA-10, Hitachi S-810/820, and NEC SX/2). The VAST system, developed by Pacific Sierra Research Corporation (Brode, 1981; Pacific Sierra Research, 1986a), served as the front end for the Alliant FX/8, Cyber-205, ETA-10, and Intel iPSC-VX compilers.

Arnold (1982) reviews three automatic vectorizers; Callahan *et al.* (1988) provides a test suite of 100 loops, with which 18 different vectorization systems are compared.

The theoretical foundation of vectorization, as developed in Sections 6.2–6.4, is mainly due to Lamport (1974), Kuck, Allen and Kennedy. Loop transformations are described in many papers; significant collections can be found in Wolfe (1982) and Leasure (1985).

We now conclude with a number of remarks on selected issues.

Loop interchange has been treated in detail by Wolfe (1982, 1986). In Wolfe (1982), an algorithm is presented that produces all permutations of loop indices which can be obtained by a sequence of valid interchanges. The 'best' of these permutations can be selected by applying a machine-dependent cost function to the algorithm's results. The algorithm has been used in the KAP vectorization system (Huson *et al.*, 1986; Macke *et al.*, 1986; Davies *et al.*, 1986). Wolfe also considers triangular loops and loop interchange for non-perfectly nested loops. Allen and Kennedy (Allen, 1983; Allen and Kennedy, 1984b) specify criteria for interchanging non-adjacent loops by performing a sequence of interchanges for adjacent loops. They show that, for certain scalar dependences, the condition preventing c-interchange can be weakened.

Scalar expansion is described in the Parafrase documentation, together with array shrinking (Leasure, 1985); see also Wolfe (1982) and Kuck *et al.* (1984a).

Variable copying is discussed in more detail in Kuck *et al.* (1981).

Index set splitting was proposed in Banerjee's Ph.D. thesis (Banerjee, 1979) and has considerable practical relevance in the context of vectorization (Wolfe, 1982; Callahan *et al.*, 1988). Banerjee specifies an algorithm for determining the value where the dependence changes direction.

If-conversion was developed by Allen and Kennedy (Allen, 1983; Allen *et al.*, 1983; Allen and Kennedy, 1987) and implemented in PFC. One of the related problems is that the resulting programs are difficult for the user to read and understand. Thus, if a loop cannot be vectorized after if-conversion has been performed, the original form of the loop should be regenerated.

The major merits of if-conversion are related to vectorization. A more general approach for the treatment of control dependences has been developed in the PTRAN system, based on control dependence graphs (Allen *et al.*, 1988b; Ferrante *et al.*, 1987; see also Section 7.6).

Vector register allocation is discussed in Allen and Kennedy (1988).

Until now, we have completely excluded input/output from our discussion. Relatively little can be done for these statements owing to their inherent side effects. One possibility for optimization is the reduction of the number of library calls that have to be executed at run time.[†] A technique that can be used is **blocking** of I/O lists. For example, the following transformation can be performed:

```
DO I=1,1000
   WRITE(6,100) C(I)    ⟹        WRITE(6,100) C
END DO                        100 FORMAT(E12.6)
100 FORMAT(E12.6)
```

Some recent research examines knowledge-based approaches to vectorization. This includes work by Brandes (1988), which develops formal methods for the specification of automatic vectorization, and research at IBM (Bose, 1988a, 1988b).

[†] Parafrase (Leasure, 1985) has the inverse transformation which splits all I/O statements in such a way that each one reads or writes exactly one variable. This is no optimization, but is used to simplify program timing.

Chapter 7

Parallelization

7.1 Introduction

This chapter discusses the transformation of sequential programs into parallel programs for a multiprocessing architecture, which may be a shared-memory (SMS) or distributed-memory (DMS) system, or a combination of both.

Our interest focusses on large application programs that are executed as a system of parallel processes which use the entire machine (**multitasking**). The goal is to run as much of the program in parallel as is feasible, and to balance the computational load as evenly as possible among the processors. Many systems offer special hardware support for scheduling and synchronization in a multitasking environment, as some of the protection mechanisms required in a multi-user system can then be circumvented.

For an SMS with only a few processors, parallelization can be realized by **function partitioning**, where a small number of program segments performs different tasks on a shared data set. Typical examples for programs to which this approach can be successfully applied are database systems, compilers, flight simulators, and process control systems. Function partitioning will not be further explored here, since our primary objective is to exploit massive parallelism, as it can be found in MIMD machines with a large number of processors such as the INTEL iPSC, the IBM RP3, the NCube, and SUPRENUM.

As a consequence, our search for parallelism will concentrate on loops. Whereas the approach to parallelization for an SMS is closely related to the analysis of loop concurrency described in the previous

266

chapter, we will have to develop new concepts for DMSs. This will be outlined below.

Let us first consider the parallelization problem for an SMS. The language element for expressing parallelism is the **parallel loop**, whose iterations are executed concurrently (in parallel) by different processes. A process that performs one specific iteration of a parallel loop executes the loop body, with the do-variable replaced by the number of the iteration. Since loop-independent dependences are then satisfied automatically, only loop-carried dependences need to be considered in this context. We distinguish two kinds of parallel loops, namely doall-loops and doacross-loops. Whereas the iterations of a doall-loop must be completely independent, the processes executing the iterations of a doacross-loop may be synchronized. We will see that a do-loop can be validly transformed into a doall-loop iff it does not contain a loop-carried dependence. In contrast, every do-loop can be transformed into a doacross-loop if all dependences are satisfied by proper synchronization between loop iterations. We illustrate this by two examples.

Example 7.1

The loop

```
L:  DO I = 1, 100
       A(I) = B(I) * C(I) + D(I)
       B(I) = C(I)/D(I - 1) + A(I)
       IF C(I) < 0 THEN C(I) = A(I) * B(I) FI
    END DO
```

contains no loop-carried dependence, and thus it can be validly rewritten as a doall-loop:

```
L': DOALL I = 1, 100
       A(I) = B(I) * C(I) + D(I)
       B(I) = C(I)/D(I - 1) + A(I)
       IF C(I) < 0 THEN C(I) = A(I) * B(I) FI
    ENDALL
```

Suppose that 100 processes p_i ($1 \leq i \leq 100$) are available for the execution of L', and for every i, p_i performs iteration i:

```
A(i) = B(i) * C(i) + D(i)
B(i) = C(i)/D(i - 1) + A(i)
IF C(i) < 0 THEN C(i) = A(i) * B(i) FI
```

All processes work independently in parallel.

Example 7.2

In the following loop, a loop-carried dependence $S \delta S'$ exists:

```
L:  DO I = 1, 100
      S:   A(I) = B(I) * C(I) + D(I)
      S':  B(I) = C(I)/D(I - 1) + A(I - 3)
    END DO
```

L cannot be transformed into a doall-loop. However, a doacross-loop with synchronization can be generated :

```
L':  DOACROSS I = 1, 100
       S:   A(I) = B(I) * C(I) + D(I)
            SEND_SIGNAL(S)
            WAIT_SIGNAL(S, I - 3)
       S':  B(I) = C(I)/D(I - 1) + A(I - 3)
     ENDACROSS
```

Assume that for every i ($1 \leqslant i \leqslant 100$), iteration i is performed by process p_i, and select i arbitrarily with $1 \leqslant i \leqslant 97$. The execution of SEND_SIGNAL(S) in p_i signals to the other processes that $S(i)$ has completed its execution. The only process actually interested in this message is p_{i+3}, since $S'(i + 3)$ cannot be executed before $A(i)$ has been defined in $S(i)$. The synchronization required is expressed by the statement WAIT_SIGNAL(S,I-3). Whereas the process executing SEND_SIGNAL can proceed after the message has been sent, the execution of WAIT_SIGNAL implies the conditional blocking of a process, depending on whether or not the 'matching' SEND_SIGNAL has already been performed.

We now turn to the problem of parallelization for a DMS. In the above example – which was discussed in the context of an SMS – communication between two processes related by a true dependence is established by sending a synchronization signal notifying the receiving process that the required data is available in shared memory. In contrast, processes in a DMS may only access their local address space directly: in order to satisfy a true dependence from a process p to a process p' ($p \neq p'$), the value of the variable defined in p must be sent across the interconnection network to p'. Such message-passing communication incurs a significant run-time penalty. The approach to parallelization for a DMS is motivated by the observation that many numerical programs operate on a large data domain in a uniform way, characterized by a high degree of spatial locality. This is exploited as follows. The data domain of the sequential program is partitioned into disjoint blocks, which are allocated in the local address spaces of different processes. All processes execute the same program, operating essentially in parallel on their local data, except when involved in communication with other processes. With a suitable choice of data partition, the ratio between communication and computation time can be kept low. While the data partition must be provided by the user, the compiler takes this information to automatically create a parallel program for a DMS, in particular inserting and optimizing all required communication and synchronization.

Chapter 7 consists of six sections. Sections 7.2–7.4 are based on the shared-memory paradigm, whereas Section 7.5 describes parallelization for a DMS. Bibliographical notes conclude the chapter.

Section 7.2 presents an algorithm for parallel code generation based on the premise that synchronization between the iterations of a parallel loop is too expensive and should therefore be avoided. As a consequence, the only means provided to express parallelism is the doall-loop. In some aspects, this method for parallelization is similar to that used for vector code generation; in particular, the dependence graph and its acyclic condensation are the principal data structures operated upon, and statement reordering as well as loop distribution are the main transformations applied. However, whereas vector code generation transforms individual statements, our algorithm attempts to parallelize the outermost loop of a nest and to build parallel regions of maximum size, so that the overhead for scheduling and synchronization can be reduced.

Section 7.3 uses the doacross-loop, in combination with the pair of synchronization primitives introduced in Example 7.2, as a means for the specification of parallelism. The approach to the automatic generation of synchronization is outlined, and techniques for the detection and elimination of redundant synchronization are discussed.

Section 7.4 discusses the scheduling of parallel loops, and then examines transformations from the viewpoint of parallelization.

In Section 7.5, we discuss parallelization by data partitioning for a DMS consisting of a host and a massively parallel kernel system (an example for such an architecture is the SUPRENUM machine; see Section 2.3.4). The sequential program is split into two program units, one for execution on the host (performing essentially I/O and control functions), and the other for spawning a set of processes on the kernel.

7.2   Parallel code generation for doall-loops

7.2.1   A single-program–multiple-data model for shared memory

We begin by describing a **single-program–multiple-data** (SPMD) model for parallel programs and their execution on an SMS (Darema-Rogers *et al.*, 1985; Stone, 1985). The underlying hardware architecture is assumed to

Table 7.1 Syntax of the program model.

program	$\rightarrow$	*section*$^+$
section	$\rightarrow$	*serial-section|parallel-section|replicate-section*
serial-section	$\rightarrow$	`"SERIAL"` *statement** `"ENDSERIAL"`
parallel-section	$\rightarrow$	`"DOALL"` *do-control body* `"ENDALL"` [*do-variable*]
replicate-section	$\rightarrow$	(*statement|barrier|serial-section|parallel-section*)*
barrier	$\rightarrow$	`"BARRIER"` | `"IF"` *condition* `"THEN"` `"BARRIER"` `"FI"`
condition	$\rightarrow$	*expression*

provide a large number of processors, all of which can access a global shared memory. Parallelism is expressed by the doall-loop.

The syntax of programs is specified in Table 7.1 (see also Table 4.1).

A program is a sequence of one or more **sections**, which may be serial, parallel, or replicate. Note that sections are not defined recursively; in particular, serial sections and parallel sections may not contain any other sections. Any serial or parallel section that is nested within a replicate section is considered not to be a part of the replicate section.

For each program, a set of processes is created, all of which execute the same code. At any given time, different processes may perform different instructions and operate on different data. Tasks are assigned to processes dynamically according to the following rules.

A **serial section** is executed by exactly one process. The first process to arrive at a serial section is assigned to it, while all other processes skip the section and proceed with the following code. For example, code which initializes a parallel computation will be a serial section.

The iterations of the doall-loop which constitutes a **parallel section** are executed in parallel without synchronization. Iterations are dynamically assigned to processes when they reach the section. After a process has completed its iteration, it returns to compete for another one. Any process which reaches the parallel section after all iterations have been executed skips the section and proceeds. If the number of iterations is large compared with the number of processes, then it may be preferable to assign each process a 'chunk' of iterations rather than a single iteration (see Section 7.4.1).

A **replicate section** is a (usually small) portion of the program which is executed in all processes. It could, in principle, be executed by a single process. Replicate sections are preferred to serial sections if the synchronization overhead of serialization is large compared with the time required for the computation.

For the purpose of expressing synchronization, our model provides the barrier statement, each instance of which is called a **synchronization point**. When a process reaches `BARRIER`, it must wait for all other processes to arrive at this point before it can proceed.

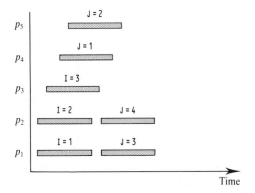

Figure 7.1 Execution of the first program in Example 7.3 on a system with five processes.

Example 7.3

Suppose we have a sequential program consisting of two do-loops, in which there are no interloop dependences, and neither loop contains loop-carried dependences:

```
DO I = 1, 3
  S₁; ...; Sₚ
END DO

DO J = 1, 4
  S'₁; ...; S'ᵧ
END DO
```

Then all iterations of both loops can be executed in parallel. An equivalent parallel program is:

```
DOALL I = 1, 3
  S₁; ...; Sₚ
ENDALL

DOALL J = 1, 4
  S'₁; ...; S'ᵧ
ENDALL
```

A possible execution sequence for this program on a system with five processes p_i $(1 \leq i \leq 5)$ is given in Figure 7.1.

Now assume that we have a program that differs from the above in that there are interloop dependences from the first to the second loop. We

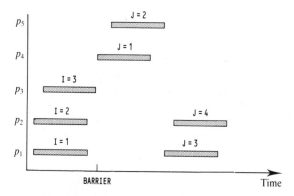

Figure 7.2 Execution of the second program in Example 7.3 on a system with five processes.

can then generate the following parallel program:

```
DOALL I = 1, 3
  S₁; ...; Sₚ
ENDALL

BARRIER

DOALL J = 1, 4
  S′₁; ...; S′q
ENDALL
```

We need the barrier to ensure that all iterations of the first loop are executed before all iterations of the second loop, this being enough to satisfy the interloop dependences. A possible execution sequence – again for a system with five processes – is indicated in Figure 7.2

If a serial or parallel section is contained in a do-loop, synchronization must be inserted in order to maintain the program semantics, as demonstrated in the following example.

Example 7.4

Consider the following sequential program:

```
DO I = 1, N
  DO J = 1, M
    S₁; ...; Sₚ
  END DO
END DO
```

Now assume that the outer loop must be executed sequentially, while the inner loop may be parallelized. We attempt to do so as follows:

```
DO I = 1, N
  DOALL J = 1, M
    S₁; ...; Sₚ
  ENDALL
END DO
```

This is, however, not a semantically valid solution, since it could lead to the parallel execution of iterations of the J loop for different values of I. Synchronization is required to obtain a correct parallel program:

```
DO I = 1, N
  DOALL J = 1, M
    S₁; ...; Sₚ
  ENDALL
  IF I < N THEN BARRIER FI
END DO
```

We need synchronization to deal with dependences. Whenever we have a dependence between different sections, a barrier must be inserted between them. In contrast, dependences between statements within a section are satisfied automatically and require no synchronization.

Our aim is to parallelize as many do-loops as possible, while keeping the number of synchronization points small. The second objective can be achieved by fusing sections: if, for instance, a serial section SC' depends on a serial section SC, then fusing these two sections removes the need for a barrier between them. We can always fuse serial sections and replicate sections; parallel sections may only be fused under certain conditions. This is discussed in more detail in Section 7.2.3.

7.2.2 Theoretical foundation

Consider a loop L and a statement S at level n of L. In the previous chapter, we saw that all instances of S at a level $c \in [1{:}n]$ can be executed concurrently if S is not contained in a cycle of $D := DG(L)$ at level c (Theorem 6.5). We used this result to develop a strategy for vector code generation.

Rather than only considering single statements, we now want to find large regions of code which can be executed in parallel, since only these will offset the overhead caused by scheduling and synchronization. As a consequence, we generalize the concepts and results of Section 6.3 to include regions that correspond to one or more nodes of the acyclic condensation of a (layered) dependence graph.

In the following, we assume that for an arbitrary $c \geqslant 1$, $D_c :=$ constrain(D,c) is the level c dependence graph of L, and $G' = AC(D_c) = (N',E')$ is its acyclic condensation. Each $n' \in N'$ represents a strongly connected component $G_i = (N_i,E_i)$ of D_c, which is called a **region** at level c. G_i and n' will be used synonymously.

Definition 7.1   Let $G_i = (N_i,E_i)$ denote a region at level c:

(1) G_i is **scalar** iff there is a statement $S \in N_i$ that is scalar at level c.

(2) G_i is **serial** iff there is a statement $S \in N_i$ that is serial at level c.

(3) G_i is **parallel** iff G_i is not serial.   ■

Note that a region which is scalar at level c is always serial at that level.

Theorem 7.2   Let G_i denote a region at level c.

(1)   If G_i is serial, then all statements of G_i are serial at level c. G_i is either a trivial graph (if it is scalar) or a cyclic strongly connected region with a cycle at level c.

(2)   If G_i is parallel, then all statements of G_i are concurrent at level c. G_i is then either a trivial graph or a cyclic strongly connected component, whose cycles are all at levels $\geqslant c + 1$.   ■

Proof   If G_i is serial, then it contains a statement S that is serial at level c. If S is scalar, then it is the only statement in G_i, and the theorem holds. Otherwise, S is contained in a cyclic path π at level c in D_c, which is also a path in G_i and contains all statements of G_i. Therefore, all statements of G_i are serial at level c. This proves (1). (2) follows immediately from the definition of a parallel region and (1).   ■

Corollary

(1)   Any region G_i is either serial or parallel, but not both.

(2)   A region G_i at level c is parallel iff G_i is not scalar and has no edge at level c.

(3)   All iterations of a parallel region can be executed in parallel without synchronization.   ■

Note that the last item above is more than just the obvious extension of Theorem 6.5: not only can the individual statements of G_i be performed separately in parallel, but the whole region can be executed in parallel without the need to break it up via loop distribution.

In the following, we will use the term 'concurrent' for the characterization of a statement in a loop synonymously with 'parallel'.

If a region is scalar at level c, then it contains a statement at a level less than c. If a region is serial, but not scalar, then in general its iterations cannot be executed in parallel without synchronization (see the discussion in Sections 6.3 and 6.5.7).

7.2.3 Loop fusion

Loop fusion is a transformation that combines two adjacent loops into one loop. In this subsection, we look for conditions which tell us when two sequential loops or two doall-loops can be fused. We use the results in Section 7.2.4 to define the concept of a cluster of regions precisely.

We first consider the fusion of do-loops, and begin by looking at an example.

Example 7.5

The two adjacent loops:

```
L:  DO I = 1, N
       A(I) = A(I - 3) + C(I)
    END DO

L': DO I = 1, N
       D(I) = A(I - 1) * D(I - 2)
    END DO
```

can be fused to form:

```
L": DO I = 1, N
       A(I) = A(I - 3) + C(I)
       D(I) = A(I - 1) * D(I - 2)
    END DO
```

L'' is equivalent to the sequence $L;L'$, so the transformation is valid. Note that the loop-independent dependence caused by A(I) and A(I-1) in the original program has been transformed into a loop-carried dependence in

L''. If we were to replace A(I-1) in L' by A(I+1), then loop fusion would change the program semantics, and thus could not be validly applied (see Example 7.6).

Loop fusion will be defined for the more general case where L and L' are a pair of adjacent loops at the same level c of a loop nest LL ($c \geqslant 1$). (If $c = 1$, then L and L' are top-level loops. As usual in such a case, we assume that an implicit loop encloses L and L'.)

TRANSFORMATION 7.1: Loop fusion for do-loops

> **Input**   A loop nest LL, and adjacent do-loops L and L', both at level c of LL ($c \geqslant 1$):
>
> > L: DO I = t, u
> >   *SEQ*
> >   END DO
> >
> > L': DO I = t, u
> >   *SEQ'*
> >   END DO
>
> > t and u are assumed to be invariant within L. *SEQ* and *SEQ'* are statement sequences.
>
> **Output**   A do-loop L'' at level c of LL, replacing $L;L'$:
>
> > L'': DO I = t, u
> >   *SEQ*
> >   *SEQ'*
> >   END DO   ■

Remarks

(1)   Loop fusion is defined for two loops only when the expressions for their lower and upper bounds are identical and, in the first loop, invariant (this guarantees identical values of the bounds in both loops). If the values of these expressions differ by a small amount only, an adjustment can be made by loop unrolling or loop peeling (Wolfe, 1982).

(2)   We can easily extend the definition to loops with forward branches.   ■

Definition 7.2   Assume that we have a pair of adjacent do-loops L and L' at level c of a loop LL (specified as in Transformation 7.1), and that S and S' are statements within L and L', respectively.

A dependence $S\,\delta_\infty\,S'$ is **serial-fusion preventing** iff there are iteration vectors $\mathbf{i} \in [S]$, $\mathbf{i}' \in [S']$ such that the dependence is caused by the instances $S(\mathbf{i})$ and $S'(\mathbf{i}')$, where $i_c > i'_c$.[†]　■

Example 7.6

The dependence of Example 7.5 is not serial-fusion preventing ($c = 1$). If, however, we modify the second loop to obtain

```
L:   DO I = 1, N
        A(I) = A(I - 3) + C(I)
     END DO

L':  DO I = 1, N
        D(I) = A(I + 1) * D(I - 2)
     END DO
```

then A(I) and A(I + 1) give rise to a dependence which is serial-fusion preventing. Fusion would produce a loop with a different semantics.

Theorem 7.2　Loop fusion for do-loops L and L' is valid iff there exists no serial-fusion preventing dependence from L to L'.　■

Proof　Suppose first that S and S' are statements in L and L', respectively, and that there is a serial-fusion preventing dependence from S to S' caused by iteration vectors $\mathbf{i}$ and $\mathbf{i}'$. Then $S(\mathbf{i}) \ll_\infty S'(\mathbf{i}')$. Loop fusion inverts the ordering of the two statement instances since $i_c > i'_c$. This destroys the dependence.

It can be easily verified that the above case is the only one in which a dependence can be destroyed by fusion.　■

A remark on the use of this transformation in practice: we have introduced loop fusion for do-loops here because we want to combine serial regions in order to generate efficient parallel code. This is similar to the way the transformation is used in compilers for sequential machines, where loop fusion enables a reduction in the overhead caused by loop control. It can also be used to reduce traffic in a memory hierarchy (the fused loops may share references to variables; see Kuck *et al.* (1984a)).

Loop fusion for doall-loops is now defined similarly as for do-loops.

[†] Note that the maximum common loop level of S and S' is $c - 1$, which implies that for all j, $1 \leq j < c$, $i_j = i'_j$).

TRANSFORMATION 7.2: Loop fusion for doall-loops

Input A loop LL, and adjacent doall-loops L and L', both at
level c of LL ($c \geqslant 1$):

```
L:   DOALL I = t, u
        SEQ
     ENDALL
```

```
L':  DOALL I = t, u
        SEQ'
     ENDALL
```

t and u are assumed to be invariant within L. SEQ and
SEQ' are statement sequences. All loops enclosing L and
L' (if they exist) are sequential do-loops.[†]

Output A doall-loop L'' at level c of LL:

```
L'':  DOALL I = t, u
         SEQ
         SEQ'
      ENDALL
```
■

While the mechanism of fusing is the same for both do-loops and doall-loops, the criteria for their correct application are not.

Definition 7.3 Assume that we have a pair of adjacent doall-loops L and L' at level c of a loop LL (specified as in Transformation 7.2), and that S and S' are statements within L and L', respectively.

A dependence $S \delta_\infty S'$ is **parallel-fusion preventing** iff there are iteration vectors $\mathbf{i} \in [S]$, $\mathbf{i}' \in [S']$ such that the dependence is caused by the instances $S(\mathbf{i})$ and $S'(\mathbf{i}')$, where $i_c \neq i'_c$. ■

Theorem 7.3 Loop fusion for doall-loops L and L' is valid iff there exists no parallel-fusion preventing dependence from L to L'. ■

Proof If a parallel-fusion preventing dependence occurs, then after fusion the order between $S(\mathbf{i})$ and $S'(\mathbf{i}')$ is lost, as the iterations of a doall-loop are executed in parallel. Thus the dependence $S \delta S'$ would be destroyed by fusion. This is the only case which prevents valid fusion of doall-loops.

[†] Loop fusion is applied *before* the insertion of barriers into the code. At this point, the doall-loops are assumed to be executed sequentially. ■

7.2.4 Clusters

Let $G' = (N', E')$ be the acyclic condensation of a level c dependence graph, and $n' \in N'$ represent a region G_i of G'. We say that **serial** or **parallel code** is generated for G_i at level c depending on whether, for each statement S of G_i, the level c loop enclosing S remains sequential or is transformed into a doall-loop. Parallel code can be validly generated for a region iff the region is parallel.[†] The code generation algorithm produces parallel code for the outermost parallel region of a nest, and serial code for all other levels. Whenever we consider, in the context of parallel code generation, a region G_i at level c, we assume that for all levels less than c serial code has been generated. The code generation algorithm attempts to combine regions whenever it is possible to do so without having to generate a synchronization point. We call such a set of regions a **cluster**. In the following, we characterize clusters and develop methods for their construction.

Assume that we have two loops L and L', and that the statements in their bodies are serial at all levels. Then we can build separate serial sections, SC and SC', around L and L':

```
SC:   SERIAL L ENDSERIAL
SC':  SERIAL L' ENDSERIAL
```

In principle, these sections can be executed in parallel; but if a dependence between them exists, a barrier must be generated. SC and SC' can always be combined by fusing the serial sections:

```
SERIAL L;L' ENDSERIAL
```

Alternatively, if L and L' satisfy the input conditions of the first loop fusion transformation (Transformation 7.1) and there are no serial-fusion preventing dependences, the two loops can be fused to generate

```
SERIAL L" ENDSERIAL
```

where L'' is the loop resulting from this transformation. The algorithm will always combine sequential loops in this manner. The method can be extended to replicate sections.

The fusion of parallel sections, when possible and semantically valid, is always a fusion of doall-loops (see Transformation 7.2 and Theorem 7.3). If parallel sections cannot be fused, they will be separated by a barrier.

[†] Here we ignore special cases in which parallel code generation is possible for serial regions (see the remarks at the end of Section 7.2.2, and Sections 6.3 and 6.5.7).

We are now in a position to specify clusters precisely. In the first step, all edges of E' are classified according to whether or not they cause the generation of a barrier.

Definition 7.4

(1)   An edge $e' = (n'',n') \in E'$ is a **barrier-free edge** $:\Longleftrightarrow$

   (a) n'' and n' are both serial regions, or
   (b) n'' and n' are two parallel regions that can be validly fused.

(2) $e' \in E'$ is a **barrier-edge** iff e' is not a barrier-free edge.
(3)   A path in G' is **barrier-free** iff all its edges are barrier-free.   ∎

If $e' = (n'',n')$ is an edge in E', then the code generation algorithm will insert a barrier between n'' and n' iff e' is a barrier-edge.

We now introduce the concept of a consistent partition of N' (Allen *et al.*, 1987).

Definition 7.5   Let $h \geqslant 1$ and $TS := \{T_j: 1 \leqslant j \leqslant h\}$ be an ordered partition of N', which can be characterized as follows:

(1)   For every $(n'',n') \in E'$ such that $n'' \in T_{j_1}$ and $n' \in T_{j_2}$: $j1 \leqslant j2$.
(2)   For every $e \in E'$ and every $T \in TS$: e is an edge in $G'|T$ only if e is a barrier-free edge.

TS is called a **consistent partition**.   ∎

In general, there may be more than one consistent partition for N'; for instance, any two isolated nodes of N' may be either combined or put into different elements of the partition. We aim to find a consistent partition with a minimum number of elements, as this will also minimize the number of synchronization points. The following algorithm constructs such a partition, which is uniquely determined by G' and will be called the **cluster partition**.

ALGORITHM 7.1: Construction of the cluster partition CS

   Input   Loop L, $D := DG(L)$, $c \geqslant 1$, and $G' = (N',E') = AC(constrain(D,c))$.

Output   A consistent partition $CS = \{C_j: 1 \leqslant j \leqslant h\}$ of N', which is called the **cluster partition**; each C_j $(1 \leqslant j \leqslant h)$ is called a **cluster**.

Method

```
begin
N₀ := ∅; j := 0;
repeat
  j := j + 1;
  initials(Cⱼ) := {n' ∈ N' − Nⱼ₋₁: pred(n') ⊆ Nⱼ₋₁};
  Cⱼ := initials(Cⱼ) ∪
        {n': n' ∈ N' − Nⱼ₋₁, and
            n' can be reached from initials(Cⱼ), and
            (n'',n') ∈ E' implies n'' ∈ Nⱼ₋₁ or (n'' ∈ Cⱼ and
            (n'',n') is barrier-free)};
  Nⱼ := ∪{Cₜ: 1 ⩽ t ⩽ j}
until Nⱼ = N';
h := j;
CS := {Cⱼ: 1 ⩽ j ⩽ h}
end
```

∎

The algorithm begins by constructing $initials(C_1)$ as the set of all nodes in N' without predecessor; since G' is acyclic, this is non-empty. C_1 is then defined as the set of all nodes that are either in $initials(C_1)$ or can be reached from $initials(C_1)$ only along barrier-free paths in G'. Now assume that $C_1, \ldots, C_{j-1}$ $(j > 1)$ have already been constructed. If $N_{j-1} = N'$, then $h := j - 1$ and the construction process terminates. Otherwise, the next cluster, C_j, is constructed similarly to C_1 above.

The cluster partition is a consistent partition of N' which is uniquely determined by G'. Furthermore, among all consistent partitions the cluster partition is the one with the minimum number of elements. As a consequence, if code generation is controlled by the cluster partition, then a minimum number of barriers (namely $h - 1$) is created at any level (which, however, does not guarantee that the overall number of barrier statements dynamically executed is minimal – see Example 7.10).

We finally note that each cluster C can be decomposed into a set of **segments**, where a segment is a connected subgraph of C whose regions are all:

(1)   scalar, or
(2)   serial, but not scalar, or
(3)   parallel.

In the last two cases, we additionally require that all level c loops contained in the segment can be fused. Depending on which of these cases holds, we speak of a scalar, serial, or parallel segment.

Example 7.7

Consider the program

```
LL₁:  DO I = 1, N
          DO J = 1, N
              S₁:  A(I, J) = A(I, J - 1)
              S₂:  B(I, J) = A(I, J - 2) + 2
          END DO J
      END DO I


LL₂:  DO I = 1, N
          DO J = 1, N
              DO K = 1, UB
                  S₃:  C(I, J, K) = (C(I - 1, J, K) + C(I, J - 2, K) +
                                     C(I, J, K - 3))/3 * A(I, J)
              END DO K
          END DO J
      END DO I


LL₃:  DO I = 1, N
          DO J = 1, N
              S₄:  D(I, J) = D(I - 3, J) + A(I, J) * 2
          END DO J
      END DO I
```

The dependence graph D for this program is displayed, together with its acyclic condensation, in Figure 7.3. It can be easily verified that S_1 is parallel at level 1 and serial at level 2, S_2 is parallel at levels 1 and 2, S_3 is serial at levels 1, 2, and 3, and S_4 is serial at level 1 and parallel at level 2.

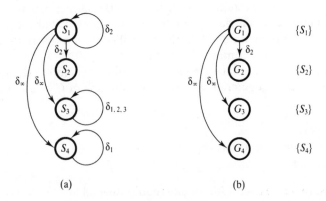

(a)   (b)

Figure 7.3   (a) Dependence graph D and (b) acyclic condensation $AC(D)$ for the program of Example 7.7.

For $c = 1$, the edge (G_1, G_2) – which connects two fusable parallel regions – is barrier-free. In contrast, the edges (G_1, G_3) and (G_1, G_4), which connect a parallel with a serial region, are barrier-edges. There are four consistent partitions, the last of which is the cluster partition:

$$\{\{G_1\}, \{G_2\}, \{G_3\}, \{G_4\}\}$$
$$\{\{G_1\}, \{G_2\}, \{G_3, G_4\}\}$$
$$\{\{G_1, G_2\}, \{G_3\}, \{G_4\}\}$$
$$\{\{G_1, G_2\}, \{G_3, G_4\}\}$$

7.2.5 The code generation algorithm

In this subsection we present a code generation algorithm due to Allen, Callahan, and Kennedy (Allen *et al.*, 1987; Callahan, 1987). It creates code for the model introduced in Section 7.2.1 and is based on the concepts discussed in the preceding subsections. The algorithm determines loops whose iterations can be executed in parallel without synchronization and transforms them into doall-loops; if such a transformation is possible at more than one level, then it is performed at the outermost possible level.

ALGORITHM 7.2: Parallel code generation

Input   Loop L with dependence graph $D = DG(L)$ and statement set *STAT*.

Output   A parallelized program L_{par}, equivalent to L.

Method

procedure parallelize($R,c,doall\_flag$);

/* R is a set of assignment statements in L, $c \in \mathbb{N}$ is a level, and *doall_flag* is a boolean output parameter that is used to signal to the calling procedure whether or not this call generates a doall-loop.

This procedure (excluding recursive calls) generates code at level c for R. If $c > 1$, then the statements in R are contained in serial regions at all levels $\leq c - 1$, and sequential do-loops have been created at these levels.

We use the following notation:

- $G' = (N', E')$: the acyclic condensation of the level c dependence graph, restricted to R
- *visited* $\subseteq N'$. At any time, the value of *visited* is the set of all regions that have already been processed by the call
- *initials* is a shorthand for the expression:
  $\{n': (n' \in N' - visited) \wedge (pred(n') \subseteq visited)\}$

- *new_regions*: an auxiliary variable whose values are sets of regions
- *CLUSTER* ⊆ *N'*: a set of regions that can be combined
- *old_CLUSTER*: an auxiliary variable needed for the stabilization test
- *STAT(SEG)*: the set of statements contained in a segment *SEG*
- *local_flag*: a local boolean variable
- a call generate_body(*STATS,c*) generates serial code for the set of statements in *STATS* at all levels ≥ *c*. */

begin
$G' = (N',E') := AC(constrain(D,c)|R)$;
visited := ∅;
doall_flag := false;

/* The while loop below performs exactly *h* iterations, where *h* ≥ 1 is the cardinality of the cluster partition. Iteration *j* (1 ≤ *j* ≤ *h*) first constructs C_j (collecting its elements in the variable *CLUSTER*) and then generates code for the cluster */

while *initials* ≠ ∅ **do**

/* Step 1: construct the next cluster C_j */

CLUSTER := *initials*;
visited **plus** *initials*;   •
repeat
    old_CLUSTER := *CLUSTER*;
    new_regions := {*n'*: *pred(n')* ⊆ *visited* ∧
                                    ∀ *n''* ∈ *pred(n')* ∩ *CLUSTER*:
                                    (*n'',n'*) is a barrier-free edge};
    CLUSTER **plus** *new_regions*;
    visited **plus** *new_regions*
until *old_CLUSTER* = *CLUSTER*;

/* Step 2: generate code for C_j */

for every segment *SEG* ⊆ CLUSTER in topological order **do**
    if *SEG* is scalar at level *c*
    then generate_body(*STAT(SEG),c*)
    else   /* *SEG* is serial or parallel: let I_c, T_c and U_c be the do-variable, the lower and the upper bound of the loop associated with *SEG* at level *c* */
    if *SEG* is serial at level *c*
    then generate(" DO I_c = T_c,U_c ");
                parallelize(*STAT(SEG),c* + 1,*local_flag*);
                if *local_flag*
                then   /* a doall-loop has been generated at level *c* + 1: this enforces synchronization for the level *c* loop (see Example 7.4) */
                generate(" IF I_c < U_c THEN BARRIER FI ")
                fi;
                generate(" END DO I_c ")

```
    else   /* SEG is parallel at level c */
        doall_flag := true;
        generate(" DOALL I_c = T_c,U_c ");
        generate_body(STAT(SEG),c + 1);
        generate(" ENDALL I_c ")
    fi
  fi
end for;
/* Step 3: if this is not the last cluster, generate a barrier */
if visited ≠ N' then generate(" BARRIER ") fi
end while
end   /* parallelize */
/* MAIN PROGRAM */
begin parallelize(STAT,1,doall_flag) end                    ■
```

Remark We avoid unnecessary complications above by not explicitly generating the parentheses SERIAL and ENDSERIAL around serial sections. Assume in the following that all maximum substructures of composite sections that do not contain serial or parallel sections are transformed into serial sections.   ■

Example 7.8

We apply the algorithm to the program:

```
DO I = 1, N
  DO J = 1, N
    S:  A(I, J) = A(I, J - 1)
  END DO J
END DO I
```

As the dependence graph shows, S is parallel at level 1 and serial at level 2. The call parallelize($\{S\}$,1,doall_flag) produces $G' = (N',E')$ with $N' = \{n'\}$ and $E' = \emptyset$, where n' represents the cyclic region $(\{S\},\{(S,S)\})$ shown above. Step 1 sets CLUSTER and visited to $\{n'\}$; the repeat loop changes nothing. Thus the partition constructed is $CS = \{\{n'\}\}$, where n' is parallel at level 1; and step 2 generates the code shown below. Since step 3 has no effect, and no further iteration of the while loop must be performed, this completes code generation:

```
DOALL I = 1, N
  DO J = 1, N
    S:  A(I, J) = A(I, J - 1)
  END DO J
ENDALL I
```

Example 7.9

We now generate code for the program of Example 7.7 (see also Figure 7.3). The call parallelize($\{S_1,S_2,S_3,S_4\}$,1,*doall_flag*) causes the while-loop to perform two iterations, which in step 1 produce the cluster partition $\{\{G_1,G_2\},\{G_3,G_4\}\}$. The first cluster, $\{G_1,G_2\}$, consists of exactly one parallel segment, while the second cluster contains two different serial segments G_3 and G_4.

Step 2 and step 3 generate the following code for the parallel segment $\{G_1,G_2\}$:

```
DOALL I = 1, N
  DO J = 1, N
    S₁:  A(I, J) = A(I, J - 1)
    S₂:  B(I, J) = A(I, J - 2) + 2
  END DO J
ENDALL I
BARRIER
```

Consider now G_3. Since S_3 is serial in all levels, four recursive calls of parallelize are needed to reproduce the code equivalent to LL_2. In contrast, the algorithm generates for S_4 a serial loop at level 1, and a doall-loop at level 2. The final code produced (after creating serial regions as required) is shown in Program 7.1.

We summarize the effect of the code generation algorithm in the following theorem.

Theorem 7.4 Suppose that Algorithm 7.2 is applied to a loop L, S is an assignment statement at level n of L, and L_j ($1 \leqslant j \leqslant n$) denotes the level j loop enclosing S.

(1) The algorithm terminates.

(2) If S is serial at all levels, then the instances of S in the transformed program are executed in standard order.

(3) If S is parallel at a level, then let $cmin := min\{c: S$ is parallel at level $c\}$. The algorithm validly rearranges the execution of L in such a way that all instances of S in L_{cmin} are executed in parallel; at all other levels, serial code is generated for S.

(4) The algorithm generates all synchronization that is required to maintain the semantics of the program. ∎

Program 7.1 Parallel code for the program in Example 7.7.

```
DOALL I = 1, N
  DO J = 1, N
    S₁:  A(I, J) = A(I, J - 1)
    S₂:  B(I, J) = A(I, J - 2) + 2
  END DO J
ENDALL I

BARRIER

SERIAL
  DO I = 1, N
    DO J = 1, N
      DO K = 1, UB
        S₃:  C(I, J, K) = (C(I - 1, J, K) + C(I, J - 2, K) +
                          C(I, J, K - 3))/3 * A(I, J)
      END DO K
    END DO J
  END DO I
ENDSERIAL

DO I = 1, N
  DOALL J = 1, N
    S₄:  D(I, J) = D(I - 3, J) + A(I, J) * 2
  ENDALL J
  IF I < N THEN BARRIER
END DO I
```

The number of barrier synchronization points generated is minimal at any particular level. However, the following example demonstrates that the total number of times a barrier statement has to be executed may be improved upon. This problem can be solved if we do not fuse two serial regions when one of these regions contains a nested parallel loop. The required modification of the algorithm is elaborated in detail in Allen *et al.* (1987) and Callahan (1987).

Example 7.10

The following program has the dependence graph given at the right-hand side:

```
DO I = 1, N
  DO J = 1, N
    S₁:  X(I, J) = 1/3 * (X(I - 1, J + 1) + X(I, J - 2) + Y(I, J))
  END DO J
```

```
DO J = 1, N
  S₂: Y(I, J) = Y(I - 3, J - 2) * 4
END DO J
END DO I
```

At level 1, a partition $CS_1 = \{\{n_{11}, n_{12}\}\}$ is created, where n_{1i} represents the cyclic region containing S_i ($i = 1,2$). Both regions are serial, can be fused, and thus are put into a single serial segment (that is, the original form of the outer loop is regenerated after the distribution implied by the construction of the two regions). The recursive call parallelize ($\{S_1, S_2\}, 2, local\_flag$) produces the partition $CS_2 = \{\{n_{21}\}, \{n_{22}\}\}$, where n_{21} is associated with S_1 and is serial, whereas n_{22} is associated with S_2 and is parallel. The final code produced is:

```
DO I = 1, N
  SERIAL
    DO J = 1, N
      S₁: X(I, J) = 1/3 * (X(I - 1, J + 1) + X(I, J - 2) + Y(I, J))
    END DO J
  ENDSERIAL
  BARRIER
  DOALL J = 1, N
    S₂: Y(I, J) = Y(I - 3, J - 2) * 4
  ENDALL J
  IF I < N THEN BARRIER
END DO I
```

A system of processes executing this loop encounters $2N - 1$ barrier statements. In contrast, the following equivalent code, requires only N synchronizations. This is achieved by avoiding fusion at level 1, thus distributing the level 1 loop and moving the barrier between S_1 and S_2 one level out.

```
SERIAL
DO I = 1, N
  DO J = 1, N
    S₁: X(I, J) = 1/3 * (X(I - 1, J + 1) + X(I, J - 2) + Y(I, J))
  END DO J
END DO I
ENDSERIAL
BARRIER
DO I = 1, N
  DOALL J = 1, N
    S₂: Y(I, J) = Y(I - 3, J - 2) * 4
  ENDALL J
  IF I < N THEN BARRIER FI
END DO I
```

Algorithm 7.2, as discussed in this section, is the basic version of an algorithm for parallel code generation. It can be improved by including additional transformations such as loop interchange, loop alignment, and loop replication (see Section 7.4). With these transformations included, the problem of generating optimal code (in the sense of minimizing the number of barrier statements to be executed) becomes computationally intractable, and we are forced to use heuristical methods (Allen *et al.*, 1987; Callahan, 1987).

7.3 Parallel code generation for doacross-loops

The approach to parallelization discussed in the previous section essentially transformed loops without loop-carried dependences into doall-loops. Here, we deal with a more general situation by considering the parallelization of loops with arbitrary dependences. If the iterations of such loops are executed in parallel, different iterations may have to be synchronized.

7.3.1 Language features

Parallel loops are specified as doacross-loops with the following syntax (see Table 4.1):

doacross-loop → "DOACROSS" *do-control body* "ENDACROSS" [*do-variable*]

Doacross-loops may not be nested. We define the manner in which a loop

DOACROSS I = t, u *body* ENDACROSS

is executed as follows. After their initiation, the iterations $I = T, \dots, U$ (T and U are the respective values of t and u) are executed in parallel, subject only to synchronization constraints in the body. Where there are no such constraints, a doacross-loop is equivalent to a doall-loop. If there is a dependence cycle, then the loop may be executed sequentially, like a do-loop, but with scheduling and synchronization overhead. (Note that a variety of semantics for doacross-loops are to be found in the literature, for example Cytron (1984), Polychronopoulos (1986), and Wolfe (1987b), which may be different from our interpretation).

For the remainder of this section, we assume that different iterations of a doacross-loop are mapped to different processes. The send and wait statements, as described in the following, can be used to enforce synchronization between processes.

Suppose we have a doacross-loop with iteration range $[T:U]$, containing the statement S_1 and the send statement SS: SEND_SIGNAL(S_1). The execution of instance $SS(i)$ $(T \le i \le U)$ signals the completion of $S_1(i)$. SEND_SIGNAL is a non-blocking operation, that is the process may proceed after its execution.

A wait statement has the form WS: WAIT_SIGNAL(S_2,exp). We then say that $SS(i)$ **matches** $WS(j)$ $(T \le i < j \le U)$ iff $S_2 = S_1$ and the value of $exp(j)$ is equal to i. If a matching statement has been executed before we reach $WS(j)$, then the wait statement will have no effect on the process performing iteration j. Otherwise, this process is delayed until a matching statement is executed.

A more general form of wait statement permits us to specify a list of pairs (*statement,expression*) and requires that each of these be matched by a corresponding send statement. We need this to avoid deadlocks if more than one dependence arc points to the same statement. If the value of exp is less than 1 for some $WS(i)$, then we assume that this is equivalent to an empty statement.

There are several ways to implement the synchronization primitives; which is best depends on the expected length of the delays associated with wait statements (see Section 2.3.2).

7.3.2   Generating synchronization in a loop

Assume we have a do-loop L with iteration range $[T:U]$, in which there are no backward or exit branches. Then we can always transform L into a doacross-loop, regardless of its dependence graph, by inserting the appropriate synchronization statements into the loop's body. To do this, we must consider the loop-carried dependences involved: the basic approach is as follows.

Let $S(i)\,\delta(d)\,S'(i')$ be a loop-carried dependence $(T \le i < i' \le U)$, where $d := i' - i$ is the dependence distance (see Section 4.3.2). We assume that neither statement is control dependent on another statement, and that S' does not depend on another statement. Then we

(1)   generate a send statement immediately[†] following S in the program text: SEND_SIGNAL(S), and

(2)   generate a wait statement immediately[†] before S': WAIT_SIGNAL(S,I $- d$).

[†] In general, this restriction may be relaxed. The position immediately after the source, and immediately before the sink of a dependence is the first or last position, respectively, where the synchronization statement can be inserted.

Whenever a synchronization statement is conditionally executed, then we must generate a corresponding synchronization statement in the other branch of the condition to avoid deadlock (see Example 7.14). If a statement is the target of two or more dependences that cannot be combined, we must use the extended form of the wait statement.

We begin with a simple example.

Example 7.11

Consider the following do-loop:

```
DO I = M, N
  S:   A(I) = B(I) - 1
  S':  C(I) = A(I - 3)/B(I - 2)
END DO
```

Here, there is a loop-carried dependence $S \delta(3) S'$. So the loop cannot be transformed into a doall-loop (although we could apply loop distribution and then generate two doall-loops). We transform it into the doacross-loop

```
DOACROSS I = M, N
  S:   A(I) = B(I) - 1
       SEND_SIGNAL(S)
       WAIT_SIGNAL(S, I - 3)
  S':  C(I) = A(I - 3)/B(I - 2)
ENDACROSS
```

Even a cyclic dependence graph will not, at least in principle, prevent transformation into a doacross-loop.

Example 7.12

```
DO I = 1, N
  S:   A(I) = B(I - 1) + 2
  S':  B(I) = A(I - 3)/C(I - 2)
END DO
```

In this loop there are two loop-carried dependences, $S \delta(3) S'$ and $S' \delta(1) S$.

The transformation into a doacross-loop results in:

```
DOACROSS I = 1, N
        WAIT_SIGNAL(S', I - 1)
    S:  A(I) = B(I - 1) + 2
        SEND_SIGNAL(S)
        WAIT_SIGNAL(S, I - 3)
    S': B(I) = A(I - 3)/C(I - 2)
        SEND_SIGNAL(S')
ENDACROSS
```

In each iteration apart from the first one, the execution of WAIT_SIGNAL (S',I-1) is blocked until the matching SEND_SIGNAL(S') in the previous iteration has been executed: thus the loop is effectively executed sequentially. The scheduling and synchronization overhead, however, make it far more time consuming than the original do-loop. Even if we eliminate synchronization for the dependence $S \, \delta \, S'$ (which is semantically valid), a significant overhead remains.

Thus the fact, as remarked at the outset, that every loop can be rewritten as a doacross-loop, is of theoretical value only. In practice, we must analyze the degree of parallelism in the doacross-loop, and the overhead for synchronization and scheduling. Such investigations go beyond the scope of this book (Polychronopoulos, 1986, 1988). The problems encountered shed additional light on the importance of the rigorous scheme on which the code generation algorithm of the previous section has been based.

We restrict our discussion to two further examples which indicate when synchronization statements can be eliminated.

Example 7.13

Consider the following loop, with the associated graph of loop-carried dependences:

```
DO I = 1, N
    S₁:  A(I) = B(I) * C(I)
    S₂:  B(I) = A(I - 2) + 2
    S₃:  C(I) = B(I - 4) - B(I)/2
    S₄:  D(I) = A(I - 2) * 3
END DO
```

Remember that we can ignore all loop-independent dependences. If no further analysis is carried out, the following code is generated:

```
DOACROSS I = 1, N
  S₁:  A(I) = B(I) * C(I)
       SEND_SIGNAL(S₁)
       WAIT_SIGNAL(S₁, I - 2)
  S₂:  B(I) = A(I - 2) + 2
       SEND_SIGNAL(S₂)
       WAIT_SIGNAL(S₂, I - 4)
  S₃:  C(I) = B(I - 4) - B(I)/2
       WAIT_SIGNAL(S₁, I - 2)
  S₄:  D(I) = A(I - 2) * 3
ENDACROSS
```

Closer examination reveals the fact that if $S_1 \, \delta(2) \, S_2$ is satisfied, then the other loop-carried dependences will be satisfied as well. The code can thus be simplified to:

```
DOACROSS I = 1, N
  S₁:  A(I) = B(I) * C(I)
       SEND_SIGNAL(S₁)
       WAIT_SIGNAL(S₁, I - 2)
  S₂:  B(I) = A(I - 2) + 2
  S₃:  C(I) = B(I - 4) - B(I)/2
  S₄:  D(I) = A(I - 2) * 3
ENDACROSS
```

Suppose that we are transforming a sequential do-loop line by line into a doacross-loop by inserting appropriate synchronization statements, and that at any given time the restrictions imposed by the dependences thus far processed have been encoded into the loop body (note that all loop-independent dependences are satisfied from the outset). Then, when we come upon a new dependence, either the restriction it imposes is implied by others already implemented, in which case no new synchronization statements need be generated, or it is not, and we need additional synchronization. The resulting doacross-loop may depend on the order in which the dependences are processed.

There are a set of rules to help us decide which sychronization statements must be generated. Here are two of them:

(1)   If $S \, \delta \, S'$ is a 'transitive dependence', that is if there is a $t \geqslant 2$ such that $S_{i-1} \, \delta \, S_i$ for all i ($1 \leqslant i \leqslant t$) with $S = S_0$ and $S' = S_t$, and the $S_{i-1} \, \delta \, S_i$ are all in the set of dependences already processed, then we need not generate synchronization for $S \, \delta \, S'$.

(2)   Suppose that there are no branches in a loop containing statements
       S, S', S_1 and S_2, and that there are loop-carried dependences
       $S \delta(d) S'$ and $S_1 \delta(d') S_2$, where d is a multiple of d'. If S_2 bef S', and
       $S_1 \delta(d') S_2$ has already been processed, then no synchronization
       must be generated for $S \delta(d) S'$ (as in Example 7.13).

We conclude by illustrating how we handle loops with conditional
statements.

Example 7.14

The following do-loop is a slightly modified version of that in Example
7.11:

```
DO I = 1, N
  IF C(I) ≥ 0 THEN
    S:   A(I) = B(I) - 1
    S':  C(I) = A(I - 3)/B(I - 2)
  FI
END DO
```

We may transform this loop into

```
DOACROSS I = 1, N
  IF C(I) ≥ 0
    THEN
      S:   A(I) = B(I) - 1
           SEND_SIGNAL(S)
           WAIT_SIGNAL(S, I - 3)
      S':  C(I) = A(I - 3)/B(I - 2)
    ELSE SEND_SIGNAL(S)
  FI
ENDACROSS
```

The transformation must guarantee that a SEND_SIGNAL is executed in every
branch of the conditional: if we omit the ELSE-clause, then we have a
potential deadlock in the transformed program.

The above approach can be significantly improved for mutual exclusion
(see Section 2.3.2). We can then avoid the serialization of the loop iterations by enclosing the accesses to a variable which must be protected into a
critical region.

Example 7.15

The program

```
        MIN_DIST = maximum integer number
    L:  DO I = 1, N
            DIST = SQRT((MY_X - CITY_X(I))**2 +
                    (MY_Y - CITY_Y(I))**2)
            IF DIST < MIN_DIST
              THEN NEAREST = I
                    MIN_DIST = DIST
            FI
        END DO
```

computes the distances between a city with coordinates (MY_X,MY_Y) and N other cities, whose coordinates are given by (CITY_X(i),CITY_Y(i)), where $1 \leqslant i \leqslant N$. The index of the nearest city, and the associated distance are stored in the variables NEAREST and MIN_DIST.

The cyclic dependence involving DIST can be eliminated by creating a local copy %DIST of DIST for each process, by a transformation similar to scalar expansion (see Sections 6.5.2 and 7.4). The dependences caused by NEAREST and MIN_DIST require a different treatment: the analysis of the if-statement reveals that the order in which it is executed in different iterations is immaterial, as long as it is guaranteed that no two iterations execute it concurrently. In other words, the if-statement must be protected by a critical region. Thus L can be transformed into the parallel loop

```
    DOACROSS I = 1, N
      %DIST(I) = SQRT((MY_X - CITY_X(I))**2 + (MY_Y - CITY_Y(I))**2)
      WITH (NEAREST, MIN_DIST) DO
        IF %DIST(I) < MIN_DIST
          THEN NEAREST = I
                MIN_DIST = %DIST(I)
        FI
      END WITH
    END DO
```

where the statement WITH *vlist* DO *statements* END WITH denotes a critical region, which manipulates the variables in *vlist*. The iterations of this loop can be executed in parallel, subject to the constraint of the critical region.

7.4 Shared-memory parallelization: final remarks

7.4.1 Scheduling parallel loops

The iterations of a parallel loop must be **scheduled**, that is mapped to the set of available processes. There are two commonly used methods for doing this: prescheduling and self-scheduling.

For **prescheduling**, the mapping is performed in some predefined way. Each process determines which iterations it must execute, and waits for the other processes to finish after it has completed its work. The iterations may be spread either vertically or horizontally.

Vertical spreading assigns a contiguous block of iterations to each process: let $NP \geqslant 1$ be the number of processes available, p_i the ith process $(1 \leqslant i \leqslant NP)$, and N the number of iterations. If $N \leqslant NP$, then for all i iterations i may be simply mapped to p_i. Otherwise, let $B = CEIL(N/NP)$. For all i with $1 \leqslant i < NP$, the block of iterations $(i - 1)B + q$ is mapped to p_i, where q ranges from 1 to B; the iterations $(NP - 1)B + 1$ through N are mapped to p_{NP} (see Table 7.2).

Example 7.16

Assume $NP = 4$ and $N = 18$. Then $B = CEIL(18/4) = 5$, and vertical spreading maps the iterations to processes as follows:

Iteration	1 2 3 4 5	6 7 8 9 10	11 12 13 14 15	16 17 18
Process number	1	2	3	4

Horizontal spreading maps the set of iterations given by $i + q \times NP$ $(0 \leqslant q < B)$ to p_i, making suitable adjustments for the case where $B > N/NP$ (see Table 7.3).

Table 7.2 Vertical spreading.

Iteration	$1 \ldots B$	$B+1 \ldots 2B$	$\ldots$	$(NP-2)B+1 \ldots (NP-1)B$	$(NP-1)B+1 \ldots N$
Process number	1	2	$\ldots$	$NP-1$	NP

Table 7.3 Horizontal spreading.

Iteration	1	$2...NP$	$NP+1$	$NP+2...2NP$	$...q \times NP+1$	$q \times NP+2...q \times (NP+1)...$
Process number	1	$2...NP$	1	2	... NP ... 1	2 ... NP ...

Example 7.17

Assume $NP = 4$ and $N = 18$ as in Example 7.16. Horizontal spreading results in the following mapping:

Iteration	1	2	3	4	5	6	7	8	9	10	11	12	13	14	15	16	17	18
	↓	↓	↓	↓	↓	...												
Process number	1	2	3	4	1	2	3	4	1	2	3	4	1	2	3	4	1	2

Deciding which of these options is appropriate in a particular case is not a trivial matter: we must consider, among other things, the dependence structure of the loop and properties of the target machine. Vertical spreading may, for example, serialize a loop that contains a loop-carried dependence with distance 1. On the other hand, when a processor has a cache memory, vertical spreading will often be the better method.

When we have a fixed number of processes and use prescheduling, the same processes will execute the same iterations in different executions of a loop. The scheduling overhead will be relatively small, but processes may be idle part of the time.

This is not the case if we choose **self-scheduling**, where the iterations are dynamically mapped to processors (see Section 7.2.1). This can be modeled as follows. Let *global_I* be a global variable which counts the iterations of the loop, *local_I* the corresponding local variable of a process, and *chunk_size* ≥ 1 the number of iterations to be mapped to each process. Assume that $[T:U]$ is the iteration range of the loop; *global_I* must then be initialized to T. A process that is ready to accept a new chunk of iterations executes the following piece of program (the access to *global_I* is protected by a critical region):

```
with global_I do local_I := global_I;
              global_I plus chunk_size
end with;
if local_I > U
    then finish   /* All iterations have already been mapped to processes:
                  nothing remains to be done */
```

else execute iterations in the interval
[*local_I*:*MIN*(*local_I* + *chunk_size* − 1,*U*)]

fi

If the amount of work to be done varies from iteration to iteration, as may be the case when there are if-statements and/or procedure calls in the loop, then self-scheduling is to be preferred to prescheduling: all processes keep working as long as there is work to be done. Its disadvantage is the larger run-time overhead, which can, however, be reduced by increasing the size of chunks.

7.4.2   Transformations to support parallelization

We begin by reviewing some transformations we already know. We do not, however, discuss the standard transformations such as subscript normalization and scalar renaming (see Chapter 5) which are as important for parallelization as they are for vectorization, and select only a few of the transformations introduced in Section 6.5 for our further discussion.

Statement reordering and loop distribution (defined in Section 6.2) play a vital role in parallelization. They are the principal tools of Algorithm 7.2. Loop distribution in particular can be seen as a transformation to convert a loop-carried forward dependence $S \delta S'$ (S bef S') into a loop-independent dependence, thus reducing the number of synchronization statements to be executed in the parallel version of a loop with the form:

```
DO I = 1, N
  A(I) = ...
  ... = A(I - 1) ...
END DO
```

from $N - 1$ to 1.

Scalar expansion (see Section 6.5.2) can be easily adapted for parallelization if the processors have local memories. The variable is then no longer expanded into an array, but instead becomes local to each process. This may eliminate a dependence cycle in the same way as actual scalar expansion does (see Example 7.15).

Loop interchange, defined in Section 6.5.1, is a powerful tool which can be used in a variety of ways to support parallelization. As we already know, we want to move a parallelizable loop as far out as possible to reduce scheduling and synchronization overhead. The number of iterations in a parallel loop, and the amount of work to be done in each iteration, should be maximized. The following example illustrates this.

Example 7.18

```
L:  DO I = 1, N
       DO J = 1, N
         A(I, J) = A(I - 1, J) + C(I, J)
       END DO J
     END DO I
```

L contains a loop-carried dependence at level 1; parallelization is possible at level 2. If we parallelize the inner loop, scheduling would have to be performed N times, once for each iteration of the outer loop. After loop interchange (which is semantically valid), scheduling is required once only.

Use of loop interchange in a compiler must in general be guided by efficient heuristics rather than by optimization of a cost function. Callahan (1987) has shown that the problem of minimizing the number of barrier synchronization points when loop interchange is included in Algorithm 7.2 is NP-complete. Similar results have been obtained elsewhere.

We now look at a transformation specifically designed for parallelization. **Loop alignment** attempts to transform a loop-carried dependence into a loop-independent dependence without distributing the loop. The basic idea is as follows. Suppose that $S(i) \, \delta \, S'(i + 1)$ is a loop-carried dependence. If we can replace S' by a statement S'' such that $S''(i)$ and $S'(i + 1)$ have the same effect, then the dependence $S(i) \, \delta \, S'(i + 1)$ will be converted to a loop-independent dependence $S(i) \, \delta \, S''(i)$. We achieve this by moving variable references from one iteration to another, that is by aligning them. We then need to make a few other modifications – in particular, some statements will have to be executed conditionally – to preserve the semantics of the program.

Example 7.19

```
L:  DO I = 1, N
       S:   A(I) = B(I + 1) * C(I - 1)
       S':  D(I) = A(I - 1) + 2
     END DO
```

In this example, L contains a loop-carried dependence and requires synchronization statements to be inserted between S and S'; loop alignment will produce the following loop L':

```
L':  DO I = 0, N
       IF I > 0 THEN A(I) = B(I + 1) * C(I - 1) FI
       IF I < N THEN D(I + 1) = A(I) + 2 FI
     END DO
```

L' may be executed as a parallel loop without synchronization, that is as a doall-loop.

Loop alignment is not always a valid transformation: if we replace S' in the above example by `D(I) = A(I - 1) + A(I)`, then it would change the program semantics by destroying a loop-independent dependence. We can use **code replication**, that is statement copying together with the introduction of temporary arrays, to remove any loop-carried dependence that is not part of a dependence cycle. The problem of minimizing code replication is, however, NP-hard. A detailed discussion of this problem can be found in Callahan (1987).

7.5   Parallelization for distributed-memory architectures

7.5.1   Overview

In this section we discuss parallelization by data partitioning, an approach to the parallelization of sequential programs for DMSs, which is based upon a user-specified partition of the data domain. A dominating feature of DMSs is the high cost of communication: whereas communication can be realized on an SMS by synchronizing processes via special registers or the global memory, on a DMS, data involved in a true dependence may have to be physically transferred from one local memory to another via the communication network. Depending on how the network is realized and how efficient the operating system is, the time taken to transmit a single data item between two processors may reach the order of a millisecond. So it becomes vital to control communication effectively.

In our approach, communication is controlled jointly by the user – who is primarily responsible for the specification of a partition – and the system, which provides analysis information upon which the choice of a partition can be based. The system automatically inserts all communication that is implied by a given partition and the sequential program, and attempts to reduce the number of communication statements to be executed while increasing the amount of data transferred during one communication.

The method works in principle for arbitrary programs – that is, it correctly translates any sequential program, for which data partitioning has been specified, into an equivalent parallel program for a DMS – but a reasonable efficiency of the target program can only be achieved if the application satisfies certain criteria. The approach is specifically oriented towards the parallelization of numerical algorithms that can be characterized as follows: (1) the programs work on a mesh; (2) the computations at the mesh points are local, that is depend only on the values of a small number of points in the neighborhood; and (3) the size of the data domain may be very large: a typical program may operate on up to 10^9 grid points.

We describe here the salient features of the interactive parallelization system SUPERB (Zima *et al.*, 1988), which is the first automatic tool developed to support parallelization for a DMS. The target machine of SUPERB is the SUPRENUM computer (see Section 2.3.4); the validity of the approach extends, however, to arbitrary DMSs.

The method of parallelization is outlined in Section 7.5.2; the subsequent subsections discuss the design in more detail. We conclude by providing the reader with a complex example illustrating the mapping from a Fortran 77 program for an eigenvalue computation to a parallel program with message passing communication.

7.5.2 The parallelization method

We assume a DMS consisting of a kernel system with a large number of processing nodes, and a host that controls I/O and performs global management tasks. Each node contains a local memory; there is no global memory in the system.

Our target language provides a new type of program unit which is called a **task unit**. A process is created when a task unit is activated. Different processes have disjoint local address spaces; communication with other processes may be established using asynchronous SEND and synchronous RECEIVE message passing primitives (see Section 2.3.2).

The parallelization system takes as input a sequential Fortran program, together with a specification of data partitioning, and produces a parallel program for a DMS (see Figure 7.4). Parallelization is performed in three steps:

- *Step 1: Splitting*
  The program is split into a **host task unit** which includes all I/O and is executed on the host, and a **kernel task unit** that describes the actual computation (Figure 7.5). The processes of the kernel system are created by activations of the kernel task unit.
  Splitting is further discussed in Section 7.5.3.

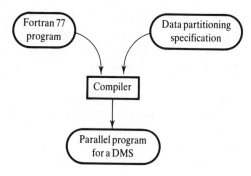

Figure 7.4 Compiling for a DMS.

- *Step 2: Partitioning the data domain*
  The data domain of the sequential program is partitioned under the control of the user. The partition is determined by subdividing arrays into rectangular blocks, and mapping the blocks to processes. This mapping establishes which process **owns** each block – storage for the block is allocated in the local address space of its owner and any assignment to an element of a block must be performed by its owner.

  The way we partition our data determines the process structure of the resulting parallelized program. When we select a suitable partition we must take into account, among other things, the size of the application, the ranges of do-loops, and the structure of the dependences between the statements of a loop.

  Partitioning is discussed in more detail in Section 7.5.4.

- *Step 3: Transforming the kernel task unit*
  The choice of a partition determines a set of requirements for the transformation of the kernel task unit. Its assignment statements must in general be masked in order to guarantee that they write exclusively into the local address space of the executing process, loop bounds must be adjusted, and communication statements have to be inserted in order to satisfy dependences between statements executed in different processes.

  This transformation will be discussed in Section 7.5.5.

7.5.3 Splitting

A parallelized program consists of an host task unit and a kernel task unit. The operating system begins execution of an application program by

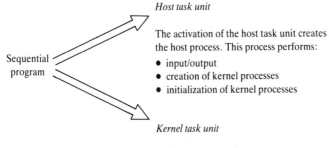

Host task unit

The activation of the host task unit creates
the host process. This process performs:

- input/output
- creation of kernel processes
- initialization of kernel processes

Kernel task unit

The activations of the kernel task unit create
the processes executing on the kernel system.

Figure 7.5   Splitting.

starting the host task unit. This creates the **host process**, which runs on the
host. All I/O operations must be performed in this process. The host
process also activates the kernel task unit, thereby creating the processes
(**kernel processes**) that are executed in the kernel system, and sends them
initialization messages. Only one host process exists for an application; it is
terminated only after all kernel processes have terminated.

This organization means that each unit of the sequential program
must be split into code for the host task unit and the kernel task unit
(Figure 7.5). Essentially, all I/O statements must be collected in the host
task unit, and the corresponding communication statements must be generated in both the host task and the kernel task unit. We can see this in the
following simple example.

Example 7.20: Splitting the program

---

(1)   *Original program*

```
            AMAX = 0.0
            DO I = 1, 10000
              READ (5, 1) A
              IF ABS(A) > AMAX THEN AMAX = ABS(A)  FI
            END DO
            WRITE (6, 1) AMAX
            STOP
        1   FORMAT (F10.2)
            END
```

(2)   *Result of transformation – basic version (abridged)*

Host task unit   Kernel task unit

```
    ...                   ...
                          AMAX=0.0
DO I=1,10000              DO I=1,10000
    READ (5,1) A              RECEIVE A
    SEND A                    IF ABS(A)>AMAX THEN AMAX=ABS(A) FI
END DO                    END DO
RECEIVE AMAX              SEND AMAX
WRITE (6,1) AMAX          ...
    ...
1  FORMAT (F10.2)
   END
```

Although this example gives us an idea of how we can handle I/O operations when splitting, it is completely unrealistic. The start-up time for messages is considerable and dominates the time taken to actually send small messages. Thus the execution of 10000 SEND/RECEIVE operations in the loop would slow things down by an intolerable degree. This can be improved by scalar expansion (see Section 6.5.2): we expand scalar A in the do-loop to %AA(1:10000) and transfer the whole array in a single message.

(3)   *Result of transformation – optimized version (abridged)*

Host task unit   Kernel task unit

```
    ...                   ...
READ (5,1) %AA            AMAX=0.0
SEND %AA                  RECEIVE %AA
RECEIVE AMAX              DO I=1,10000
WRITE (6,1) AMAX              IF ABS(%AA(I))>AMAX THEN AMAX=ABS(%AA(I)) FI
    ...                   END DO
1  FORMAT (F10.2)         SEND AMAX
   END                    ...
```

7.5.4 Partitioning the data domain

The major part of the kernel task unit's data domain consists of arrays. Partitioning of arrays is performed by subdividing them into blocks, which are mapped to processes. The way in which we partition an array will influence the subsequent communication overhead, which in turn influences the speed of the parallel program considerably. The problem of determining an optimal partition with regard to a cost function which minimizes communication cost and maximizes the degree of parallelism is intractable, and no adequate heuristic methods are known so far. This is the background motivating the design decision that requires the user to specify the partition.

Let:

NP denote the number of kernel processes,

$P = \{p_i: 1 \leqslant i \leqslant NP\}$ denote the set of these processes, and

A denote an arbitrary array to be partitioned; A is interpreted as a set of subscripted variables.

The blocks of A are specified by decomposing A into NP mutually disjoint subsets A_i of A ($1 \leqslant i \leqslant NP$) such that the following holds:

(1) $A = \bigcup_{1 \leqslant i \leqslant NP} A_i.$

(2) Each A_i is a rectangular section of A.

(3) A_i is owned by process p_i ($1 \leqslant i \leqslant NP$). All variables in A_i are allocated in the local address space of process p_i, and all statements assigning a value to one of these variables must be executed in p_i.

We need not always partition an array. If a small array A is needed in several processes, then it may be more efficient to make each process an owner of A. Scalar variables are generally handled in this way. Thus, unpartitioned arrays and scalar variables are manipulated in all processes in exactly the same way; they do not cause communication.

Suppose that SI and SJ are statement instances that are executed in processes p_i and p_j respectively ($i \neq j$), and that there is a variable v such that p_j owns v, p_i does not own v, and v causes a dependence $SJ\, \delta^t\, SI$. Then v belongs to the address space of p_j, but its value is also needed by p_i. Thus the value of v must be sent from p_j to p_i via the system's communication mechanisms, and p_i has to allocate space for a copy of v in its local memory. All such variables will be collected in p_i's **overlap area**.

We can now see that the following objects are in the local address space of a process:

(1) the code of the program to be executed,

(2) all blocks owned by the process, together with associated overlap areas,

(3) all unpartitioned arrays, and

(4) all scalar variables.

Example 7.21

Let A(0:101,0:101) be a two-dimensional array and assume that new values are computed for A by the statement below:

```
DO J = 1, 100
  DO I = 1, 100
    ...
    A(I, J) = 0.25 * (A(I, J + 1) + A(I, J - 1) + A(I - 1, J) +
              A(I + 1, J))
    ...
  END DO I
END DO J
```

Now assume that $NP = 100$, and the blocks of A are defined to be 'squares' with 10 elements in every dimension. Then each block is of the form:

$$A(L_1:R_1, L_2:R_2)$$

where $L_1 = s \cdot 10 + 1$, $L_2 = t \cdot 10 + 1$ for some integers s,t $(0 \leqslant s,t \leqslant 9)$, and $R_i = L_i + 9$ for $i = 1,2$.

If we examine the assignment statement in the loop, we see that each inner block must be supplemented by an overlap area including exactly one element to the left and right in each dimension. Thus the block and overlap area together comprise the elements (see Figure 7.6):

$$A(L_1 - 1:R_1 + 1, L_2 - 1:R_2 + 1)$$

We see that the overlap area depends on what computations are performed on the array. The choice of partition and the dependences together determine what communication is necessary.

The parallelizer is able to generate the data declarations and communication statements required when it is provided with a partition. It can also automatically modify the loops in the kernel task unit by adjusting their ranges and/or masking the statements in the body.

7.5.5 Transforming the kernel task unit

We assume the SPMD model of computation, in its DMS version (Karp, 1987). All processes are created when an application program is initiated, and terminated at its end. Each process essentially executes the same program, but on different sets of data.

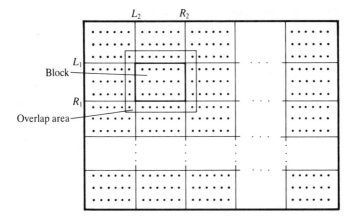

Figure 7.6 The blocks of array A in Example 7.21.

In the remainder of this subsection we ignore splitting and consider only the problem of compiling the kernel task unit.

The basic compilation scheme transforms a program in three steps:

(1) To each assignment statement S a boolean expression *MASK* is attached that determines under which conditions S must be executed – that is, S is transformed into $MASK \rightarrow S$, where the value of $MASK$ at execution time is true iff the process executing S assigns to a variable it owns.

(2) Communication is inserted: for each potentially non-local reference, explicit message passing must be performed.

(3) The resulting program is optimized by the elimination of masks (essentially by translating them into loop bounds) and reduction of communication.

Example 7.22

Consider arrays D and E, declared by DIMENSION D(1:M), E(1:M), and suppose that we have processes p_i $(1 \leq i \leq NP)$, where NP divides M, $q = M/NP$ and p_i owns the blocks D$((i - 1) * q + 1 : i * q)$ and E$((i - 1) * q + 1 : i * q)$ (see Figure 7.7).

The statement S in the do-loop

```
DO I = 1, M - 1
  ...
  S:  E(I) = D(I) + D(I + 1)
  ...
END DO
```

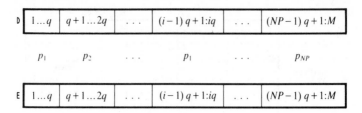

Figure 7.7   Partition of the arrays in Example 7.22.

will be transformed into

```
EXCH(D(I + 1))
owned(E(I)) → S:   E(I) = D(I) + D(I + 1)
```

where *owned*(x) is a predicate that yields **true** iff x is owned by the actually executing process. Now consider the right-hand side of S. D is partitioned in the same way as E, so any process that owns E(I) also owns D(I). Therefore, the occurrence of D(I) does not generate synchronization. In contrast, communication may be required for the access to D(I + 1). This is expressed by the exchange statement EXCH(D(I + 1)), which can be roughly described as follows:

```
if this_process owns D(I + 1)
    then SEND D(I + 1) to all processes p such that:
            (i)   p reads D(I + 1), and
            (ii)  p does not own D(I + 1), and
            (iii) the mask of S in p is true
    else
      if this_process owns D(I)
          then RECEIVE D(I + 1)
      fi
fi
```

This is rather inefficient code; but it allows optimization by moving the information in the mask to the loop bounds, and pulling the communication out of the loop, resulting in:

```
SEND D(L)
RECEIVE D(R + 1)
DO I = L, R
    ...
  S:   E(I) = D(I) + D(I + 1)
    ...
END DO
```

where L and R are functions that describe the lower and upper bounds of blocks in the current process (that is, for p_i, $L = (i - 1)q + 1$, $R = iq$).

In the following, we look at a number of additional examples that illustrate the relationship between partitioning and communication.

As we already know, when a process is to execute a particular iteration of a loop, then it must have the required code and data items in its local address space. We must aim to map loop iterations to the processes as uniformly as possible with a minimum of communication overhead. In the ideal case, the structure of a loop will match the partitions of the arrays accessed in it perfectly and there will be few dependences between statements executed in different processes.

The code executed in one process is sequential; so all dependences inside it are automatically satisfied. Thus, we need only to examine interprocess dependences and can ignore all loop-independent dependencies. Output dependences, if they exist (for data owned by more than one process), are irrelevant; true and anti dependences must be resolved by communication.

In the examples below, we no longer show the intermediate steps of code generation in which masks and exchange statements occur, but illustrate the transformed version of the parallel program by specifying the code executed by one representative process in a loop with an iteration range of $[L:R]$, if nothing else is specified explicitly.

Example 7.23

Let the arrays A, B, C be declared as A(0:1000), B(1:1000), C(1:1000). Assume that process p owns the blocks A(L:R) and C(L:R), and the whole array B (that is, B is unpartitioned). The overlap area associated with A(L:R) contains A(L-1). The overlap area for the blocks of C is empty.

```
DO I = 1, 1000
  S₁:  A(I) = B(I) + A(I)
  S₂:  C(I) = A(I - 1)
END DO
```

Here, the only dependence is a loop-carried true dependence from S_1 to S_2 and loop distribution is thus possible. However, we must insert communication:

```
DO I = L, R
  A(I) = B(I) + A(I)
END DO
```

```
SEND A(R)
RECEIVE A(L - 1)
DO I = L, R
   C(I) = A(I - 1)
END DO
```

If we had attempted to parallelize the loop without distribution, then we would have produced a synchronized loop resulting in serial execution.

Example 7.24

Assume that A, B, and C are defined and partitioned as in Example 7.23, with the exception that the overlap area associated with A(L:R) consists of the variable A(R+1). Now consider the following loop:

```
DO I = 1, 1000
   S₁:  A(I) = B(I)
   S₂:  C(I) = A(I + 1) + A(I)
END DO
```

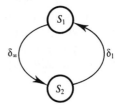

Here, the dependence graph is cyclic. However, if we examine it more closely, we see that the loop-independent dependence is irrelevant, and the anti dependence can be satisfied by communication. Parallel code can therefore be generated as follows:

```
SEND A(L)
RECEIVE A(R + 1)
DO I = L, R
  A(I) = B(I)
  C(I) = A(I + 1) + A(I)
END DO
```

A final example shows that we must insert communication statements judiciously to minimize the start-up overheads. We encountered a similar problem in splitting (see Example 7.20).

Example 7.25

We modify the above loop slightly to obtain:

```
DO I = 1, 1000
  S₁:  A(I) = B(I)
  S₂:  C(I + 1) = A(I + 1) + A(I)
END DO
```

The loop has the same dependences as above, but now the overlap area associated with A(L:R) consists of the variable A(L-1). This can be seen as follows. Let p_i denote two processes which own the block $A(L_i, R_i)$ and $C(L_i, R_i)$ $(i = 1, 2)$, where $L_2 = R_1 + 1$. When process p_1 executes $S_1(R_1)$, it defines $A(R_1)$. However, $S_2(R_1)$ must be executed by process p_2, since the variable $C(R_1 + 1) = C(L_2)$, which is defined in this assignment, is owned by p_2. Since p_2 uses the value of $A(R_1)$ computed by p_1, we must synchronize the processes p_1 and p_2.

We can transform the loop to:

```
DO I = L - 1, R
  IF (L ≤ I ≤ R)     THEN A(I) = B(I) FI
  IF (I = R)         THEN SEND A(I) FI
  IF (I = L - 1)     THEN RECEIVE A(I) FI
  IF (L ≤ I + 1 ≤ R) THEN C(I + 1) = A(I + 1) + A(I) FI
END DO
```

This has effectively serialized the processes. However, we can change the partition of C from $C(L_i : R_i)$ to $C(L_{i+1} : R_{i+1})$ and the overlap area of A to $A(R_{i+1})$. The loop can then be transformed as in the previous example.

So we see that the communication of processes depends, in general, on our choice of partition. In the first case, we require synchronizing communication because there is a true dependence between S_1 and S_2: A(I) is defined in S_1 and used in S_2 and our partitioning means that definition and use are not always in the same process. Once we change the partitioning, communication is necessitated by the occurrence of A(I+1) in S_2. In contrast, this time there is no true dependence involved and we are able to perform the communication before the processes are actually executed.

7.5.6   An example

The following is part of the program MISES, a Fortran 77 program based on the method of Mises (Engeln-Müllges and Reutter, 1985), to compute the eigenvalue and corresponding eigenvector of a $10\,000 \times 10\,000$ matrix A. The parallelized version of the program is then given.

I: The sequential program

The main subroutine in MISES is EIVALUE. Its parameters are:

(1) Input parameters

> A   : two-dimensional input matrix
>
> N   : dimension of A
>
> MO   : maximal iteration count
>
> EPSI : accuracy criterion
>
> X   : working space

(2)   Output parameters

> Y   : eigenvector
>
> Z   : residuum vector
>
> EV   : eigenvalue
>
> IER   : error code (0: successful, 1: unsuccessful)

```
      PROGRAM MISES
      PARAMETER (N = 10000)
      DOUBLE PRECISION A(N, N), X(N), Y(N), Z(N), EV
C*** READ A ***
      DO I = 1, N
        DO J = 1, N
          READ(*, 100) A(I, J)
        END DO J
      END DO I
100   FORMAT(1D20.12)
      CALL EIVALUE(A, N, 1000, 1.0D - 6, X, Y, Z, EV, IER)
C*** WRITE RESULTS ***
      WRITE (*, 200) Y, Z, EV, IER
200   FORMAT(' EIGENVECTOR = '/, N D16.3/, 'RESIDUALS = ', N D16.3/,
     '          ' EV = ', D16.3/, ' IER = ', I5)
      STOP
      END
C******************************************************************
C******************************************************************
      SUBROUTINE EIVALUE(A, N, MO, EPSI, X, Y, Z, EV, IER)
      IMPLICIT DOUBLE PRECISION (A - H, O - Z)
      DIMENSION A(N, N), Z(N), X(N), Y(N)
      IER = 0
C*** INITIALIZATION: Y(1:N) = 1.0D0 ***
      DO I = 1, N
        Y(I) = 1.0D0
      END DO
```

```
      CALL NORM(Y, N)
      EV = 0.0D0
      ITER = 0
  200 ITER = ITER + 1
      EM = EV
   C**** TRANSFER TO WORK SPACE: X(1:N) = Y(1:N) ***

      DO I = 1, N
        X(I) = Y(I)
      END DO
      CALL MAVE(A, X, Y, N)
      ...
      CALL NORM(Y, N)
      ...
      IF(S > EPSI OR DABS(EV - EM) > EPSI) THEN GOTO 200 FI
  500 RETURN
      END

   C********************************************************************
   C********************************************************************

      SUBROUTINE MAVE(A, X, Y, N)
      IMPLICIT DOUBLE PRECISION (A - H, O - Z)
      DIMENSION A(N, N),  X(N),  Y(N)

   C*** Y(1:N) = A(1:N, 1:N) * Xᵗ(1:N) ***

      DO I = 1, N
        Y(I) = 0.0D0
        DO J = 1, N
          Y(I) = Y(I) + A(I, J)*X(J)
        END DO J
      END DO I
      RETURN
      END

   C********************************************************************
   C********************************************************************

      SUBROUTINE NORM(X, N)
      IMPLICIT DOUBLE PRECISION (A - H, O - Z)
      DIMENSION X(N)
      ...
      S = DSQRT(S)
      IF (S.NE.0.0D0) THEN

   C*** X(1:N) = X(1:N) / S ***

      DO I = 1, N
        X(I) = X(I)/S
      END DO
      FI
      RETURN
      END
```

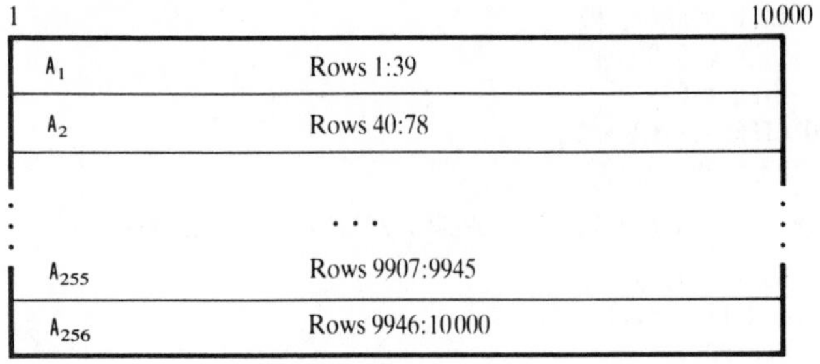

1   10000

A_1	Rows 1:39
A_2	Rows 40:78
	. . .
A_{255}	Rows 9907:9945
A_{256}	Rows 9946:10000

Figure 7.8   Partition of array A.

II: The parallelized version

Array A is partitioned into 256 blocks denoted by A_i $(1 \leq i \leq 256)$: 255 blocks have 39 rows, one block has 55 rows (see Figure 7.8).

$$A_i = A(39(i-1) + 1:39i, 1:10000) \quad 1 \leq i \leq 255$$
$$A_{256} = A(9946:10000, 1:10000)$$

The one-dimensional array X is similarly partitioned into 256 blocks X_i (255 blocks with 39 points, one with 55 points, see Figure 7.9):

$$X_i = X(39(i-1) + 1:39i) \quad 1 \leq i \leq 255$$
$$X_{256} = X(9946:10000)$$

Y and Z are partitioned in the same way as X. The overlap area for the blocks of X is the whole array X. The overlap areas for all other blocks are empty.

In the kernel task unit, the arrays implementing the blocks are specified according to the largest block. The array implementing the blocks of X and their overlap area is declared by %X(N). All variables introduced by the parallelizer are preceded by a '%'. Values of the type PROCESSID are process identifiers.

```
C *** SPECIFICATION OF THE HOST TASK UNIT ***
  HOST TASK PROGRAM MISES
C ===========================
  PARAMETER (%INIT=1,%STOP=2,%MAVEM=3,%QUOTM=4,%QSKALM=5)
  PARAMETER (N=10000, %SEGDIM=55, %NP=256)
  DOUBLE PRECISION A(N,N), Y(N), Z(N), EV, %HELPY(%SEGDIM),
                   %HELPZ(%SEGDIM)
  INTEGER %I,%J,I,J,IER
  PROCESSID %PROCESSES(%NP)
```

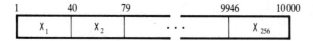

Figure 7.9 Partition of array X.

```
C *** READ A ***
   DO I = 1,N
     DO J = 1,N
       READ(*,100) A(I,J)
     END DO J
   END DO I
100 FORMAT(1D20.12)
  C*** CREATE KERNEL PROCESSES ***
   DO %I = 1,%NP
     %PROCESSES(%I) = NEWTASK(KERNELTASK)
   END DO
  C*** TRANSFER BLOCKS OF A TO THE PROCESSES ***
   %L = 1
   DO %I = 1,%NP-1
     %R = %L+38
     SEND (TAG=%INIT, PROCESSID=%PROCESSES(%I)) A(%L:%R,1:N), %L,%R
     %L = %L+39
   END DO
   SEND (TAG=%INIT, PROCESSID=%PROCESSES(%NP))
        A(9946:10000,1:N),9946,10000
  C*** RECEIVE RESULTS ***
   DO %I = 1,%NP
     RECEIVE (TAG=%STOP) %HELPY,%HELPZ,EV,IER,%L,%R
     Y(%L:%R) = %HELPY(1:%R-%L+1)
     Z(%L:%R) = %HELPZ(1:%R-%L+1)
   END DO
  C*** WRITE RESULTS ***
   WRITE (*,200) Y,Z,EV,IER
200 FORMAT(' EIGENVECTOR= '/,N D16.3/,'RESIDUALS = ',
   *        N D16.3/,' EV=',D16.3/, ' IER= ',I5)
   STOP
   END
 C *** SPECIFICATION OF THE KERNEL TASK UNIT ***
   TASK PROGRAM KERNELTASK
 C =======================
   PARAMETER (%INIT=1,%STOP=2,%MAVEM=3,%QUOTM=4,%QSKALM=5)
   PARAMETER (N=10000, %SEGDIM=55, %NP=256)
   DOUBLE PRECISION %A(%SEGDIM,N),%X(N),%Y(%SEGDIM),
                    %Z(%SEGDIM),EV,IER
   INTEGER %L,%R
   PROCESSID %INITPROC
```

```
C*** RECEIVE BLOCK OF A ***
   RECEIVE (TAG=%INIT,SENDER=%INITPROC) %A(1:%R-%L+1,N),%L,%R
   CALL EIVALUE(%A,N,1000,1.0D-6,%X,%Y(1:%R-%L+1),
              %Z(1:%R-%L+1),EV,IER,%L,%R,%NP)
C*** SEND RESULTS ***
   SEND (TAG=%STOP,PROCESSID=%INITPROC) %Y,%Z,EV,IER,%L,%R
   STOP
   END
C*******************************************************************
C*******************************************************************
   SUBROUTINE EIVALUE(A,N,MO,EPSI,X,Y,Z,EV,IER,%L,%R,%NP)
   IMPLICIT DOUBLE PRECISION (A-H,O-Z)
   DIMENSION A(%L:%R,N),Z(%L:%R),X(N),Y(%L:%R)
   INTEGER %L,%R,%NP
   IER=0
C*** INITIALIZATION: Y(%L:%R) = 1.0D0 ***
   DO I = %L,%R
     Y(I) = 1.0D0
   END DO
   CALL NORM(Y,%L,%R,%NP)
   EV = 0.0D0
   ITER = 0
200 ITER = ITER+1
   EM = EV
C*** TRANSFER TO WORK SPACE: X(%L:%R) = Y(%L:%R) ***
   DO I = %L,%R
     X(I) = Y(I)
   END DO
   CALL MAVE(A,X,Y,N,%L,%R,%NP)
   ...
   CALL NORM(Y,%L,%R,%NP)
   ...
   IF(S > EPSI OR DABS(EV-EM) > EPSI) THEN GOTO 200 FI
500 RETURN
   END
   C*******************************************************************
   C*******************************************************************
   SUBROUTINE MAVE(A,X,Y,N,%L,%R,%NP)
   PARAMETER (%INIT=1,%STOP=2,%MAVEM=3,%QUOTM=4,%QSKALM=5)
   IMPLICIT DOUBLE PRECISION (A-H,O-Z)
   INTEGER %L,%R,%NP,%L1,%R1,%I
   DIMENSION A(%L:%R,N), X(N), Y(%L:%R)
C*** SEND X(%L:%R) TO ALL PROCESSES ***
   SEND (TAG=%MAVEM,PROCESSID=KERNELTASK) %L,%R,X(%L:%R)
C*** RECEIVE THE BLOCKS OF X FROM ALL PROCESSES ***
   DO %I = 1,%NP-1
     RECEIVE (TAG=%MAVEM) %L1,%R1,X(%L1:%R1)
   END DO
```

```
C*** Y(%L:%R) = A(%L:%R,1:N) * X^t(1:N) ***
   DO I = %L,%R
     Y(I) = 0.0D0
     DO J = 1,N
       Y(I)=Y(I)+A(I,J)*X(J)
     END DO J
   END DO I
   RETURN
   END
C****************************************************************
C****************************************************************
   SUBROUTINE NORM(X,%L,%R,%NP)
   IMPLICIT DOUBLE PRECISION (A-H,O-Z)
   INTEGER %L,%R,%NP
   DIMENSION X(%L:%R)
   ...
   S = DSQRT(S)
   IF (S.NE.0.0D0) THEN
C*** X(%L:%R) = X(%L:%R) / S ***
     DO I = %L,%R
       X(I)=X(I)/S
     END DO
   FI
   RETURN
   END
```

BIBLIOGRAPHICAL NOTES

The algorithm for shared-memory parallelization (Algorithm 7.2) was developed by K. Kennedy and his group at Rice University. It was first published in Callahan's Ph.D. thesis (Callahan, 1987) and in Allen *et al.* (1987). Both the thesis and the paper discuss the consequences of including loop interchange, loop alignment and code replication. The execution model given in Section 7.2.1, upon which parallel code generation is based, is essentially the SPMD model designed at IBM in the context of the RP3 development (Pfister *et al.*, 1987). The code generation algorithm was implemented for that system. The scheduling of tasks in the model can be efficiently implemented by low-level synchronization mechanisms such as semaphores or FETCH_AND_ADD. The existence of all processes for the whole lifetime of an application minimizes operating system overhead, compared with a fork/join mechanism (at the cost of reduced flexibility). The model is discussed in Darema-Rogers *et al.* (1985); it has been extended to include nested parallelism (Stone, 1985).

D. Kuck and colleagues at the University of Illinois have investigated several kinds of parallel loops, and their generation, scheduling, and synchronization. The most important papers on their Parafrase system and aspects of its implementation have already been mentioned (Kuck and Padua, 1979; Kuck *et al.*, 1984a, 1984b; Leasure, 1985). Padua's Ph.D. thesis (Padua, 1979) discusses a broad range of topics in the context of parallelization for SMSs, including the problem of scheduling. Davies (1981) explores pipelining as a method of executing parallel loops. Cytron (1984, 1985, 1986) introduces a particular form of doacross-loop (which differs from that of Section 7.3): he attaches a positive number d, the delay, to each loop. The iterations of the loop are scheduled so that the first statement of iteration i is executed with a delay of $(i - 1)d$. Since d may take on any value between 0 and the time needed for a complete iteration, this models anything from fully parallel doall-loops to serial do-loops. It must be complemented by a synchronization mechanism. Cytron develops methods for the automatic computation of d from the loop characteristics. Polychronopoulos (1986, 1988) explores the relationships between program restructuring, scheduling, synchronization and communication for SMSs, with the objective of maximizing program speed-up. He investigates 'horizontal' (that is inter-iteration) as well as 'vertical' (that is interloop) parallelism, and presents a number of optimal or near-optimal solutions for the optimization problem mentioned above (which is NP-complete in general), using static and dynamic scheduling techniques. Part of the material in Section 7.3 relates to work done by M. Wolfe, as presented in Wolfe (1987a, 1987b). The first of these describes a version of the KAP restructuring system implemented for the Sequent Balance computer. The second paper is a more general discussion of various methods for the automatic generation of synchronization. Beginning with 'random' synchronization (that is, synchronization in the sense of Section 7.3.3), Wolfe discusses pipelining, barrier synchronization, and synchronization using critical regions. In another paper (Wolfe, 1986), he treats the wavefront method for the execution of parallel loops. The generation of synchronization and its optimization has also been treated by Midkiff, Padua, Li and Abu-Sufah (Midkiff and Padua, 1986, 1987; Li and Abu-Sufah, 1985).

Material related to the transformations we discussed in Section 7.4 is spread over a large number of papers, some of them of a general nature (Padua and Wolfe, 1986). In particular, Callahan's thesis (Callahan, 1987) includes a detailed treatment of alignment and code replication; related topics are discussed in Peir's work (Peir, 1986). Polychronopoulos (1988) specifies loop coalescing as a technique supporting parallelization.

A systematic approach to the treatment of control dependences has been developed within the framework of the PTRAN (parallel translator) system, which is being implemented at IBM's T.J. Watson Research Center (Allen *et al.*, 1988a, 1988b). PTRAN handles sequential as well as parallel programs. The 'useful' parallelism of a program – that is, the appropriate parallelism for a given program and a specific SMS – is determined as follows. In the first step, the control dependence graph (see

Section 3.3.5) is constructed from the flowgraph of a program. This graph displays the maximal parallelism of the program (since data dependences are ignored at this stage). From the control dependence graph, a process tree is formed, which represents nested fork/join parallelism. Now, data dependences are taken into consideration. Interprocess dependences are reduced by introducing shared and local storage (see below) and applying renaming. Finally, a set of useful processes is determined by coalescing and sequencing processes in the process tree, thus reducing the amount of synchronization required.

PTRAN performs an elaborate interprocedural analysis (see Sections 3.7 and 4.7 (Burke and Cytron, 1986)). The parallelization of programs with procedures is also treated by Triolet (Triolet, 1984; Triolet *et al.*, 1986) and in the ParaScope system developed at Rice University.

Our discussion of parallelization for SMSs was primarily guided by the data dependences between the statements of a loop. A closely related viewpoint classifies variables according to their use in a loop. We outline an approach described in Osterhaug (1989), in which the user determines the classification and inserts corresponding directives into the program. Five classes of variables are distinguished: shared, local, reduction, shared ordered, and shared locked.

Shared variables are not involved in a loop-carried dependence. Their use does not restrict parallel execution. Examples for shared variables are A and B in the I loop of loop LL_1 of Example 7.7. **Local variables** are variables which are not shared, but initialized in each iteration before their first use. Such variables could be renamed in each iteration without affecting the result of the program. The do-variables and certain scalar temporaries belong in this category (an example is DIST in Example 7.15). A **reduction variable** is a variable which is used in only one associative and commutative operation of the form $v = v \mu exp$, where v does not occur in *exp*. For reduction variables, special transformations exist (see Section 6.5.7). A **shared ordered variable** is one that does not belong in any of the above classes, and requires the ordering (that is, synchronization) of iterations. Examples are the variables A and B in Example 7.12. Finally, a **shared locked variable** does not belong in any of the above categories; it must be protected by a critical region (examples are the variables NEAREST and MIN_DIST in Example 7.15).

The approach to parallelization for a DMS is based on techniques developed in the context of the SUPRENUM project (Giloi, 1988; Zima, 1988), in particular on the SUPERB parallelization system which was implemented at Bonn University (Zima *et al.*, 1986a, 1986b; Kremer *et al.*, 1988; Zima *et al.*, 1988; Gerndt and Zima, 1988). Gerndt's Ph.D. thesis (1989) provides a full account of the theory of this approach, together with a detailed discussion of the major optimization techniques. Callahan and Kennedy independently developed a similar scheme in the ParaScope system, based on user-supplied annotations of Fortran programs by

DECOMPOSE and DISTRIBUTE statements, which provide language features for a (static) data partitioning scheme (Callahan and Kennedy, 1988b). The compilation mechanism is similar to that in SUPERB. Based on this approach, Rogers and Pingali (1989) describe the parallelization of programs of the functional language ID-Nouveau.

Koelbel *et al.* (1987) translate BLAZE, an explicitly parallel language, into E-BLAZE, a language with low-level process manipulation features. The compilation mechanism they have developed basically works analogously to the one developed in SUPERB and ParaScope.

Kennedy and Zima (1989) generalize the static partitioning schemes of SUPERB, ParaScope, and BLAZE by defining a data partitioning language that allows dynamic array decomposition and distribution, and extending the compilation method correspondingly. This expands the range of applications to include adaptive methods and other problem solutions in which the distribution pattern of data changes dynamically (as, for instance, in adaptive multigrid and systolic matrix algorithms). In addition, they explore methods for the analysis of sequential programs to automatically derive elements of a data partitioning strategy.

The parallelization systems for DMSs, as discussed above, can all be seen as tools that provide the user with the abstraction of a virtual shared-memory for a DMS. Such abstractions can also be realized by using a suitable language. We mention three language-based approaches (C*, Linda, Dino) below.

C*, developed for the Connection Machine (Rose and Steele, 1987), is an SIMD language. Programmers declare replicated variables, which can be manipulated as aggregates in an extension of the C language. Explicit message passing is eliminated in the virtual machine provided by the system.

Linda, developed at Yale (Carriero and Gelernter, 1985), supports virtual shared data structures, but forces the programmer to use special primitives for the access of these structures. Each node has to be programmed explicitly.

DINO, developed at the University of Colorado, Boulder (Rosing and Schnabel, 1988), allows the programmer to specify distributed data structures and invoke replicated functions on these data structures. Programmers must mark variable references that indicate updates and thus are forced to program message passing.

Chapter 8

Supercompilers and their Environments

8.1 Introduction

Three existing supercompilers – Parafrase, PFC, and SUPERB – are reviewed in Section 8.2, and the most important elements of advanced programming environments for concurrent machines are discussed (Section 8.3). The role of user–machine interaction in restructuring systems is outlined, and some performance issues (Section 8.3.4) and graphics (Section 8.3.5) are briefly dealt with.

8.2 Case studies

8.2.1 Parafrase

Parafrase was the first restructuring tool to address the problem of transforming sequential Fortran programs into concurrent programs systematically for a variety of architectures. The system, whose development by D. Kuck and coworkers at the University of Illinois at Urbana–Champaign reaches back to 1970, has had a profound influence on most of the work in automatic vectorization and parallelization since then.

Parafrase is a source-to-source transformer: applied to a Fortran 66 or Fortran 77 program, it yields a semantically equivalent extended Fortran program that is tailored to a specific machine. The system can be retargeted to produce code for different classes of concurrent architectures, including register-to-register and memory-to-memory vector

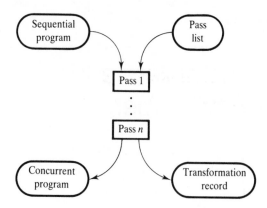

Figure 8.1   The organization of Parafrase.

machines, array processors, and shared-memory multiprocessors. The transformed program can be translated by a non-optimizing Fortran compiler. Parafrase also contains facilities for detecting concurrency in expressions and in basic blocks (Kuck, 1977).

The input to Parafrase consists of the sequential program and a **pass list** – a list of pass names and related switch settings – that specifies the tasks to be performed. Each pass name identifies a procedure that may read and/or write the program; passes are applied in the order specified in the list and each one performs a source-to-source transformation. A particular pass (for example, cleanup) may occur more than once. Parafrase contains more than 100 transformations, which are encoded as passes.

This organization is highly flexible: it enables the construction of pass lists that are optimized towards specific architectures and makes it easy to extend the system by including new passes. Global and local (that is, pass-related) parameters, called **switches**, control the execution of the system. Examples for system functions parameterized by switches are debug and print options, as well as range specifications for certain transformations.

The application of Parafrase to a source program and a pass list (see Figure 8.1) results in a concurrent program and a **transformation record**, describing the sequence of actions taken by the system, a list of errors, and timing tables that indicate the expected speed-up of the resulting program. The units of a program are processed sequentially.[†]

Parafrase distinguishes between three rings of optimization, which differ in their degree of machine dependence (Kuck *et al.*, 1984).

[†] Triolet (1985, 1986) has implemented a variant of this scheme for interprocedural analysis.

Architecture-independent passes perform analysis and optimization for general concurrent architectures: this includes scalar data flow analysis and optimization, dependence analysis, normalization, induction variable substitution, forward substitution, scalar renaming, scalar expansion, and subroutine expansion. Parafrase normalizes do-loops and represents dependences by direction vectors. The gcd and Banerjee tests are the principal dependence tests used.

The **intermediate** passes adapt the program to the requirements of a given architecture, for example a vector processor, without taking into consideration the facilities (such as registers) of a specific machine. The translation of conditional statements into a sequence of masked assignment statements belongs to this group.

Finally, the **machine-dependent** passes adapt the program to the requirements of a target machine. If this machine is a pipelined register-to-register vector architecture, for example, such passes would include loop distribution, sectioning and interchange. Particular emphasis has been placed on the recognition of linear recurrences and their substitution by library routines.

Parafrase allows the user to convey information to the system by means of **assertions** and **commands** which can be embedded into the source program. They can be used for the following purposes:

(1)   specifying the value of program variables;

(2)   enforcing concurrent execution for a group of statements;

(3)   enforcing serialization for a given loop;

(4)   enforcing serialization for all loops in which certain constructs, such as branches and procedure calls, occur.

Parafrase does not produce code for the validation of assertions: thus, the use of information supplied in this manner may lead to semantically invalid transformations.

It is difficult to measure the performance of a restructuring tool in a general and objective way, since its results depend on the specific benchmark used, the size of input data, and the actual configuration of the target machine. Parafrase provides statistics that show the fraction of vectorized loops in a program depending on various parameters such as size and the occurrence of certain statement types (Kuck *et al.*, 1984a). The effect of applying Parafrase, enhanced by manual restructuring, to the LINPACK and EISPACK benchmarks is evaluated for two types of architectures in Kuck *et al.* (1984b).

The implementation language of Parafrase is PL/I.

Parafrase-2, a multilingual successor to this system which can also handle programs written in C and Pascal, is currently being developed at the University of Illinois (Polychronopoulos *et al.*, 1989).

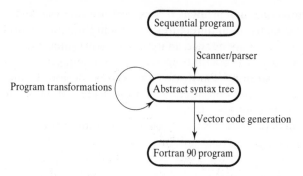

Figure 8.2   The organization of PFC.

8.2.2   PFC and PFC⁺

PFC (parallel Fortran converter) is an automatic source-to-source vectorizer that translates from Fortran 66 or 77 into Fortran 90. PFC has been under development since 1979 by K. Kennedy and his group at Rice University, Houston, and was initially based on Parafrase.

In a first step, PFC transforms the source program into an internal representation similar to those used in conventional compilers, and essentially based upon an abstract syntax tree and the associated symbol table. All PFC transformations manipulate the internal representation (see Figure 8.2).

The initial abstract syntax tree is transformed by PFC in four steps, each of which consists of one or more passes over the program (Allen and Kennedy, 1987):

(1)   *Interprocedural analysis is performed*
      The call graph is constructed and interprocedural flow-insensitive summary information is collected.

(2)   *Standard transformations are applied*
      These include if-conversion, do-loop normalization, induction variable recognition and substitution, forward substitution, subscript simplification and standardization, constant propagation and folding, and recognition and deletion of dead code.

      A global data flow analysis algorithm, which uses a worklist version of the iterative algorithm, constructs use–definition chains on which most transformations of this step are based. After if-conversion, only simple statements and do-loops exist in the program.

(3) *Dependence analysis is performed*
     Dependence analysis applies the separability, gcd, and Banerjee tests (the latter with an adaptation for triangular loops). During the construction of the dependence graph for nested loops, the interchange sensitivity of edges is determined. Data dependence edges are marked as deletable if they can be removed by scalar expansion or scalar renaming.

(4) *Vector code is generated*
     Vector code generation is based on the algorithm described in Section 6.4; scalar expansion, renaming, and loop interchange have been built into the code generator.

PFC$^+$, a recent extension of PFC, implements Callahan's parallel code generation algorithm (Algorithm 7.2) for shared memory systems. In addition, elements of an interprocedural dependence test have been implemented.

A major strength of PFC is the efficiency of the transformation process, which is comparable to that of a compiler for a sequential machine: while each Parafrase pass performs a source-to-source transformation, PFC transformations manipulate the internal representation, resulting in a speed-up of more than one order of magnitude (Allen and Kennedy, 1987). The number of transformations provided by PFC is much smaller than that of Parafrase, and fewer options are available to the user. Parafrase also implements a more elaborate pattern matching facility than PFC for recognizing linear recurrences. PFC has been written in PL/I.

8.2.3 SUPERB

SUPERB is an interactive source-to-source restructuring tool which was developed at Bonn University from 1985 to 1989 by Hans Zima and coworkers. It translates Fortran 77 programs into concurrent SUPRENUM Fortran programs for the SUPRENUM machine. The structure of the system is shown in Figure 8.3; the restructuring process can be outlined as follows.

The **front end** transforms a Fortran 77 program into an intermediate representation consisting of an attributed abstract tree, an associated symbol table, flow graphs, and initial data flow information. The core of the system contains a set of routines combined in the analysis component and the transformation catalog; these routines operate on the program's intermediate representation. The **analysis component** furnishes a collection of tools for program flow and dependence analysis. Intraprocedural data flow analysis is based on the iterative algorithm; interprocedural analysis applies techniques discussed in Section 3.7. Dependence analysis uses the separability, gcd and Banerjee tests (with an adaptation to triangular

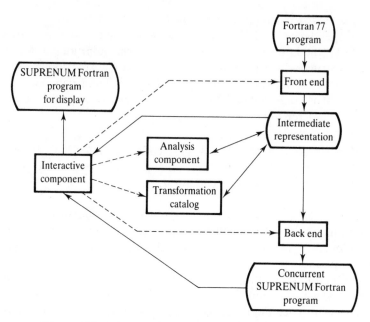

Figure 8.3   The structure of SUPERB (——, data flow;
-----, control flow).

loops), in the framework of a hierarchical approach. The services offered
by the analysis component can best be described by specifying the three
main tasks it performs: (1) verifying the existence of preconditions necessary for the application of transformations and helping to establish criteria
for making a selection from a number of valid transformations; (2) providing the information to clean up after a transformation sequence has been
applied; and (3) supplying the user of the system with details about the
program. The last item is particularly important for parallelization, which
is inherently interactive when the target is a distributed-memory machine;
it requires a powerful service facility within the analysis component.

     At the outset of the restructuring process, the intermediate repres-
entation of a program is normalized, making the subsequent transformations easier to apply and more efficient. This includes do-loop
normalization and if-conversion. Corresponding to the machine architecture which, from a global point of view, is a distributed-memory system,
but, on the level of the basic processing node, contains a pipelined vector
unit, restructuring is performed in two phases. First, coarse-grained parallelism is determined, and program execution is distributed over a set of
processes (parallelization, as described in Section 7.5); secondly, the process code is vectorized.

     The **interactive component** allows control of the other system ser-
vices by establishing a two-way communication link between the user and

the modules of the system. The information contained in the transformed intermediate representation is used during **code generation** to produce a concurrent SUPRENUM Fortran program. Directives are included to enhance the efficiency of a compiler creating object code for the SUPRENUM system.

8.3 Advanced programming environments for concurrent computers

8.3.1 Overview

In this section, we deal with criteria and requirements for advanced software environments that support program development for concurrent computers.

Despite the dominating role of Fortran in the world of scientific programming, most programming environments developed so far have been based on other languages, apparently as a result of the unpopularity of Fortran among most computer scientists (Teitelman, 1977; Teitelbaum and Reps, 1981; Habermann and Notkin, 1982; Goldberg and Robson, 1983). There are a few notable exceptions, including TOOLPACK (Osterweil, 1981), $\mathbf{R}^n$ (Cooper *et al.*, 1986), PTOOL (Allen *et al.*, 1986), and FAUST (Guarna *et al.*, 1988).

Parallel programs are much harder to develop, debug, maintain, and understand than their sequential counterparts. One reason is the difficulty in establishing correctness – which must take into account temporal conditions such as liveness, deadlock–freeness, process synchronization and communication. Another reason is the diversity of concurrent architectures and the need to produce a highly efficient program, fine tuned to the specific target architecture. The impact of task granularity on a concurrent algorithm, the properties of the memory hierarchy, and the intricacies involved in the exploitation of multilevel concurrency, for example, must all be carefully analyzed and used to devise a transformation strategy for the program. The adaptation of an initially inefficient algorithm to a specific hardware is often called **performance debugging**, a term that suggests that the correctness criteria for a concurrent algorithm should include requirements for its performance on a given architecture. An inefficient, but otherwise correct, program is of practically no use for execution on a supercomputer.

Portability is a closely related issue: a program that executes effectively on one concurrent machine (for example, a Cray X-MP) cannot in general be assumed to work with comparable efficiency on another concurrent architecture (for instance, a Cosmic Cube), and it is difficult to make the necessary transformation.

Even a program with a few hundred lines of code may contain thousands of dependences, which define its implicit concurrency and the options open to a restructuring system. Thus automatic tools which analyze programs and their execution behavior are essential. In particular, tools are needed which are able to present copious amounts of information in a form which can be readily understood by the programmer.

However, automatic tools cannot perform without assistance from the user. One of the main reasons for this is the undecidability or intractability of many relevant problems; furthermore, a static analyzer will have no information at all on variables whose value is input during program execution. For example, assume we want to vectorize the loop

```
L:  DO I = 1, N
      S:  A(I) = A(I - K) + 1
    END DO
```

Vectorization is valid iff S is not involved in an elementary cycle of true dependences, which in turn is true iff $K \leq 0$ or $K \geq N$. However, even when this condition is fulfilled, the value of N may not exceed the vector breakeven length, meaning that vectorization is not profitable and should therefore be avoided (see Section 2.2.5). If the restructurer does not succeed in obtaining information on the value of K, and no other information is at its disposal, then worst-case assumptions must be made and the loop cannot be vectorized. In such a situation, the user may make an assertion that rules out dependence, or, alternatively, may explicitly enforce or suppress vectorization.

We have seen how difficult it may be for an automatic tool to make the right decision in a rather simple situation; it is even harder to do so in more complex cases, in particular where parallelization is concerned. The knowledgeable user will play an important role, informing the system of global relationships (some of which may be due to high-level properties of the algorithm) which an automatic state-of-the-art tool cannot detect.

Thus the programming environment should provide an **interactive interface**, enabling the user to formulate assertions about program objects and to issue commands to the system. In turn, the system should be able to relay information to the user. The tools provided by the programming environment should be usable in batch mode as well as in interactive mode; in the latter case, they can be thought of as service routines that may be individually activated.

The set of tools should be **integrated**: there ought to be a well-defined interface between tools and the user on the one hand, and information stored in the system on the other hand. This information is best organized as a central **database**, which can be thought of as a knowledge base containing information about the application program. It must be interactively accessible by the user and all tools in the system. The database can provide support for **independent compilation** in a natural way. It contains objects and related information:

Objects in the database may include:

(1)   Units: procedures, declaration libraries, macros;

(2)   Modules: a structured collection of units;

(3)   Programs.

Objects are stored in an internal representation (procedures, for example, may be represented as abstract trees, together with a symbol table). They may exist in more than one version (for instance, a program may be present in the sequential and a restructured form).

Information about objects may include:

(1)   their control flowgraphs;

(2)   results of data flow analysis;

(3)   the call graph;

(4)   the dependence graph;

(5)   performance information;

(6)   linkage information.

Finally, an advanced programming environment should be organized as a collection of **knowledge-based subsystems** with different levels of expertise. Explanation facilities should guide the user in the complex process of program restructuring.

Table 8.1 gives an overview of elements that may be contained in a programming environment.

8.3.2   A program development paradigm based on Fortran 77

Although several concurrent programming languages already exist, there are some important reasons for choosing Fortran 77 as the basis of a supercomputer programming environment. Firstly, there may already be a Fortran 77 program that is to be run on the target machine. This may be an old, dusty-deck program, or one that was written for another concurrent computer. Secondly, there are well-established methods for the development and debugging of sequential programs, which make the initial development of a sequential program comparatively easy. At the same time, this will provide the programmer with sound knowledge of the numerical characteristics of the algorithm, help him or her to identify the computationally critical areas of the program, and supply information on how the program may best be restructured.

Table 8.1   Elements of a programming environment for concurrent machines.

Languages and their compilers
   Sequential languages
   Concurrent languages
   Very-high-level languages

Static analysis tools
   Control flow analysis
   Data flow analysis
   Dependence analysis
   Performance analysis

Transformation catalog
   A catalog of restructuring tools for architecture-independent, architecture-specific and machine-specific transformations

Execution analysis tools
   Execution flow analysis
   Performance analysis

Debugging tools

Experts

Graphics and visualization tools

Simulation systems

Editors

Assertion prover

Software libraries
   Communication
   Mapping
   Micro tasking
   Linear algebra
   Application packages

Project management tools

The program development cycle based on this paradigm is illustrated in Figure 8.4. It includes the following steps:

Step 1: A Fortran 77 program $P1$ is written

$P1$ is typically developed on a host computer or a workstation, without requiring any access to the target machine. It is assumed to be correct at the end of step 1.

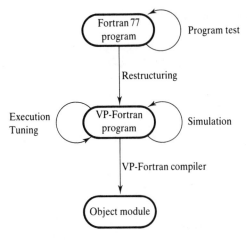

Figure 8.4 A program development paradigm based on Fortran 77.

Step 2: A concurrent Fortran program *P2* is created

The sequential program *P1* is restructured, resulting in a concurrent program *P2* in VP-Fortran.

Step 3: A revised program version *P3* is developed

P2 is analyzed and compared with *P1*, but not actually executed on the target machine. The analysis may include the use of automatic tools that compare the estimated run-time behaviors of the programs, particularly in the critical areas identified in step 1. The application of a target machine simulator to *P2* may yield statistical data reflecting properties of actual executions, such as the number of iterations of do-loops, the TRUE-ratio of conditionals in if-statements, load balancing, and the volume of communication.

Depending on the results of analysis and simulation, and the severity of any errors and/or performance problems, step 3 (and possibly step 2) will have to be repeated.

Step 4: *P3* is run on the target machine, debugged and tuned; a revised program version *P4* is created

Program *P3* may not execute successfully on the target machine as a result of features of the real machine which are not modeled by the tools used in step 3: a static analysis tool or simulator will not always accurately predict the communication behavior, performance characteristics, and load balancing observed during actual execution. As a result, step 4 may have to be repeated, or, in more severe cases, the repetition of earlier steps may be necessary.

8.3.3 Interactive restructuring

If a program is interactively vectorized and/or parallelized, then the system cooperates with the user in determining the best transformation strategy. Consider loop L:

```
L:  DO I = 1, N
        ...
    S:    A(I) = 1/2(B(I - 1) + C(I + 1)) + T * B(I)
        ...
    S':   CALL SUB(A, B(I), C)
        ...
    END DO
```

Questions that may be relevant for deciding upon an appropriate restructuring strategy will not always be able to be automatically answered. They include the following:

- What is the value (range) of T?
- Does the call to SUB have any side effects on the loop?
- How much time is spent in the procedure call?
- Can the procedure call be taken out of the loop?
- How many iterations of the loop will be performed?

These are questions which the user may put to the system, to see whether and how the loop can be restructured; alternatively, the system may prompt the user for information it cannot derive automatically.

The system–user interface in the context of interactive restructuring (aside from such technical aspects as screen layout and graphics) should offer the following features:

(1)   The user should be able to do the following:

    (a)   Activate individual services of the system directly, such as the computation of specific analysis information (for example, the dependence graph for a certain area of the program) or the application of individual transformations.

    (b)   Specify assertions and commands, which convey information to the system and may override decisions made by the system concerning the application or non-application of transformations. Assertions can be prompted by the system or be entered on the initiative of the user.

    (c)   Control the volume and detail of information output by the system.

(2)   System services should be provided to carry out the following:

    (a)   'Unparse': at any time during the restructuring process, the program should be representable as a source program.

    (b)   Illustrate the relationship between the original and restructured programs.

    (c)   Represent information in an intelligible form and at different levels of abstraction. This applies to analysis information of any kind, including data flow, dependence, and performance analysis.

    (d)   Generate validation code for the dynamic checking of user-specified assertions or commands whose semantic validity cannot be established statically.

    (e)   Perform standard restructuring procedures. These should be parameterized sequences of (possibly conditional) analysis and transformation functions, which allow batch-oriented processing wherever applicable.

    (f)   Keep a log of transformations and associated program states, and enable the transformation process to be restarted at a previous state (setting of breakpoints).

In the following, we examine the transfer of information between the user and the restructuring system more closely.

Transfer of information from the system to the user

We restrict our attention to vectorization. The discussion may be generalized to parallelization in an obvious manner.

For each loop L, the system must inform the user whether L is a candidate for restructuring. If so, then it must indicate, for each statement S in L, whether or not S can be vectorized. When this is the case, details of the transformation should be provided. If vectorization is not possible, the reasons should be stated as precisely as possible. In either case, tuning messages should refer to possible methods for the improvement of the code. Three kinds of system information are described in (1) to (3) below:

(1) L is a candidate for vectorization, but a statement S in L cannot be vectorized because it is involved in a recurrence or a potential recurrence.

(2) L contains a statement S that can be vectorized. Two sets of information may be provided. They are characterized in (a) and (b)

(a) Details of the transformation:

- number of loops in which S can be vectorized;
- do-variables involved;
- loop range information;
- method of vectorization: for example, the realization of conditional execution by masking, gather/scatter, or indexing;
- insertion of instrumentation for performance monitoring;
- user-supplied information on which the transformation has been based;
- insertion of validation code for such information;
- default assumptions, for example on the TRUE-ratio of conditionals in if-statements, if no other information is available.

(b) Tuning messages. It may be that potential improvements in the code were not realized because not enough information was available: for example, a loop interchange could conceivably lead to longer vectors in the innermost loop, but was not performed owing to lack of information on iteration ranges. This helps the user to understand where assertions or commands could support the system.

(3) Now assume that a loop L cannot be vectorized. Then the system should give the user the following information:

   (a) Inhibitor analysis – the reason why L is not a candidate for vectorization. This may, for example, be caused by the presence of a:

- backward goto;
- exit goto;
- computed/assigned goto;
- procedure call with unknown side effects;
- RETURN, STOP, or PAUSE;
- input/output

   (b) Tuning messages suggesting, for instance, that the user should:

- eliminate a potential recurrence by an assertion;
- transform a while-loop or if/goto-loop into a do-loop;

- specify the side effects of a procedure by an assertion;
- expand a procedure;
- split out input/output or procedure calls from the loop;
- change the algorithm (restructuring advice).

Example 8.1: System information regarding a vectorizable statement

---

We distinguish user assertions or commands by a leading '&DIR'. Information provided by the system is enclosed by '%'.

Consider the loop L and its vectorized version L':

```
      &DIR 100≤M≤200
L:    DO I=1,1000                    L':  DO I=1,1000
        DO J=1,M                            A(I,1:M)=A(I-K,1:M)*
      S:  A(I,J)=A(I-K,J)*B(I,J)                   B(I,1:M)
        END DO                             END DO
      END DO
```

% Statement S has been vectorized in the level 2 loop (loop variable J with range 1:M). The assertion $100 \leq M \leq 200$ was used. No validation code has been generated.

A potential recurrence prevented vectorization of the level 1 loop (loop variable I with range 1:1000). If $K \leq 0$ or $K \geq M$, then vectorization is possible (assertion?). Level 1 and level 2 loops could then be interchanged, yielding a vector length of 1000 and stride 1 for the references to A and B.

Example 8.2

Consider the loop

```
L:   DO I = 1, 1000
       DO J = 1, M
     S:   A(I, J) = B(I, J) * C(J)
            CALL INK(A, B, C, I)
     S':   C(J) = C(J)/B(I, J + 2)
       END DO
     END DO
```

% L is not a candidate for vectorization because it contains a call statement INK(A,B,C,I) with unknown side effects.

Possible user action to enable vectorization:

- Specify the side effects of INK(A,B,C,I) by an assertion
- Expand the call INK(A,B,C,I)
- Split the call out of the loop.%

The interaction between the user and the system is similar when a loop is parallelized. The generation of doall-loops or doacross-loops, synchronization and its effect on the degree of parallelism, scheduling overhead, and load balancing are some of the specific issues that are important in this context. If we compile parallel code for a distributed-memory system according to the strategy described in Section 7.5, then the user must specify data partitioning (possibly after having requested input from the system concerning dependences, or after having completed one cycle of the program development process and discovering that the selected partition involves too much communication). A combination of heuristics and user-specified knowledge is crucial in this context.

We discuss methods with which the user can (partially) control restructuring.

Control of restructuring by the user

The user is able to control the restructuring process by formulating assertions and issuing commands.

An **assertion** either states a relationship between variables, which is assumed to hold at a certain point of the program, or specifies some property such as timing characteristics of a loop or procedure. Assertions will typically be used when static analysis is not able to compute sufficient information: as a consequence, they will in general not be statically verifiable. A transformation based on an assertion may be semantically invalid. So, if possible, the correctness of assertions should be checked by validation code inserted by the system. This can be omitted if only the efficiency of the generated code is affected: for example, if the assertion regarding M in Example 8.1 were wrong, and M could assume small values such as 1 or 2, then the generated vector code would be inefficient, but the program would nevertheless still be correct.

Some examples for relationships that can be specified by assertions are:

- the value of a program variable: $C = 1.41421356$;
- the value range of a program variable: $1.0 \leqslant C \leqslant 2.71828$;
- a relational expression involving one or more program variables: $A \leqslant B + 3.$;

- the existence or non-existence of a (certain type of) dependence between two statements;
- the TRUE-ratio for the conditional expression in an if-statement;
- summary information for a procedure;
- the side effects of a procedure call;
- the frequency of communication between processes, and the volume of the data transfers;
- performance data for statements, loops or procedures: frequency of execution, execution cost in terms of time and memory consumption.

Commands provide the user with a means to explicitly control the system's actions, including the possibility of overriding decisions made by the system. Some important classes of commands are:

- *Set system parameters*
  This tunes the operation of the system to the specific needs of a target architecture. Parafrase has more than 100 'switches' which can be used for this purpose.
- *Enforce vectorization/parallelization*
  This enforces the transformation of programs in situations where the system does not have sufficient information to ensure the semantic validity.
- *Enforce scalarization*
  This enforces scalar execution of a loop which in, principle, could be vectorized or parallelized.
- *Compute analysis information*
  This command computes selected analysis information for parts of the program.
- *Apply transformations*
  This command allows the selective application of individual transformations. In principle, any transformation provided by the system could be organized as a system service routine and thus be independently activated.

While most currently existing systems provide at best some limited features for specifying directives (that is, assertions or commands in the form of annotations to the source program), a few interactive restructuring systems already exist: they include the vectorizer VECTUNE for the Fujitsu VP-System (Amdahl; 1984), Pacific Sierra's FORGE, a restructurer for Cray systems (Pacific Sierra Research, 1986b), PTOOL (Allen *et al.*, 1986), SUPERB (Zima *et al.*, 1986b, 1988), and ParaScope. Most of the discussion in this section is based on the capabilities of VECTUNE, FORGE, and SUPERB.

An interactive restructuring system must regularly update the analysis information associated with statements, loops and procedures. In order to reduce the amount of recomputation, incremental analysis methods have been examined by a number of authors, including Zadeck (1983) and Kremer *et al.* (1988).

Finally, it can be expected that future systems will make use of more sophisticated methods. This may include the realization of transformations as rules in a rule-based system, knowledge bases that support the decision process with respect to the applicability and the effect of transformations, and, in the long run, automated learning by analyzing transformation strategies applied to certain classes of problems. So far, these issues have seldom been addressed (Brandes, 1988; Bose, 1988a, 1988b).

8.3.4 Performance analysis

When a program is restructured, it is necessary to obtain information on the performance of both the original program and its transformed version, and to identify those parts that critically determine its overall execution time. This information is required in all steps of the program development cycle.

Performance data can be obtained by:

(1) static analysis tools,

(2) monitored program execution,

(3) execution of the program on a simulator for the target machine, or

(4) the actual execution of the program for typical loads on the target machine.

Static analysis tools calculate the approximate execution costs based on assumptions about critical parameters. One tool that obtains performance data by monitoring program execution is FORTUNE (Fortran tuner), which is part of the Fujitsu VP-System (Amdahl, 1984). FORTUNE consists of an editor and an analyzer and provides timing information for the execution of a scalar program, with the aim of identifying those parts of the program that are executed most frequently and/or consume most execution time. FORTUNE is applied to a program in five steps: edit, compile, link, execute/analyze, and report. The program is linked to a special analyzer library; analysis is tied to the execution. It provides the following results:

● for each statement and each procedure: the number of executions and the associated cost in terms of time;

● for each logical expression in a logical IF, block IF, or ELSE IF: its TRUE-ratio.

In a similar way, performance data can be obtained for the transformed version of the program without the need to execute it on the target machine. Of course, performance data yielded by a simulator or the actual hardware may be more precise.

When performance data for the original and the transformed version of the program are available, the effect of restructuring can be estimated. This in turn allows the identification of those parts of the program where the transformation does not have the desired effect, which may lead to another iteration of the program development cycle.

8.3.5 Graphics and visualization

The volume of data produced by a supercomputer can in general no longer be communicated to the user in the conventional way. Rather than printing long rows of numbers, the human–machine interface must be suitably adapted to the power of the machine: this implies the use of data reduction, graphics, and visualization techniques. A movie that illustrates the flow of air along the wings of an aircraft can express compactly and in an intelligible way the information contained in millions of numerical data.

Visualization makes it possible for critical problem areas to be located rapidly. The results of a computation are not only better understood, it is also much easier to communicate them. It may even sometimes be possible to modify experiments during their execution: for example, by indicating a special area of interest on the screen display for more intense computation.

A graphics component for a supercomputer must satisfy the following minimum requirements. A user must be able to see not only a global display, but also have the possibility of zooming in on an area to examine it in more depth. Both the screen resolution and the coloring scheme must be able to handle a sufficient level of detail. It should be possible to make surfaces transparent to see what is happening behind them. In general, three-dimensional images will be appropriate. Sound will sometimes be a useful aid, perhaps increasing in level when some force increases in intensity. The graphics display must show changes in behavior patterns fast enough to enable informed observers to understand the dynamic features of an experiment.

Graphics may also be used in restructuring and to visualize certain aspects of programs and their execution, for example

- to specify data partitioning,
- to represent analysis information during restructuring,
- to represent the process and communication structure of a parallel program, and
- to illustrate the execution behavior of a program.

Appendix A

Tarjan's Algorithm

In this section we specify an algorithm due to Tarjan (Tarjan, 1972; Aho *et al.*, 1974) which uses a variant of depth-first search to determine the strongly connnected components of a directed graph. This was the first algorithm that solved the problem in linear time (see Theorem A.1). The reader is referred to Aho *et al.* (1974) for an explanation of the underlying theory. However, the specification of the algorithm is self-contained and complete.

ALGORITHM A.1: Strongly connected components of a graph

Input   A directed graph $G = (N,E)$.

Output   A list of the strongly connected components of G.

Method

/* The algorithm uses a push-down *STACK*. With every node $n \in N$ three variables are associated: *visited*(n), *dfn*(n), and *link*(n). Furthermore, the algorithm uses counters *df-count* and *r*.

The number *link*(n) computed in search(n) can be characterized as follows:

link$(n) = min(\{dfn(w): w = n$ or there is a descendant n' of n and an edge (n',w) with $dfn(n') \geq dfn(w)$ such that the root of the strongly connected component containing w is an ancestor of $n\})$

According to this definition, *link*$(n) \leq dfn(n)$ for all $n \in N$.

A node n is the root of a strongly connected component iff *link*$(n) = n$.
*/

```
procedure search(n);
begin
visited(n) := true;
dfn(n)    := df_count;
link(n)   := df_count;
df_count plus 1;
push(n);
for every n' ∈ succ(n) do
   if not(visited(n'))
     then search(n'); link(n) := min(link(n),link(n'))
     else   //* ⊢ visited(n') *//
       if dfn(n') < dfn(n) and in_stack(n')
         then   /* n' is in the same strongly connected component as an
                    ancestor of n */
            link(n): = min(link(n),dfn(n'))
       fi
   fi
end for;


if link(n) = dfn(n)
   then   /* n is the root of a strongly connected component whose nodes are
             the topmost elements of STACK, up to and including n. These
             elements are output and popped off the STACK */
   r plus 1; write("Strongly connected component number ", r);
   repeat
     x := top_of_stack; pop; write(x)
   until x = n
fi
end search;


/* MAIN PROGRAM: */


begin
init_stack;
df_count := 1;
r := 0;
for every n ∈ N do visited(n) := false end for;
while ∃ n ∈ N such that not(visited(n)) do search(n) end while
end
```

We cite the following theorem without proof.

Theorem A.1   The   time   complexity   of   Algorithm   A.1   is
$O(max(|N|,|E|))$.

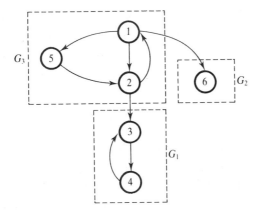

Figure A.1   Graph G.

Example A.1: Finding the strongly connected components of a graph

---

Consider the graph $G = (N,E)$ as given in Figure A.1. In order to simplify matters, the nodes of the graph have been identified with their number in a depth-first search. Table A.1 illustrates the action of the algorithm, applied to G. There are two entries for each activation of search which represent the time immediately after the call, and the time of the test whether or not the actual node is a root. These entries are represented for a node n by n and n^*, respectively. Recursion is indicated by indentation. The stack is represented by a list, with the top element at the right. The final values of $link(n)$ are given in Table A.2. The strongly connected components found by the algorithm are $G_1 = (\{3,4\},\{(3,4),(4,3)\})$, $G_2 = (\{6\},\varnothing)$, and $G_3 = (\{1,2,5\},\{(1,2),(2,1),(1,5),(5,2)\})$. Note that the edges $(1,6)$ and $(2,3)$ of G are not contained in any strongly connected component; they are edges of the acyclic condensation $AC(G)$, which is shown in Figure A.2.

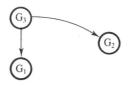

Figure A.2 $AC(G)$.

Table A.1 Application of Algorithm A.1 to *G*.

Calls to search	Edges	Stack	Comments
–	–	Empty	Initial state
1	(1,2)	(1)	
2	(2,1)	(1,2)	
	(2,3)	(1,2)	
3	(3,4)	(1,2,3)	
4	(4,3)	(1,2,3,4)	
4*		(1,2,3,4)	4 is not a root
3*		(1,2,3,4)	3 is a root
2*		(1,2)	2 is not a root
	(1,5)	(1,2)	
5	(5,2)	(1,2,5)	
5*		(1,2,5)	5 is not a root
	(1,6)	(1,2,5)	
6		(1,2,5,6)	
6*		(1,2,5,6)	6 is a root
1*		(1,2,5)	1 is a root

Table A.2 Values of *link(n)*.

n	link(n)
1	1
2	1
3	3
4	3
5	2
6	6

Appendix B

The Banerjee Test

Theorem 4.9: Banerjee test Consider a dependence system, where all bounds T_j, U_j, T'_j, and U'_j are constant. Then $S\,\delta\theta\,S'$ or $S'\,\delta\theta^{-1}\,S$ implies:

$$\sum_{1\leqslant j\leqslant m} LC_j + \sum_{m<j\leqslant n} LA_j + \sum_{m<j\leqslant n'} LB_j \;\leqslant\; b_0 - a_0 \;\leqslant$$

$$\sum_{1<j\leqslant m} UC_j + \sum_{m<j\leqslant n} UA_j + \sum_{m<j\leqslant n'} UB_j$$

where:

$$(1)\quad LC_j = \begin{cases} -(a_j^- + b_j)^+(U_j - T_j - 1) + (a_j - b_j)T_j - b_j & \text{for } j \in lt \\ -(a_j - b_j)^-(U_j - T_j) + (a_j - b_j)T_j & \text{for } j \in eq \\ -(b_j^+ - a_j)^+(U_j - T_j - 1) + (a_j - b_j)T_j + a_j & \text{for } j \in gt \\ -(a_j^- + b_j^+)(U_j - T_j) + (a_j - b_j)T_j & \text{for } j \in st \end{cases}$$

$$(2)\quad LA_j = -a_j^-(U_j - T_j) + a_j T_j \quad \text{for } m < j \leqslant n$$

$$(3)\quad LB_j = -b_j^+(U'_j - T'_j) - b_j T'_j \quad \text{for } m < j \leqslant n'$$

$$(4)\quad UC_j = \begin{cases} (a_j^+ - b_j)^+(U_j - T_j - 1) + (a_j - b_j)T_j - b_j & \text{for } j \in lt \\ (a_j - b_j)^+(U_j - T_j) + (a_j - b_j)T_j & \text{for } j \in eq \\ (b_j^- + a_j)^+(U_j - T_j - 1) + (a_j - b_j)T_j + a_j & \text{for } j \in gt \\ (a_j^+ + b_j^-)(U_j - T_j) + (a_j - b_j)T_j & \text{for } j \in st \end{cases}$$

$$(5)\quad UA_j = a_j^+(U_j - T_j) + a_j T_j \quad \text{for } m < j \leqslant n$$

$$(6)\quad UB_j = b_j^-(U'_j - T'_j) - b_j T'_j \quad \text{for } m < j \leqslant n' \qquad \blacksquare$$

Proof   Under the assumptions of the theorem, the dependence system can be solved under the constraints of θ, that is, there exist $\mathbf{i} \in [S]$ and $\mathbf{i}' \in [S']$ such that $h(\mathbf{i},\mathbf{i}') = f(\mathbf{i}) - f'(\mathbf{i}') = 0$, $i_j \in [T_j : U_j]$ for all $j \in [1:n]$, $i'_j \in [T'_j : U'_j]$ for all $j \in [1:n']$, and $\theta = dir(\mathbf{i},\mathbf{i}')$.

Thus,

$$\text{(MIN–MAX)} \quad min(h(\mathbf{x},\mathbf{y})) \leq 0 \leq max(h(\mathbf{x},\mathbf{y}))$$

for all $\mathbf{x} \in \mathbb{Z}^n$ and $\mathbf{y} \in \mathbb{Z}^{n'}$ with $x_j \in [T_j : U_j]$ for all $j \in [1:n]$, $y'_j \in [T'_j : U'_j]$ for all $j \in [1:n']$, and $\theta = dir(\mathbf{i},\mathbf{i}')$.

Using the representation of f and f' in (DEQ), we obtain:

$$h(\mathbf{x},\mathbf{y}) = f(\mathbf{x}) - f'(\mathbf{y}) = f(x_1, \ldots, x_n) - f'(y_1, \ldots, y'_n)$$

$$\text{(E)} \qquad = \sum_{1 \leq j \leq n} a_j x_j - \sum_{1 \leq j \leq n'} b_j y_j + a_0 - b_0$$

In the following, we will determine the minimum and maximum of (E) in the given region. This will be done by decomposing (E), based on the index sets specified by the classes *eq*, *lt*, *gt*, and *st*, and then treating each class separately. The result of this, when put together and substituted into (MIN–MAX), will yield the assertion of the theorem.

$$\text{(E)} \qquad \sum_{1 \leq j \leq n} a_j x_j - \sum_{1 \leq j \leq n'} b_j y_j + a_0 - b_0 =$$

$$\text{(E-1)} \qquad \sum_{j \in lt} (a_j x_j - b_j y_j) +$$

$$\text{(E-2)} \qquad \sum_{j \in eq} (a_j - b_j) x_j \; +$$

$$\text{(E-3)} \qquad \sum_{j \in gt} (a_j x_j - b_j y_j) +$$

$$\text{(E-4)} \qquad \sum_{j \in st} (a_j x_j - b_j y_j) +$$

$$\text{(E-5)} \qquad \sum_{m < j \leq n} a_j x_j \qquad -$$

$$\text{(E-6)} \qquad \sum_{m < j \leq n'} b_j y_j \qquad +$$

$$\text{(E-7)} \qquad a_0 - b_0$$

We shall prove the theorem for lines 1,2 and 4 of case (1) (the definition of LC_j). The remaining cases can be treated similarly. In the proof, we will assume that the sets *lt*, *eq* and *st* are non-empty (if they are empty, nothing has to be shown).

Case (1), line 1 (E-1):

Let $j \in lt$ be arbitrarily selected. We prove:

$$a_j x_j - b_j y_j \geq -(a_j^- + b_j)^+ (U_j - T_j - 1) + (a_j - b_j) T_j - b_j$$

We can transform the left-hand side as follows:

[1] $a_j x_j - b_j y_j = (-b_j)(y_j - T_j - 1) + a_j(x_j - T_j) + (a_j - b_j) T_j - b_j$

From $j \in lt$ and $x_j, y_j \in [T_j : U_j]$ we obtain $T_j \leq x_j \leq y_j - 1 \leq U_j - 1$, which further yields:

[2] $0 \leq y_j - T_j - 1 \leq U_j - T_j - 1$
[3] $0 \leq x_j - T_j \leq y_j - T_j - 1$

Here, $x'' := y_j - T_j - 1$ and $y'' := x_j - T_j$ can be viewed as 'normalized' subscripts. Now we can apply Lemma 4.11 ($x = x''$, $y = y''$, $U = U_j - T_j - 1$) to the function $(-b_j)x'' + a_j y''$. This yields:

[4] $-(-b_j - a_j^-)^- (U_j - T_j - 1) \leq (-b_j)x'' + a_j y''$

By combining [1] and [4], we obtain:

$$
\begin{aligned}
a_j x_j - b_j y_j &= (-b_j)x'' + a_j y'' + (a_j - b_j) T_j - b_j \\
&\geq -(-b_j - a_j^-)^- (U_j - T_j - 1) + (a_j - b_j) T_j - b_j \\
&= -(a_j^- + b_j)^+ (U_j - T_j - 1) + (a_j - b_j) T_j - b_j
\end{aligned}
$$

Case (1), line 2 (E-2):

Let $j \in eq$ be arbitrarily selected. We prove:

$$(a_j - b_j) x_j \geq -(a_j - b_j)^- (U_j - T_j) + (a_j - b_j) T_j$$

Using $x_j \in [T_j : U_j]$, we can apply Lemma 4.10 to the function $(a_j - b_j) x_j$. Thus:

$$
\begin{aligned}
&(a_j - b_j) x_j \\
&\geq (a_j - b_j)^+ T_j - (a_j - b_j)^- U_j \\
&= -(a_j - b_j)^- (U_j - T_j) + (a_j - b_j)^+ T_j - (a_j - b_j)^- T_j \\
&= -(a_j - b_j)^- (U_j - T_j) + ((a_j - b_j)^+ - (a_j - b_j)^-) T_j \\
&= -(a_j - b_j)^- (U_j - T_j) + (a_j - b_j) T_j
\end{aligned}
$$

Case (1), line 4 (E-4):

Let $j \in st$ be arbitrarily selected. We prove:

$$a_j x_j - b_j y_j \geq -(a_j^- + b_j^+)(U_j - T_j) + (a_j - b_j)T_j$$

We begin by applying Theorem 4.6 to the function $a_j x_j - b_j y_j$. This yields:

$$a_j x_j - b_j y_j \geq a_j^+ T_j - a_j^- U_j + (-b_j)^+ T_j - (-b_j)^- U_j$$
$$= a_j^+ T_j - a_j^- U_j + b_j^- T_j - b_j^+ U_j$$
$$= -(a_j^- + b_j^+)(U_j - T_j) + (a_j^+ - a_j^- - b_j^+ + b_j^-)T_j$$
$$= -(a_j^- + b_j^+)(U_j - T_j) + (a_j - b_j)T_j$$

This completes our partial proof of the theorem.   ■

Appendix C

Mathematical Notation

In the following sections, the basic mathematical concepts and notation that are used throughout the book are summarized. Most of the terminology should be familiar to readers with a mathematical background. This is followed by a description of the notation used to specify algorithms.

C.1 Logic

The connectives of the propositional calculus are represented by $\neg$ (not), $\wedge$ (and), $\vee$ (or), $\rightarrow$ (implication) and $\leftrightarrow$ (coimplication). The quantifiers of predicate logic are denoted by $\exists$ (there exists) and $\forall$ (for all).

If Q is a well-formed formula, then $\vdash Q$ asserts the validity of Q.

In proofs, we use $\Longrightarrow$ as an abbreviation for 'if–then', and $\Longleftrightarrow$ for 'if, and only if', for which we also often write 'iff'. For example, $Q \Longleftrightarrow R$ can be also expressed as Q iff R, and is equivalent to $Q \Longrightarrow R$ and $R \Longrightarrow Q$.

In definitions, a colon at the left-hand side of '$=$' or '$\Longleftrightarrow$' indicates the item being defined: for example, $T := \{\textbf{true}, \textbf{false}\}$ defines T as the set of truth values.

C.2 Sets

The empty set is written as $\emptyset$, set membership is denoted by $\in$, and the symbols $\cup$ (union), $\cap$ (intersection), $\times$ (cartesian product), $-$ (difference), and $\subseteq$ (inclusion) are used in the conventional sense. The cardinality of a set M is denoted by $|M|$, its powerset by $\mathcal{P}(M)$.

Let M_1 denote a set, and p be a predicate defined for all elements of M_1. Then the subset M_2 of all elements of M_1 that satisfy p can be written in the form: $M_2 := \{a : a \in M_1 \wedge p(a)\}$, or $M_2 := \{a \in M_1 : p(a)\}$.

Let $\mathbf{F} = \{M_i : i = 1, 2, \ldots\}$ be a collection of sets. Then we write $\bigcup \mathbf{F}$, $\bigcap \mathbf{F}$, $\times \mathbf{F}$ for the union, intersection and cartesian product, respectively, of all sets M_i. For $\mathbf{F} = \emptyset$ we obtain $\bigcup \mathbf{F} = \emptyset$, $\bigcap \mathbf{F} = \emptyset$, and $\times \mathbf{F} = \{\emptyset\}$.

A **partition** of a non-empty set M is a collection of non-empty subsets of M whose members are pairwise disjoint and whose union is M. For example, the set of all natural numbers can be partitioned into the sets of even and odd numbers.

For the sets of natural, integer, and real numbers we employ the standard notation:

$\mathbb{N}$ $:= \{1, 2, \ldots\}$ set of natural numbers

$\mathbb{N}_0$ $:= \{0\} \cup \mathbb{N}$

$\mathbb{Z}$ set of integer numbers

$\mathbb{R}$ set of real numbers.

For arbitrary integers i, j we introduce the notation $[i:j]$ for the set of all integer numbers between i and j: $[i:j] := \{k \in \mathbb{Z} : i \leq k \leq j\}$. For example, $[-1:2] = \{-1, 0, 1, 2\}$ and $[3:2] = \varnothing$. If no ambiguity can arise, we may omit the brackets.

C.3   Lists and strings

Let a non-empty set M be given, and let $M_i := M$ for all $i \geq 1$. We define:

$$M^n := \underset{1 \leq i \leq n}{\bigtimes} M_i \text{ for all } n \geq 0$$

$$M^* := \bigcup_{n \geq 0} M^n \quad \text{and} \quad M^+ := \bigcup_{n \geq 1} M^n$$

The elements of M^n are referred to as **(ordered) tuples** or **lists**, depending on the context in which they are used; they can be written in the form $\mathbf{a} = (a_1, \ldots, a_n)$, where $a_i \in M$ for all i, and n is called the **length** of $\mathbf{a}$, denoted by $|\mathbf{a}|$. A list of length 0 will be referred to as the **empty list**, and will be written as ε. Let $\mathbf{a} = (a_1, \ldots, a_n)$ and i, j be arbitrary integer numbers. Then $\mathbf{a}(i:j)$ designates the sublist $(a_i, \ldots, a_j)$ of $\mathbf{a}$ iff $1 \leq i \leq j \leq n$, and the empty list otherwise. The access to element i ($1 \leq i \leq n$) is specified in the form $\mathbf{a}(i)$. By $\mathbf{a}^R$ we denote the **reverse** of $\mathbf{a}$, that is the list $(a_n, \ldots, a_1)$. Let $\mathbf{a} = (a_1, \ldots, a_n)$ and $\mathbf{b} = (b_1, \ldots, b_m)$ denote two elements of M^*. The **concatenation** of $\mathbf{a}$ and $\mathbf{b}$, written as $\mathbf{a} \| \mathbf{b}$, yields the element $(a_1, \ldots, a_n, b_1, \ldots, b_m)$ in M^*. Two lists are **equal** iff they have the same lengths, and corresponding elements are equal. Finally, for every $a \in M$ and $n \geq 0$, a^n denotes the list which consists of exactly n instances of a.

An **alphabet** Σ is a finite, non-empty set of **symbols**. We do not make any specific assumptions about the symbols; examples are letters, digits, or special characters such as '+', '*' or '%'.

Let Σ be arbitrarily selected. Σ^n for all $n \geq 0$, Σ^+ and Σ^* are defined as above; however, for the elements of these sets we adopt the following

special notation and terminology. An element of Σ^n $(n \geq 0)$ is called a
string or **word** of **length** n over Σ, and is written in the form $a_1 a_2 \ldots a_n$
($a_i \in \Sigma$ for all i, $1 \leq i \leq n$). A string of length 0 is called the **empty string**
and is written as ε. The concatenation of two strings can be expressed by
juxtaposition of the two operands. Depending on the context in which they
are used, strings may be enclosed in double quotes.

For example, let $\Sigma := \{A, B, \ldots, Z, 0, 1, \ldots, 9\}$. Then ε, A, 0001Y,
and Z1Y2X3 are strings over Σ. Their lengths are 0, 1, 5, and 6, respectively. Let $x = $ B07: then $x^R = $ 70B, $x^0 = \varepsilon$, and $x^3 = $ B07B07B07.

C.4   Relations

Let M_1 and M_2 be sets. A **relation** R from M_1 to M_2 is a subset
$R \subseteq M_1 \times M_2$. M_1 is called the **domain**, and M_2 the **range**, of R. We write
$a_1 R a_2$ iff $(a_1, a_2) \in R$. If $M_1 = M_2$, we speak of a relation **on** M_1. The
inverse of R, written R^{-1}, is the set of all pairs (a_2, a_1) such that (a_1, a_2) is in
R.

The sets $DEF(R)$ and $VAL(R)$ specify those elements of M_1 or M_2,
which occur as the first or second element of a pair in R, respectively:

$$DEF(R) := \{a_1 \in M_1 : \exists a_2 \in M_2 : a_1 R a_2\}$$
$$VAL(R) := \{a_2 \in M_2 : \exists a_1 \in M_1 : a_1 R a_2\}$$

For the following, let R be a relation on M.

R is **reflexive**	iff $\forall a \in M : a R a$
R is **irreflexive**	iff $\forall a \in M : \neg(a R a)$
R is **symmetric**	iff $\forall a, b \in M : a R b \to b R a$
R is **asymmetric**	iff $\forall a, b \in M : a R b \to \neg(b R a)$
R is **antisymmetric**	iff $\forall a, b \in M : a R b \wedge b R a \to a = b$
R is **transitive**	iff $\forall a, b, c \in M : a R b \wedge b R c \to a R c$

A relation which is reflexive, symmetric, and transitive is called an **equivalence relation**. Let $\equiv$ be an equivalence relation on M, and $a \in M$
arbitrarily selected. Then we define the **equivalence class** of a, $[a]$, as the
set $[a] := \{b \in M : a \equiv b\}$. The set $\{[a] : a \in M\}$ is a partition of M.

Let R and S be relations on a set M. The **product** of R and S, written
$S \circ R$, is defined by: $S \circ R := \{(a, c) \in M^2 : \exists b \in M : a R b \wedge b S c\}$. The
n-fold product, R^n, of R is given by $R^0 := \{(a, a) : a \in M\}$, and
$R^n := R \circ R^{n-1}$ for all $n \geq 1$.

The **transitive closure**, R^+, of R is defined by $R^+ := \{(a, b) \in M^2 :$
$\exists n \geq 1 : a R^n b\}$. R^+ is the smallest transitive relation that includes R. The
reflexive and transitive closure of R, R^*, is given by $R^* := R^0 \cup R^+$. R^* is
the smallest reflexive and transitive relation that includes R. The **reflexive
reduction** of a relation R is the relation $R - R^0$.

Partial orders are special relations on a set M. They include reflexive and irreflexive orders, which are defined as follows: R is a **reflexive order** on M iff R is reflexive, antisymmetric, and transitive. R is an **irreflexive order** iff R is irreflexive and transitive. A partial order R is **linear** iff for all $a, b \in M$, $a \, R \, b$ or $b \, R \, a$ or $a = b$ holds. An example for a linear reflexive order is the relation $\geqslant$ on the set $\mathbb{R}$; the relation $>$ on $\mathbb{R}$ is a linear irreflexive order. For every set M, the relation $\subseteq$ and its inverse are reflexive orders on $\mathcal{P}(M)$. If $|M| \geqslant 2$, these orders are not linear.

If we define an irreflexive partial order $<$ on a set M, then we will always denote by $\leqslant$ the corresponding reflexive partial order, that is $\leqslant := \, < \cup \, R^0$, and $>$, $\geqslant$ will respectively denote the inverses of these two relations.

Let R denote a partial order on a set M. Then we say that a linear partial order S **topologically sorts** R iff $R \subseteq S$.

C.5 Functions

Let M_1 and M_2 be sets. We define a **(partial) function** f from M_1 to M_2, denoted by $f \colon M_1 \to M_2$, as a relation from M_1 to M_2 such that $a_1 f a_2$ and $a_1 f a_2'$ always implies $a_2 = a_2'$. If $a_1 f a_2$ for a function f, then we write $f(a_1) = a_2$. We say that f is **defined** in $DEF(f)$. f is **total** iff $DEF(f)$ is M_1.

Let $f \colon M_1 \to M_2$ be a total function.

- f is an **injection** iff $f(a_1) = a_2$ and $f(a_1') = a_2$ implies $a_1' = a_1$. An injection is also called a **one-to-one mapping** from M_1 **into** M_2.
- f is a **surjection**, or a function from M_1 **onto** M_2, iff $VAL(f) = M_2$.
- f is a **bijection** iff f is an injection and a surjection. In this case, we also say that f is a **one-to-one correspondence** between M_1 and M_2.

Let $f \colon M_1 \to M_2$, and $M_1' \subseteq M_1$. Then, $f|M_1'$, the **restriction** of f to M_1', is the function $f' \colon M_1' \to M_2$ with $DEF(f') := M_1' \cap DEF(f)$ and $f'(a') := f(a')$ for all $a' \in DEF(f')$.

For any set M, the **identity function** $id \colon M \to M$ on M is a total function with $id(a) := a$ for all $a \in M$.

Finally, we introduce the O notation, which is useful for discussing approximations. For any given function $f \colon \mathbb{N} \to \mathbb{R}$, an occurrence of $O(f(n))$ represents a quantity that is less than $c \cdot |f(n)|$, where $c > 0$ is a suitable real constant. For different occurrences of $O(n)$, different values of c may have to be selected. For example, we may write $c_0 n^2 + c_1 n + c_2 \log(n) + c_3 = O(n^2)$, where the c_i are real constants. In a few places, we will use $\alpha(n) \geqslant 1$ to denote a very slowly growing function, which is related to a functional inverse of Ackermann's function (Tarjan, 1975).

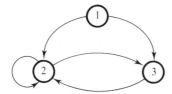

Figure C.1 Representation of a graph.

C.6 Graphs

A (**directed**) **graph** G is a pair $G = (N,E)$, where N is the set of **nodes** (or **vertices**), and $E \subseteq N^2$ is the set of **edges** (or **arcs**). Both N and E are finite sets. We can draw a picture of a graph by representing its nodes as points and connecting two points n,n' by an arrow from n to n' iff (n,n') is in E. For example, the graph $G = (\{1,2,3\}, \{(1,2),(1,3),(2,2),(2,3),(3,2)\})$ is shown in Figure C.1. A graph with one node and no edges, that is $(\{n\},\emptyset)$, is called a **trivial graph**.

Let $G = (N,E)$ be given, and select an arbitrary node $n \in N$. We define the sets $pred(n)$ and $succ(n)$ of the (**immediate**) **predecessors** and **successors**, respectively, of n by:

$$pred(n) := \{n' \in N: (n',n) \in E\}$$
$$succ(n) := \{n' \in N: (n,n') \in E\}$$

For example, in the graph G of Figure C.1, $pred(2) = \{1,2,3\}$ and $succ(2) = \{2,3\}$. The cardinality of the sets $|pred(n)|$ and $|succ(n)|$ is called the **in-degree** and **out-degree**, respectively, of n.

We now explain the concept of paths in a graph $G = (N,E)$: A sequence $\pi = (n_1,n_2, \ldots, n_m)$ with $m \geq 1$ and $n_i \in N$ for all i, $1 \leq i \leq m$, is a **path of length** $m - 1$ iff for all $i \in [1:m - 1]$, (n_i,n_{i+1}) is in E.

If $\pi = (n_1, \ldots, n_m)$ is a path, then we say that n_m can be **reached** from n_1. If $m = 1$, we call π a **trivial** path. π is a **cycle** iff $m \geq 2$ and $n_1 = n_m$. A cycle of length 1 is called an **elementary loop**. π is called **cycle-free** if it does not contain any cycles. A path is **simple** if all nodes in the path, except possibly the first and last nodes, are distinct.

A graph is **cyclic** iff it contains a cycle, and otherwise **acyclic**.

Graph G of Figure C.1 is a cyclic graph, containing (among others) the cyclic paths (2,2) and (2,3,2,2,2,3,2). The first, a path of length 1, is an elementary loop, while the second path has length 6. The nodes 2 and 3 can be reached from every node, but 1 can only be reached from itself.

Relations and graphs are connected in an obvious way, as the set of edges of a graph can be considered to be a relation in its node set. We will say that the graph (N,E) is a **representation** of the relation E on N.

Let $G = (N,E)$ be a directed graph. We now introduce the concepts of subgraph and partial graph.

A subset $N' \subseteq N$ of nodes **generates** the **subgraph** $G|N' := (N',E')$ of G, where $E' := E \cap (N' \times N')$. A **partial graph** of G is any graph $G'' := (N',E'')$, where $N' \subseteq N$ and $E'' \subseteq E \cap (N' \times N')$. For example, the graph $G|N' := (\{2,3\}, \{(2,2),(2,3),(3,2)\})$ is the subgraph of G (in Figure C.1) which is generated by the node set $N' = \{2,3\}$. In contrast, $G'' := (\{2,3\}, \{(2,3)\})$ is a partial graph of G, but not a subgraph.

A **labeled** graph is a triple $G = (N,E,\mu)$, where (N,E) is a graph, Σ is an alphabet, and $\mu: (N \cup E) \to \Sigma^*$ is a **labeling function**. Labeling functions are used to associate information with nodes and/or edges of a graph.

Let us define an equivalence relation on the node set of a graph by relating two nodes iff there is a path from the first to the second node and vice versa. The subgraphs generated by the associated equivalence classes are called the **strongly connected components** of the graph; if we replace them by nodes, we obtain the **acyclic condensation** of the graph. This abstraction process will play a crucial role in program restructuring. We now describe these concepts more precisely.

Definition C.1: Strongly connected components of a directed graph   Let $G = (N,E)$ be a graph.

(1)   For arbitrary $n_1, n_2 \in N$: $n_1 \equiv n_2 :\Longleftrightarrow$ there is a path from n_1 to n_2 and a path from n_2 to n_1.

(2)   Let $\{N_i: 1 \leqslant i \leqslant p\}$ denote the partition of N created by $\equiv$ (which is an equivalence relation). Then each graph $G_i := G|N_i$ is a **strongly connected component** (SCC) of G.

(3) G is **strongly connected** iff it has exactly one SCC.   ■

Note that paths may be of length 0; thus an SCC may be a trivial graph.

Tarjan found an algorithm which computes the SCCs of a directed graph in time $O(max(|N|,|E|))$. We describe his algorithm in Appendix A.

The acyclic condensation can be constructed by making each SCC a node and connecting different SCCs by edges iff such connections existed in the original graph.

Definition C.2: Acyclic condensation   Let $G = (N,E)$ be a graph, and $G_i = (N_i,E_i)$ its SCCs $(1 \leqslant i \leqslant p)$. The **acyclic condensation** of G, denoted by $AC(G)$, is a directed graph, (N',E'), such that:

(1) $N' := \{G_i: 1 \leqslant i \leqslant p\}$.

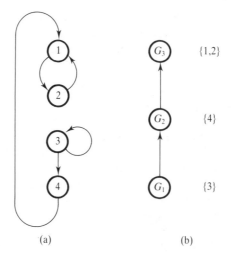

Figure C.2   (a) A graph G and (b) its acyclic condensation $AC(G)$.

(2)   Let G_{i_1}, G_{i_2} be arbitrarily selected from N'. Then $(G_{i_1},G_{i_2}) \in E'$ iff $i_1 \neq i_2$ and there are vertices $n_1 \in N_{i_1}$ and $n_2 \in N_{i_2}$ such that $(n_1,n_2) \in E$.   ∎

Example C.1

Consider the graph G of Figure C.2(a). G consists of three SCCs: $G_1 = (\{3\},\{(3,3)\})$, $G_2 = (\{4\},\varnothing)$, and $G_3 = (\{1,2\},\{(1,2),(2,1)\})$. $AC(G)$ is the graph $(\{G_1,G_2,G_3\}, \{(G_1,G_2),(G_2,G_3)\})$ shown in Figure C.2(b). (The numbering adopted here for the G_i $(1 \leqslant i \leqslant 3)$ is not the one obtained by Tarjan's algorithm (Algorithm A.1), but one that topologically sorts the SCCs.)

In Appendix A, we discuss another example for the construction of the acyclic condensation (Example A.1).

We will frequently work with a special class of graphs called trees: a **tree** is a directed acyclic graph $T = (N,E)$ with a special node $r \in N$, the **root** of T, such that the in-degree is 0 for the root and 1 for all other nodes. In a tree, every node can be reached from the root by a unique path. Let $n,n' \in N$ be arbitrarily selected. If there is a non-trivial path from n' to n then n' is an **ancestor** of n, and n a descendant of n'. If (n',n) is in E, then n' is the **father** of n, and n the **son** of n'. A node n of a tree is a **leaf** iff its out-degree is 0, and an **inner node** otherwise. A tree is **ordered** if a linear order is defined in each set $succ(n)$, $n \in N$. The successors of a node in an ordered tree are arranged from left to right in a graphical representation of the tree. An *n*-ary tree is a tree where each inner node has at most *n* sons ($n \geq 1$). For $n = 2$ and $n = 3$ we speak of a **binary** and a **ternary** tree, respectively.

C.7   Extended Backus Naur form

We will use **extended Backus Naur form** to specify the context-free grammar of a language. We write non-terminals as strings of letters, enclose terminals between double quotes, and separate the left- and right-hand sides of rules by arrows. If X is a symbol of the grammar, then X^+ and X^* represent X^n, with an arbitrary $n \geq 1$ or $n \geq 0$, respectively. We illustrate the notation by a simple example:

$$
\begin{aligned}
\textit{Letter} &\rightarrow \text{"A"}|\text{"B"}|\ldots|\text{"Z"} \\
\textit{Digit} &\rightarrow \text{"0"}|\text{"1"}|\ldots|\text{"9"} \\
\textit{Alpha} &\rightarrow \textit{Letter}|\textit{Digit} \\
\textit{Number} &\rightarrow \textit{Digit}^+ \\
\textit{Identifier} &\rightarrow \textit{Letter Alpha}^*
\end{aligned}
$$

C.8   Specification of algorithms

Algorithms are specified in a Pascal-like notation with a number of self-explanatory modifications. We first describe some general features of our language below, and discuss a number of special elements subsequently.

Variables are normally used without an explicit declaration; they may take on values of standard types or they may represent sets, graphs and other objects. We make free use of the mathematical notation introduced in the preceding section.

All composite statements are terminated by a closing symbol; as a consequence, we do not need to enclose the statement sequences occurring in their bodies between **begin** and **end**. For example:

if $A \leq B$ **then** $A := A + 1$; $F1(A)$ **else** $A := B$; $F2(C + 1)$ **fi**.

Comments are enclosed between /* and */. A special type of comment is an **assertion** which is written between //* and *//. An assertion specifies a condition that is valid immediately after the statement to which it is attached. For example:

$A := 0$;   /* Initialization */
while $A \leq 100$ **do** ... ;$A := A + 1$ **end**;   /* A is only changed as shown */
//* $\models A = 101$ *//

Let M denote a non-empty set. Then the built-in function *select*(M) can be called to provide us with an arbitrary element of M; it does not modify M. In contrast, a call to *select_and_remove*(M) combines the selection of an element of M with its subsequent removal from the set.

Assume now that M represents a set, v is a variable, p a predicate defined on the elements of M, and *SEQ* a statement sequence. The effect of the statement:

for every $v \in M$ **such that** $p(v)$ **do** *SEQ* **end for**

is equivalent to:

$MV := \{x \in M: p(x)\}$;
while $MV \neq \emptyset$ **do**
   $v := $ *select_and_remove*(MV);
   SEQ
end

The statement:

for every $v \in M$ **do** *SEQ* **end for**

is equivalent to

for every $v \in M$ **such that true do** *SEQ* **end for**

Algorithms may use a push-down stack. The following built-in procedures can be applied:

init_stack	initializes the stack to empty
push(x)	pushes the value of x on top of stack
pop	pops top of stack, if the stack is non-empty, and is undefined otherwise
empty_stack	returns a boolean value that indicates whether or not the stack is empty
top_of_stack	returns the top element of the stack, if the stack is non-empty, and is undefined otherwise
in_stack(x)	returns a boolean value that indicates whether or not x is in the stack

Finally, we introduce special notation for a type of assignment statement which occurs frequently. Let v denote an integer or real variable, and x an expression. Then:

v **plus** x is equivalent to $v := v + x$

v **minus** x is equivalent to $v := v - x$

Similarly, if Y is a variable whose values are sets, and x is an expression, then:

Y **plus** x is equivalent to $Y := Y \cup x$

Y **minus** x is equivalent to $Y := Y - x$

C.9 Performance measures

To compare the performance of computer systems, several units of measurement have been introduced. One is the number of floating point operations a system can perform in one second (**FLOPS**) and another is the number of instructions it can execute in one second (**IPS**). Memory sizes may be described in bytes (**B**) or 64-bit words (**W**). A word can hold a double-precision floating point number, the standard precision for scientific computations. The prefixes K (kilo), M (mega), G (giga) and T (tera) stand for the scaling factors 10^3, 10^6, 10^9, and 10^{12}, respectively.

References

Aho A.V., Hopcroft J.E. and Ullman J.D. (1974). *The Design and Analysis of Computer Algorithms*. Reading MA: Addison-Wesley

Aho A.V., Sethi R. and Ullman J.D. (1986). *Compilers. Principles, Techniques and Tools*. Reading MA: Addison-Wesley

Allen F.E. (1969). Program optimization. In *Annual Review of Automatic Programming* Vol. 5, pp.239–307. Elmsford NY: Pergamon

Allen F.E. (1974). Interprocedural data flow analysis. In *Information Processing*, **74**, 398–402. Amsterdam: North-Holland

Allen F.E. and Cocke J. (1972). A catalogue of optimizing transformations. In *Design and Optimization of Compilers* (Rustin, R., ed.), pp.1–30. Englewood Cliffs NJ: Prentice-Hall

Allen F.E. and Cocke J. (1976). A program data flow analysis procedure. *Comm. ACM*, **19**, 137–47

Allen F.E., Burke M., Cytron R., Ferrante J., Sarkar V. and Hsieh W. (1988a). A framework for determining useful parallelism. In *Proc. 1988 Int. Conf. on Supercomputing*, St. Malo, pp.207–15. New York NY: ACM Press

Allen F.E., Burke M., Charles P., Cytron R. and Ferrante J. (1988b). An overview of the PTRAN analysis system for multiprocessing. *Parallel and Distributed Computing*, **5**, 617–40

Allen J.R. (1983). *Dependence Analysis for Subscripted Variables and its Applications to Program Transformations*. Ph.D. Dissertation, Department of Mathematical Sciences, Rice University, Houston TX

Allen J.R. and Kennedy K. (1982). PFC: a program to convert Fortran to parallel form. In *Proc. IBM Conf. Parallel Computing and Scientific Computations*

Allen J.R. and Kennedy K. (1984a). *Automatic Translation of Fortran Programs to Vector Form*. Computer Science Technical Report COMP TR84-9, Rice University, Houston TX

Allen J.R. and Kennedy K. (1984b). Automatic loop interchange. In *Proc. ACM SIGPLAN '84 Sym. on Compiler Construction. SIGPLAN Notices*, **19**(6), 233–46

Allen J.R. and Kennedy K. (1987). Automatic translation of FORTRAN programs to vector form. *ACM TOPLAS*, **9**, 491–542

Allen J.R. and Kennedy K. (1988). *Vector Register Allocation*. Computer Science Technical Report COMP TR86-45 (revised, August 1988), Rice University, Houston TX

Allen J.R., Kennedy K., Porterfield C. and Warren J. (1983). Conversion of control dependence to data dependence. In *Conf. Rec. 10th ACM Sym. Principles of Programming Languages* (POPL), pp.177–89

Allen J.R., Baumgartner D., Kennedy K. and Porterfield A. (1986). *PTOOL: A Semi-Automatic Parallel Programming Assistant*. Computer Science Technical Report COMP TR86-31, Rice University, Houston TX

Allen J.R., Callahan D. and Kennedy K. (1987). Automatic decomposition of scientific programs for parallel execution. In *Conf. Rec. 14th ACM Sym. Principles of Programming Languages* (POPL), pp.63–76

Amdahl G. (1967). The validity of the single processor approach to achieving large scale computing capabilities. In *AFIPS Conf. Proc.* Vol. 30, pp.483–85

Amdahl Corp. (1984). *Vector Processor. Technical Overview*. Publication No. G1065.0-01A

Andrews G.R. and Schneider F.B. (1983). Concepts and notations for concurrent programming. *ACM Computing Surveys*, **15**, 3–44

Andersen D.W., Sparacio F.J. and Tamaluso R.M. (1967). The IBM System/360 Model 91: system philosophy and instruction handling. *IBM J. Research and Development*, **11**(1), 8–24

ANSI (1976). *American National Standard Programming Language PL/I*. American National Standards Institute X3.53-1976

ANSI (1978). *American National Standard Programming Language FORTRAN 77*. American National Standards Institute X3.9-1978

ANSI (1989). *Fortran 8X Draft S8, Version 111*. American National Standards Institute X3J3 (1989)

Arnold C.N. (1982). Performance evaluation of three automatic vectorization packages. In *Proc. 1982 Int. Conf. Parallel Processing*, pp.235–42. IEEE Computer Society

Arnold C.N. (1983). Vector optimization on the CYBER 205. In *Proc. 1983 Int. Conf. Parallel Processing*, pp.530–6. IEEE Computer Society

Babb II R.G., ed. (1988). *Programming Parallel Processors*. Reading MA: Addison-Wesley

Baer J.L. (1973). A survey of some theoretical aspects of multiprocessing. *ACM Computing Surveys*, **5**, 31–80

Balasundaram V. (1989). *Interactive Parallelization of Numerical Scientific Programs*. Ph.D. Dissertation, Computer Science Technical Report COMP TR89-95, Rice University, Houston TX

Banerjee U. (1976). *Data Dependence in Ordinary Programs*. M.S. Thesis, Technical Report UIUCDCS-R-76-837, Department of Computer Science, University of Illinois at Urbana–Champaign

Banerjee U. (1979). *Speedup of Ordinary Programs*. Ph.D. Dissertation, Technical Report UIUCDCS-R-79-989, Department of Computer Science, University of Illinois at Urbana–Champaign

Banerjee U. (1988). *Dependence Analysis for Supercomputing*. Boston MA: Kluwer

Banning J.P. (1979). An efficient way to find the side effects of procedure calls and the aliases of variables. In *Conf. Rec. 6th ACM Sym. Principles of Programming Languages* (POPL), pp.29–41

Barth J.M. (1978). A practical interprocedural data flow analysis algorithm. *Comm. ACM*, **21**, 724–36

Batcher K.E. (1980). Design of a massively parallel processor. *IEEE Trans. Computers*, **29**, 836–40

BBN Laboratories Inc. (1986). *Butterfly Parallel Processor Overview*. BBN Report No. 6149, Version 2

Beatty J.C. (1972). An axiomatic approach to code optimization for expressions. *J. ACM*, **19**, 613–40

Benner R., Gustafson J. and Montry G. (1988). Analysis of scientific application programs on a 1024-processor hypercube. *SIAM J. Scientific Statistical Computing*, **9**, 609–38

Bernstein A.J. (1966). Analysis of programs for parallel processing. *IEEE Trans. Electronic Computers*, **15**, 757–62

Bertsekas D.P. and Tsitsiklis J.N. (1989). *Parallel and Distributed Computation. Numerical Methods*. Englewood Cliffs NJ: Prentice-Hall

Booth M. and Misegades K. (1986). Microtasking: a new way to harness multiprocessors. *Cray Channels*, **6**(5), 24–7

Bose P. (1988a). Heuristic rule-based program transformations for enhanced vectorization. In *Proc. 1988 Int. Conf. Parallel Processing*, pp.63–6. IEEE Computer Society

Bose P. (1988b). Interactive program improvement via EAVE: an expert adviser for vectorization. In *Proc. 1988 Int. Conf. on Supercomputing*, St. Malo, pp.119–30. New York NY: ACM Press

Brandes T. (1988). *Formale Methoden zur Spezifikation automatischer Parallelisierung*. Ph.D. Dissertation, University of Marburg, FRG

Brinch Hansen P. (1975). The programming language Concurrent Pascal. *IEEE Trans. Software Engineering*, **1**, 199–206

Brode B. (1981). Precompilation of Fortran programs to facilitate array processing. *IEEE Computer*, **14**, 46–51

Buchholz W. (1986). The IBM System/370 vector architecture. *IBM Systems J.*, **25**(1), 51–62

Burke M. and Cytron R. (1986). Interprocedural dependence analysis and parallelization. In *Proc. SIGPLAN '86 Sym. on Compiler Construction*, pp.162–75

Callahan D. (1987). *A Global Approach to Detection of Parallelism*. Ph.D. Dissertation, Department of Computer Science, Rice University, Houston TX

Callahan D. and Kennedy K. (1988a). Analysis of interprocedural side effects in a parallel programming environment. In *Supercomputing. Proc. 1st Conf.* (Houstis E.N., Papatheodorou T.S. and Polychronopoulos C.D., eds.), Athens, Greece, June 1987, Lecture Notes in Computer Science 297, pp.138–71. Berlin: Springer

Callahan D. and Kennedy K. (1988b). Compiling programs for distributed-memory multiprocessors. *J. Supercomputing*, **2**(2), 151–69

Callahan D., Cooper K.D., Kennedy K. and Torczon L. (1986). Interprocedural constant propagation. In *Proc. SIGPLAN '86 Symposium on Compiler Construction*, pp.152–61. *SIGPLAN Notices*, **21**(7), pp.152–61.

Callahan D., Dongarra J. and Levine D. (1988). *Vectorizing Compilers: a Test Suite and Results*. Technical Memorandum ANL/MCS-TM-109, Mathematics and Computer Science Division, Argonne National Laboratory

Carriero N. and Gelernter D. (1985). *The S/Nets Linda Kernel*. Research Report YALEU/DCS/RR-383, Department of Computer Science, Yale University

Charlesworth A.E. (1981). An approach to scientific array processing: the architectural design of the AP-120B/FPS-164 family. *IEEE Computer*, **14**(9), 18–27

Chen S.S. (1984). Large-scale and high-speed multiprocessor system for scientific applications: CRAY-X-MP Series. In: *High-Speed Computation* (Kowalik J.S., ed.), NATO ASI Series F: Computer and System Sciences, Vol. 7. Berlin: Springer

Cocke J. and Schwartz J.T. (1970). *Programming Languages and Their Compilers*. Preliminary Notes, 2nd revised ed, Courant Institute, New York NY

Cohagan W.L. (1973). Vector optimization for the ASC. In *Proc. 7th Annual Conf. on Information and System Sciences*, pp.169–74

Conway M. (1963). A multiprocessor system design. In *Proc. AFIPS Fall Joint Computer Conf.*, pp.139–46. New York NY: Spartan Books

Cooper K.D. and Kennedy K. (1988). Interprocedural side-effect analysis in linear time. In *Proc. SIGPLAN '88 Conf. on Programming Language Design and Implementation. SIGPLAN Notices*, **19**(6), 247–58

Cooper K.D. and Kennedy K. (1989). Fast interprocedural alias analysis. In *Conf. Rec. 16th ACM Sym. Principles of Programming Languages* (POPL), pp.49–59

Cooper K.D., Kennedy K. and Torczon L. (1986). The impact of interprocedural analysis and optimization in the R^n programming environment. *ACM TOPLAS*, **8**, 491–523

Cowell W.R. and Thompson C.P. (1986). *Transforming Fortran DO Loops to Improve Performance on Vector Architectures*. Technical Report NP 1168, Numerical Algorithms Group, Oxford, UK, and Downers Grove IL

Cray Research Inc. (1980). *Cray-1 Computer System Fortran (CFT) Reference Manual*. Publication 224000, Cray Research Inc., Mendota Heights MN

Cytron R.G. (1984). *Compile-Time Scheduling and Optimization for Asynchronous Machines*. Ph.D. Dissertation, Department of Computer Science, University of Illinois at Urbana–Champaign

Cytron R.G. (1985). Useful parallelism in a multiprocessor environment. In *Proc. 1985 Int. Conf. Parallel Processing*, pp.450–7. IEEE Computer Society

Cytron R.G. (1986). Doacross: beyond vectorization for multiprocessors (extended abstract). In *Proc. 1986 Int. Conf. Parallel Processing*, pp.226–34. IEEE Computer Society

Darema-Rogers F., Norton V.A. and Pfister G.F. (1985). *Using a Single-Program–Multiple-Data Computational Model for Parallel Execution of Scientific Applications*. Research Report RC 11552, IBM T.J. Watson Research Center, Yorktown Heights

Davies J.R.B. (1981). *Parallel Loop Constructs for Multiprocessors*. M.S. Thesis, Technical Report UIUCDCS-R-81-1070, Department of Computer Science, University of Illinois at Urbana–Champaign

Davies J., Huson C.A., Macke T., Leasure B.R. and Wolfe M.J. (1986). The KAP/S-1: an advanced source-to-source vectorizer for the S-1 Mark IIa supercomputer. In *Proc. 1986 Int. Conf. Parallel Processing*, pp.833–5, IEEE Computer Society

Denelcor Inc. (1981). *Heterogenous Element Processor: Principles of Operation*

Department of Defense (1981). *Programming Language Ada: Reference Manual*, Lecture Notes in Computer Science 106. Berlin: Springer

DiNucci D.C. (1988). Alliant FX/8. In: *Programming Parallel Processors* (Babb II R.G., ed.), pp.27–42. Reading MA: Addison-Wesley

Dongarra J.J., ed. (1987). *Experimental Parallel Computing Architectures, Special Topics in Supercomputing Vol. 1*. Amsterdam: North-Holland

Dongarra J.J. and Eisenstat S.C. (1984). Squeezing the most out of an algorithm in Cray Fortran. *ACM Trans. Mathematical Software*, **10**(3), 221–30

Ehses E. and Mevenkamp M. (1986). *MIMD-Fortran*. Technical Report, Gesellschaft für Mathematik und Datenverarbeitung (GMD), Bonn

Engeln-Müllges G. and Reutter F. (1985). *Formelsammlung zur Numerischen Mathematik mit Standard Fortran 77 Programmen*. Mannheim: Bibliographisches Institut

Ercegovac M.D. and Lang T. (1986). Vector processing, In *Supercomputers. Class VI Systems, Hardware and Software* (Fernbach S., ed.), pp.29–57. Amsterdam: North-Holland

Faber V., Lubeck O.M. and White Jr. A.B. (1986). Superlinear speedup of an efficient sequential algorithm is not possible. *Parallel Computing*, **3**, 259–60

Fernbach S., ed. (1986). *Supercomputers. Class VI Systems, Hardware and Software*. Amsterdam: North-Holland

Ferrante J., Ottenstein K.J. and Warren J.D. (1987). The program dependence graph and its use in optimization. *ACM TOPLAS*, **9**, 319–49

Flanders P.M., Hunt D.J., Reddaway S.F. and Parkinson D. (1977). Efficient high-speed computing with the distributed array processor. In: *High Speed Computer and Algorithm Organization*, pp.113–28. New York NY: Academic Press

Flynn M. (1966). Very high-speed computing systems. *Proc. IEEE*, **54**, 1901–9

Fosdick L.D. and Osterweil L.J. (1976). Data flow analysis in software reliability. *ACM Computing Surveys*, **8**, 305–30

Fox G.C. and Otto S.W. (1984). Algorithms for concurrent processors. *Physics Today*, May, 50–9

Fox G.C., Johnson M., Lyzenga G., Otto S.W., Salmon J. and Walker D. (1988). *Solving Problems on Concurrent Processors Vol. I*. Englewood Cliffs NJ: Prentice-Hall

Gehani N.H. and Roome W.D. (1986). Concurrent C. *Software: Practice and Experience*, **16**(9), 821–44

Gerndt H.M. (1989). *Automatic Parallelization for Distributed-Memory Multiprocessing Systems*. Ph.D. Dissertation, University of Bonn, Technical Report Series ACPC/TR 90-1, Austrian Center for Parallel Computation

Gerndt H.M. and Zima H.P. (1988). MIMD-parallelization for SUPRENUM. In *Supercomputing. Proc. 1st Conf.* (Houstis E.N., Papatheodorou T.S. and Polychronopoulos C.D., eds.), Athens, Greece, June 1987, Lecture Notes in Computer Science 297, pp.278–93 Berlin: Springer

Gilmore P.A. (1986). The massively parallel processor. In *Supercomputers. Class VI Systems. Hardware and Software* (Fernbach S., ed.), pp.183–219. Amsterdam: North-Holland

Giloi W.K. (1988). SUPRENUM: a trendsetter in modern supercomputer development. *Parallel Computing*, **7**, 283–96

Goldberg A. and Robson D. (1983). *Smalltalk-80: the Language and its Implementation*. Reading MA: Addison-Wesley

Gottlieb A., Grishman R., Kruskal C.P., McAuliffe K.P., Rudolph L. and Suir M. (1983). The NYU ultracomputer – designing an MIMD shared memory parallel computer. *IEEE Trans. Computers*, **32**, 175–89

Griffin H. (1954). *Elementary Theory of Numbers*. New York NY: McGraw-Hill

Guarna V.A., Gannon, D., Gaur Y. and Jablonowski D. (1988). FAUST: an environment for programming parallel scientific applications. *Supercomputing 1988*. IEEE Computer Society

Habermann A.N. and Notkin D.S. (1982). *The GANDALF Software Development Environment*. Research Report, Computer Science Department, Carnegie–Mellon University, Pittsburgh PA

Harel D. (1985). A linear time algorithm for finding dominators in flow graphs and related problems. In *Proc. 17th ACM Sym. on Theory of Computing*, pp.185–94

Hecht M.S. (1977). *Flow Analysis of Computer Programs*. Amsterdam: North-Holland

Hecht M.S. and Ullman J.D. (1975). A simple algorithm for global data flow analysis programs. *SIAM J. Computing*, **4**, 519–32

Helmbold D.P. and McDowell C.E. (1989). Modeling Speedup(n) greater than n. In *Proc. 1989 Int. Conf. Parallel Processing*, pp.III-219–III-225. IEEE Computer Society

Higbee L. (1979). *Vectorization and Conversion of Fortran Programs for the Cray-1 CFT Compiler*. Publication 2240207, Cray Research Inc., Mendota Heights MN

Hillis W.D. (1985). *The Connection Machine*. Cambridge MA: MIT Press

Hoare C.A.R. (1978). Communicating sequential processes. *Comm. ACM*, **21**, 666–77

Hockney R.W. and Jesshope C.R. (1981). *Parallel Computers*. Bristol: Adam Hilger

Huson C.A. (1982). *An In-Line Subroutine Expander for PARAFRASE*. Technical Report UIUCDCS-R-82-118, M.S. Thesis, Department of Computer Science, University of Illinois at Urbana–Champaign

Huson C.A., Macke T., Davies J., Wolfe M.J. and Leasure B.R. (1986). The KAP/205: an advanced source-to-source vectorizer for the Cyber 205 supercomputer. In *Proc. 1986 Int. Conf. Parallel Processing*, pp.827–32. IEEE Computer Society

Hwang K., ed. (1984a). *Supercomputers: Design and Applications Tutorial*. IEEE Catalog Number EHO219-6, IEEE Society Press, Silver Spring MD

Hwang K. (1984b). Evolution of modern supercomputers. In *Supercomputers: Design and Applications Tutorial* (Hwang K. ed.), pp.5-8. IEEE Catalog Number EHO219-6, IEEE Society Press, Silver Spring MD

Hwang K. and Briggs F.A. (1984). *Computer Architecture and Parallel Processing*. New York NY: McGraw-Hill

IBM (1988). *Parallel Fortran*. Language and Library Reference, First Edition, International Business Machines Corporation

INMOS (1988). *OCCAM 2 Reference Manual*. Prentice Hall International Series in Computer Science. New York NY: Prentice-Hall

Kam J.B. and Ullman J.D. (1976). Global flow analysis and iterative algorithms. *J. ACM*, **23**, 158–71

Kam J.B. and Ullman J.D. (1977). Monotone data flow analysis frameworks. *Acta Informatica*, **7**, 305–17

Karp A.H. (1987). Programming for parallelism. *IEEE Computer*, **20**, May, 43–57

Karp A.H. and Babb II R.G. (1988). A comparison of 12 parallel Fortran dialects. *IEEE Software*, **5**, September, 52–67

Kashiwagi H. (1984). Japanese super-speed computer project. In *High-Speed Computation* (Kowalik J.S., ed.), NATO ASI Series F: Computer and System Sciences, Vol. 7, pp.117–26. Berlin: Springer

Kennedy K. (1975). Node listing applied to data flow analysis. In *Conf. Rec. 2nd ACM Sym. Principles of Programming Languages* (POPL), pp.10–21

Kennedy K. (1976). A comparison of two algorithms for global data flow analysis. *SIAM J. Computing*, **5**, 158–80

Kennedy K. (1981). A survey of data flow analysis techniques. In *Program Flow Analysis. Theory and Applications* (Muchnick S.S. and Jones N.D., eds.), pp.5–54. Englewood Cliffs NJ: Prentice-Hall

Kennedy K. and Zima H.P. (1989). Virtual shared memory for distributed-memory machines. In *Proc. 4th Conf. on Hypercubes, Concurrent Computers and Applications*, **1**, 361–6, Monterey CA

Kildall G.A. (1973). A unified approach to global program optimization. In *Conf. Rec. ACM Sym. Principles of Programming Languages* (POPL), pp.194-206

Knuth D.E. (1971). An empirical study of Fortran programs. *Software Practice and Experience*, **1**(2), 105–34

Koelbel C., Mehrotra P. and van Rosendale J. (1987). Semi-automatic domain decomposition in BLAZE. In *Proc. 1987 Int. Conf. Parallel Processing*, pp.521–4 IEEE Computer Society

Kotov V.E. (1984). Automatic construction of parallel programs. In *Algorithms, Software and Hardware for Parallel Computers* (Miklosko J. and Kotov V.E., eds.). Berlin: Springer

Kotov V.E. and Narinyani A.S. (1969). On transformation of sequential programs into asynchronous parallel programs. In *Information Processing 68*, pp.351–7. Amsterdam: North-Holland

Kremer U., Bast H.-J., Gerndt H.M. and Zima H.P. (1988). Advanced tools for automatic parallelization. In *Proc. of the 2nd Int. SUPRENUM Colloq., Parallel Computing*, **7**, 387–93

Kuck D.J (1973a). Multioperation machine computational complexity. In *Complexity of Sequential and Parallel Numerical Algorithms* (Traub F.J., ed.), pp.17–48. New York NY: Academic Press

Kuck D.J. (1973b). Measurements of parallelism in ordinary Fortran programs. In *Proc. 1973 Sagamore Conf. on Parallel Processing*

Kuck D.J. (1977). A survey of parallel machine organization and programming. *ACM Computing Surveys*, **9**, 29–59

Kuck D.J. and Padua D.A. (1979). High-speed multiprocessors and their compilers. In *Proc. 1979 Int. Conf. Parallel Processing*, pp.5–16. IEEE Computer Society

Kuck D.J. and Stokes R.A. (1982). The Burroughs Scientific Processor (BSP). *IEEE Trans. Computers*, **31**, 363–76

Kuck D.J., Muraoka Y. and Chen S.C. (1972). On the number of operations simultaneously executable in Fortran-like programs and their resulting speed-up. *IEEE Trans. Computers*, **21**, 1293–310

Kuck D.J., Kuhn R.H., Padua D.A., Leasure B.R. and Wolfe M.J. (1981). Dependence graphs and compiler optimizations. In *Conf. Rec. 8th ACM Sym. Principles of Programming Languages* (POPL), pp.207–18

Kuck D.J., Kuhn R.H., Leasure B.R. and Wolfe M.J. (1984a). The structure of an advanced retargetable vectorizer. In *Supercomputers: Design and Applications Tutorial* (Hwang K., ed.), pp.967–74. IEEE Catalog Number EHO219-6, IEEE Society Press, Silver Spring MD

Kuck D.J., Sameh A.H., Cytron R.G., Veidenbaum A.V., Polychronopoulos L.D., Lee G., McDaniel T., Leasure B.R., Beckman C., Davies J.R. and Kruskal C.P. (1984). The effects of program restructuring, algorithm change, and architectural choice on program performance. In *Proc. 1984 Int. Conf. Parallel Processing*, pp.129–38 IEEE Computer Society

Kuck D.J., Davidson E.S., Lawrie D.H. and Sameh A.H. (1986). Parallel supercomputing today and the CEDAR approach. *Science Mag.*, **231**, 967–74 (revised version in Dongarra J.J., ed. 1987. *Experimental Parallel Computing Architectures*, Special Topics in Supercomputing Vol. 1, pp.1–23. Amsterdam: North-Holland)

Kuhn R.H. (1980). *Optimization and Interconnection Complexity for Parallel Processors, Single-Stage Networks, and Decision Trees*. Ph.D. Dissertation, Department of Computer Science, University of Illinois at Urbana–Champaign

Lamport L. (1974). The parallel execution of DO loops. *Comm. ACM*, **17**, 83–93

Lawrie D. (1975). Access and alignment of data in an array processor. *IEEE Trans. Computers*, **24**, 1145–55

Leasure B.R. (1985). *The Parafrase Project's Fortran Analyzer. Major Module Documentation*. Technical Report CSRD-504, Department of Computer Science, University of Illinois at Urbana–Champaign

Leasure B.R., Furtney M., Kuhn B. and Pinsky E. (1988). *PCF Fortran: Language Definition Version 1 Parallel Computing Forum*. Kuck & Associates, 1906 Fox Drive, Champaign IL 61820

Lengauer T. and Tarjan R.E. (1979). A fast algorithm for finding dominators in a flow graph. *ACM TOPLAS*, **1**, 121–41

Levesque J.M. and Williamson J.W. (1989). *A Guidebook to Fortran on Supercomputers*. New York NY: Academic Press

Li Z. (1989). *Intraprocedural and Interprocedural Data Dependence Analysis for Parallel Computing*. Ph.D. Dissertation, Department of Computer Science, University of Illinois at Urbana–Champaign

Li Z. and Abu-Sufah W. (1985). A technique for reducing synchronization overhead in large-scale multiprocessors. In *Proc. 12th Int. Sym. on Computer Architecture*, pp.284–91

Lichnewsky A. and Thomasset F. (1988). Introducing symbolic program solving techniques into the dependence testing phase of a vectorizer. In *Proc. 1988 Int. Conf. on Supercomputing*, St. Malo, pp.396–406. New York NY: ACM Press

Lincoln N.R. (1986). Technology and design tradeoffs in the creation of·a modern supercomputer. In *Supercomputers. Class VI Systems, Hardware and Software* (Fernbach S., ed.), pp.83–111. Amsterdam: North-Holland

Macke T., Huson C.A., Davies J.R., Leasure B.R. and Wolfe M.J. (1986). The KAP/ST-100: a Fortran translator for the ST-100 attached processor. In *Proc. 1986 Int. Conf. Parallel Processing*, pp.171–5. IEEE Computer Society

McCluskey E.J. (1956). Minimization of boolean functions. *Bell System Technical J.*, **35**, 1417–44

McGraw J.R., Skedzielewski S., Allan S., Oldehoeft R., Glauert J., Kirkham C., Noyce B. and Thomas R. (1985). SISAL: *Streams and Iteration in a Single-Assignment Language*. Language Reference Manual, M-146, Version 1.2, Rev. 1, Lawrence Livermore National Laboratory

Mehrotra P. and van Rosendale J. (1985). *The BLAZE Language: a Parallel Language for Scientific Programming*. Report 85-29, Institute for Computer Applications in Science and Engineering, NASA Langley Research Center, Hampton VA

Midkiff S.P. and Padua D.A. (1986). Compiler generated synchronization for DO loops. *Proc. 1986 Int. Conf. Parallel Processing*, pp.544–51. IEEE Computer Society

Midkiff S.P. and Padua D.A. (1987). Compiler algorithms for synchronization. *IEEE Trans. Computers*, **36**, 1485–95

Miller P.C., John C.E.S. and Hawkinson S.W. (1988). FPS T series parallel processor. In *Programming Parallel Processors* (Babb II R.G., ed.), pp.73–91. Reading MA: Addison-Wesley

Miura K. and Uchida K. (1984). FACOM vector processor VP-100/VP-200. In *High-Speed Computation* (Kowalik J.S., ed.), NATO ASI Series F: Computer and System Sciences, Vol. 7, pp.127–38. Berlin: Springer

Muchnick S.S. and Jones N.D., eds. (1981). *Program Flow Analysis. Theory and Applications*. Englewood Cliffs NJ: Prentice-Hall

Myers E.W. (1981). A precise inter-procedural data flow algorithm. In *Conf. Rec. 8th ACM Sym. Principles of Programming Languages* (POPL), pp.219–30

Odaka T., Nagashima S. and Kawabe S. (1986). Hitachi supercomputer S-810 array processor system. In *Supercomputers. Class VI Systems, Hardware and Software* (Fernbach S., ed.), pp.113–36. Amsterdam: North-Holland

Osterhaug A., ed. (1989). *Guide to Parallel Programming on Sequent Computer Systems* 2nd edn. Englewood Cliffs NJ: Prentice-Hall

Osterweil L. (1981). *TOOLPACK Architectural Design*. Toolpack Ref. LO-10304, University of Colorado, Boulder CO

Pacific Sierra Research (1986a). *VAST-2 User's Guide, Fortran 8x Output Option Version 2.0*. Pacific Sierra Research Corporation, Los Angeles CA

Pacific Sierra Research (1986b). *Forge. A Fortran Expert Workstation User's Handbook*. Pacific Sierra Research Corporation, Los Angeles CA

Padua D.A. (1979). *Multiprocessors: Discussion of Some Theoretical and Practical Problems*. Ph.D. Dissertation, Technical Report UIUCDCS-R-79-990, Department of Computer Science, University of Illinois at Urbana–Champaign

Padua D.A. and Wolfe M.J. (1986). Advanced compiler optimizations for supercomputers. *Comm. ACM*, **29**, 1184–201

Parkinson D. (1986). Parallel efficiency can be greater than unity. *Parallel Computing*, **3**, 261–2

Pase D.M. and Larrabee A.R. (1988). Intel iPSC concurrent computer. In *Programming Parallel Processors* (Babb II R.G., ed.), pp.105–24. Reading MA: Addison-Wesley

Paul G. and Wilson M.W. (1978). An introduction to VECTRAN and its use in scientific applications programming. In *Proc. 1978 LASL Workshop on Vector and Parallel Processors*. Technical Report LA-7491-C, Los Alamos Scientific Laboratory

Peir J.K. (1986). *Program Partitioning and Synchronization on Multiprocessor Systems*. Ph.D. Dissertation, Technical Report UIUCDCS-R-86-1259, Department of Computer Science, University of Illinois at Urbana–Champaign

Perrott R.H. (1979). A language for array and vector processors. *ACM TOPLAS*, **1**, 176–95

Perrott R.H. (1987). *Parallel Programming*. Reading MA: Addison-Wesley

Perrott R.H., Crookes D. and Milligan P. (1983). The programming language ACTUS. *Software Practice Experience*, **13**, 305–22

Pfister G.F., Brantley W.C., George D.A., Harvey S.L., Klienfelder W.J., McAuliffe K.P., Melton E.A., Norton V.A. and Weiss J. (1987). An introduction to the IBM Research parallel processor prototype (RP3). In *Experimental Parallel Computing Architectures* (Dongarra J.J., ed.), Special Topics in Supercomputing Vol. 1, pp.123–40. Amsterdam: North-Holland

Polychronopoulos C.D. (1986). *On Program Restructuring, Scheduling, and Communication for Parallel Processor Systems*. Ph.D. Dissertation, Technical Report SCRD No. 595, Center for Supercomputing Research and Development, University of Illinois at Urbana–Champaign

Polychronopoulos C.D. (1988). *Parallel Programming and Compilers*. Boston MA: Kluwer

Polychronopoulos C.D., Girkar M., Haghighat M.R., Lee C.L., Leung B. and Schouten D. (1989). Parafrase-2: an environment for parallelizing, partitioning, synchronizing, and scheduling programs on multiprocessors. In *Proc. 1989 Int. Conf. Parallel Processing*, pp.II-39–II-48. IEEE Computer Society

Quine W.V. (1952). The problem of simplifying truth functions. *American Mathematical Monthly*, **59**(8), 521–31

Quinn M.J. (1987). *Designing Efficient Algorithms for Parallel Computers*. New York NY: McGraw-Hill

Ramamoorthy C.V. and Gonzalez M.J. (1969). A survey of techniques for recognizing parallel processable streams in computer programs. In *Proc. AFIPS 1969 Fall Joint Computing Conf.*, pp.1–15

Ramamoorthy C.V. and Gonzalez M.J. (1971). Subexpression ordering in the execution of arithmetic expressions. *Comm. ACM*, **14**, 479–85

Rogers A. and Pingali K. (1989). Process decomposition through locality of reference. In *Proc. ACM SIGPLAN 1989 Conf. on Programming Language Design and Implementation*

Rose J. and Steele G. (1987). *C*: an Extended C Language for Data Parallel Programming*. Technical Report PL87-5, Thinking Machines, Inc., Cambridge MA

Rosing M. and Schnabel R.B. (1988). *An Overview of DINO – a New Language for Numerical Computation on Distributed-Memory Multiprocessors*. Technical Report TR CU-CS-385-88, Department of Computer Science, University of Colorado, Boulder CO

Roucairol G. (1977). On parallelization of single-assignment programs. In *Parallel Computers–Parallel Mathematics* (Feilmeier M., ed.), pp.203–6. International Association for Mathematics and Computers in Simulation

Ruppelt T. and Wirtz G. (1988). From mathematical specifications to parallel programs on a message-based system. In *Proc. 1988 Int. Conf. on Supercomputing*, St. Malo, pp.108–18. New York NY: ACM Press

Ruppelt T. and Wirtz G. (1989). Automatic transformation of high-level object-oriented specifications into parallel programs. *Parallel Computing*, **10**, 15–28

Russell E.C. (1969). *Automatic Program Analysis*. Ph.D. Dissertation, Department of Electrical Engineering, University of California, Los Angeles CA

Russell R.M. (1978). The CRAY-1 computer system. *Comm. ACM*, **21**, 63–72

Ryder B.G. (1979). Constructing the call graph of a program. *IEEE Trans. Software Engineering*, **5**(3), 216–26

Scarborough R.G. and Kolsky H.G. (1986). A vectorizing Fortran compiler. *IBM J. Research Development*, **30**(2), 163–71

Schaefer M. (1973). *A Mathematical Theory of Global Program Optimization*. Englewood Cliffs NJ: Prentice-Hall

Seitz C.L. (1985). The Cosmic Cube. *Comm. ACM*, **29**, 22–33

Shostak R. (1981). Deciding linear inequalities by computing loop residues. *J. ACM*, **28**, 769–79

Smith B.J. (1981). Architecture and applications of the HEP multiprocessor computer system, real-time signal processing IV. *Proc. SPIE*, August, 241–8

Spillman T.C. (1972). Exposing side-effects in a PL/I optimizing compiler. *Information Processing*. **71**, 376–81

Stone H.S. (1967). One-pass compilation for arithmetic expressions for a parallel processor. *Comm. ACM*, **10**, 220–3

Stone H.S. (1987). *High-performance Computer Architecture*. Addison-Wesley Series in Electrical and Computer Engineering. Reading MA: Addison-Wesley

Stone J.M. (1985). *Nested Parallelism in a Parallel Fortran Environment*. Research Report RC 11506, IBM T.J. Watson Research Center, Yorktown Heights

Tarjan R.E. (1972). Depth first search and linear graph algorithms. *SIAM J. Computing*, **1**, 146–60

Tarjan R.E. (1975). *Application of Path Compression on Balanced Trees*. Technical Report STAN-75-512, Computer Science Department, Stanford University

Teitelbaum R.T. and Reps T. (1981). The Cornell Program Synthesizer: a syntax-directed programming environment. *Comm. ACM*, **24**, 563–73

Teitelman W. (1977). A display-oriented programmer's assistant. In *Proc. 5th Int. Joint Conf. on Artificial Intelligence*, pp.905–15

Towle R.A. (1976). *Control and Data Dependence for Program Transformations*. Ph.D. Dissertation, Report 76-788, Department of Computer Science, University of Illinois at Urbana–Champaign

Triolet R.J. (1984). *Contribution a la Parallelisation Automatique des Programmes Fortran Comportant des Appels de Procedure*. Ph.D. Dissertation, l'Universite Pierre et Marie Curie (Paris VI)

Triolet R.J. (1985). *Interprocedural Analysis for Program Restructuring with Parafrase*. Technical Report CSRD-538, Department of Computer Science, University of Illinois at Urbana–Champaign

Triolet R.J. (1986). Interprocedural analysis based restructuring of programs. In *Parallel Algorithms and Architectures* (Cosnard M., Quinton P., Robert Y, and Tchuente M., eds.), pp.203–17. Amsterdam: North-Holland

Triolet R.J., Irigoin F. and Feautrier P. (1986). Direct parallelization of call statements. In *Proc. SIGPLAN '86 Symposium on Compiler Construction*, pp.176–85

Tucker S.G. (1986). The IBM 3090 system: an overview. *IBM Systems J.*, **25**(1), 4–19

Ullman J.D. (1973). Fast algorithms for the elimination of common subexpressions. *Acta Informatica*, **2**, 191–213

Urschler G. (1973). The transformation of flow diagrams into maximally parallel form. In *Proc. 1973 Sagamore Computer Conf. on Parallel Processing*

Watanabe T., Katayama H. and Iwaya A. (1986). Introduction of NEC supercomputer SX system. In *Supercomputers. Class VI Systems, Hardware and Software* (Fernbach S., ed.), pp.153–67. Amsterdam: North-Holland

Wedel D. (1975). Fortran for the Texas Instruments ASC system. *SIGPLAN Notices*, **10**(3), 119–32

van Wijngaarden A., Mailloux B.J., Peck J.E.L., Koster C.H.A., Sintzoff M., Lindsey C.H., Meertens L.G.L.T. and Fisker R.G. (1975). Revised report on the algorithmic language ALGOL68. *Acta Informatica*, **5**, 1-236

Wirtz G. (1989). Transforming numerical specifications into parallel programs. In *Proc. CONPAR 1988* (Jesshope C.R. and Reinartz K.D., eds.) Manchester. Cambridge: Cambridge University Press

Wolfe M.J. and Banerjee U. (1987). Data dependence and its application to parallel processing. *International J. of Parallel Programming*, **16**(2), 137–78

Wolfe M.J. (1978). *Techniques for improving the inherent parallelism in programs*. M.S. Thesis, Technical Report UIUCDCS-R-78-929, Department of Computer Science, University of Illinois at Urbana–Champaign

Wolfe M.J. (1982). *Optimizing Supercompilers for Supercomputers*. Ph.D. Dissertation, Technical Report 82-1009, Department of Computer Science, University of Illinois at Urbana–Champaign

Wolfe M.J. (1986). Advanced loop interchanging. In *Proc. 1986 Int. Conf. Parallel Processing*, pp.536–42. IEEE Computer Society

Wolfe M.J. (1987a). *Automatic Detection of Concurrency for Shared-Memory Multiprocessors*. Technical Report, Kuck and Associates, Savoy IL

Wolfe M.J. (1987b). *Multiprocessor Synchronization for Concurrent Loops*. Technical Report, Kuck and Associates, Savoy IL

Zadeck F.K. (1983). *Incremental Data Flow Analysis in a Structured Program Editor*. Ph.D. Dissertation, Department of Mathematical Sciences, Rice University, Houston TX

Zima H.P. (1983). *Compilerbau II: Synthese und Optimierung*, Reihe Informatik Band 37. Mannheim: Bibliographisches Institut

Zima H.P. (1986). *Betriebssysteme: Parallele Prozesse* 3rd (revised) edn., Reihe Informatik Band 20. Mannheim: Bibliographisches Institut

Zima H.P. (1988). Das SUPRENUM System: Architektur, Software und Anwendungen. In *Proc. GI/ITG-Fachtagung Architektur und Betrieb von Rechensystemen* (Kastens U. and Rammig F.J., eds.), Informatik Fachberichte 168, pp.1–20. Berlin: Springer

Zima H.P. (1989). *Compilerbau I: Analyse* 2nd (revised) edn., Reihe Informatik Band 36. Mannheim: Bibliographisches Institut

Zima H.P., Bast H.-J., Gerndt H.M. and Hoppen P.J. (1986a). Semi-automatic parallelization of Fortran programs. In *CONPAR 86. Conf. on Algorithms and Hardware for Parallel Processing* (Händler W., Haupt D., Leusch K., Juling W. and Lange O., eds.), Lecture Notes in Computer Science 237, pp.287–94. Berlin: Springer

Zima H.P., Bast H.-J., Gerndt H.M. and Hoppen P.J. (1986b). *SUPERB: the SUPRENUM Parallelizer Bonn*. Research Report SUPRENUM 861203, Bonn University

Zima H.P., Bast H.-J. and Gerndt H.M. (1988). SUPERB – a tool for semi-automatic MIMD/SIMD parallelization. *Parallel Computing*, **6**, 1–18

Index